# Katie Hickman

# SHE-MERCHANTS, BUCCANEERS & GENTLEWOMEN

## British Women in India

D1634431

virago

VIRAGO

First published in Great Britain in 2019 by Virago Press
This paperback edition published in 2020 by Virago Press

1 3 5 7 9 10 8 6 4 2

A CIP catalogue record for this book
is available from the British Library.

ISBN 978-0-349-00827-1

Typeset in Garamond by M Rules
Printed and bound in Great Britain by Clays Ltd, Elcograf S.p.A.

Papers used by Virago are from well-managed forests
and other responsible sources.

MIX
Paper from
responsible sources
FSC® C104740

Virago Press
An imprint of
Little, Brown Book Group
Carmelite House
50 Victoria Embankment
London EC4Y 0DZ

An Hachette UK Company
www.hachette.co.uk

www.virago.co.uk

*For Matthew Ruscombe-King,*
*who listened to my stories*

# CONTENTS

List of Maps                                                    viii
Author's Note                                                    ix
Preface                                                           1
Introduction                                                      5

PART ONE: The Seventeenth Century:
'A Series of Preposterous Gambles'                               15

PART TWO: The Eighteenth Century                                 45

PART THREE: First Half of the
Nineteenth Century                                              133

PART FOUR: The Uprisings: 'Nothing has
ever happened in the world like this'                           273

PART FIVE: In the Aftermath of the
Uprisings: Kaisar-i-Hind                                        317

Acknowledgements                                                363
Notes                                                           365
Bibliography                                                    371
Index                                                           377

# LIST OF MAPS

Map 1: British East India Company Factories in the
      17th century     16

Map 2: Territories of the British East India Company, 1765     46

Map 3: Territories of the British East India Company, 1805     134

Map 4: Territories of the British East India Company at
      the time of the Indian Uprisings, 1857     274

# AUTHOR'S NOTE

The time frame of this book – 1600–1900 – covers the centuries between the very first stumbling English attempts to make contact with India to, approximately, the death of Queen Victoria, self-styled Empress of India, who died in 1901. Thus, although I do include a few memsahibs of the Imperial era (that is, post 1858), this book was never intended to be about them, nor their twentieth century successors, about whom much has already been written.

I have chosen instead to concentrate on the women of the seventeenth, eighteenth and nineteenth centuries, about whom far less has been written (and in the case of the seventeenth century, so far as I am aware, almost nothing) and whose experiences, in each century, have proved to be so radically different from the ones that came before.

The names of many places on the Indian subcontinent have changed since the events described in this book. For the sake of clarity I have stuck to those that were in use among English speakers at the time they were writing: Bombay for Mumbai, Madras for Chennai, and Calcutta for Kolkata being the most obvious examples. For less commonly known places, or where the sources are very old, I have either silently corrected their spellings, or included their modern equivalents in brackets afterwards, such as Cawnpore (Kanpur), Oudh (Awadh) and Plassey (Palashi).

Where the names of individual women are concerned, I have tried, where style allows, to avoid infantilising them by using only their first names. Hence, for example, I refer to 'Flora Annie Steel', or 'Mrs Steel', rather than merely 'Flora Annie'. No historian that I am aware of has ever referred to Warren Hastings as 'Warren'.

*Katie Hickman*
*September, 2019*

# PREFACE

On a sultry midsummer night, 22 June 1782, a young Englishwoman named Charlotte Hickey was rowed across the bay of Lisbon to take up her passage on board the *Raynha de Portugal*, a vessel bound for the East Indies.

Mrs Hickey and her husband, William, had come directly from a farewell dinner and a ball given in their honour by the British Ambassador to Lisbon, Mr Walpole, and his wife. All the English residents of any standing had assembled at their residence to bid the couple goodbye, and the party had still been going strong at two o'clock in the morning, when the ambassador himself had insisted on lending them his private barge on which they were now being rowed, still in full evening dress, across the moonlit bay.

Everything about Mrs Hickey, from her expensive silk gown and elaborately dressed and powdered hair to the soberly clad lady's maid who accompanied her, marked her out as a lady of high fashion. Her husband, a thirty-two-year-old attorney in the employ of the East India Company, was returning to India after a leave of several years. He too was clearly a man of means, although his preferred costume – a gaudily embroidered scarlet velvet *banian* coat, with a profusion of spangled and foiled lace at the neck and cuffs – might have raised an amused eyebrow or two had he dared to wear it down Bond Street.

William Hickey had taken pains to arrange the most comfortable accommodation possible for his new wife, on what was her first voyage to India. He secured for her not only the state cabin on board the *Raynha de Portugal*, but also the luxury of an adjoining cabin for her maid, Harriette, which would double as Charlotte's dressing room, and every other convenience besides.

Carpenters had been busy for the last few weeks fitting up their quarters with all the furniture they would require for the year-long voyage: a bed, closets, even a writing desk. William had also taken the precaution of laying down a generous supply of the finest wines available to help pass the time. (Madeira is said to have been especially popular on the long voyages to India, as a good tossing on the high seas was thought to improve its taste.)

Although we do not know exactly what was going through Mrs Hickey's mind as she boarded the *Raynha de Portugal* that night, one of her feelings was likely to have been that of relief. For, ever since she had left London six months previously, she had been playing a part. For all the glamorous outward show, Charlotte was not the gentlewoman she appeared to be. She was not, in fact, even Mrs Hickey, but Charlotte Barry, one of London's most notorious courtesans.

The first leg of her journey had involved travelling under conditions of the utmost secrecy. To avoid being seen together (William's relatives had an unfortunate habit of popping up when they were least expected) the couple had taken the precaution of travelling from London to the coast in separate carriages. En route they had passed the night in Exeter in a '*hotel*',* one of the first of its kind in England, hoping to find it a more discreet establishment than a smaller and more gossipy wayside inn.

The most risky part of their enterprise, however, had been boarding the packet from Falmouth to Lisbon. Charlotte Barry may have been Hickey's 'darling girl', whom he considered a paragon among women; but to almost everyone else she was no better than a common

---

*This was almost certainly the Royal Clarence Hotel. According to Hickey, the word *hotel* was 'a term then little known in England, though now in general use, every dirty little coffee house in London being dignified with the name of *hotel*.' He was writing in 1810 (see *The Memoirs of William Hickey*).

prostitute. Despite leaving behind a string of rich protectors and a fashionable address in Queen Anne Street, she was a woman whose tarnished reputation was such that no 'respectable' woman would have tolerated her presence, and the ship's captain, had he had any inkling about her past, would have had no hesitation in refusing her passage. A Portuguese captain, however, on board a Portuguese ship was likely to be far less vigilant than one employed by the East India Company.

Since leaving London, in January that year, Charlotte Barry had successfully passed herself off as 'Mrs Hickey' in mixed company several times. In Lisbon, where many dyspeptic and otherwise convalescent English went to enjoy the mild climate, she seems to have pulled it off with equal aplomb, although 'disrespectful' gossip about her was already beginning to circulate among their acquaintances. It was not until she embarked on the *Raynha de Portugal* that hot June night to set sail for India that her true transformation would take place. Stepping on to the vessel as plain Charlotte Barry, she would step off it the other end in Calcutta as Mrs Hickey, a married lady of unimpeachable virtue, ready to take a full place in Calcutta society.

So far away from home, surely no one would be any the wiser?

# INTRODUCTION

I first came across the story of Charlotte Barry almost twenty years ago.

I was writing a book about eighteenth- and nineteenth-century English courtesans, and had turned to the diaries of William Hickey, the man whose wife Charlotte would one day pretend to be, as part of my research. Hickey's memoirs of a riotously dissipated youth among the fleshpots of late eighteenth-century London proved to be an enormously entertaining source of information, but not all of it was germane to my book.

The young William's debauchery and extravagance had eventually reached such a pitch that his despairing family decided that something had to be done. As did so many families with dissolute, bankrupt or otherwise badly behaved offspring, they packed him off to India to seek employment with the East India Company. Once in Calcutta, Hickey was overjoyed to meet many of his former school-fellows and drinking partners, most of whom had also been sent there by their families, and for exactly the same reasons, whereupon the party continued more or less as before – except it was hotter, and there was even less parental control.

Apart from leaving an interesting question mark over what English society in India was like at this period, the story of Charlotte Barry was a distraction from my theme. Her life seemed to have more to do with travelling and adventure than it did with the hothouse world of London's demi-monde. Regretfully, I put her story aside.

It was not until many years later, when I came to research this book, that I began to wonder about Charlotte Barry again. The sheer improbability of her story – not to mention her dazzling chutzpah in carrying it off – had stayed with me. It made me question all my assumptions about the conventional world of the British memsahib. What had become of her, I wondered. Had she survived that terrible voyage, which included not only being captured by the French, but also being shipwrecked after a violent hurricane literally blew the *Raynha de Portugal* to bits? Had she really managed to reinvent herself, once and for all, as 'Mrs Hickey', and become the darling of English society in Calcutta – if there even was such a thing in the 1780s?

To my great surprise, and on all counts, the answer was yes.

The history of Englishwomen in India has turned out to be not at all what I was expecting it to be.

Before I began, I had thought that I already knew something about British memsahibs. As a child I had once spent an unusual amount of time looking at photographs of them. I was aged about eleven and at boarding school in England for the first time when I was befriended by an elderly relative of my father's, who turned out to live nearby. Phyllis was the second or third wife of a distant Hickman cousin. I remember my parents, who lived abroad, alluding vaguely to the fact that she had once been some sort of Gaiety Girl, a dancer or possibly an actress on the London stage. Even as an eleven-year-old I was aware of a faint but exhilarating whiff of the demi-monde about her (although I would not have known to call it by that name). Her husband, who had something to do with horses and racing – a world of which I was equally ignorant – was frequently away from home, and it occurs to me now that Phyllis was probably as lonely as I was. It would certainly explain why she took so much trouble over an unknown little girl.*

*Phyllis turns out to have been a real celebrity in her day. Known as 'The Great Broadcasting Star' in the 1930s, she sang with Henry Hall's Band and went on to star in several films.

Even in a family such as mine, blessed with more than its fair share of eccentrics, Phyllis was odd. She was a tiny woman, no more than five feet tall, who arrived one Sunday afternoon at my school in an old Humber of such antiquity it was amazing she had managed to get it on to the road at all. Despite the fact that it was a warm day she was wearing a fur coat and a pair of enormous tinted spectacles, which gave her a faintly Cruella de Vil-ish air, an impression that was greatly magnified the moment she began driving. Although she could barely see over the steering wheel, we screeched off at terrifying speed through the tiny Buckinghamshire lanes, with me hanging on, as best I could, to the door strap.

When we arrived at her house, she took me into her sitting room in which my entertainment for the afternoon – the first of many – had been set out. Photograph albums, most of them very old, lay across every conceivable surface. They contained the usual family portraits and gatherings, and one or two boasted some stage memorabilia, but the ones I remember best were the photographs taken in India.

These showed Edwardian ladies in flowing white lace sitting about languidly on the verandas of their bungalows. Sometimes these same women (for somehow it was always the women who stood out) were in shooting parties, or on elephants, or picnicking by rivers. Other pictures had been taken at various clubs, and featured hearty outdoor pursuits: tennis, croquet and golf. There were very few Indians in these images. Sometimes there was a solitary bearer standing behind a chair, or a turbaned syce (groom) holding a horse's reins; but the presence of scores of other servants could be felt, hovering just out of sight: the punkah-wallah (the servant who pulled the fan strings), the ayah (nanny or lady's maid), the dhobi (washerman). There were photographs of children, too, miniature versions of their parents all dressed alike in jodhpurs and sola topis. None of them was older than six or seven since it was at that age that English children were always sent home to school (how I sympathised!). In the vacuum left by these older siblings were potted palms and tiger skins, and a pervasive air of melancholy.

Unlike the groups of women I have written about in the past –
English courtesans of the eighteenth and nineteenth centuries
(*Courtesans*), and women married to British diplomats (*Daughters of
Britannia*), about whom very little was generally known – when I
came to research this book I found that absolutely everybody had an
opinion on the subject.

Usually, it was the same opinion. For example, everyone *knew* that
the widening of the cultural divide between the British and Indians
was entirely due to the increasing numbers of women who made their
way to India on the 'fishing fleets' of the late nineteenth and twentieth centuries. Everyone *knew* it was the women who had somehow
poisoned that which had come before (never very clearly defined).
Everyone *knew* that if it were not for the snobbery and racial prejudice
of the memsahibs there would, somehow, have been far greater har-
mony and accord between the races.

This queasy view of British women in India, which Phyllis's photos
seemed to uphold, has proved extraordinarily difficult to dislodge. In
the last thirty years there have been a handful of histories that have
attempted to present a more nuanced account of women's experiences,
but the stereotype persists. The perception that everything was the
fault of the memsahibs remains stubbornly embedded in our consciousness. Why is this? I do not mean to suggest that prejudice of
every kind – racial, social, imperial, religious – did not cloud many
aspects of British involvement in India. It did. But neither was it
invariably the case. Even the most cursory reading of the archives suggests a far more complex story, and one that goes back much further
than we might think.

The testaments left behind by these women reveal an incredible
range of experiences and responses to India. Many, it is true, were
bored or frightened or sometimes even repelled by cultures and
peoples they never fully understood; but just as many delighted in
their experiences there. Yet whatever their qualities were as individual
human beings, the context in which they lived out their lives is a vexed
one for the modern historian. Except for the very earliest to venture

to the subcontinent, these women were members of a colonising race, and it is impossible for our judgement of them not to be coloured by this fact. While having no agency themselves in the land-grabbing ventures of the East India Company, they rapidly became part of the system that it created. It was their men – their husbands, brothers and sons – who from the mid-eighteenth century onwards carved up the subcontinent and took it for their own.

It is striking how few of them, if any, questioned their right to be there, and perhaps it would be anachronistic to hope otherwise. Very few of Henrietta Clive's contemporaries would have thought it at all strange, let along wrong, when in 1800 she wrote: 'What a wonderful people we are really, having command of the whole world. It makes me very proud of being an Englishwoman.' Even Fanny Parkes, that most enthusiastic and open-minded lover of all things Indian, seems never to have questioned the British presence there. Most of them, particularly in the later part of the nineteenth century, believed that they were doing good by being there. They were convinced, quite genuinely, not only that the Empire they helped to build was a benevolent one, but also that most Indians – not that they were ever asked – must think so too.

We know better today. Or do we? In his recent book, *Inglorious Empire*, the Indian historian Shashi Tharoor has accused the British public of being 'woefully ignorant of the realities of the British empire, and what it meant to its subject peoples[1],' and goes on to cite what he sees as a 'yearning for the Raj' in the success of the recent television series *Indian Summers*, which built upon earlier 'Anglo-nostalgic productions' such as *The Far Pavilions* and *The Jewel in the Crown*: comforting narratives, perhaps, but ones that, on their own, no longer hold good. More importantly still, Tharoor goes on to summarise, to devastating effect, what many critics of Empire have been pointing out for decades: that the rule of the British Government during the period of the Raj was, if anything, even more detrimental to the material and social flourishing of India than the excesses and corruption of the East India Company before it. The Raj was run by the British, for the British (by which, naturally, he means British men).

It is important to remind ourselves that before the mid-nineteenth century, there was no Raj; and yet the first British women to travel to India did so in the very early seventeenth century, nearly two hundred and fifty years previously. What of them? Just as there is a tendency to think that race relations between Britain and India were largely the fault of the women who went there, so there is a tendency to think of memsahibs as one historically homogeneous group; as having sprung, fully formed, into the clubs, bungalows and hill stations of the imperial high noon. But the very first British women to set foot on Indian soil bear no resemblance to the languid Edwardian ladies that had so fascinated me as a child. These women were tough adventurers, every bit as intrepid as their men, the quarrelsome, buccaneering sea captains and traders in whose wake they followed. Their voyages to India were extraordinarily daring leaps into the unknown.

Women made their way to India for exactly the same reasons that men did: to carve out a better life for themselves. They did so under the auspices of the East India Company, a British trading entity that began its life as a handful of tiny mosquito-infested trading posts along the Indian littoral – at Surat (in present-day Gujarat), Bombay, Madras and Calcutta. One day, the Company would swell to become the world's most powerful paramilitary corporation, de facto ruler of most of the subcontinent, but in the seventeenth century, and for most of the eighteenth, it was no such thing. In fact, its mettle was for many years tested, and found wanting, when pitted against the far more successful Dutch and Portuguese traders in the spice islands of modern-day Indonesia. English attempts to establish footholds in India were initiated largely as a result of their failures elsewhere.

In those early days, India was the British 'Wild East': a hunting ground in which vast fortunes could be made; the slates of 'blotted pedigrees' wiped clean; bankrupts given a chance to make good; a taste for adventure satisfied. There were – as the story of Charlotte Hickey shows – almost endless possibilities for reinvention.

It is well known that as often as not women went to India either to follow husbands or to fish for them (and why wouldn't they, in a world in which, according to conventional wisdom, marriage was the only career available to them). What is almost completely unknown is that from the seventeenth century onwards large numbers of them also worked there as independent women in their own right: as milliners, bakers, dressmakers, actresses, portrait painters, maids, shopkeepers, governesses, teachers, boarding house proprietors, midwives, nurses, missionaries, doctors, geologists, plant-collectors, writers, travellers and – most surprising of all – even traders.

One of the very first women to travel to India, Mrs Hudson, who arrived in the great Mughal port of Surat in 1617, brought with her the considerable sum of £100 (around £24,000 in today's money) with which to invest in the indigo trade, but was rebuffed by the East India Company factors, eager to protect their monopoly. They allowed her to trade in cloth instead.

Later, they would have more success. 'Women drove as large a trade as men, and with no less judgement,' wrote one observer in Madras in the eighteenth century. 'Nay ... some are so forward as to have invoyces, accounts current etc, in their own names, though their husbands are in being.'[2] The she-merchant was already a familiar, not to say formidable, figure by this time. During the Restoration, Constance Pley ran an extremely successful business dealing in the canvas cloth used for sailing boats. 'Pray be punctual with her,' wrote a fellow merchant, 'she being as famous a she-merchant as you have met with in England one who turns and winds thirty thousand pounds a year.'[3] Women were also able to acquire shares in the East India Company itself, and the records are full of references to the women who invested in goods, and claimed their dividends. There were fifty-six female shareholders by the end of the seventeenth century; and less than a hundred years later more than 16 per cent of all EIC stock was owned by women, who attended shareholder meetings, and had their say on any issues put to the vote, on exactly the same footing as men.[4]

In the 1760s a woman known as 'Poll Puff' was a familiar figure on the streets of Calcutta. She derived her name from the exquisitely light apple puffs for which she was famous. Each day Poll would take up her position at the gateway to one of the English schools in Calcutta, an overflowing basket on her arm. She would sell her puffs for three half-pence, a trade she was to follow 'for upwards of thirty years, growing grey in the service'.⁵ Poll Puff became such a beloved fixture among the English in Calcutta that in her declining years a group of her former customers – including the hard-living, hard-drinking, rackety young attorney and future diarist William Hickey – clubbed together to buy her an annuity 'so as to provide the necessary comforts for her in old age', but, prudently, and after much discussion, not so much 'as to encourage the vice of dram drinking to excess, to which she was known to be addicted'. (Something of an irony, given their own pro-digious capacity for alcohol.)

Hickey's diaries are unusual – and fascinating – because he loved women and often wrote about them, even quite humble ones such as Poll Puff. This is not the case with most histories of the British in India, even the most up-to-date ones, which have an annoying habit of confining women's experiences to just one chapter, usually a rather short one, and invariably tucked away at the back. Luckily, the ten miles of archives that there are said to be in the India Office section of the British Library proved to contain an extraordinarily rich collection of female voices.

Most of these are domestic documents, by which I mean diaries, letters and memoirs, some published, many still in manuscript form, the majority of them intended only for private readership. They are addressed for the most part to friends, family, children and grand-children, and range from a single letter – such as the one, fragile, elfin-sized (three- by four-inch) note, covered in almost illegible sepia copperplate, written by Lady Sale when in captivity near Kabul during the First Afghan War – to the two gold-embossed volumes of diaries published as *Our Viceregal Life in India*, written by the Vicereine, the Marchioness of Dufferin and Ava, in the 1880s.

Collectively, they make up a narrative that is very different from the one we have been used to, and a great deal longer. While we might, quite rightly, criticise them as colonisers, in the early days of the East

India Company that is not how they thought of themselves. With the success of the Company often balanced on a knife-edge, most women's lives in India were far rougher, ruder – in both senses of the word – and a great deal less secure than we might imagine.

For several centuries they were a vulnerable, alien people in a world that was often hostile to them. Elizabeth Marsh, her palanquin surrounded by a mob of howling, sword-wielding Marathas on her travels through south India in 1773, or Margaret Fowke, the daughter of a diamond merchant, writing home anxiously from Calcutta in the 1780s in what she was convinced were the last days of Company rule in the subcontinent, would have been astonished to think that a queen of England would one day pronounce herself Empress of India.

In 1909, the novelist Maud Diver published a book, *The Englishwoman in India*, which made a sympathetic case for those women whose lives, with all their dangers and difficulties, were so little understood at home. 'English men and women in India are, as it were, members of one great family, aliens under one sky,' she wrote. 'Their social conditions have been handed down to them from the days when India practically meant life-long banishment; and so long as they hold by these India will be a pleasant friendly land, even though it be a land of exile.'[6]

But how did this 'one great family' and the social conditions that ruled it – with its brutal hierarchies, its Warrant of Precedence, its codes of etiquette more rigid than anything that women would experience at 'home' – come about? How did the tiny band of tough women adventurers, who in the seventeenth century chanced their all to follow their men to the Wild East, evolve into the many hundreds of women, in full court dress, who were received in Delhi by the Vicereine, Edith Lytton, during the celebrations that pronounced Queen Victoria Empress of India? What were their lives really like? What was their relationship to the vast country, and its people, that they would, bit by bit, take as their own?

Above all, who were they, and how had they come to be there at all?

# PART ONE

# THE SEVENTEENTH CENTURY:
## 'A Series of Preposterous Gambles'

*In which the East India Company is founded in 1600, and its first tiny trading posts are established along the Indian littoral, including factories at Surat, Calcutta and Madras – William Hawkins travels to the court of the Mughal Emperor at Agra to negotiate trading rights, and finds one of the most opulent and sophisticated courts in the world – the first three English women arrive in Surat – Charles II acquires the archipelago of Bombay from his Portuguese wife, Catherine of Braganza, and in 1668 the Company leases it from the Crown, thereby acquiring its first sovereign Indian possession.*

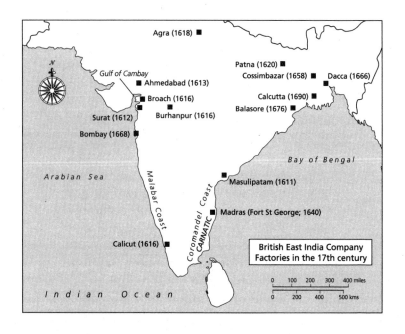

Agra (1618) ■

Patna (1620) ■
Cossimbazar (1658) ■     Dacca (1666) ■
■ Ahmedabad (1613)
Broach (1616) ■                Calcutta (1690) ■
Burhanpur (1616)           Balasore (1676) ■
Surat (1612)
Bombay (1668) ■

*Gulf of Cambay*

N

*Arabian Sea*

*Bay of Bengal*

*Malabar Coast*

*Coromandel Coast*

*CARNATIC*

■ Masulipatam (1611)

Madras (Fort St George; 1640) ■

Calicut (1616) ■

**British East India Company
Factories in the 17th century**

0   100   200   300   400 miles
0        200        400        500 kms

*Indian Ocean*

# CHAPTER 1

'Before I pass the equinoctal, I am to acquaint your Honours and Worships with a strange accident which hath happened contrary I do think to any of your expectations.'

The source of this unwelcome news was Nathaniel Salmon, master of the *New Year's Gift*, one of a small convoy of East India Company ships making the voyage from London to Surat, in present-day Gujarat, in 1617. The 'accident' he was referring to concerned a woman named Frances Webb, who together with her fellow countrywoman Mrs Hudson, had somehow succeeded in being granted permission to travel to India as companions to Mrs Towerson, the wife of an East India Company captain.

Already, by virtue of her sex, an unwelcome addition to the voyage, it transpired that Frances Webb had smuggled another, even less welcome passenger on board. 'One of the gentlewomen which came with Captain Towerson and his wife is great with child,' Nathaniel Salmon continued in his letter to the East India Company directors in London on 9 July, hardly believing the news himself, 'and at this present is so big that I fear that if she have not twins she will hardly hold out to Surat. But the best is she hath a father for it in the fleet, yet none aboard the *Gift*, (where haply it might be judged, were not the contrary known) but aboard the *Anne*.'

The father of the unborn stowaway was discovered to be Richard Steele, an unusually intrepid English merchant, even in that great age of seafaring entrepreneurs, who had obtained permission to travel out to India with Captain Towerson. Steele, it transpired, had secretly married Frances Webb 'under a tree' at some point on the journey, 'and since the acknowledgement of it hath been resident aboard our ship'. The Towersons, apparently, had been as ignorant of Frances's condition as anyone else, until it could no longer be concealed. Mr and Mrs Steele (as from now on Frances Webb would be referred to in the East India Company records) had machinated to get the Towersons to 'entertain' her on board the *Gift* (in other words, to sponsor her journey), and were clearly – and somewhat ludicrously, given how long the voyage was likely to be – hoping that her condition could be kept secret until their arrival in India: 'but that her belly told tales,' Salmon noted acerbically in his report, 'and could no longer be hid under the name of a timpany'.[1]

In the early seventeenth century, the English presence in India began with the arrival of a handful of quarrelsome, drunken, sea- and battle-hardened sailors. They had no thought of territorial conquest. They looked only for trading opportunities; thought only of their share, even if it were only a few crumbs, of a global market that was then dominated by the far greater powers of Portugal, France and Holland.

For in 1617, when Frances Webb first set sail into the unknown, the British were the underdogs in terms of world trade. For a long time it looked as though they would stay that way. Knowing, as we do, the outcome of history, it is tempting to see the Raj as an immutable and inevitable fact, but the East India Company with which it all began, and which on many occasions so nearly failed in its endeavours, stands out, in the words of the historian John Keay, 'as a robust association of adventurers engaged in hazarding all in a series of preposterous gambles'.[2]

And when it came to preposterous gambles, their women were not going to be left out. Mrs Towerson, Mrs Hudson and Mrs Steele were not the first Englishwomen to set foot on Indian soil, but they are the first for whom a narrative of any significance can be traced;* and their stories, even in these very early days of a British presence in India, contain all the seeds of women's experiences there over the next three hundred and fifty years. By this I mean not only the usual women's lot of love, marriage and childbirth, but almost always, it seems to me, something far more robust: the quest for a better life and a fearless spirit of adventure.

What else could possibly have induced them to go? In 1617 the voyage alone, let alone the unknown perils they might find when they got there, was as lengthy and dangerous as a voyage into outer space might be today. For safety's sake, ships sailing from England did so in small flotillas, although circumstances often separated them. The *New Year's Gift*, a ship of 867 tons (about the size of three double-decker buses), sailed in company with three sister ships: the *James Royal* (1000 tons), the *Anne Royal* (700 tons) and the *Bee* (150 tons). Even in convoy, they were prey to many dangers: not only to storms, shipwrecks, piracy and attacks by their trading competitors, but also to the winds themselves on which sailing ships depended, which could sweep them as far west as the northern shores of South America before they were able to round the Cape of Good Hope. The vagaries of the winds meant that round trips to the Indies took two to three years. The *New Year's Gift*, which set forth from Gravesend on 4 February 1617, did not arrive in Surat until 20 September 1617.

It is hard to imagine what resilience it must have taken to survive nearly eight months at sea. Although none of the women on board the *Gift* have left a written account of their voyage, women in later years left plenty of such descriptions. The conditions they describe,

---

*The first British woman in India for whom I can find a reference is Lady Powell, wife of Sir Thomas Powell, who was sent as James I's ambassador to the Court of the Mughal Emperor Jahangir in 1613. They were in company with the Persian Ambassador to London, another extraordinarily colourful and intrepid Englishman, Sir Robert Shirley, one of two Catholic brothers to enter the service of Shah Abbas during the reign of Queen Elizabeth I. After many misadventures, the party landed in Sind, near modern-day Karachi, where Sir Thomas promptly died, followed almost immediately by his wife, who died in childbirth. Their baby is said to have survived them only by a few days. Robert Shirley and his extravagantly beautiful Circassian wife, Teresia, seem to have been rather more robust than the Powells, and survived the experience. Life-size double portraits of what was surely one of the most glamorous couples of the seventeenth century were painted in 1627.

endured over such a long time, are almost unimaginably awful. Sea captains were reluctant to take female passengers at all (they considered them to be unlucky), and often confined them to the very lowest decks, where it was more usual to house the terrified horses, dogs and other animals which would have been taken on the journey.

Treated like so much livestock themselves, these early travellers were obliged to endure living conditions in which there was little or no air or light, and ceilings so low that they were never able to stand upright. These miserable quarters were especially the lot of lower-class women who, unlike their betters, could not afford to pay for a share of a more decent cabin. There was no privacy. And, if unmarried, no escape from predatory, sex-starved sailors.

In a feeble attempt to allow the air to circulate in these lower decks, women were forbidden to hang up blankets or linen as screens during the day, so they were obliged to eat, sleep, dress, undress and even use the 'necessary' under the gaze of their fellow passengers. Sanitary arrangements amounted to a few buckets, which regularly spilt over when the weather was rough, flooding the floor space with vomit and other effluvia until the fetid air became no more than 'a sickening, foul, repulsive breath'. Even trips on to the deck, to breathe some sea air and take some exercise, were often seriously limited, or even forbidden, by some misogynist captains. Eliza Fay, who travelled to India and back again three times in the mid-eighteenth century, recounted how on her voyage home in 1784 the captain of the ship only allowed her and her six female travelling companions to go on deck five times over the course of a sixteen-month voyage. And pity the poor woman whose story was recounted by Henrietta Clive in a letter to her brother sent from Madras in 1799. This unfortunate had apparently taken a passage from Deal to Portsmouth, on a ship whose captain then decided not to stop off in Portsmouth at all, but to head straight for Madras. 'Think of anybody coming to the East Indies by mistake!!!' she wrote in horror.[3]

Under these conditions, disease was rife. John Jourdain, an East India Company merchant of the early 1600s, recounted how he went to meet one ship in Batavia (modern-day Jakarta) expecting an enthusiastic welcome from his countrymen, only to be met by an eerily deserted and silent vessel. With the exception of four factors, 'all of them like ghosts of men freighted', everyone else on board had died from the 'bloody flux' (dysentery). 'I demanded for the General and all the rest of our friends in particular; but I could not name any man of note but was dead, to the number of 140 persons; and the rest remaining were all sick, these four being the strongest of them and they scarce able to go on their legges.'[4]

Mrs Towerson, Mrs Hudson and Mrs Steele survived both the seas and sickness, and made it safely to Surat, where after the dangers of the voyage, Frances Steele was almost immediately confronted with the greatest danger of all. 'Mrs Steele shortly after her sea travel travailed on shore, and brought forth, to the no small joy of her husband, a goodly young son,' reported one of the factors, Edward Monox, to the East India Company directors in London, adding with the typical self-interest of the Company man, 'of whom you may hope one day to have as good service as that from his father'.[5]

It was possibly the last charitable thing anyone had to say about Frances Steele. Even with two husbands to shield them, the women found themselves in a hostile all-male environment in which 'drunkenness, dicing and swearing' were the norm – and where absolutely nobody was pleased to see them.

The truth was that the addition of three women and a baby to the tiny English community on the Gujarati coast was extremely disagreeable to everyone, and they made no bones about it. The East India Company 'factory' (so-called, although nothing was actually made there) at Surat was, in those early days, a communal, almost monastic affair, run much along the lines of an Oxford or Cambridge college. No one was cheered by a set of new fresh faces from England, even female ones. Instead, everyone grumbled loudly at the thought of three extra mouths to feed. And everyone wanted someone else to blame.

A flurry of bad-tempered correspondence ensued, between the

various factors at Surat and Ahmedabad* and the English ambassador, Sir Thomas Roe, who was then following the Mughal Court on one of its progresses, trying in vain to coax a trading agreement out of the Emperor Jahangir. Their initial complaints were mostly about the expense of these women and the disruption they would cause in the all-male community. Edward Monox, who had been the first to inform the East India Company of the birth of Baby Steele, was quick to rub in the state of confusion that prevailed after the women's arrival: 'the house being so pestered with them, and Captain Towerson and their retinue,' he wrote, 'that for my own part during my abode there I had neither chamber to lie in nor place to write in, which caused me unwillingly to omit duties which otherwise I should have performed'.

In the end the newcomers took matters into their own hands, and very sensibly acquired a separate property in which to house themselves. This did not go down well either. 'I hope the house kept apart is at their own charge,' grumbled Thomas Roe to Thomas Kerridge, the most senior merchant at Surat, 'for I perceive not that the Company intended to keep their families ... If I find any fault it is at *you*,' he continued, 'that will suffer Mr Steele to run out at the beginning, to take the Company's money to lay out for a house, or to waste in his expense anyway. If he will be vain, let him do it at his own cost. For, roundly, I will not allow any extraordinary charge for his wife, and therefore I pray reckon with him.'

Others blamed the situation on Roe himself. William Biddulph, an English merchant based at Ahmedabad, wrote a letter of complaint to the Company directors in London, roundly criticising the ambassador for not getting rid of both Steele and his wife immediately. '[It is] an article of your commission', he reminded them, 'that whoever shall have a wife in these parts shall upon knowledge thereof be forthwith dismissed of his place and service and sent home.'

While it was true that the Company directors explicitly forbade its

---

*By 1618 there were five fledgling English factories in north-western India: at Agra, Ahmedabad, Burhanpur, Broach and Surat. Surat, being the only port, was the oldest and the most important.

factors to take their wives with them, it was not a decision they had taken lightly. A man's wife was held to be 'very fitting for the quiet of his mind and the good of his soul, as a curse befalleth those that keep man and wife asunder', but there were other more important considerations. Although the records show that they debated the question three times, the good of the Company won out over the good of their employees' souls, and once they had made up their minds, there was no turning them. Even EIC veterans such as Thomas Keeling, one of the captains on the Company's third voyage to the Indies in 1607, could not persuade them to bend the regulations. Although he wrote 'wonderful many arguments and requests to have his wife sent unto him or permit him to come home (in what fashion so ever)'[6] all fell upon deaf ears. Mrs Keeling had at one point even smuggled herself aboard her husband's ship, but was discovered while still in English waters, and ignominiously sent back to shore.

Thomas Roe, having left his own new bride back in England after only seven weeks of marriage, was of the same view as the directors. 'I desire noe weomans company,' he declared, 'but labour to leave such incumberances behind.' Now he took the decision that the only thing for it was to try to persuade Frances Steele to leave as soon as possible. 'I know not his means; but if the Company gave her not leave as his wife I will not consent she shall be a charge upon them, nor travel this way,' he wrote to Thomas Kerridge. 'I pray advise him to take such a course as I be not enforced to see his fault. To this purpose I have dealt freely with [Mr Steele], to let him see the inconveniences that will follow us, the charge to him, the displeasure of the Company, all of which will be restored by a good course, to persuade [Mrs Steele] to return home, which I have prevailed so far in as that his own reason hath drawn his consent and to that end promised his endeavour to satisfy the gentlewoman, whom I am sorry for.'[7]

Then, perhaps realising that plain reason might not be enough, he offered an inducement. 'If she return and he stay I will do him all kindness according to his desert, and recommend her to the

Company's care. Excuse what is past, but let them not smart for it that are innocent. You that have the Company's purse must order it. Money is dear ware in India. I would have you use her and Captain Towerson with courtesy,' he wrote, but could not help adding anxiously, 'but not live upon you, lest they stay too long.'[8]

A month later he was writing to Kerridge again. 'I know Mr Steele as well as any other. I hope he will be comfortable and his own friend . . . ' he wrote, adding in a rather more flinty tone, 'His wife *will* be ruled, and will return; and therefore consider her sex. Use her lovingly, assist her, and lend her all fit comforts.'[9]

Roe's appeals were all in vain. After nearly eight months cooped up on the *Gift*, Frances Steele had no intention of returning home. Besides, she and her husband had other plans. Their ambition was not to remain in Surat at all, but to travel to Agra with the Towersons, where Richard Steele had ambitious plans to design waterworks for the Mughal Emperor's city – to which end he had brought out with him on the *Anne* a number of English 'artificers'. Gabriel Towerson, a veteran of several previous East India Company expeditions, and a captain of the *Hector* in 1611, was also intending to trade on his own account. His wife, Maryam, as we shall see, was crucial to this enterprise.

As for Mrs Hudson, the records are almost silent about her, except in one respect: once she had arrived in India, she had the audacity to think that she too could trade in her own right, with the £100 she had brought with her. 'I received Mrs Hudson's desires for herself,' Roe added. "Her demand is to have the Company's [indigo] for money, or to invest it for her.' In the end they decided, grudgingly, that she might invest not in indigo, but in cloth. 'She may be lucky as a calling duck,' wrote Thomas Roe with heavy irony, 'and therefore try her.'*[10]

---

*The English were never very successful when it came to selling their cloth, which was generally far too heavy for the hot Indian climate, but in these early days they were still trying. A letter from Surat, sent on 25 January 1612, includes a request for the following: '500 Venice red cloths, 100 popinjay greens and light greens, 100 straw colours, yellows and horseflesh; 100 light blues commonly called Hulings; and 200 Murries in grave and other pleasant colours.'

If the expense and the bother of having women present were not enough, their presence also had an undesirable effect on the other men. One of these, a Mr Goulding, who had been the preacher on board the *Anne*, seems to have lost his head completely. At this point an already unstable and thoroughly bad-tempered situation descended into what can only be described as farce.

'When the gentlewomen were to depart from Surat to goe to [Agra], he [Mr Goulding] was strangely importunate with me to give him leave to goe,' reported the sea captain Matthew Duke to the overall commander of the 1617 fleet, Captain Pring. '[This request] I utterly denied, commanded him to stay, and gave charge to Mr Kerridge [the chief factor at Surat] to stop his passage.'

Maddened with lust, the preacher was clearly not going to be deflected from his scheme to follow the women to Agra. 'For a day or two he dissembled his intent,' Duke fumed, 'in which time he fitted himself secretly with Moores apparel, which being procured and all thinges else fitt for a fugtive hee takes his leave of Mr Kerridge, pretending to come aboard the *Anne*.'[11]

What became of Mr Goulding is not known. His 'Moores' disguise seems not to have fooled anyone, however, as in February 1618 Thomas Roe was writing to Captain Pring to say that the unfortunate Goulding had been apprehended, and would forthwith be packed off back to Surat again in disgrace.

Maryam Towerson, under whose protection Mrs Hudson and Mrs Steele had both travelled on the *New Year's Gift*, is a shadowy but extraordinary figure in the history of early women in India. An Armenian Christian from Agra, she became, through a series of extraordinary events, the wife of not one, but two, East India Company captains.

Maryam's first husband, whom she married in 1609, was William Hawkins. The captain of the *Hector* on the East India Company's third voyage to 'the Indies'*, Hawkins almost certainly belonged

*In the seventeenth century the terms 'India' and 'the Indies' were interchangeable.

to the great seafaring dynasty of Devon Hawkins, a quiverful of Richards, Williams and Johns whose extraordinary and pioneering voyages ranged from exploring the coasts of Brazil in the reign of Henry VIII to fighting alongside Francis Drake against the Spanish Armada.

Whatever his family history, William Hawkins belonged to the aristocracy of English mariners. For all this, it is hard to imagine how a rough English sea captain from a tiny, unknown and as yet entirely insignificant European island could have made any kind of impression on the perfumed, jewel-encrusted, silken majesty of the Mughal Emperor, but somehow Hawkins seems to have managed it. All that we know about him – including his unlikely marriage – has come down to us by the greatest good chance: the manuscript of the journal which he wrote during his travels in India was for a long time thought to have been lost, only surfacing in the British Museum in the late nineteenth century.

Hawkins's presence in India was, from the very start, a highly vulnerable one. Arriving in Surat on 28 August 1608, he was very soon left to his own devices by the rest of his countrymen, who almost immediately pushed off with the rest of the fleet to Bantam, in present-day Indonesia, leaving him alone with just one other merchant to try his luck at the Mughal Court. His mission: to secure the right to set up a trading post on the Indian coast, where he hoped, among other things, to buy the lightweight Indian cottons that could be taken to Indonesia and exchanged for spices. Hawkins's only companion, a merchant named William Finch, within weeks succumbed to 'the bloody flux' and was 'not able to stirre abroad to doe any business'. Hawkins's only other support during his time in India were his two servants, 'a cook and my Boy'.

'These were the [only] companie I had,' Hawkins wrote, 'to defend ourselves from so many enemies, which lay lurking to destroy us, aiming at me for the stopping of my passage to the great Mughal.' They were formidable enemies. Not only the Portuguese, who had been profitably established in Surat for some time, and who did not take at all kindly to the thought of the English muscling in on their trade, but also the Mughal officials, who fleeced Hawkins at every opportunity of both money and goods, and had no compunction about playing off one European trader against another (which they did most successfully). When Hawkins complained, specifying the peace that now existed between England and Portugal, and insisting that he should be allowed freely to go about his business, the Portuguese factors scoffed at him. 'These Seas belonged unto the King of Portugal,' they insisted, 'and none ought to come here without his licence.' In addition, 'they most vilely abused his Majesties, terming him the King of Fishermen, and of an Island of no import, and a fart for his commission'.

Hawkins, however, was nothing if not resourceful. Despite 'so many enemies, who daily did nothing else but plot to murther me, and cosen me of my goods' (there were at least two attempts on his life while he was in Surat), he eventually managed to get permission to travel to Agra, the Mughal capital, making the journey in some style having secured a guard of fifty horsemen to accompany him there – 'valiant Pattens [Pathans] a people much feared in these parts: for if I had not done it, I had beene over-throwne'.[12]

Protected by his bodyguard of Pathan warriors, Hawkins finally arrived in Agra – 'after much labour, toyle, and many dangers' – on 16 April 1609. As 'Embassadour' from King James I, with suitable letters of credence, he was quickly taken to see the Emperor – so quickly, in fact, that the travel-stained Hawkins was almost wholly unprepared for the audience. Hearing of his arrival, the Emperor 'presently charged both Horsemen and Footmen in many troupes ... commanding his Knight-Marshall to accompany me with great state to the Court, as an Embassadour of a king ought to be; which he did with a great traine, making such extraordinary haste that I admired much, for I could scarce obtayne time to apparel myself in my best attire.'

It was not an auspicious beginning. For a start, in addition to his dishevelled appearance, Hawkins did not have the right gift to present to the Emperor* – an almost insurmountable solecism when meeting an eastern potentate – most of his valuables having been frisked off him, and then confiscated, by 'that dogge Mocreb-chan' the Emperor's Viceroy in Surat. 'I came with a slight present, having nothing but cloth, and that not esteemed.'[13] As if this were not enough to mar his first crucial encounter with the Emperor, a Jesuit interpreter had been summoned to be present at their audience, who did not at all appreciate the presence of a Protestant intruder on his territory. And yet, despite all these difficulties Hawkins found himself received by the Emperor 'with the most kind and smiling countenance'.

Hawkins, it turned out, had two great assets: he could speak Turkish, and therefore was able to communicate with the Emperor directly; and he had the ability to consume vast quantities of alcohol. Jahangir was among the most sophisticated and cultured of all the Mughal emperors, but he was also much addicted to the pleasures of the flesh, alcohol and opium chief among them. In Hawkins he found the perfect bingeing companion.

'Perceuing I had the Turkish Tongue, which himselfe well understood, he commanded me to follow him unto his Chamber of Presence, being then risen from that place of Open Audience, desiring to have further conference with me,' Hawkins recorded of his first meeting with the Emperor, 'in which place I stayed some two hours, till the King came forth with his women.'

Jahangir took an instant shine to him. Not only did he appoint one of his captains to house him and assist the Englishman in his every

---

*The quest for the right gift to send the Mughal Emperor vexed the East India Company factors for many years. They spent a great deal of time puzzling over what best to send. A 'small pair of organs' was one of the top choices, 'having here a skillful musician to play on them'; followed by 'a very fair case of bottles filled with several sorts of the best strong waters' – perhaps not the most felicitous idea given the Muslim court was, albeit in name only, teetotal. This was followed by two or three pairs of 'rich strong knives', and 'some fair pictures' – and 'if you send the King's picture it will be the more highly esteemed'. To this was added two or three 'fair spaniels and a fair greyhound or two', and on another occasion a sad mastiff, the only dog to have survived the journey out of an entire pack. The portrait of 'a citizen wife', an anonymous beauty, was requested to be sent to Agra in 1615, one of a pair: the other was of Sir Thomas Smythe, the first Governor of the EIC. When Thomas Roe met with the Jahangir, he observed the portrait of the beautiful 'citizen wife', together with a number of portraits of the English royal family, in pride of place in an alcove behind the Emperor's throne.

need, but he gave the command that he should be brought every day into his presence. 'According to his command, I resorted to the Court where I had daily conference with the King,' Hawkins wrote, no doubt thoroughly enjoying the discomfiture of his Portuguese rivals. 'Both night and day, his delight was very much to talke with me, both of the Affaires of England and other Countries, as also many demands of the West Indies, whereof hee had notice long before, being in doubt if there were any such place, till he had spoken with me, who had beene in the Countrey.'

Within weeks of arriving at the Mughal Court, Hawkins had charmed his way into the Emperor's inner circle. On ceremonial occasions he earned himself a place of honour along with the 'chiefest sort of nobles', behind the 'red rayle', which was three steps higher than the space reserved for ordinary onlookers. 'Many dayes and weeks being past, and I now in great favour with the King,' he wrote, 'to the grief of all my enemies . . .'

Hawkins now found himself at a court that was the most sumptuous and sophisticated in the world. The luxury and scale of everything amazed him. On feast days, such as the Persian New Year, when all the nobles in the land would gather for eighteen days of festivities, he was particularly impressed by the tent that was pitched for the Emperor, 'so rich,' he noted, 'that I think the like cannot be found in the world'. This tent, which he judged to be two acres in size, in which the Emperor placed his 'Chairs of Estate', was shaded from the sun on all sides by blinds made from wrought velvet embroidered with gold. The floor was covered with silk and gold carpets, the interiors hung with cloths adorned with gold, pearls and precious stones. In addition to the Emperor's tent, and the adjoining harem quarters set aside for his women, was some five acres of ground on which his nobles had their own quarters, each one striving to see 'who may adorn his roome the richest'.

Not only was Jahangir a passionate patron of science and the arts, he was also a builder of palaces and exquisite water gardens. The gardens in his numerous palaces, set with pavilions amid marble channels running with water, splashing fountains and rills, and a myriad flowers and fruit trees, were one of the wonders of the world.

He was also one of the richest monarchs in existence. In his journal, Hawkins describes in detail the great stores of treasure that the Emperor had amassed, being the combined plunder 'of so many Kings as his forefathers had conquered'. 'He is exceeding rich in Diamants,' he went on, 'and all other precious stones, and usually weareth every day a fair Diamant of great price, and that which he weareth this day, till his time be come about to weare it again, he weareth not the same; that is to say, all his faire Jewels are divided into a certain quantitie or proportion to wear every day.' When a diamond cutter of Hawkins's acquaintance was asked to facet a huge diamond 'of three Mettegals and a halfe', the man asked for a smaller 'foul' diamond with which to do the cutting, and was brought a chest 'of three spannes long and a spanne and a half broad, and a spanne and a halfe deep'* overflowing with stones of all sizes and sorts.

In addition to his daily diamond fix, Jahangir also had huge stores of gold, silver and other jewels at his disposal. He was often seen wearing a great chain of pearls, 'very fair and great', and another of emeralds and rubies. He wore huge aigrettes of diamonds and rubies (a stone more esteemed in the East than diamonds) in his turban. In his treasury there were also 'two hundred rich glasses; a hundred vases for wine ... very fair and rich and set with Jewels', and five hundred drinking cups, fifty of which were particularly valuable, being fashioned from solid rubies, emeralds and other precious stones. In addition there were 'an infinite number' of chains, made from pearls and precious stones, and rings set with diamonds, rubies and emeralds. Also noted were swords, scabbards, poniards, saddles, lances and kittasoles [state umbrellas] all marvellously wrought and encrusted with jewels.

On the feast of his birthday every year, Jahangir would go into 'a very fair room' in the treasury, fitted out with a pair of giant scales

---

*A span is equivalent to nine inches, so the chest would have been two and a half feet long, and just over a foot in width and height.

made of beaten gold. The Emperor would sit on one end of the scales, while the other was filled with gold, silver, gemstones and grain, which would later be distributed to the poor. Altogether, Hawkins estimated that the value of this treasure was ten thousand pounds.

It was not just the treasures of the counting house that impressed Hawkins. Everything at Jahangir's court was on a scale he could never have imagined before. 'Of horses there are twelve thousand ... of elephants there be twelve thousand ... of camels there be two thousand,' he wrote breathlessly. In addition there were ten thousand oxen 'for the cart', one thousand mules, four hundred hunting dogs and greyhounds, four thousand hawks, ten thousand pigeons 'for the sport of flying', four thousand singing birds, a hundred 'tame' lions and 'an infinite' number of dromedaries.

But possibly the most impressive feature of the Mughal Court was when Jahangir, the descendant of Mongol nomads, made a progress away from the city. Hawkins described the tented cities* that accompanied the Emperor on his journeys as being so vast that they were 'the compass of London or more', each one of which might be attended by a retinue of as many as two hundred thousand people 'of all sorts'. In addition to servants, courtiers and soldiers were forty thousand elephants, of which half were 'trayned elephants for the Warre'.

But Jahangir's was also a decadent court. Games and entertainments were cruel and bloody – one of his favourites was to pit men against wild animals – and the Emperor himself, for all his learning and refinement, was a self-confessed alcoholic and opium addict. 'He would come forth into a private room where none can come but such as himself nominateth (for two years I was one of his attendants here.) In this place he drinketh other fine cupfuls, which is the portion that the Physicians alot him. This done he eateth opium, and then he ariseth, and being in the hight of his drinke, he layeth him down to sleepe.' When he woke again the Emperor was so incapable that even

---

*These extraordinary encampments were the prototypes of those that would later become such a feature of British life in India, copied most faithfully perhaps at the Imperial Assemblage of 1877, see Part Five.

when his supper was brought to him he could not feed himself, his food being 'thrust into his mouth by others, and . . . then he sleepeth the rest of the night'.

In between his drinking bouts, Jahangir did 'many idle things . . . and whatsoever he doeth, either without or within, drunken or sober, he hath writers, who by turnes set downed every thing in writing which he doth'. These writers recorded every aspect of Jahangir's life, 'so that nothing passeth in his life time which is not noted; no, not so much as going to the necessary; and how often he lieth with his women, and with whom; and all this is done unto this end, that when he dieth, these writings of [his] actions and speeches, which are worthy to be set downe, might be recorded in the Chronicles.'

Hawkins's enemies, the Portuguese and the Jesuits, who until now had known uninterrupted high favour with Jahangir, had good reason to feel aggrieved. They watched with envy and amazement as the Emperor showered the upstart English 'Embassadour' with honours, promising him a generous stipend for each year that he stayed at the Mughal court, together with the right to a cavalcade of four hundred horses, rising to a thousand horses – an honour that would have put him on a par with an English duke.* Hawkins, the briny English sea captain, had almost overnight become 'the Inglis Khan' – the English Lord.

For the moment all was well; but his closeness to the Emperor was no guarantee of his safety. Hawkins remained convinced that behind the scenes 'the Portugalls were like madde Dogges, labouring to worke my passage out of the World'. He had good reason to be alarmed. His 'Boy', Stephen Gravoner, died in mysterious circumstances, and his cook, Nicholas Ufflet, also became 'extreame sick'. Hawkins himself was also beginning to feel unwell, and suspected that he was being poisoned.

The Emperor, possibly after one of his all-night drinking binges with his new friend, had a brilliant idea. He would find Hawkins a wife – 'a white Mayden out of his Palace' – who would look after

---

*'For the nobility of India have their Titles by the number of their Horses, that is to say from fortie to twelve thousand, which pay belongeth to Princes and their Sonnes' (*Hawkins' Voyages*).

him, and ensure his safety; 'and by this means my meates and drinkes should be looked unto by them, and I should live without fear'.

Hawkins was in a quandary. The thought of taking a woman, sight unseen, as his wife clearly horrified him, but the gift of one of the Mughal Emperor's 'maydens' was something that could not with safety be refused. At first he tried to excuse himself on the grounds that as the 'mayden' was likely to be a 'Moore', he could not think of it, 'but if so bee there could bee a Christian found, I would accept it. At which my speech,' he added naively, 'I little thought a Christian's daughter could bee found.'

No sooner were Hawkins's words out of his mouth than the Emperor recalled to mind one Mubarik Khan, an Armenian, 'of the race of the most ancient Christians', who had been a captain in the service of Jahangir's father, the mighty Akbar, and in great favour with him. Mubarik had died unexpectedly, leaving his daughter, Maryam Khan, with nothing except a few jewels to her name.

What could he do? 'I seeing she was of so honest a Descent, having passed my word to the King, could not withstand my fortunes,' Hawkins wrote. 'Therefore I tooke her, and for want of a Minister, before Christian Witnesses, I marryed her.'

Against all the odds, the couple took to one another. From the few sentences that Hawkins recorded about her in his journal (and it is telling that he wrote anything about her at all) it seems that real affection blossomed between them. 'For ever after I lived content and without fear,' he wrote, 'she being willing to goe where I went, and live as I lived.'[14]

Unfortunately, William Hawkins did not live long. He may have found personal happiness at the Mughal Court, but his professional venture ended in failure. After two and a half years kicking his heels in Agra, binge-drinking with the Emperor, court politics eventually won out: the Portuguese and their factions triumphed. Hawkins, having fallen from favour, retreated back to the coast without the promised *ferman*, or imperial decree, which would have granted the English 'Articles for our Factorie'.

William and Maryam finally set sail for England in January 1611; but after a circuitous voyage via the spice islands, Hawkins died while rounding the Cape in 1613, as did most of the other men on board. He was buried in Ireland.

Maryam Hawkins, left alone among strangers, must have felt his loss deeply. She was, however, still in possession of the gemstones which had been her only inheritance. These 'few' jewels turned out to be a single diamond worth £2000 and smaller ones worth £4000[15] – immense sums – and so whether from her wealth or her personal charms, she soon succeeded in attracting another Englishman as her husband.

It is not certain when she remarried, but since her new husband was Gabriel Towerson, who had taken over as captain of the *Hector*, the ship on which she had been sailing back to England when William Hawkins died, she was clearly not one to waste time.

Like Hawkins, Towerson was a veteran of the East India Company. He had been on the Company's first voyage to the Indies in 1601, and would go on to have a long, if turbulent, career with them, long after he married his Armenian wife.*

It is not known exactly what Towerson intended trading on his own account at the Emperor's Court at Agra, but it would clearly have been impossible were it not for his wife's connections (since Maryam's mother had remarried a Dutch diamond cutter from Antwerp in the employ of Jahangir's son, the future Shah Jehan, it may have been gemstones, which were highly sought-after trading commodities). Richard and Frances Steele, with their enterprising plans for designing a new water system for the Emperor's capital city, also hoped to benefit from Maryam Towerson's connections.

---

*Captain Towerson was murdered in 1624 in what became known as the Amboyna Massacre. This gruesome incident, which took place on the Indonesian island of Amboyna, involved ten of the East India Company men who were set upon, tortured and then killed by their rivals in the Dutch East India Company. It was typical of the brutal high-stakes surrounding the spice trade. The tortures the Dutch inflicted included throttling them, tying them to stakes, whipping them in the open market-place after washing them in vinegar and salt, and 'tumbling' them down rocks until their crushed and bruised 'carcasses' were unrecognisable. The incident became something of a *cause célèbre*, inspiring a play, *The Tragedy of Amboyna*; an equally gory painting, 'wherein those several bloody tortures and executions is lively, largely, and artificially set forth'; and a printed pamphlet.

Having set the English colony at Surat on its heels, the four rene-gades, together with the would-be trader, Mrs Hudson, went off to try their fortunes in Agra (hotly pursued by the preacher, Mr Goulding, in his 'Moores' disguise). No one was happy about the situation. Even though both Richard Steele's and Gabriel Towerson's projects had been sanctioned by the directors in London, the Company's merchants in India saw both these independent enterprises as unwelcome intrusions on their own attempts to secure business there; but there was noth-ing they could do. They consoled themselves by writing grumbling letters to one another, predicting disaster. 'Perhaps they thought his [Gabriel Towerson's] greatness could do them some pleasure,' Thomas Roe wrote stuffily to William Kerridge, on 18 December 1617. 'If so they mistake their friends, it is well if she [Mrs Towerson] can return as she came ... ' Edward Monox was even more scathing. 'What he [Towerson] intends to do I think no man knows, no, not himself ... I fear a bootless errand he is come out and of a sleeveless one he must return home ... '[16]

Maryam Towerson, however, was not going to be put off by a few whingeing English merchants. She was not some *feringee* trader wait-ing around, cap in hand, to get the attention of the Emperor. Maryam was going home.* She had connections and family at court. Moreover, she knew how things should be done.

'[Gabriel Towerson] is here arrived with many servants, and a trum-pet [trumpeter], and more show than *I* use,' Roe complained. 'If it may stead him I am glad, but I think it had been fitter to have kept the Company's servants about their own business, for I know not when he will return, nor what his presence here will produce.'[17]

Unfortunately, it is not known exactly how the Towersons fared at Agra, although it is later recorded that they were 'disappointed in their hopes' and blamed Roe for hindering their private trade.[18] Neither do

*It was probably for this reason that the EIC made her an exception to their rule, allowing her to travel back to India with her new husband. No one would have expected a gentlewoman to travel without either a female companion or a female servant, and it was in this way that Mrs Hudson and Frances Webb also slipped through the net. Frances Webb's mistake seems to have been becoming a Company wife, for I can find no record of any objection to the presence of Mrs Hudson.

we have any first-hand account of how Richard Steele's designs for a new water system for Agra were received, although since he and his wife returned to England in 1619, they too were clearly unsuccessful. The enterprising Mrs Hudson, on the other hand, turns out to have been much luckier – and certainly more astute – than the 'calling duck' predicted by Thomas Roe. When she too returned to England in 1619 she had amassed a cargo of goods so considerable that the cost of freighting them alone was £30 (more than £7000 in today's money)[19], making her the first of many successful she-merchants to ply her trade in India.

Of Frances Steele's time in India, however, some delightful details are known, thanks to the energies of Samuel Purchas, an English clergyman who devoted much of his time to collecting travellers' tales. Purchas quizzed Richard Steele on his return from India and, more unusually, his wife too, who told him of her experiences of 'the Women of these parts'. Frances Steele, the former lady's maid, had found herself living in unaccustomed style in Agra, with a coach, a 'palinke' [palanquin], seven horses and ten servants at her command, when she came to the notice of a daughter of Abdul Rahim Khan-i-Khana, the head of Jahangir's household and a very senior courtier. This woman, who was also the widow of one of the Emperor's brothers, expressed a desire to see Mrs Steele, and the arrangements were soon made. As far as I know this is the first ever description of an Englishwoman's visit to a high-ranking Indian woman in her home.

She was fetched in a close Chariot drawne by white Oxen, attended by Eunuchs; and was first brought into an open Court, in midst of which was a Tanke or Well of Water, where sate many women, slaves to Chan-Channa's daughter, of diuers nations and complexions: some blacke, exceedingly lovely and comely of person, whose hare before did stand vp with right tufts, as if it had growne vpward, nor would ruffling disorder them; some browne, of Indian complexion; others very white, but pale, and not ruddy; many of them seemed goodly and louely, all sitting in their sight, but rich garments on the floore couered with carpets. The Lady came forth in meaner attire, whereat they all arose and did her reuerence, with their faces to the ground. Mistress Steele made her three courtsies, after the English fashion (being also in English attire) and deliured her a present (without which there is no visitation of great persons) and the Lady caused her to sit by her, and after discourse, entertained her with a Banquet; and began familiarity with her, continued and increased with often visitations, and rewarded with many gifts, as of womens vestments of those parts; some of which I saw, the vpper garment like a smoke, of thin Calico, vnder which they weare a paire of breeches close about the nether parts very long and slendor, loosely ruffling about their legs, of thin stuffe also.[20]

# CHAPTER 2

Just twenty years after its foundation on New Year's Eve 1600, the East India Company had become not only a thriving mercantile enterprise, with nearly two hundred factors spread over more than a dozen trading centres in the East, but an industrial one too. Its dockyards at Deptford and Blackwall, complete with foundries, timber yards and cordage works, were among the sights of London.

The next thirty years of the Company's existence, however, were characterised by a series of disasters, both natural and man-made, that very nearly brought an end to its ventures altogether. First there came increasing hostilities with the Dutch; followed by a decline in the price of pepper, still the most valuable commodity being traded from the spice islands where the majority of EIC trade still lay. In India, too, disaster struck. Following one another in quick succession, both famine and floods swept through Gujarat. It is thought that over a million people died, and several times that number fled the area. Not only was there nothing to buy, but no one to buy it from. 'We are always so bestraited that all is little enough to hold buckle and thong together,'[1] lamented one factor in his report to the directors. Starving villagers picked through 'the very excrement of beastes', reported another factor, Peter Mundy, on his return to Surat from Agra. 'Women were seen to roast their children, men travelling in the waie were laid hold of to be eaten.'[2]

By 1633, the English factory at Surat, once so thriving, had been all but wiped out. Out of the twenty-one English factors who had once worked there, just seven were still alive. Three more would be dead within days of Mundy's return.

Nothing, however, had a more disastrous effect on the successes of the Company than the English Civil War. Their monopoly lapsed, and there was little or no investment capital available. For three years Cromwell dithered over the terms on which the Company's charter might be reissued, and how it would be regulated. Eventually, in despair, on 14 January 1657, the directors declared for liquidation, putting the Company up for auction. They were effectively bankrupt. An asking price of £14,000 was mentioned, 'not much to show for nearly sixty years of trade'.

However, a few months later, a new charter was issued. Slowly, trade picked up again. After Cromwell's death in 1658, and the restoration of Charles II in 1660, another similar charter was granted. Crucially for the future of the Company, this second charter, which was to be permanent, included a grant 'authorising the Company to fortify and colonize any of its establishments and to transport to them settlers, stores, and ammunition'.[3] And if settlers were needed in these new colonies, then it went without saying that women would be needed too.

In a satisfying historical twist, it was a woman who would eventually bring this about: not an Englishwoman, but a Portuguese one. Two years after his restoration, Charles II married the Portuguese princess Catherine of Braganza. As part of her dowry she brought with her the islands of Bombay, just down the coast from Surat. And it was at Bombay that the first truly English settlement was made.

Initially the King seemed not to know what to do with his new territory. The Seven Islands of Bombay were a tiny archipelago, only twenty miles across, at the far end of the world. During the six years that Bombay belonged to the Crown, it was to bring the King nothing but trouble and expense. There was even talk of the Portuguese buying it back. Eventually, in 1668, with a metaphorical sigh of relief, he leased it to the East India Company, for a rent of £10 a year, which was to be paid 'in gold, on 30th day of September, yearly, forever'. For the first time, the EIC was in possession of a sovereign settlement in India.

At first Bombay did not seem to be worth much, even to the Company. There was no trade there to speak of, and the merchants claimed that they had only taken it off His Majesty's hands to ease him 'of that great burthen and expense which the keeping of it hath hitherto beene'. But from its beginnings as an English settlement, Bombay was a very different proposition to the dissolute, all-male factory of semi-pirates at Surat. Although by mid-century the English settlement there was once more thriving, and could boast 'the best accommodation of any in the city', complete with lush roof gardens and a grand dining hall, its presence depended entirely on the whims of the Emperor. Although they were allowed to govern their people according to English laws, the English had never been allowed to own land or property in Surat, or anywhere else in India; and under Company laws, women – and with them any chance of family life – were still strictly forbidden. With Bombay, on the other hand, the Company found itself with a colony to manage, protect – and populate.

Shortly after he acquired Bombay, and before he passed it on to the East India Company, Charles II had sent a squadron of five ships and four hundred troops to the islands with the idea that they would build a fort and a garrison there; but when the commander of the fleet, the Earl of Marlborough (no relation to the future Duke of Marlborough), arrived it was only to become embroiled in a series of interminable wrangles with the outgoing Portuguese Governor, who had not been informed of the new arrangement, and was not going anywhere soon.

The unfortunate troops, marooned on their ships while the two governors slugged it out, were moved from pillar to post and eventually deposited on a desert island, Anjediva, near Goa, which, although it had water, measured only a mile long and three hundred paces broad. 'Then, for most of a year, they paced the 300 paces, drank the water, and died miserably . . . Out of Marlborough's force of 400, just 97 emaciated castaways finally sailed north and at last scrambled ashore at Bombay.'[4]

It was at least partly to service the needs of these 'emaciated cast-aways' that the EIC now changed its policy towards women altogether.

For the new colony to succeed it was not only more settlers – soldiers and 'artificers', preferably both rolled into one – who must be enticed to the East Indies; their women must be persuaded to go with them. From being an expensive nuisance, they were now a necessary evil. Ever pragmatic, the Company did not waste time. Barely two months after the lease was signed they put out an advertisement. 'Any willing to enlist should come to the Company's house on Wednesdays and Fridays,' declared the Court of Committees on 4 December 1668, 'when they will hear the terms of entertainment and the accommodation for themselves and their wives.'

But what of the men who were already there, the ninety-seven 'emaciated castaways', the remains of Marlborough's troops? Some provision needed to be made for them also. For the first time, single women too – so long as they could prove themselves 'of sober and civil lives' – were actively encouraged to join the enterprise.

The surprisingly favourable terms with which the Company tried to tempt these women across the seas is indicative of how much they were needed. 'That if any single women or maids, related to the soldiers or others ... shall be willing to go to Bombay,' it was announced in the EIC Court Minutes of 30 December 1668, '20 shall be permitted to do so at the Company's expense.'

While there was clearly an expectation that these women would take their pick from the soldiers already at large on the island, sensible and humane provision was put in place for them should this not come about. 'And, if they desire it, and do not marry Englishmen,' the Minutes announced, 'then for one year after their arrival the company are to provide them with food and a set of clothes according to the fashion of the country, during which time they are to be employed in the Company's service, but not in planting. These women are not to be permitted to marry any but those of their own nation, or such as are Protestants, and upon marriage they are to be free.'[5]

This first attempt to lure soldiers and their wives to Bombay to form the first colonisers was not a success – 'none were entertained' – largely because no provision was made for them to take their children with them. So when, six years later, the Company tried again, they modified their terms and conditions accordingly. This time it was decreed that 'any subjects of the King under 40 years of age should be allowed to go to Bombay in the Company's ships, with their wives, servants, estates, and such of their children as are over seven years of age'.[6] Moreover, to make it even more appealing, the colonisers would now be allowed to trade on their own account (albeit with certain restrictions, and so long as they took out a bond or covenant for £500 limiting their activities to Bombay itself).

It is hard to know how many wives took advantage of this opportunity, but it is certain that at least some did. To find a supply of single women who were brave enough to venture their all and sail to Bombay (with precious little chance of ever returning should they change their mind) was, hardly surprisingly, to prove even more difficult.

In 1675, the Court Minutes of the East India Company recorded: 'Mary Barker to be allowed to go in one of the Company's ships … paying her own passage.'[7] The following year they were considering the petition of Sarah and Anne Mace, and 'if they are of condition and degree proper to be the wives of soldiers, to permit them to go as passengers to Bombay according to the rules of the Company'.[8] But it was still not enough.

The EIC then came up with an ingenious idea. In order that there might be a 'supply of young maidens, that have had a virtuous education', those on the EIC committees who were also governors of Christ's Hospital were urged to find 'young women bred up there to be disposed of in this way'. Founded by Edward VI in 1552, Christ's Hospital was a charitable institution that provided food, clothing and 'a little learning for fatherless children and other poor men's children'. Both the president and the treasurer were to be approached, to see whether there were any young women there (they specified that they should be between the ages of twelve and thirty) who might be willing – rather like a job lot ordered on eBay – to be dispatched to

Bombay. If so, they would be offered their passage on the same terms that had been set out previously.

It is sobering to imagine what an otherwise destitute twelve-year-old must have endured as she made her way, friendless and alone, to that *ultima Thule*, the west coast of India in the 1670s. What would have become of her? How would she have made her way in that strange new world? All we know is that this time the advertisement worked. Despite its notoriously unhealthy climate – the island had a higher mortality rate than anywhere else in India: 'two mussouns [monsoons] are the age of man' claimed one of the colony's chaplains, adding that of children born on the island 'not one in twenty lived beyond their infant days'[9] – Bombay prospered.

From the cloak-and-dagger antics of William Hawkins, dodging Portuguese plots to 'murther' him in his bed, the East India Company's concerns become almost touchingly domestic. The Court Minutes of 1674–1676 speak of the need for 'a church or chapel for divine service'; for 'a hospital for the sick families of English, or other [of] his Majesties Protestant subjects'; and for houses and warehouses for foreign merchants who might desire to live on the islands. Little by little, a picture emerges of something enduring in the making: not only of bricks and mortar, but also of a culture and a way of life.

Against all the odds – pestilence, disease, even mutiny – the English colony at Bombay survived its early days. By the third quarter of the seventeenth century it had become a thriving settlement of some sixty thousand people, men and women, both Indian and European. Other English colonies also thrived at this time, particularly at Madraspatnam (the patnam was quickly dropped), where the local *naik*, or ruler, had been persuaded to lease the EIC a small plot of land on which to build a fort. By the 1680s, despite the Company strictures, there were just over a hundred Englishwomen, tolerated mainly as a means to stop the factors there from marrying Portuguese, and therefore Catholic, women. But as is so often the case, those pioneering women are tantalisingly silent about their experiences. They left no testimonies of their own, and we come to them only obliquely, through the records of others.

Those that exist, it has to be said, do not make very edifying reading. The Company's new policy of trying to entice 'plain, honest' women to the subcontinent, which they also attempted at Madras in this period, had been only a moderate success. Women's behaviour was frequently not much better than that of the men: their conduct, complained the directors back in London, had grown 'scandalous to our nation, religion and government', and they were warned that if they did not 'apply themselves to a more sober and Christian conversation' they would be imprisoned on a diet of bread and water, and then shipped home. At the general table at which the factors and their dependants would continue to dine together until the custom was abolished in 1722, rows of musketeers were needed to keep order.

By the turn of the century, however, the situation was changing. The British foothold in India, so tenuous throughout the seventeenth century, was about to become something more substantial. As if on cue, women's voices, in all their glory, come bursting loudly on to the scene.

PART TWO

# THE EIGHTEENTH CENTURY

*In which, in 1717, the East India Company finally acquires the long-coveted* ferman, *granting it permanent trading privileges, just as the once mighty Mughal Empire begins to crumble – the Company, taking political advantage of the ensuing chaos, brings in more troops to protect its interests – the French take over from the Dutch and the Portuguese as the Company's main trading rivals, and the Battle of Plassey is won decisively by Robert Clive against a combined force of Mughal and French troops; a puppet Nawab is installed by the EIC in Bengal – and in 1765 a* diwani, *or governorship, is granted to the Company, making it de facto ruler of a vast area of north-western India.*

Territories of the British
East India Company, 1765

N

KASHMIR

PUNJAB

MUGHAL

DELHI •

SIND

RAJPUT

H i m a l a y a s

OUDH

Allahabad •

• Benares

MARATHA

BENGAL
Plassey •

TERRITORY

CALCUTTA •

• Surat

Cuttack •

BOMBAY •

• Puri

Arabian Sea

NIZAM

Hyderabad •

Bay of Bengal

Karwar •

MYSORE

MADRAS

Seringapatam •

Vellore •

Arcot •

Tellicherry •

• Mysore

Calicut •

Cochin •

Anjengo •

Malabar Coast

Coromandel Coast

CARNATIC

Indian Ocean

British

Hindu

Muslim

# CHAPTER 3

On the morning of Sunday 17 November 1782, a few leagues west of Sri Lanka, Charlotte Hickey was startled awake on board the *Raynha de Portugal*. The ship was moving in such an unusual way that she knew immediately that something was terribly wrong and hurried up on to the deck to investigate. There she was confronted by a scene so terrifying that she never forgot the shock.

As far as the eye could see, the horizon 'was of a blackish purple, above which rolled great masses of cloud of a deep copper colour, moving in every direction with uncommon rapidity'. Lightning flashed 'in every quarter', thunder rumbled, the surf crashed. The wind came whistling as shrill 'as a boatswain's pipe' through the blocks and rigging. The scene, as she and her 'husband' William witnessed it, 'was enough to appal the bravest men on board'. Perhaps more frightening still was the deathly silence of all the sailors around them, 'not a syllable uttered by anyone, all looking in stupid amazement', as the hurricane approached.

By eight o'clock that morning it was upon them. Torrents of rain poured down, making it as dark as night. Charlotte Hickey went to her cabin, secured as many of her possessions as she could, and prepared for the worst.

Orders were given immediately to take in the top-gallant and reef topsails, but it was too late. The instant the sails were lowered they were 'blown to atoms, being torn from their respective yards in shreds'.

Soon, the sea had increased 'to an almost unbelievable height', the wind now roaring to such a degree that the officers on board could not make themselves heard by the crew, even with the largest speaking trumpets. Between nine and ten the hurricane was upon them in all its force. 'As it veered all round the compass so did the sea increase infinitely beyond imagination, one wave encountering another from every direction, and by their mutual force in thus meeting ran up apparently to a sharp point, there breaking at a height that is actually incredible but to those who unhappily saw it.' Within minutes the foretopmast, yard rigging and all, went over the side, 'the noise of it being imperceptible amidst the roaring of wind and sea'. Seconds later it was followed by the mizzen mast, which 'snapped like a walking stick'. Meanwhile, 'the entire ocean was in a foam as white as soap-suds'. At half past eleven the foremast also snapped, 'being shivered into splinters quite down to the gun deck. The fall of it drew the main-mast forward, whereby the levers upon which the pumps worked ... were totally destroyed. Before noon the main-mast and the bolt-sprit both collapsed at the same instant.'

With all the masts down, the ship immediately began to roll 'with unparalleled velocity from side to side, with half the quarter-deck being submerged in water each roll, so that we every moment expected she would be bottom uttermost or roll her sides out'. Next, three out of the five stern windows, frames and all, suddenly burst inward from the force of the wind, the noise so tremendous that both Charlotte and William were to imagine that 'the last scene of the tragedy had arrived'.

In the space of just four hours their 'noble vessel' was in a state of distress 'as few have ever been in. Our situation seemed hopeless,' William Hickey would later recall, 'not a creature on board but thought any minute would be the last of their lives.'[1]

The ship by now was filled with so much water that they were both sure it was only moments before it would begin to sink. But somehow the *Raynha de Portugal* kept going, although 'the velocity and depth of her rolling abated nothing'. The couple watched helplessly as all their possessions were smashed into a pulp. 'Not a bureau, not a chest or trunk but broke loose and was soon demolished, the contents from the quickness and constant splashing from one side to the other of the ship becoming a perfect paste, adhering to the deck between the beams, many depths in thickness, so as near the sides actually to fill up the space to the deck.'

By two in the afternoon every bulkhead between the decks, except that of the Hickeys' cabin, had collapsed from the violent thrashings of the ship. Suddenly, the folding doors that opened into their cabin were torn off their hinges and smashed to pieces, 'exposing to our view the foaming surges through the great cabin's stern windows'.

Even with the terrifying sight of a boiling sea just a few feet away from them, the Hickeys had at least some measure of protection from the tempest while they remained below deck. Their hellish experience was nothing compared to that of the crew. Their captain, who had been confined to his cabin for days in a delirious fever, somehow found his strength again. He jumped from his bed and went on deck to give orders, but within a short space of time a giant wave came crashing over the decks, throwing him down with such force that it broke his arm and gave him such a severe concussion that it 'rendered him insensible'. The chief mate, an active and clever seaman, was actually washed overboard, but then, by amazing good fortune, washed back again into the galley below the forecastle, where he remained too bruised and wounded to move.

The second mate was of even less use. As he was nowhere to be seen after eight o'clock in the morning, everyone assumed that he too must have been carried overboard; but this turned out not to be the case. Clearly believing that there was no possibility of the ship being saved, he was found to have shut himself up in a small booby hutch, or cabin, on one of the upper decks, where he spent the day 'between the brandy bottle and the prayer book'. The third officer, while struggling on nobly, eventually was so overcome with fatigue that he simply collapsed on to the deck, where he remained 'secured by a rope on the spot where he fell'.

Meanwhile, through what remained of their cabin door, the Hickeys had the unnerving experience of hearing the Portuguese crew weeping and wailing in terror of their lives, clinging to their completely overwhelmed priest and 'screeching out prayers for pardon and mercy in such dismal and frantic yells as was horrible to hear. So eager were the miserable enthusiasts to embrace the image of Jesus Christ upon the Cross,' wrote William with disgust, '. . . that they, in their endeavours to do so, actually tore it to pieces.'[2]

Having supported his wife as best he could, Hickey turned to her at this point and warned her that all must soon be over, 'it being quite impossible that wood and iron could long sustain such extraordinary and terrific motion'. Charlotte, his 'dear woman', he would recall, 'with a composure and a serenity that struck me most forcibly, mildly replied, "God's will be done, to that I bend with humble resignation, blessing a benevolent providence for permitting me, my dearest William, to expire with you, whose fate I am content to share, but Oh! My dearest love, let us in the agonies of death be not separated"; and she clasped me in her arms.'*

'At this awful hour did it occur to me what I had somewhere read that death by shipwreck is the most terrible of deaths . . . In a storm at sea the scene is not more terrible than disgusting, in a miserable cabin, on a filthy wet bed, in a confined and putrid air, where it is as impossible to think as to breathe freely. The fatigue, the motion, the want of rest and food, give a kind of hysteric sensibility to the frame, which makes it alive to the slightest danger,' he wrote. 'If we look round the miserable group that surrounds us, no eye beams comfort, no tongue speaks consolation, and when we throw our imagination beyond – to the death-like darkness, the howling blast, the raging and merciless element, expected every moment to become our horrid habitation – surely, surely it is the most terrible of deaths.'[3]

In this state of acute apprehension Charlotte Hickey remained for

---

*Since Hickey wrote his famous memoirs some twenty years after the events he was recalling, we must allow him a certain licence when it comes to remembering Charlotte's precise words at that fateful moment.

hour after hour – only to find, to her amazement, that the *Raynha de Portugal* remained afloat. By six in the evening she had the sense that the fury of the storm was gradually abating. By eight, the gale had greatly subsided; by midnight the swell had gone down sufficiently to make it possible for some of the seamen to rig up one of the pumps. By dawn, the clouds were still scudding over them with great velocity, but the wind, although it blew strongly, seemed hourly more moderate. By ten on the morning of the 18th a bright sun shone forth.

Against all the odds, Charlotte Hickey had survived.

Not so some of the crew, thirteen of whom lost their lives to the hurricane. Most had been simply washed out to sea; three were later found dead in various places on the ruined skeleton of the ship. One of them was discovered between the copper and the ship's side, a space of only a few inches wide. 'It was a shocking spectacle, for being so jammed in by the working of the ship the intestines were squeezed out and the head forced completely round, the face being towards the back.'[4]

Somehow the remaining crew managed to patch up the ship just enough to sail her again, and a week later they spotted land. On 30 November, the *Raynha de Portugal* finally limped into harbour at Trincomalee, in present-day Sri Lanka.

Charlotte Hickey was a famous beauty in her day. Although she herself left no written records, and no portrait of her has survived, we know a great deal about her, and her journey to India, thanks to her protector's famous memoirs. According to William (who may have been partial), she made herself a favourite wherever she went, not only because of her beauty but because of 'the peculiar gentleness and suavity of her manners'. When the great hurricane was finally over she became, Hickey wrote proudly, 'the first object and immediate care of, I may safely say, everybody on board'.

But their troubles were not yet over. To their dismay, the first thing they saw on entering the harbour was a French flag flying over the fort on the summit of a hill. Before they could even drop anchor, a French pilot had come on board and taken charge of the ship, informing them that the British garrison they were expecting to find there had surrendered the previous September. Instead of having reached a safe haven, they had unwittingly sailed into enemy territory.*

The acting Governor, the Chevalier de Roys, believing the ship to be English and not Portuguese, refused to allow them to disembark. Half-starved and destitute, having lost everything they possessed, the Hickeys were also now prisoners of the French.

Luckily for them both, Charlotte Hickey seems to have had the same miraculous effect on the enemy – apart from the tyrannical de Roys – as she had had on the Portuguese crew. The French commanding officer of the frigate that arrived soon after to take possession of their ship turned out to be 'a very gentlemanlike man' called L'Anglade. Despite giving orders that a sentry with his musket and bayonet fixed should be put on guard at each gangway, he nonetheless pronounced himself quite shocked at the situation in which he found Mrs Hickey, 'without food, without clothing, or the common comfort of a female attendant' (her maid, Harriette, the only other female passenger on the *Raynha de Portugal*, had died early on during the voyage). He took one look at Mrs Hickey and promptly declared that it was a disgrace to Frenchmen to permit a lady such as herself to remain an hour in so unbecoming a state.

No sooner had the news been broadcast that there was a woman, albeit a married one, on board the shattered ship than food, clothing and offers of help came pouring in from other quarters too. Captain Malle of the French ship *Consolante*, which was moored nearby, immediately jumped into his barge to bring them gifts of tea, coffee, sugar, chocolate, biscuits, liqueurs 'and various other articles for the table'. Monsieur Chevillard De Montesson, the Port Captain, followed soon after 'with a quantity of fruit and eggs, a few fowls, some fish, and what was more acceptable than all, a small loaf of excellent bread'. He

---

*Throughout much of the second half of the eighteenth century, the British and the French were at war with one another: wars in Europe played out in the geopolitics of the subcontinent, and combined in the struggle for its control – see below.

too took one look at Charlotte and declared that he would go forthwith to the Governor 'and in the name of the King call upon him to act more like one of his liberal nation'.

'No-one could be more attentive or kind than these three gentlemen,' Hickey declared, 'by whose benevolent care my darling girl's sufferings were greatly alleviated.'

Not altogether true. Soon, eager Frenchmen positively queued up to offer her their gallantry. A trunk containing two suits of women's apparel appeared anonymously in her cabin. A Captain Gautier sent her a present of some good loaves of bread, some lemons and some speciality biscuits from the island of Bourbon. These came together with 'a little pot of candy sugar for the use of Mrs Hickey when she takes her tea'. Another visit brought ladies' shoes and stockings, with a variety of different sorts of cloth, and no fewer than four tailors to sew a new wardrobe for her. When she was ill, a Mr de Boissières procured a Malay maid to attend her. Best of all was the special dispensation they were given allowing them to leave the ship for a short while and enjoy a dinner party on board the *Consolante.*

When the Hickeys were eventually allowed to leave the *Raynha de Portugal*, they were invited to stay by Monsieur Chevillard de Montesson. They found his house to be exactly the quiet haven that they needed after their ordeal at sea, with only 'half a dozen very worthy men' as their fellow guests. Among these gentlemen the lovely Mrs Hickey was, of course, an instant hit, entertaining them with her fine singing voice. (Her most admired pieces, we are told, were 'No, t'was neither shape nor feature', 'Kate of Aberdeen' and 'Tally Ho!')

Their tranquillity did not last long. As the days went on, and the news of the beautiful and accomplished Englishwoman spread – 'for under such a description [Charlotte] had been represented' – so the

---

*The other passengers, cooped up miserably on board the filthy wreck of a Portuguese ship, looked upon this favouritism with an understandably jaundiced eye. One of them, Mr Bateman, went so far as 'impudently insinuating it was the charms of Mrs Hickey ... that had occasioned such evident and unjust partiality to us'. Not surprisingly 'a violent quarrel ensued' and from being the best of friends, they became thereafter 'inveterate enemies'. In Calcutta, they would later fight a duel over the harsh words that had been uttered (neither was hurt).

bustle and confusion at the house seemed mysteriously to increase, until it was overrun from morning till night with officers and seamen on matters of business. This disagreeable change, it gradually dawned on Hickey, was due to the fact that many of the visitors were only making a pretence of having business to conduct: their real purpose was to catch a glimpse of his wife. Indeed, before long she 'could not stir from home without being overwhelmed with fulsome compliments'. Some 'disagreeable coxcombs' even had the temerity to send her anonymous love letters – a fact, Hickey claims, he would have let pass 'with silent contempt' had he not perceived that they annoyed Charlotte so much 'as to affect her health'.

Clearly there was something about Charlotte Hickey, even in her new, virtuous guise as William's wife, that attracted an unusual amount of attention. The mobbing, the love letters, which would continue, even after she had reached Calcutta, all seem to indicate that the men she met were under no illusions about her past.

Improbable as it sounds, there was nothing unusual in Charlotte Barry's transformation into the respectably married 'Mrs Hickey' halfway across the Indian Ocean. In those early days of travel to India, women were able to move up and down the social scale with much greater ease than would have been possible at home.

In the previous century, when the East India Company factors wrote to the Court of Committees (Directors) in London suggesting that it would be 'convenient' to send a job lot of females to help populate the new colony at Bombay, it was generally recognised that women came in two varieties: 'gentlewomen', for the factors and officers, and 'other women', for the troops and labourers. In 'the mad rush to nuptials', that matching of pedigrees had soon gone by the way.

'Be they what they will, at their arrival all pretend to be gentlewomen, high born, great parentage and relations, and scorn to marry under a factor or commissioned officer, though ready to starve.'

'They goe pretty fast,' added one Governor, with a barely perceptible lift of an eyebrow, 'some married, some sure, some in a fair way.'[5]

Women who already regarded themselves as 'respectable' did not always take such a carefree view. 'Mrs Hickey' had been the only woman on board the *Raynha de Portugal*, but if Eliza Fay, Charlotte Hickey's contemporary, had been one of her fellow passengers, I have the feeling she would have sniffed her out immediately. 'The woman, of whom I entertained some suspicion from the first, is I am now credibly informed, one of the very lowest creatures taken off the streets of London,' Mrs Fay wrote home about one of her fellow passengers aboard the *Nathalia* in 1779. 'She is so *perfectly* depraved in disposition, that her supreme delight consists in rendering everyone around her miserable – It would be doing her too much honour to stain my paper with a detail of the various artifices she daily practices to that end.' You can almost see a disdainful toss of the head. 'Her *pretended* husband,'* she went on (her italics), 'having been in India before, and giving himself many airs, is looked upon as a person of mighty consequence, whom nobody chooses to offend.'[6]

Mrs Fay's whispered criticism is very telling. In the eighteenth century, no woman travelling to India for the first time really knew what, or who, she would find when she arrived. What would the rules of engagement be, they must have wondered, in this strange new place, the English Wild East?

---

*Thought to have been Mr Tulloh, an eminent Calcutta auctioneer. The painter Zoffany is said to have quarrelled with him a few years earlier, and drawn his likeness into the face of Judas Iscariot in a painting of the Last Supper, which is said to be still in St John's Church, Calcutta. See E. M. Forster's introduction to *Letters from India*.

# CHAPTER 4

The world in which Charlotte Hickey and Eliza Fay found themselves was an indescribably alien place for a young Englishwoman.

In the hot season, before the annual migration to the hill stations became possible, the heat was intolerable, often deadly. 'Every article of furniture is burning to the touch; the hardest wood, if not well covered with blankets, will split with a report like that of a pistol, and liver taken from the drawers appears as if just removed from a kitchen fire.'[1] Even the most resilient travellers among them complained about the heat, which could be so tremendous it was 'like putting one's head inside an oven', one complained.[2] Another shuddered at the thought of a too-soon return to the plains from the cool of the hill stations, thinking it 'about as rational as if a slice of bread were to get off the plate and put itself on a toasting fork'.[3]

The memory of it, for those who survived long enough to return to England, remained with them all their lives. In the early nineteenth century, one woman remembered visiting her grandmother in Great Cumberland Street, an old lady 'who never allowed a ray of sunshine into her room – a relic of her fear of sun in India'.[4] And on first arriving in India herself as a young married bride, the same woman was struck down by sunstroke, which left a permanent streak of grey in her hair.

In addition to the terrifying heat, their senses were assaulted by the startling colours of the tropical vegetation – 'I never saw a more vivid green than adorns the surrounding fields'.[5] They were no less astonished by the immense throngs of people, the smell of spices, the strange wildlife – elephants, camels and snakes; the variety of dress – or lack of it; and above all the different complexions of the Indians.

One woman, who left England for Madras in 1798, recorded her two daughters' absolute refusal to believe that 'the people dressed in *long* muslin *dresses* were not women, though some had *long grey beards*'.[6] While some found much to enjoy in observing these differences, others reacted with horror. On arriving in Galle in 1757, another wrote: 'The Dutch people are white but their servants are all Black. They wear nothing at all about them but a little piece of rag about their waist, which to us at first appeared very shocking.'[7] A third, arriving in the Dutch settlement of Nagapatam in 1765, thought the same: 'I could not be reconciled to the vast numbers of black people who flocked to the shore ... at first sight I believed them all to be women from the effeminacy both of their persons and dress ... The almost stark naked-ness of the lower classes is disgusting.'[8] Some found their first sight of Indians positively frightening. 'God knows what would become of me left quite alone with the black people,' exclaimed one early traveller in a letter home in 1770. 'God forgive me, I cannot bear the sight of them.'[9] For those arriving in Madras for the first time, their unease was compounded by the discovery that they would be entirely dependent on these semi-naked 'natives' to make it to the shore.

By the eighteenth century, the East India Company merchants had made themselves overlords of three thriving Presidencies (so-called because the chief factor in each became known as the President), at Bombay, Madras and Calcutta. Madras, founded in 1640, was the first of these. Of all the many mistakes made by the EIC in their early days in India, their choice of Madras as one of their principal settlements was one of the worst. Francis Day, the Company agent responsible for choosing the site, was said to have had a 'mistris' in the nearby Portuguese settlement of San Thomé, which seems entirely likely given the unsuitability of Madras itself in every other respect: 'a few acres of surf-swept beach, dune and lagoon' at the edge of a fishing village.

There was no port at Madras, nor even the possibility of one. Instead, the most ferocious surf on the entire Coromandel Coast pounded its beaches, day and night. Not only could no ship land there, they would not even dare come close, not only because of the surf but also because of the 'bar', the great reef of sand running parallel to the beach. Instead, all passengers alike, high and low – including their assorted children, pets, furniture and any home comforts they might have brought with them – were obliged to scramble into *mussoola* boats to be rowed ashore. These large but lightweight vessels were constructed of special planks that were sewn rather than nailed together 'by the fibers of the Cocoa-nut', so as to bear being 'dashed upon the beach by the unresting surf without instantly breaking to pieces'. And as if this were not enough, as the travellers approached the shore at last, they found themselves unceremoniously hauled on to the beach on the back of a wet, slippery and semi-naked fisherman.

The sheer terror of 'crossing the bar' became part of the Madras mythology, and gave rise to some hair-raising stories. 'Nothing is more terrible at Madras than the surf, which . . . is not only alarming but dangerous.' Another described in detail how each *mussoola* was usually accompanied by two or three small catamarans made from bamboo and paddled by just one man, which 'in case of [the *mussoola*] being overset usually pick up the drowning passengers'. On the day that she had attempted to land, there had been what was called a black surf which was deemed very dangerous indeed; even the specially built local boats were frequently smashed to a pulp, their passengers injured, some even killed, by the pounding waves. She and her husband survived, but the experience was something she never forgot. 'There were moments when I really thought we were nearly gone,' she lamented; 'for how could I in my weak state have buffeted the waves had the boat overset? How I saved myself from falling Heaven knows.'[10]

Besides the crowds of people, the heat and the tropical vegetation throbbing with insects, spiders and venomous snakes, they found another, even more fundamental difference: the almost total absence of Indian women. As they would soon discover, it was not only Muslims who kept their wives and daughters in purdah. *All* women in India, whatever their creed, other than the lowest servant classes, were strictly secluded.

It took a great deal of adjustment to get used to this idea. 'No people in the world have stricter notions of the honour of their women, particularly those of higher castes,' explained Jemima Kindersley, the wife of a Company army officer who wrote about her experiences in the 1760s. She went on to observe that it was 'an idea of delicacy and dignity' which obliged them to conceal themselves 'from vulgar eyes'.

'Of the Hindoo we can know little,' she added, 'as none but the very lowest are visible: they are almost in their infancy married by the care of their parents to some of their own caste ... They live retired in the zennanahs [women's quarters], and amuse themselves with each other, smoking the hookah, bathing, and seeing their servants dance.'[11] A 'Mahommedan never speaks of his wives, and it is thought a great affront and an indelicacy to enquire after them.' Others agreed. 'The Hindoo ladies are never seen abroad; when they go out their carriages are closely covered with curtains, so that one has little chance of satisfying curiosity.'[12]

It is no accident that the first written account of India by an Englishwoman was penned in order to satisfy this intense curiosity women felt about their Indian sisters. In her *Letter from a Lady at Madras to her Friends in England*, Jane Smart described in detail her visit to the Nawab's harem in 1743.*

The Nawab (the Mughal Emperor's representative) had come to pay a visit to the English Governor of Madras. His wife and her women attendants accompanied him. 'He and she are Moors,' Jane Smart explained, 'whose Women are never seen by any Man upon earth, except their Husbands.' Despite her strict seclusion from the outside world, her high status was made abundantly clear by the fact that

---

*To the best of my knowledge, this is the earliest published travel narrative written by a British woman. The more famous *Letters from Constantinople* by Lady Mary Wortley-Montagu describing her time at the Ottoman Court in 1713 were published posthumously in the 1760s.

the guns around Fort St George fired a salute on her arrival. When the highest-ranking Englishwomen at the settlement, comprising the Governor's wife, Mrs Benyon, and her eldest daughter, and Jane Smart herself, were chosen to make the 'Lady' a visit of etiquette, they did so in just as much state as the Governor had done when paying his visit to the Nawab. 'We had all the Governor's Attendants, as well as his Lady's, and his Musick playing before us all the Way, and Thousands of People looking at us on our Way thither.'[13]

When we arriv'd, Mrs B. [the Governor's wife] was handed by a Lady, who was to introduce her, through two Halls, which brought us into a large Garden and a Pavilion at the End of it, where the *Nabob's* [Nawab's] Lady was seated. A grand *Moor*-Lady of her Acquaintance came to receive Mrs B. in the Middle of the Garden, and presented her to the *Nabob's* Lady, who was seated in the Middle of the Pavilion, upon a Settee cover'd with rich Embroidery upon Crimson Velvet; an embroider'd Carpet hung over it, which went all round her Feet. She received our Governess with the utmost Gentility and good Breeding, and paid her proper Compliments to us.

Her Person was thin, genteel, and middle-sized, her Complexion tawny, as the Moors all are; eyes as black as possible, large and fine, and painted at the Edges, which is what most of the *Moors* do; her lips painted red; and between every Tooth, which was fine and regular, she was painted black, that they might look like Ebony. All her Attendants, which were about thirty Ladies, were the same. Her Face was done over, like frotted [fret] Work, with Leaf-gold; the Nails of her Fingers and Toes, for they were bare-footed, were painted red, and likewise the Middle of her Hands.

You will perhaps think this a strange Description, but I assure you it is literally true.

Her hair was black as Jet, very long and thick, which was combed back neatly, and then braided; it hung a great deal below her Waist; she had a Fillet of Diamonds round her Head, edged with Pearls of a large Size. Her Ear-rings were as broad as my Hand, made of Diamonds and Pearls, so as they almost cover'd each side of her Face; then she had a Nose-Jewel that went through her left Nostril. Round her Neck she had twenty Rows of Pearls, none smaller than a Pea, but a great number of them as large as the End of my little Finger. From her Necklace there hung a great Number of Rows of large Pearls, which came down below her Waist, at the end of which hung an emerald as large as my Hand, and as thick. Her Coat which she had on was made of fine Gold-Muslin, made close to her, and a slash'd Sleeve: a Gold-Veil, which she hung carelessly over her Head, and went over her Body, all the Front-Part of it was trim'd with a Row of large Pearls; she had a Girdle, or rather a Hoop, made of Diamonds, which went round the Bottom of her Waist; it was above an Inch broad; several Strings of large Pearls around her Waist, which hung down almost to her Knees, and great Knots of Pearl at the End of them; ten rows of large Pearls round her Wrist, and ten Rows round her Arms a little above her Elbow, and her Fingers every one of them adorn'd with rich Rings of all Sorts and Sizes: her Feet and Ankles were, if possible, richer, and more adorn'd than her Hands and Arms. In short, Mrs B. and myself computed that she had many more Diamonds and Pearls about her than would fill a Peck-Measure [two dry gallons].

At the Entrance of the Pavilion, there was a long embroidered Carpet, with a Pillow of the same Work at each End, which was opposite the Settee the Lady sat upon, for us to walk over; there was something like an Arning [awning], made of Crimson Silk, which went all on the outside of the Pavilion, and was supported with Pillars of Gold. We had two Gold Censors of Incense and Sandal Wood, that almost suffocated us with the Perfume.[14]

They were given tea for their refreshment, but even that was strange, as it came spiced with rose water and cinnamon. Later, betel nut was brought in gold 'Philligree' boxes, 'which we liked much better than what was in them, for the Beetle is a large Green Leaf, which the

*Indians* chew, of an intoxicating Nature and very Disagreeable to the *English*; but we were forced to comply with that out of Compliment'.

The presents went down better. A Moor's coat and two gold veils were presented to each of them. 'The Nabob's Lady put Mrs B's Veil upon her, so we in Compliment put on ours, which she was pleased at.' Later she sent them sixty dishes served under silver covers, and put in scarlet cloth bags made for the purpose.

Jane Smart and her companions were not the only ones who were curious. The Nawab's women inspected the Englishwomen closely. 'The *Nabob's* lady and her Attendants admir'd us all, but thought our dress very odd. Two of the Ladies examin'd my Dress till they came to my Hoop-Petticoat, which they were very much astonished at; they much admired my Tweezer* and the Trinkets in it. To end all, we were the first *English* Women they had ever seen, and I doubt not but we appeared as odd to them, as they did to us.'

Jane Smart's lengthy and beautifully precise description of her visit to the Nawab's 'Lady' is a measure not only of the thirst for information about such a visit, but also of its rarity. Other women in the eighteenth century also wrote about their visits to high-born Indians. In the 1780s Elizabeth Plowden and her husband were feasted royally by Asaf ud-Daula, the Nawab of Lucknow, who entertained them with elephant fights, fireworks and dancing *nautch* girls. Ten years earlier, Mary Morgan and her husband were visited by a local Nawab in Calcutta, who came with two hundred attendants, 'eight elephants, some fine palanquins, and a great many horses'.[15] But these invitations only rarely extended to visiting their women, it being 'a favour which they are not very fond of granting to Europeans'.[16]

The invitation to visit the Nawab's wife at Madras was clearly extended for political rather than social reasons. There is no sense in which she wanted to get to know Jane Smart and her companions, or to further their acquaintance; nor was there any suggestion that the visit might be repeated (unlike Frances Steele's friendship with

---

*A case for small instruments – scissors, button hook, thimble, and what we now think of as 'tweezers' etc. – which Jane probably wore hanging from a chain at her waist.

Khan-i-Khana's daughter, which resulted in 'often visitations'). The connection between the women was real – their amazement, and no doubt laughter, at Jane's hoop-petticoat, for instance – but it was fleeting. Their intention was to dazzle and impress, not to socialise. In this they succeeded brilliantly. When she came to write her account, Jane Smart's abiding impression was of both the opulence and the strangeness of her experience. She was afraid that her readers would think she were telling them 'some Fairy Story ... I own, I thought myself in a Dream the whole time I was there'.

Far from evincing a snobbish desire to keep Indians at arm's length, women in the eighteenth century often lamented that they were not able to mix more with Indian women. Those encounters that did occur tended to be exceptional, and never of long enough duration for any real understanding of the other to take place. Despite that, Jane Smart's description is striking for its open-mindedness, and its freedom from the racial prejudice that frequently clouds similar, later accounts. She merely recounts, quite dispassionately, what she had seen, only commenting mildly at the end: '[Her] numerous Riches are all the Enjoyment [she has], for she is not suffered to go out all the Year round; and when obliged to travel, is covered up in her Palanquin in such a Manner, that no Mortal can see her, and it would be Death to any Man to attempt to see a *Moor's* Lady.'

Englishwomen's intense curiosity about their Indian sisters was rarely reciprocated. On the whole, the latter knew little, and cared less, about the foreign women who were gathering in their country – and why should they? Although we can only speculate what the Nawab's 'Lady' at Madras really thought of Jane Smart and her companions, one thing is for sure: the fact that the foreigners did *not* observe purdah, that they were free to roam about the towns and the countryside with their faces uncovered for every low-caste sweeper to gaze upon, would have seemed to her the height of impropriety, every bit as incomprehensible as her own seclusion was to the English.

Furthermore, for all that they were decked out in their best clothes, the Englishwomen's plain dress and lack of jewellery relative to the

'Moorish' ladies would have been suggestive of inferior rank, and – worse – that their husbands and fathers held them in low esteem.

It was not only the women who found them inexplicable. Indian men, too, found much about Englishwomen that was puzzling. Their constantly changing fashions were a particular mystery. When introduced to the wife of an English acquaintance, dressed in 'gala' [formal clothes] and wearing fashionable patches, one man enquired anxiously about the outbreak of disfiguring boils on her face, and expressed the polite wish that she would recover soon. In the late nineteenth century, when bustles were in vogue, there was a widely circulated rumour that Englishwomen had tails.

Indian women and English women lived in parallel universes. Apart from the lowest servant castes, they rarely met, if at all. One fact must have been all too clear: whatever form society would take, it would not – could not – ever include any Indian women.

# CHAPTER 5

In the eighteenth century, British women were in a tiny minority in India even among their own. According to one estimate, in 1700 in Madras there were only fifty. By 1771 the numbers had risen but still totalled only eighty-five European women and children. In the same period there were said to be fewer than two hundred white women in the whole of Bengal, as against four thousand British troops, two hundred and fifty East India Company officials and an unquantifiable number of private merchants, tradesmen, servants and mariners. The world they would have to navigate was almost totally dominated by men.

So, what was life really like when they finally arrived in India? Who did they meet, and how did they meet them? In the second half of the nineteenth century a document known as the Warrant of Precedence would rigidly dictate the social positions of each and every Englishwoman, from the Vicereine down to the wife of the lowliest Superintendent of Stamps and Stationery, but in the eighteenth century no such thing existed.

When they first arrived in India, newcomers found that even the three largest English settlements, the Presidencies of Bombay, Madras and Calcutta, had the feel of frontier towns. Social life had a provincial, almost homely feel to it. One British woman, born in Bombay in 1743, remembered that when she was a child the English community was still so small 'as to partake of a family character'. Everyone knew one another, and friends and acquaintances would simply drop in on one another's houses in the evenings for a dish of tea, enlivened by music and the occasional game of cards. When she returned to Bombay after a period of some years back in England, she was struck by how much 'the traditions of simplicity' had changed in the intervening years. Anglo-Indian society was slowly solidifying. 'Etiquette, ostentation and formality had too generally supplanted the urbanity, friendship and conviviality so delightful in former times.'[1]

A neat example of this enormous change can be found in descriptions of the newly created 'Setting Up Ceremony' to which all newcomers 'of the fair sex' were obliged to submit – even a former courtesan such as Charlotte Hickey. It was, in William Hickey's words, a 'disagreeable and foolish ceremony'.

The mistress of the house, being stuck up, full dressed, in a chair at the head of the best room (the apartment brilliantly lighted), having a female friend placed on each side, thus to receive the ladies of the settlement, three gentlemen being selected for the purpose of introducing the respective visitors, male and female, for every lady that called was attended by at least two gentlemen. One of the three gentlemen received the hand of the fair visitor at the door, led her up to the stranger, announcing her name, whereupon curtseys were exchanged, the visitor accepted a proffered seat amidst the numerous circle, where after remaining five, or at the most, ten minutes she arose, the salutations were then again exchanged, and the party retired to make way for the quick successor, this moving scene continuing from seven o'clock in the morning until past eleven. The same occurred the two following evenings, to the dreadful annoyance of the poor woman condemned to go through so tiresome and unpleasant a process. A further inconvenience was the necessity of returning every one of the visits thus made.[2]

In Britain, it was usual for only women to call on other women, and then only in the mornings; in India it took place in mixed company, and at night. What might have worked when society was smaller, less sophisticated and less male-dominated became something altogether different as the numbers swelled. The disproportionate number of men eager to view the newcomer gave the ceremony an unlooked-for and unpleasing edge, and there were those who complained that it was no better than a meat market. They were right. 'For I do aver,' wrote one commentator in the *Indian Gazette*, 'that no man of sentiment can take pleasure in seeing his sister or cousin sit dressed out like the queen of Sheba in a puppet shew; exposed to the public review of every forward young fellow, who can afford one hundred rupees for a new suit of clothes.'[3]

The dramatist Mariana Starke was even more specific, lampooning the custom in her play *The Sword of Peace; Or, A Voyage of Love*, written in 1789. Her character, Eliza, strongly objects 'to be obliged to be dressed up in grand gala, stuck on a Sopha [*sic*], at the upper end of a room for three nights running, to be view'd at will – as who should say – what d'ye please to buy, gentlemen? Monstrous! And then submitting to the salute of every man who approaches me, is such an indelicate custom.'[4]

In Charlotte Hickey's day the custom was already unpopular, and by the close of the century it had almost ceased, 'persons from thenceforward selecting their acquaintances according to liking as in Europe'.

So far, the society that was gradually coalescing around the British in India was a loose simulacrum of the society they had left behind, but far more porous than anything at home. Even so, it is interesting to speculate how 'Mrs Hickey' got on, when her turn came to be introduced into Calcutta society. It must have given her more than a pang of apprehension. Would there be an Eliza Fay to 'out' her and her disreputable past? In London, it would have been absolutely out of the question that such a deception could have been carried out. But in India the rules would be very different.

In the first few weeks of Charlotte Hickey's residence in India, she was exposed to a social group made up almost exclusively of men. Their behaviour towards her, and Hickey's response to it, suggests that no one was in any doubt about her dubious past. Yet as the couple made their slow progress up the Coromandel Coast from Sri Lanka to Calcutta, it was not only the men who made Mrs Hickey welcome. 'Mrs Hickey had this day (*22 March, 1783*) a number of female visitors, among the first of whom was Mrs Nixon, with two of her daughters, Lady Gordon, Mrs Barclay, Mrs Floyd, Mrs Tanner, Mrs Latham, the lovely Widow Maclellan, the Belle Johnston, etc.,' William Hickey wrote of their stop-off in Madras. 'The return of these and many other visits, with the numerous parties made for our entertainment, occupied several days.'

One reason for this could have been the sheer paucity of women in India at that time. Perhaps it is not surprising that they were not too fussy about such an agreeable addition to their ranks. It is highly likely, too, that many of them were not 'well bred' enough themselves either to notice or to care. The very names mentioned by Hickey – the 'Belle' Johnston, 'the lovely Widow' Maclellan – carry with them more than a whiff of the demi-monde. What is certain is that Charlotte Hickey was by no means the only courtesan to have been spirited across the oceans into new-minted respectability by her doting 'keeper'. William Hickey's great friend Bob Pott had also taken his 'favourite', Emily Warren, with him out to India just a few years previously.

Emily Pott's antecedents were even more scandalous than Charlotte Hickey's. When she was just twelve, she had been found begging on the streets of London by Mrs Hayes, one of London's most notorious madams. Mrs Hayes, that 'experienced old matron' (she was all of fifty), ran a famous 'house of celebrity' – a high-class brothel – at 2 King's Place, conveniently near St James's Palace and one of the most fashionable parts of London, where she specialised in training up young girls to the trade.

When she first spotted Emily, who was leading her blind father round the streets, Mrs Hayes was so struck by the 'uncommon beauty of the child's countenance' that she set her 'myrmidons' to work and, apparently without difficulty, soon got her into her clutches. Not only did she teach Emily to walk and move gracefully, but also to speak and converse in a ladylike manner, and to eschew all 'vulgarisms'. Emily even learned how to conceal the fact that she could neither read nor write by leaving the room whenever a note was delivered to her. 'Never did I behold so perfect a beauty,' William Hickey recalled of his first sight of Emily in 1776.[5] Joshua Reynolds, who painted her many times, declared that her every limb was in 'perfect symmetry, and altogether he had never seen so faultless and finely formed a human figure'.

Transformed from 'an unripe and awkward girl' into the pride of Mrs Hayes's establishment, Emily soon attracted the attention of Robert, or Bob, Pott, who set her up in style in 'a handsome well-furnished house in Cork Street', complete with a clutch of liveried servants, a dashing bright yellow carriage (all the rage in the 1770s) with the Pott coat of arms emblazoned on the side, and a box at the opera.[6] And when he left for India, what could be more natural than that he should take her with him?

In vain did his father, 'in an agony', plead with William Hickey to intercede. 'For do you know, Mr Hickey, the unthinking boy has taken that infamous and notoriously abandoned woman, Emily ... with him to India, a step that must not only shut him out of all proper society, but prevent his being employed in any situation of respect or emolument.' Mr Pott senior had done everything in his power to save his son from 'disgrace and ruin', he told Hickey, but to no avail. He had even tried to put pressure on the ship's captain, Captain Urmston, 'admonishing him against so unpardonable a fault as permitting a common prostitute to find her way to India on board his ship', until the poor captain was in a fever of anxiety that he would lose his job. But nothing had worked. With an arrogant fingers-up at the 'cheese-mongering' Company directors in Leadenhall Street, Bob Pott merely paid the captain off, and sailed away with his mistress triumphantly in tow.

Sadly, Emily Warren never reached India. She died on the voyage out, allegedly of prickly heat, and before any attempt was made to pass her off as 'Mrs Pott' on an unsuspecting Calcutta. Bob Pott had mourned his paramour, but the violence of his grief, we are told, 'was not of long duration'. He did however construct a memorial to her, which became known as 'Pott's Folly',* in the tiger- and mosquito-infested jungles near where she died just off the coast of Bengal. Far from the disgrace and ruin that his father had predicted for him, Pott went on to make a vast fortune and became one of the original Indian Nabobs.

The dilemma now facing his friend William Hickey, as he proceeded to Calcutta with the false 'Mrs Hickey' on his arm, was one that Bob Pott was well qualified to understand. Knowing this, Hickey had written to him from Madras, informing him of the companion he had with him, and the footing she was upon; and Pott had written back, gamely assuring his friend that he was prepared to meet her in company as an 'utter stranger' and not give their secret away. 'In spite of his disposition at all times to laugh, and his having been well acquainted with her in England, he conducted himself with the utmost propriety and decorum.'

There are complex reasons why the 'ostentation and formality' of the late eighteenth century came to replace the simple life of former times.

From the uncertain, early exploits of William Hawkins and Thomas Roe, desperate to secure the coveted *ferman*, or royal decree, granting them permanent trading rights in India, the East India Company had grown out of all recognition. By the early 1700s it had become the largest and wealthiest corporation in the English-speaking world. However, the British were not alone in wanting to exploit trading opportunities in India.

From the beginning there had always been stiff competition, not to say out-and-out hostility, from other Europeans, all of whom were now slugging it out for their share of the spoils. In the early days of the EIC it had been the Portuguese and then the Dutch who were

---

*The Italian architect of both Pott's Folly and the mausoleum over Emily's grave at Calcutta was a Mr Tiretta, known for some reason among the English as 'Nosey Jargon'.

Britain's main rivals. These were followed by the Danes, the Swedes and the Hapsburgs, all of whom founded trading settlements on the subcontinent. But by far the greatest threat as the century progressed came from their arch-enemy, the French.

At this point, the Company still had no thought of territorial conquest. Rather the opposite: for, as Thomas Roe had urged, 'if you will proffit, seek it at sea and in a quiett trade; for without controversy it is an errour to effect garrisons and land warrs in India'. But the reality of the situation meant that they had to think again. By the late seventeenth century the French were already fortifying Pondicherry, on the Coromandel Coast, and in 1672 had stormed and occupied the Portuguese settlement of San Thomé, a stone's throw from Madras. It was not long before the realisation struck that they could no longer trade simply as merchants. They needed properly fortified garrisons, firepower and a substantial military presence to protect them from their competitors, not only in Madras and Bombay, where forts already existed, but wherever British interests might extend.

With so many European powers vying with one another for a share of Indian spoils, it was inevitable that events on the Continent would play out on the Indian stage as well. The distances involved made for some strange happenings. The War of the Austrian Succession, which pitted the French against the British, was over long before news of it reached India, in September 1744. It made no difference to the participants. Two years later the French stormed and sacked the British held fortification at Madras, and for the next fifteen years the two nations were at each other's throats.

Timing was everything in what came to be called the Carnatic Wars.* After the death of the Emperor Aurangzeb in 1707, and a succession of weak and dissolute heirs, for the last half century the once powerful Mughal Empire had, 'like a crumbling popadam', been slowly disintegrating. Both France and Britain were quick to take

---

*The Carnatic is the area inland from the Coromandel Coast, on the south-east Indian littoral.

advantage of the ensuing chaos. In 1717, after more than a century of nail-biting patience and bribery, the British had finally managed to wrangle the longed-for *ferman* from one of Aurangzeb's short-lived successors – an occasion that was greeted at all three Presidencies with ecstatic celebrations, processions, bonfires, music, feasting and a 151-gun salute. It was a heady moment. The Company was now convinced that it had a winning advantage over its rivals. The French had other ideas. Sanctioned by another major European conflict, the Seven Years' War (the nearest thing the eighteenth century had to a world war), which broke out in 1756, the two powers locked horns in a ferocious battle for supremacy.

Although they could neither fight one another directly nor make conquests in their own name, by allying themselves to opposing factions within the crumbling empire they quickly extended their spheres of influence. It was not until 1757, when under Robert Clive the Battle of Plassey (Palashi) was fought, and decisively won, against the Nawab of Bengal, Siraj-ud-Daulah, and his French allies, that hostilities came – more or less – to an end, and Britain emerged as the major European political power in India.

After Plassey, everything changed. In 1765, the Mughal Emperor was forced to grant the British revenue-raising powers, known as *diwani*, over the provinces of Bengal, Bihar and Orissa in northern India. With a puppet Nawab now installed in Bengal, the British had effectively become proxy rulers of a vast area of north-east India. From now on, taxes replaced trade as the principal source of revenue.[*]

This was not the first time that tax collecting had featured in British affairs. As far back as the 1660s in Bombay, the British had inherited the Portuguese system whereby its residents remitted a quarter of their income to the government. The same system was soon adopted at Madras. And in Bengal in 1698 the Nawab had granted the Company the chance to purchase tax-gathering rights to three villages amid which Calcutta was slowly taking shape. But it was not until

---

[*]In a secret letter to the Prime Minister, William Pitt the Elder, Robert Clive estimated that the anticipated annual revenue from Bengal alone was upwards of two million pounds sterling.

now that the opportunities for making money – serious amounts of money – emerged.

With the increase of riches came many more people, both men and women, all hoping to profit by it. Administrators, a judiciary and many more troops were all now needed, in addition to an already existing merchant class, to govern and protect the rapidly swelling British community. In 1773, the British Parliament passed a 'Regulating Act' which put in place an entire infrastructure through which the East India Company would effectively govern these territories. This included a Supreme Council, made up of five councillors, the principal of which was Warren Hastings in the newly created role of Governor-General, and a Supreme Court of Judicature.

Shopkeepers, victuallers, innkeepers, actors, musicians and painters were needed to feed and amuse them. No one went there without a licence from the Company. The East India Company's Bengal establishment 'grew prodigiously, and increasingly its outward-bound ships carried more in the way of troops and stores, passengers and European luxuries than they did of broadcloths'.[7]

William Hickey meant no irony when he spoke of the 'propriety and decorum' shown by his friend Robert Pott in turning a blind eye to the introduction of a notorious courtesan into Calcutta society, but these were not qualities that were much in evidence elsewhere. Those who now braved their way to India, through ocean storms and across howling deserts, were not, as the novelist E. M. Forster once put it, people of the first order; what's more, in his opinion, they 'give an account of Calcutta that would never occur to the well-bred, the highly educated, the sincerely pious, or the satisfactorily introduced'.[8] There were some men and women who fitted Forster's ideal, but a great many fell far short.

India became a dumping ground for the dissolute, the bankrupt, and those of dubious morality. Calcutta in particular was 'one of the most wicked places in the Universe', wrote Robert Clive, 'Rapacious and luxurious beyond conception'.[9] Within a matter of days of arriving in Madras, William Hickey recalled that he had met with no fewer than six old London acquaintances 'every one of who had been ruined by boundless extravagance which compelled them to abandon their native shore'.

The first of these was O'Hara, an old school-fellow from Westminster. When he was seventeen, O'Hara's father had purchased a commission for him in the Guards, but he quickly landed himself so deeply in debt that his father could no longer afford to pay his debtors 'and was driven to the necessity of sending him abroad as a cadet in the East India Company's service, then the last resource of ruined profligates'. To this he added the stories of the other five – Tomkins, 'Handsome Lee' and 'Bouquet Byde' (so-called because he always wore a large nosegay), the fox-hunting Darby, and Williams, a captain in the Light Dragoons – each tale as unedifying as the next, and usually involving cheating their creditors back in England.

These 'dissipated London dashers' were not the only unsavoury types among whom women would be obliged to mix. The new wave of political and administrative appointees now reaching Calcutta could be equally reprobate.

Government appointments were eagerly sought depending on the emoluments they were likely to bring with them. Despite much hand-wringing by critics of the East India Company back in England (of which there were many), the EIC officials themselves were shameless in their pursuit of riches. In fact, so great were the rewards that many were happy to pay for the privilege. One Resident at Rungpore left his post after less than eighteen months 'with so overgrown a fortune as to be enabled to return with all his family to England, get into the House of Commons and purchase a fine estate in Essex'.[10] The fortunes of Charlotte and William Hickey's friend Robert Pott are an even more extreme example of what rapidly became the norm in British-controlled India: corruption on a massive scale.

Pott's great object had been to secure the position of Resident at the Court of the Nawab of Bengal, in Murshidabad, which was considered the most lucrative office in the Company's service. And through his family connections with Lord Thurlow, then Lord High Chancellor of England, this he soon did. The entire stipend paid by the Company to the Nabob passed through the Resident's hands, 'in which channel', Hickey observed cheerfully, 'a considerable portion of it always stuck to his fingers'. This was not the only way to siphon money from the Nawab's exchequer. The Resident was also the middle-man when it came to purchasing any European article that the Nawab wished for, and of course took his cut. An even more advantageous post was that of Collector of Customs for Murshidabad and Cossimbazar (Kasimbazar). 'Pott, however, did not attain these enviable situations without paying exorbitantly for them.'

The directors of the East India Company, who had always, even in the happiest circumstances, been highly critical of their factors abroad, decried in vain 'the luxurious, expensive and idle manner of life' lived by their employees. Their women were thought to be equally to blame.

But what did they care? The wealth which now stuck so liberally to English fingers had vastly increased their own opportunities for self-advancement, not only in the marriage market but also in a surprising number of places elsewhere. It also began, slowly, to create an environment that was just a little more familiar, a little less alien than it had been.

# CHAPTER 6

Since its foundation by an EIC factor, Job Charnock, just under a hundred years earlier, Calcutta had changed out of all recognition. Once an unprepossessing stretch of swampland and a few mud huts on a bend of the Hooghly River, by the mid-eighteenth century it was the most important of the three Presidencies, an elegant town of white stuccoed buildings with government offices, a court house, a 'Harmonicon' (a dancing house, concert hall and tavern that stood in the Loll Bazaar, opposite the jail), a playhouse and even a church, St John's.

'The most interesting views that can possibly be imagined, greet the eye,' wrote one newcomer in 1780. 'The banks of the river are as one may say absolutely studded with elegant mansions, called here garden-houses. These houses are surrounded by groves and lawns, which descend to the waters edge, and present a constant succession of whatever can delight the eye, or bespeak wealth and elegance in the owners. The noble appearance of the river also, which is much wider than the Thames at London,' she noted approvingly, 'together with the amazing variety of vessels continually passing on its surface, add to the beauty of the scene.'[1]

Not only were trading vessels and ships of war moored there, but budgerows – covered barges large enough to accommodate a whole family – and many other varieties of pleasure boat, including the whimsically named snake boat. All of these swarmed across the waters providing 'a magnificent and beautiful moving picture'.

Garden Reach was situated nine miles upriver from Calcutta itself. Travellers approaching the city from the Bay of Bengal would pass first the new Fort William, and then the old Fort, the site of the infamous 'Black Hole' of Calcutta some twenty years previously and now in the process of being demolished. The domestic dwellings of the British were almost all within a half-mile radius.

A glance at Hickey's (no relation to William) *Bengal Gazette* – something like an eighteenth-century cross between the *Argos* catalogue and *Private Eye* – gives a snapshot of what daily life in Calcutta would have been like for a British woman arriving in Bengal around 1780. She might have visited John Richard's newly opened Pastry Cook and Confectionery Shop, 'in the lane behind the house lately inhabited by Mr Carmichael, in the Loll Bazaar'. If she were intending to travel, whether by land or by sea, the same shop could furnish her with potted meats, preserves, pickles and other foodstuffs 'that will keep a considerable time'. At the Harmonic Tavern she might meet her friends at the newly established Public Room, 'for coffee and other refreshments', perusing a different bill of fare for every day of the week, 'Sundays and Harmonic [concert] Days excepted'.

On another day the *Gazette* may have prompted her to hurry quickly to Mr Cartwell's establishment near the theatre to snap up 'A Quantity of high flavoured old Madeira in Pipes,* and Fresh Porter in Hogsheads, upon very reasonable terms'.[2] She might also have made a bid for one of two garden houses, 'very pleasantly situated, at an easy distance from Town', which had the added benefit of roads which were passable for carriages all year round, and purchased a 'neat second-hand phaeton and pair of horses with harnesses complete' in which to travel there. In fact, she could have sourced anything from a 'Ten Oared Budgerow, with a Dingy, Rigging, Sails Etc.' to planks of wood and indigo seeds. Here, too, could be found details for the horse and dog painter who had recently set up a studio at No. 488 Loll Bazaar, as well as advertisements for the latest theatrical performances.

*A cask for wine.

When it came to dress, however, women were required to be a little more inventive. This was an era of elaborately hooped dresses and outrageously decorated headdresses, and where at all possible they sent home to friends and family to make sure of acquiring the latest fashions, apparently undeterred by the grindingly slow process that it entailed, when the shopping lists alone could take a year or more to reach England.

The correspondence of Margaret Fowke, the daughter of an English diamond merchant who wrote letters from India between 1776 and 1786, is full of such sartorial shopping lists. In December 1781 she was writing to a friend asking for:

> 3 pairs of black stuff shoes
> 2 pairs of green shoes
> 6 pairs of embroidered silk shoes, not upon black ground unless the embroidery is of silver
> 4 pairs of coloured silk or satin shoes – the colours bright.

Another shopping list requested yet more shoes: 'a dozen or so pair silk or satin shoes whichever wears the best, but not to let 3 or 4 in the number be embroidered, as I believe they are very expensive'.

In addition to the huge quantities of footwear, hats, caps and trimmings for the enormous headdresses then in fashion were in hot demand. Margaret Fowke requested two beaver riding hats, one black, one white, each decorated with feathers, specifying that they should be 'handsome ostrich ones' and not the kind made 'of several little ones fastened together which never sit well'. Other trimmings on her list included:

> 6 very handsome white feathers, not the round foxtail sort
> 2 of a good black, the feathers to be in one, or at most two
> 2 of a bright not deep pink
> 2 lilac
> 2 blue.[3]

Her correspondent, Mrs Strachey, had refused to send the feathers first time round as they 'were not the *ton* in England', but Miss Fowke was determined to have them. 'Feathers are worn here thro' all the changes of fashion in England,' she explained to another friend, Mrs Weelock, 'and I have often been without them when every other lady has her head full of plumes.'[4]

Quite how such delicate items as ostrich feathers could have survived the long, turbulent sea journeys in leaky Company ships is something of a mystery, but clearly they sometimes did. In fact, such was the determination and persistence of the sartorially minded that even the more outré London fashions quickly found their way to India.

Eliza Fay had been amazed by how well dressed the women were when she first arrived. 'The ladies here are very fashionable I assure you,' she wrote home: 'I found several novelties in dress since I quitted England, which a good deal surprised me, as I had no idea that fashions travelled so fast.'[5] On 19 July 1784, Messrs Baxter & Ord put an announcement in the *Bengal Gazette* which proudly announced the sale of 'a small but elegant assortment of millinery amongst which are the much admired and New-Fashioned Lady's Balloon Hats'. Perhaps Margaret Fowke was lucky enough already to possess one of these treasures, as two of her sartorial 'agents' visiting London from Calcutta, Mrs D (von Danckelmann) and Lady C (Chambers), had been spied by a third friend, Mrs Plowden, shopping for 'all the elegances' of the current season to take back to India with them. Between September 1780 and March 1781 no fewer than five letters in Margaret Fowke's correspondence are devoted to the pursuit of the elusive colour Devonshire brown; while another, the equally recondite *couleur de corbeau* (crow black), enjoyed a brief but feverish vogue among the Calcutta fashionistas.

When Margaret Fowke and her friend Mrs Hay shared a box of millinery at auction (the contents were sold as lots, and could not be divided up) they nearly came to blows over one particular item. 'A little miracle of a cap,' was how Margaret described it, ' . . .

independent of all Fashion – a Turk – a Persian – A Raja would admire it – an uncommon kind of feather, quite white and exquisitely beautiful, a lily of the valley – a little ripe wheat – some flowers which I have seen in our garden at home and which appear in the cap with colours equally vivid – as if just gathered from one of these enchanting spots, were the ornaments.'[6] Since there was only one such object of desire they were obliged to draw lots for it. Mrs Hay won.

It was not only fashion and luxury goods that women could read about in the *Bengal Gazette*. A perusal of the same newspaper would have informed them of the latest government appointments, and of any new regulations governing the town, such as a decree banning the breaking-in of horses on the esplanade. They might even have put in an order with Captain Robert Smith, who begged leave 'to acquaint his Friends and the Public in general that he departs for China the later end of January next, and those who wish to favour him with their Commissions will be pleased to send them as soon as possible, directed to him at his House near the China Bazaar'. They might also have taken the opportunity to read of the latest births, marriages and deaths – the latter being particularly interesting as each death in the community was sure to be followed by a list of the deceased's effects, soon up for sale at bargain prices.

Most enticing of all, however, was the salacious gossip for which the *Bengal Gazette* was notorious. 'A few days ago,' reads a typical snippet, 'a dispute arose between two young gentlemen not many miles from Serampore about a lady of sooty complexion. The friends of both were of some apprehension that a duel would have been the consequence, but it happily ended in a reciprocal bastinado.'[7]

One woman who would particularly have relished such snippets was Eliza Fay. Mrs Fay is one of the great female characters in British India. Born in 1756, in Blackheath, when she was twenty-three she married Anthony Fay, a young advocate of Irish extraction, and set off to India to make her fortune. 'Her mental equipment was that of an intelligent lady's maid ... who has read Mrs Radcliffe, Pope, and

*Nubilia in Search of a Husband*, and can allude at a pinch to Queen Christina of Sweden,' was E. M. Forster's patronising opinion of her in the introduction which he wrote to her letters. She could 'splash about in French', and was quick to pick up smatterings of Italian, Portuguese, Hindustani and – weirdly – shorthand. She loved music, was 'pious without enthusiasm', and knew how to play backgammon, cards and chess (at which she was invariably beaten). She travelled with a pair of globes, 'although geography could never had been her strong point, for she thought that the Alps were only one mountain thick, and the Malabar Hills the third highest range in the world'. She and her husband 'were both of them under-bred and quarrelsome, and he was a fool to boot'.

Eliza Fay, on the other hand, was anything but a fool. No one could be further from the stereotype of the 'real Indian lady' – bored, languid, too spoiled even to pick up their own handkerchiefs. In her marriage, Mrs Fay was quite convinced that she wore the trousers. On delivering her letter of introduction to Marian Hastings, wife of Governor-General Warren Hastings, she was stung by the lady's unsympathetic hearing of the dangers she had survived on her journey (of which more later). 'Alas!' she exclaims, 'Mrs H— could not know ... that I undertook the journey with a view of preserving my husband from destruction, for had I not accompanied him, and in many instances restrained his extravagance and dissipated habits, he would never, never, I am convinced, have reached Bengal, but have fallen a wretched sacrifice to them on the way, or perhaps through the violence of his temper been involved in some dispute, which he was too ready to provoke.'[8]

Eliza Fay wrote letters to her family from India on three separate trips there between 1779 and 1797. Her grammar and use of pronouns may have been 'most personally her own', but her character – quick-witted, energetic, just a tad vulgar – shines from every page. 'This story,' she insisted in a typical aside, 'must be told in my own way, or not at all.'

And so it is. We read of her early, slightly bungled attempts at housekeeping, 'which is no little trouble in a country where the servants will not do a single thing, but that for which you expressly engage them nor even that willingly', she complained. 'I just now asked a man to place a small table near me; he began to bawl as loud as he could for the bearers to come and help him. "Why don't you do it yourself," said I, rising as I spoke to assist. *Oh no I no English. I Bengal man. I no strong like English; one, two three Bengal man cannot do like one Englishman.*'

We learn the exact price of her house – only two hundred rupees a month, as opposed to three or four hundred, 'because it is not in a part of town much esteemed'; and we are party to her mingled admiration and disdain for grander establishments. Marian Hastings's house five miles outside Calcutta is, she exclaims, 'a perfect *bijoux*' (shades of Jane Austen's Mrs Elton), 'most superbly fitted up with all that unbounded affluence can display; but still deficient in that simple elegance which the wealthy so seldom attain, from the circumstances of not being obliged to search for effect without much cost, which those but moderately rich find to be indispensable.'

Mrs Fay, who despite her best efforts would never be even moderately rich, nonetheless kept a handsome table. Although she had been led to believe that the hot weather in Bengal would destroy the appetite, she herself never saw any proof of that: 'on the contrary I cannot help thinking that I never saw an equal quantity of victuals consumed'.

Both she and her husband were themselves excellent trenchermen, despite the fact that their dinners were eaten, as was everyone's in eighteenth-century Calcutta, at two o'clock in the afternoon, the hottest time of day. 'At this moment,' she wrote, 'Mr F— is looking out with a hawk's eye for his dinner; and though still much of an invalid' – *sigh* – 'I have no doubt of being able to pick a bit myself.'

A typical dinner in the Hay household consisted of 'a soup, a roast fowl, curry and rice, a mutton pie, a fore-quarter of lamb, a rice pudding, very good cheese, fresh churned butter, fine bread, excellent

Madeira (that is expensive but eatables are very cheap)'.* Helpfully, Mrs Fay goes on to enumerate the exact cost of the ingredients. 'A whole sheep costs but two rupees; a lamb one rupee, six good fowls or ducks ditto – twelve pigeons ditto – twelve pounds of bread ditto – two pound of butter ditto; and a joint of veal ditto – good cheese two months ago sold for the enormous price of three or four rupees per pound, but now you may buy it for one and a half – English claret sells at this time for sixty rupees a dozen. There's a price for you!'

In the afternoons, most people took to their beds to sleep off these gargantuan, drunken dinners: 'for the custom ... is so general that the streets of Calcutta are from four to five in the afternoon almost as empty of Europeans as if it were midnight'.

After a siesta, the fashion was to repair to the 'Course' – the race-course – to see and be seen, and to take what air they could, 'though sure of being half suffocated with dust'. Later they returned home to drink tea, which they continued to do even in the extremes of hot weather. After tea, it was cards and music until suppertime at ten. The card games then popular were five-card loo, tré dillé and whist. A rupee a 'fish'† was the norm. 'This will strike you as being enormously high,' she noted airily, 'but it is thought nothing of here.'

Formal visits were conducted in the evening, and were generally very short, 'as each lady has a dozen to make and a party waiting for her at home besides'. The gentlemen, such as they were, also called at this time, and the etiquette was that if they were asked to put down their hat, it was considered an invitation to stay to supper. 'Many a hat have I seen vainly dangling in its owner's hand for half an hour,' Eliza

*Excessive alcohol consumption among the British in India was nothing if not traditional. In July 1716, the 'monstrous month', nineteen EIC employees at Fort Marlborough consumed '74 dozen and half of wine [mostly very expensive claret], 24 dozen and a half of Burton Ale and pale beer, 2 pipes and 42 gallons of Madeira wine, 6 flasks of Shiraz [Persian wine], 274 bottles of toddy, 3 Leaguers and 3 Quarters of Batavia arrack, and 164 gallons of Goa [toddy]'. The Directors in London were apoplectic. 'It is a wonder to us that any of you live six months, and that there are not more quarrel-lings and duellings amongst you, if half these liquors were guzzled down ... We will not have our wine spent but at meals. If you will have it at other times, pay for it yourselves.' Quoted in Keay's *The Honourable Company: A History of the English East India Company*.
†A fish was an ivory or mother-of-pearl counter used in card games, so-called not because they were in the shape of a fish (although some were), but from the French *fiche*, a peg or card counter.

Fay wrote, 'who at last has been compelled to withdraw without any one's offering to relieve him from the burthen.'

Charlotte Hickey was not the only woman to find that the rules governing society in India were different. As the wife of an attorney at the Courts of Law, Eliza Fay soon found that she had a status that was much more elevated than anything she had enjoyed at Blackheath. At first she was a little in awe of it all (for which we rather love her). Very shortly after her arrival she was visited by Sir Robert Chambers* and his wife. Due to her own ill health she had been unable to pay her respects to them first, as would have been proper, but on hearing something of her 'melancholy story' Lady Chambers 'had the goodness to waive all ceremony to visit me ... Which was a condescension that I certainly had no right to expect.'

'She is the most beautiful woman I ever beheld,' Mrs Fay recorded, 'in the bloom of youth; and there is an agreeable frankness in her manners, that enhances her loveliness, and renders her truly fascinating.'

Her encounters with Marian Hastings, the 'First Lady' of Calcutta, were altogether less comfortable. At first, Mrs Fay was not sure quite how to behave in such august company. She did not have the right dresses in which to be seen at the grander social occasions, and had to borrow some from Lady Chambers until she could have her own made up. Her manners, too, were not quite what they should have been, despite her best efforts to cover up her mistakes.

A friend had procured her a ticket to the Harmonicon, which was supported by a 'select' number of men who, in alphabetic rotation, each gave a concert, ball or supper during the cold season. At this 'elegant amusement' (more shades of Mrs Elton) she noticed Mrs Hastings coming in rather late to the party. She 'happened to place herself on the opposite side of the room, beyond a speaking distance, so strange to tell, I quite forgot that she was there!' Eliza wrote. Luckily her observant friend Mrs Jackson noticed the faux pas,

---

*A friend of Dr Johnson, Sir Robert was a judge in the Supreme Court, and later Chief Justice. He and his wife became Eliza's chief protectors in Calcutta. 'Mrs Fay does not mention them in her subsequent visits,' Forster points out in his introduction; 'possibly they had seen enough of her.'

and after a while asked her if she had paid her respects to the Lady Governess. 'I answered in the negative, having no opportunity, as she had not chanced to look towards me when I was prepared to do so. "Oh," replied the kind old lady, "you must fix your eyes on her, and never take them off 'til she notices you. Miss Chantry has done this, and so have I; it is absolutely necessary to avoid giving offence."'

Eliza Fay, although nothing if not a quick learner, was always a little in awe of Marian Hastings. 'It is easy to perceive at the first glance that she is far superior to the generality of her sex ... ' she confided to her family at home. 'She is indeed raised to a "giddy height" and expects to be treated with the most profound respect and deference.'

Nerves, one suspects, made her garrulous. When she went on at length about her 'misfortunes' on the journey out, she got short shrift from the Lady Governess, who suggested that it was her own fault for making the journey there in the first place. Eliza, although miffed to find that her adventures were not nearly so fascinating to others as they were to her, was philosophical. 'Those basking in the lap of prosperity can little appreciate the sufferings or make allowance for the errors of the unfortunate; whom they regard as almost beings of another order,' she wrote, adding loftily, 'but I excuse her.'

Mrs Hastings, formerly Anne Maria Apollonia Chapuset, was herself a bizarre and controversial figure in Anglo-India (which is perhaps the reason she was such a stickler for etiquette). She had met and fallen in love with the future Governor-General on the boat coming out to India. All would have proceeded normally had it not been for the inconvenient fact that she was accompanied by a husband, Baron Carl von Imhoff, at the time. Once arrived in Calcutta she quickly divorced the Baron and married Hastings, in 1777, but although the marriage was perfectly legal, it scandalised the British, among whom at the time divorce was extremely rare, and then only possible through an Act of Parliament. Many regarded the new Mrs Hastings as little better than an adventuress.

Several rumours circulated about Marian Hastings in Eliza Fay's time, the most persistent of which was that she had amassed a large personal fortune by the time she returned home to England. Years later, when Warren Hastings was impeached on corruption charges, he told the chairman of the EIC that his wife had a personal fortune of £40,000. In fact it was well over £100,000, an immense sum (about fourteen million pounds in today's money). But all this was in the future. In Eliza Fay's day, everything about Mrs Hastings, from the way she wore her auburn hair in loose, unpowdered ringlets around her shoulders to her highly personal style of dressing, was the subject of gossip.

Mrs Fay put Marian Hastings's eccentricity down to her funny foreign ways. 'Her whole dress too, though studiously becoming, being at variance with our present modes which are certainly not so, perhaps for that reason, she has chosen to depart from them – as a foreigner you know, she may be excused for not strictly conforming to your fashions.'[9]

Others were not so forgiving. The opulence of Mrs Hastings's wardrobe was a particular source of fascination. One of her satin riding habits, trimmed with pearls and diamonds, was said to be worth as much as £30,000.[10] Her exotic way of dressing, added to the lavish quantity of jewels that she was fond of wearing, raised many questions about her honesty. In 'The Rolliad', an anonymous satirical poem of the time, she makes a splendid appearance:

> 'Tis Mrs Hastings' self brings up the rear!'
> Gods! How her diamonds flock
> On each powdered lock!
> On every membrane see a topaz clings!
> Behold! Her joints are fewer than her rings![11]

It was not only Marian Hastings who was fond of opulence. Luxury goods, for both men and women, were easily available, as this list of elegant commodities (as Mrs Fay might have described them) advertised in the *Bengal Gazette* shows:

**STORIA DELL'INDIA.**

12.   Prima fattoria inglese, a Surat.

SAPIS, ESTRATTO DI CARNE E DI VEGETALI DELLA COMP. LIEBIG

*Riproduzione vietata.*          *Spiegazione a tergo.*

Artist's impression of the early seventeenth-century English factory at Surat, in present-day Gujarat – the first to be built in Mughal lands. Part-warehouse, part-merchants' living quarters, it was to this strictly all-male preserve that the first three Englishwomen – Mrs Hudson, Mrs Towerson and the pregnant Mrs Steel – found their way in 1617, just six years after its foundation. No one was pleased to see them.

The tiny archipelago of Bombay was part of the dowry of the Portuguese princess Catherine of Braganza on her marriage to the newly restored English king Charles II. In 1668, it was leased to the East India Company for £10 a year, in perpetuity. The need to populate their new colony made the Company directors reconsider their policy towards women, who until now they had tried to ban from travelling to India. Advertisements for single women, aged as young as twelve, and of 'sober' dispositions, willing to take the appalling risks of travelling to India, are recorded in the Company minutes.

Along with storms and sickness, piracy was one of the dangers of a sea voyage that in the seventeenth century could take anything up to eighteen months. Some women were freed because their families were able to pay ransom money to recover them; others were sold into slavery.

The steady trickle of women arriving at the English factories in the second half of the seventeenth century seems to have done little to improve the general behaviour there. Eating at a communal table was customary in some factories until well into the eighteenth century, when drunkenness, swearing and rowdy food-throwing were often so out of hand that rows of soldiers with muskets were required to keep order.

A Native Lady in her Palkee.

The apparent absence of Indian women, other than 'the lowliest servant classes', in public life was hard for their European sisters to understand. Most Indian women, whatever their caste or creed, observed strict purdah. To be invited to visit them in their *zenanas* was a privilege granted to relatively few Englishwomen.

Admiral Sir Edward and Lady Hughes. Watercolour in the Madras style, c.1783. Unlike men, who in the eighteenth century often adopted comfortable Indian clothing, women stuck to European fashions, despite their extraordinary unsuitability in a hot climate. Many women sent home for shoes, hooped skirts and even the elaborate millinery required for their enormous headdresses, even though such items could take several years to arrive.

An official of the East India Company riding in state with an escort of soldiers. As their influence and power grew, the British were quick to give themselves imperial airs. The palanquin carried on the shoulders of four bearers was probably the conveyance of a wife or mistress, which in the tolerant eighteenth century was as likely to be an Indian *bibi* as a British woman.

Photograph of Flora Annie Steel, the co-author of the hugely influential *Complete Indian Housekeeper and Cook* (1888), a handbook for British women living in India. Flora Annie Steel came to everything she did with 'quite appalling energy'. During her twenty-two years in India, she wrote more than thirty books, including *Tales of the Punjab*, a collection of folk stories. She also founded several schools, and was a lifelong crusader for education for women.

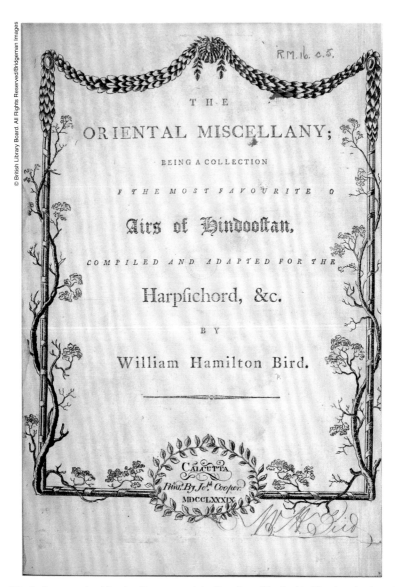

R.M.16.c.5.

THE

ORIENTAL MISCELLANY;

BEING A COLLECTION

OF THE MOST FAVOURITE

Airs of Hindoostan,

COMPILED AND ADAPTED FOR THE

Harpsichord, &c.

BY

William Hamilton Bird.

CALCUTTA

Print.d By Joh. Cooper.

MDCCLXXXIX

The Indian songs in this miscellany were originally collected by Sophia Plowden. A talented musician in her own right, Mrs Plowden first heard them at a *nautch,* or musical party, the only social occasion at which Indian women, the *nautch* girls themselves, were present in mixed company. Mrs Plowden collaborated with the famous Kashmiri courtesan and singer, Khanum Jan – a huge celebrity in her day – to adapt the songs for European instruments.

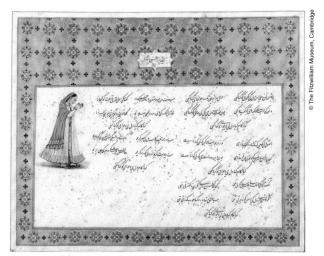

These exquisitely decorated and gold-leafed cards were found among Sophia Plowden's papers in the Fitzwilliam Museum. Originally catalogued as paintings, they in fact contain the Urdu words to the *mukhammas*, Sufi-influenced poetry, sung by Khanum Jan.

The *ferman*, or royal decree, granting Sophia Plowden the title of Begum is still held in the British Library. The honour conferred on her by the Mughal Emperor Shah Alam II, himself a renowned poet, suggests that hers was a true collaboration, recognised by Indians as well as Europeans.

Black-necked stork, by Shaikh Zain ud-Din. Calcutta, 1777. Gouache on paper. One of a series of extraordinary paintings commissioned by Mary, Lady Impey, the wife of the Calcutta Chief Justice, Sir Elijah Impey. Lady Impey employed three Patna-trained Mughal artists to make fine, large-scale natural history studies of Indian birds and animals.

Gold Enamelled Shoe and
   Knee buckles
Gold headed Canes
China and country Sugar-
   Candy of all sorts
Pictures
Looking Glasses
Silk Carpets,
   large and small
Silver and Plated
   Shoe Buckles
Silver Plate
Silk and Cotton Stockings
Lavender Water
Stoughton's Drops
Velvet Hunting Caps
Plain and Gilt Coat and
   Waistcoat Buttons
White bordered
   Handkerchiefs
Painted Handkerchiefs
Madras Muslin
Ivory Fans
Silk Gloves
Silver Watches
Diamond Rings and Rose
   Diamond Rings

Gold Snuff Boxes
Gold Watches and Chains
Lady's Watch with Seal
Pearls of all sorts
German Flutes
Gold Lace of Different Sorts
Thread Lace
Black Lace
Dimity Silk
Wax Candles
Palanquins
Muskets
Europe Vinegar in Casks
   and Bottles
Coffin Furniture
Patna Opium
Chintz of different Patterns,
   coarse and fine
Black Hats
Tweezer Cases
Spying Glasses
Quadrants
Flowered Silk
Damask of different Colours
And a variety of other
   Articles.[12]

Eliza Fay, for one, was quite shocked by the reckless way in which the British spent their money – whether they could afford to or not. 'I assure you much caution is requisite to avoid running deeply into debt – the facility of obtaining credit is beyond what I could have imagined,' she wrote. East India Company employees, according to her, were particularly prone to extravagance. Shopkeepers, both British ones anxious for custom and their Indian equivalents, known as *banias*, would offer anything between five and ten thousand rupees' worth of goods on tick. 'It is not uncommon to see *writers* [the most junior Company position] within a few months of their arrivals dashing away on the course in a *four in hand*,' she gasped: 'allowing for the inconsiderateness of youth, is it surprising that many of them become deeply embarrassed?'[13]

For all their spendthrift ways, whether it was by acquiring a four-in-hand or a phaeton, such as the one Charlotte Hickey had quickly acquired, the British were eager to demonstrate their newly elevated status. Even those from relatively humble backgrounds hired vast numbers of servants and rode about in palanquins, an elite form of transport requiring four to eight bearers. In 1771 in Dacca (Dhaka), where the Nawab of Bengal had made his capital, Elizabeth Marsh, the wife of a salt merchant, acquired not one but four *morchals*, fly-whisks made of peacock feathers, traditional Indo-Persian symbols of power (she probably just thought them decorative). The most success-ful built themselves large houses surrounded by parkland. Most telling of all, they had themselves painted.

The garden conversation piece, enormously popular with the English gentry in the mid-eighteenth century, became a favourite of British colonial officials. Typically, it showed a couple and sometimes their children standing in their own grounds, a palatial country house just glimpsed in the background. Zoffany's painting of Marian and Warren Hastings, for example, shows Mrs Hastings resplendent in a gold satin dress with an Indian servant by her side holding her hat. The aim of the paintings was 'to celebrate, commemorate and legiti-mate a family's exclusive possession of a landed estate'.[14] The newly rich in India, eager to advertise their status and power, jumped on this tradition with enthusiasm (although, as was so often the case, not before it had fallen from fashion back at home).

Those returning to England, even with modest wealth, were the focus of a mixture of unease, jealousy and ridicule. Their Indianised ways were not always found to be in good taste.

'I retired to my room to equip myself in one of my gay Indian coats, being of scarlet with a rich spangled and foil lace ... of which I was not a little vain,' wrote William Hickey on returning to London in 1780. When he appeared in this eye-catching attire, his brother merely remarked that he thought it 'a little gaudy'. His friends were less forgiving. At the theatre that night his costume created quite a stir, but not the kind that he was intending. An old acquaintance, visiting him in his box, jokingly told him he looked like nothing so much as 'the Lord Mayor's trumpeter'. This quip raised such a laugh at his expense that poor Hickey determined to get rid of it immediately, and also 'upwards of twenty coats equally ornamented and rich that I had brought from Bengal'.[15]

Like William Hickey, those returning from India with their trumpery finery, their money and their suspect foreign ways were not particularly popular. A class of the newly super rich – the so-called Nabobs* – came in for special opprobrium, not only because they were able to ape the aristocracy and landed gentry, but because they aspired to become them.

Once again, poets and playwrights found the changing status quo a source for ruthless satire. In Samuel Foote's play *The Nabob*, Sir Matthew Mite, who 'owes his rise to the ruin of thousands', comes 'thundering' among the impoverished but nobly born Sir John and Lady Oldham and their friends, 'profusely scattering the spoils of ruined provinces'. As the play opens Sir Matthew is seen in his shiny new gaming dress, taking lessons from his butler in how to throw dice in a fashionable way, and boning up on the latest oaths and phrases most in use at the Club. Although Mite is presented as a ludicrous figure, the enormous wealth at his fingertips gives him an unsettling power. He has already bought his title, but now intends to force the Oldhams to sell him their estate, and their grand house, by offering them four times its value. Worse still, he presumes (shock, horror) to offer for the Oldhams' daughter's hand in marriage: 'young girls are easily caught with titles and splendour,' he declares, 'magnificence has a kind of magic for them'. If he is successful, he will at his own expense

---

*Nabob was a corruption of Nawab. My grandmothers still used this word to describe someone with 'new money'.

transport her two younger sisters to either Calcutta or Madras 'and there procure them suitable husbands'. And so the circle would go on.

In Fanny Burney's delightful jeu d'esprit *A Busy Day*, performed for one night only in 1795, the contrast between the vulgar, newly rich Tibbses and the aristocratic family of the hero, Cleveland, is even more pronounced. In Calcutta, Cleveland has met (yet another) Eliza, the only sensible member of the Tibbs family, and on their return to England wants to marry her, but first he has to appease his formidable aunt Lady Wilhelmina. Mr Tibbs, having been told by his elder daughter Miss Tibbs (catchphrase: '*La*! Pa—') that he is 'very like a person of qualitee', is certain that he can impress Lady Wilhelmina. 'Nay, I'll bet you sixpence I can do after the manner of that Lord Thing-um, and that t'other fine Mister as was here just now, so as you would not know one of us from t'other.'

It does not go well.

Enter Lady Wilhelmina:

LW: How enormously unfortunate that the servants are not to be found. (Spotting Mr Tibbs) I know not which way to turn my eyes to avoid some disagreeable object.

Mr Tibbs: How do do.

LW: What?

Mr T: I hope you do confounded well?

LW: Heavens.

Mr T: O the Doose and the Divil, and the Plague.

LW: What inscrutable effrontery! I'll look him into a statue. (Fixes her eyes upon him and frowns)

Mr T: How do, I say (nodding familiarly).

LW: Dignity is lost upon such ignorance!

Mr T: Tol de Rol. O the Doose! (Striding about ludicrously, imitating Lord John)

LW: This is a class of person beyond any I have met with yet!

Mr T: O the Divil! (Throws himself full length on the sofa)[16]

In the end, of course, the lovers prevail, but only after Eliza turns out not only to be more attached to Cleveland than the vapid heiress, Miss Percival, whom his family had intended he should marry, but also far richer. Cleveland is heir to his uncle Sir Marmaduke, but his estates are heavily mortgaged. The fortune of £80,000 (nine million pounds today) that Eliza brings with her from India will be sufficient to pay off these debts, and the estate will then be made over to them after Sir Marmaduke dies. Money, however it had been acquired, ruled the day.

# CHAPTER 7

Whatever success the East India Company may have had in India, monetary or otherwise, it was bought at a price. For its employees and their families, India was a dangerous place in every way.

Although historians are generally agreed that by the second half of the eighteenth century Britain's status as the dominant European power in India was assured, it did not always feel like that to the people who lived through it. Even after Robert Clive's victory at Plassey there were enough skirmishes with the French – together with alarming tales of their successes, and British setbacks – to make people extremely apprehensive. 'In short, from all I heard and all I saw,' Hickey confided in his diary more than twenty years later, 'I thought the influence and power of my countrymen was completely at an end in Asia.'*

Many, if not most, believed they were living on borrowed time. Margaret Fowke, who like Charlotte Hickey and Eliza Fay found her way to Calcutta in the 1780s, confided her anxieties to an uncle back in England. 'I believe more than half the people in the place think the English will be fairly turned out of this country,' she wrote from Calcutta on 8 January 1781. 'I am no politician and know nothing of the matter, I flatter myself however they are false prophets as I think

---

*It is one of the oddities of the events recalled by Hickey in his memoirs that despite the fact that the British were almost permanently at war with the French at this time, individual Frenchmen, including several prominent naval officers, went out of their way to help him and his wife reach Calcutta.

the country not an unpleasant one, and I wish to see my brother's fortunes more advanced before we leave it.'[1]

It was not just the threat from other Europeans fighting for their share of the spoils but the combustible and constantly changing political situation within India itself which gave rise to this feeling of insecurity. When Margaret Fowke was writing her letters home, the EIC had no fewer than four separate armies fighting 'out of our own provinces'. The Company was in grave danger of overreaching itself. 'The support of all these armies depends entirely on the revenues of Bengal, which are by no means equal to so heavy an expense. Money must be raised by strong acts of violence, which will infallibly produce convulsions.'[2]

For all the huge fortunes being made by individuals at this time, the Bengal treasury was exhausted, and 'the military and civil servants are unpaid everywhere'.[3] It was not the first or the last time that the Company would be on the verge of bankruptcy. Nonetheless, as Margaret's father Joseph Fowke put it, 'it is our duty to act on the supposition of the duration of our Empire in India, but I confess to you I see not the possibility of it'.

While British traders in the Mughal-controlled lands of northern India may have celebrated the acquisition in 1717 of the Emperor's *ferman* as the 'Magna Carta' of their rights and privileges, none of it applied in the Maratha-held territories in central and eastern India; far less in the south-west, the coastline of which 'was still divided into a patchwork of minor Principalities and trading centres with a political and commercial profile more like that of the south-eastern Asian archipelago than India'.[4]

Still further south, English traders were even more vulnerable. Stretching down the coastline of modern-day Karnataka and Kerala were three tiny British trading stations – Karwar, Tellicherry and Anjengo – acquired haphazardly in the previous century, and originally administered from Surat. The factors at Tellicherry in particular were in a state of more or less perpetual war with the local rulers, the Nairs, from the early 1700s. The most southerly of these outposts,

Anjengo, acquired in 1692, is said to have been gifted to a young English emissary by the local Rani (the Nairs were a matrilineal caste) who had fallen in love with him. When the love-struck Rani died, the EIC factor, William Gyfford, decided to lead a deputation to the new queen at the royal court in Attingal to renegotiate. The 'Anjengo affair', as it became known, ended in disaster. Of the hundred-strong party who set off, only a handful made it back; the rest were brutally massacred. Gyfford had his tongue cut out and nailed to his chest. His body was then staked to a log and sent downriver. The rest of the deputation were dismembered. Only twenty 'horribly mangled' survivors made it back, to break the news.

In 1721, during the reign of George I, there were three English-women living in that lonely little outpost, one of them William Gyfford's young widow. The women were now hurried aboard a native boat and taken to Madras, where after a month-long journey they arrived, 'dishevelled and destitute' but alive.

The tale they had to tell caused a sensation, but Mrs Gyfford, for one, was no stranger either to drama or to celebrity. At the grand age of twenty-five she had already been twice widowed. Some ten years previously the ship she was sailing in to Bombay with her second husband (her first, a man old enough to be her grandfather and 'deformed' to boot, had had the good grace to die after only three years of their marriage) was attacked by a number of Maratha 'grabs' (or *ghurabs* – square-rigged frigates). Struck in the shoulder by a cannon ball, her husband, Mr Chown, bled to death in her arms. Mrs Chown, as Mrs Gyfford then was, was taken into captivity in Colaba, a Maratha stronghold under the rule of the notorious 'pirate' known to the English as Angria.* She was eventually ransomed, along with the other prisoners, for thirty thousand rupees, and is alleged to have been discovered 'in such a state of undress that the Scots Lieutenant [who had undertaken the mission], the well-named Mackintosh, "was obliged to wrap his clothes around her to

---

*Khanhoji Angrey was in fact the Grand Admiral of the Maratha fleet, and Viceroy of the Konkan, as the Maratha coastline between Bombay and Goa was known.

cover her nakedness'".[5] Around the same time another woman, Mrs Whitehall, had a similar experience, although her story is less well known, and did not make it into the East India Company annals. She too is said to have been captured by Angria and held to ransom until a substantial sum was paid by her husband for her release. Who knows how many other women, their stories unrecorded, suffered a similar fate?

Luckily, many did write about their adventures. Eliza Fay had good reason to be piqued when Marian Hastings dismissed her stories of woe. Like Charlotte Hickey, she very nearly did not get to India at all. Unlike the Hickeys, who took the sea route, the Fays chose to follow a largely overland route, which was, if possible, even more perilous.

They set off from Paris, travelling across the Alps, and then south to Genoa. From Genoa they picked up a boat to Leghorn (present-day Livorno), and then another to Alexandria. From there it was only a short distance to Cairo, where their plan was to join one of the camel caravans that crossed the desert to Suez.*

Arriving in Egypt, Mrs Fay was at first entranced by her new surroundings. Everything she saw reminded her of the Biblical stories she had learned as a child, about the children of Israel and Joseph and his coat of many colours. She saw the grand spectacle of the Pyramids ('those prodigies of human labour') which she viewed through a telescope, the flat garden roofs of the houses, smelled the intoxicating perfume from the groves of orange and lemon trees, and witnessed the camels and water buffalo drawing water from the Nile, the latter lying in the flood waters by the hundred, only their heads protruding, keeping themselves cool from the intense heat. She recorded it all with zest. 'I almost felt as if in a dream, so wonderful appeared the circumstances of my being here.'

Of special interest to her sisters back home was the dress she was advised to adopt (and in which she would later have herself fashionably painted) for entering 'Grand Cairo'. 'I had, in the first place, a pair of

*This was the 'short' desert route to India. The 'long' desert route, from Aleppo in Syria across to Bassora (Basra, in present-day Iraq), was, if possible, even more dangerous.

trowsers with yellow leather half-boots, and slippers over them; a long satin gown, with wide sleeves, open to the elbows; and a girdle round my waist, with large silver clasps; round my head a fine, coloured, muslin handkerchief, closely bound, but so arranged that one corner hung down three quarters of a yard behind. This is the dress for the House,' she wrote knowledgeably. Dress for the street required a long silk robe, 'like a surplice', and then a piece of muslin to go over her face, half a yard wide, 'which reached from the forehead to the feet, except for an opening for the eyes'. Over this cumbersome get-up went yet another layer: a piece of black silk, long and wide enough to envelop her whole form. 'So, thus equipped, stumbling at every step, I sallied forth, and with great difficulty got across my noble beast [an ass had been sent to transport her through the city]: but, as it was in the full heat of the day and the veil prevented me from breathing freely, I thought I must have died by the way.'[6]

Soon, wonder and novelty turned to fear. So great was this fear, in fact, that at first Mrs Fay would not even venture to explain it to her family. No sooner had she arrived at their lodgings than she found that 'a great change' had taken place in their situation, and the entire foreign community was in a state of uproar. 'I dare not at present enter into particulars,' she wrote anxiously, 'and can only say that something was wrong . . .'

Something *was* wrong; very wrong indeed. Only an hour after her arrival the distressing news had reached Cairo that a caravan of twelve European merchants crossing the desert, including several English, had been attacked and plundered in the most heinous way by 'Arabian robbers'. Not only had all their goods been taken, they had also been stripped of all their clothes.

'The inhuman wretches not content with stripping them to the skin, drove away their camels, and left them in a burning sandy Desert, which the feet can scarcely touch without being blistered, exposed to the scorching rays of the sun and utterly destitute of sustenance of every kind; no house, tree, or even shrub to afford them shelter,' Mrs Fay wrote. 'My heart sickens, my hand trembles as I retrace this scene.'

Her distress only grew when she heard details of what happened next. Five of the party, including one of the Englishmen, somehow managed to stumble the twenty miles back to Suez, and later were found to have survived their ordeal. Of the remaining seven who made the suicidal decision to head for Cairo, a much greater distance, only one, a Frenchman, lived to tell the tale. The rest had died horribly, scorched to death by the sun.

The terrible news, 'which seemed to involve the fate of every European alike, burst upon me like a stroke of lightning', she wrote, weeping herself almost blind at the story of how Monsieur Chevalier, the sole survivor, had tried in vain to save his dying brother. Poor Eliza. Blackheath must have seemed very far away. But this was not the end of it. Everyone around her was of the opinion that there was nothing to stop the 'Arabian robbers' striking their own caravan or, worse, falling upon them in their beds: 'not one appeared to entertain a doubt of their being immediately attacked'.

A general hysteria set in, not kind to Eliza Fay's already jangled nerves. The lady of the house where they had taken up lodgings and her daughter wrung their hands, 'crying out in agony that they were utterly ruined; that all Europeans would be murdered; and they even appeared to think that receiving another proscribed race [i.e. the English Fays] increased their danger. Imprisonment and massacre in every shape were the sole subjects of their conversation; and so many terrible images did their fears conjure up, and communicate to my already disordered mind, that there were times when the reality could scarcely have been more appalling. Oh England! Dear England! How often did I apostrophise thee, land of liberty and safety – !'

Eventually, however, a calmer frame of mind prevailed, and the Fays decided that they would join the caravan after all, but not before their eastern experience had been thoroughly leached of all its charm. Cairo itself was found to be much dirtier than she had at first suspected, and everyone came down with a violent fever. Even her charming Egyptian costume was now found to have its drawbacks. 'To show the face is considered here, an act of downright indecency,' she averred; but it was 'a terrible fashion for one like me, to whom free air seems the great requisite for existence'.

But wear it she must, even in the blistering heat of the desert. Mrs Fay described their preparations for setting off in meticulous detail. When a caravan was about to depart, large tents were pitched on the outskirts of the city, around which everyone wanting to travel would congregate, and then be put in line. Armed guards were employed to protect both the front and the rear while others flanked the sides of the caravan, completely enclosing both the merchandise to be transported and any female passengers brave enough to make the journey; the European men rode on horses, while their provisions and bedding were carried in panniers on the backs of camels. Although on this occasion Mrs Fay claimed to have been the only female, the women usually travelled in a kind of litter called a tataravan. This strange contraption was hoisted between poles fastened between two camels, one in front and one behind. The litter was topped by 'shabby, ill-contrived Venetian blinds, which in the day increase the suffocating heat, but are of use during the nights which are cold and piercing'.

Each camel carried a skin of water, which, although it started off pure, soon became a disconcerting coffee colour, and special earthenware filters were needed to make it drinkable. As well as a good supply of water, Mrs Fay had also provided herself with watermelons and hard-boiled eggs for her refreshment. As the caravan set off she was much annoyed by the constant sound of her provisions rattling around in the ill-packed baskets atop the camels, and at one point was 'saluted' by a parcel of eggs breaking loose from their net, and pelting her with their contents. 'It is fortunate that they *were* boiled,' she grumbled, 'or I should have been in pretty trim.' (It is fortunate, too, although she does not say so, that it was not the watermelons that worked their way loose.)

Lolling water buffalo and the scent of orange blossom were replaced by gritty desert winds so fiery they made the air smell like hot bricks.

It is one of the many sympathetic things about Eliza Fay, lurching along and perspiring uncomfortably in her tataravan, that although 'the late Catastrophe' was still deeply imprinted on her mind, she remained alive to the extraordinary spectacle of the desert itself. 'It is impossible,' she wrote, 'even amidst fear and suspense, not to be struck with the exquisite beauty of the nights here; a perfect cloudless sky, and the atmosphere so clear, that the stars shine with a brilliancy, infinitely surpassing any thing I witnessed elsewhere.'

For all Eliza Fay's fears of a second attack, there must have been safety in numbers. Mr Fay, well-armed against marauders, as were all the other men, estimated that their caravan was five thousand people strong. It must have been an extraordinary sight.

Willing herself to trust in God's goodness to speed them safely across the desert, Mrs Fay gradually relaxed, boasting to her family that she had behaved 'like a lion' on the crossing. Others were not so fortunate. One of their fellow English travellers, Mr Taylor, was so overcome by heat and fatigue that he slid off his horse on to the burning sand and would have died there and then if Mr Fay had not run to help him remount. The horses fared even worse. 'The wretched creatures suffered so much from heat and thirst, that their groanings were terrible, and added to this an involuntary rattling in the throat, as if they were on the point of expiring, so that one heard them with a mixture of compassion and horror piti-ful to hear.'

Eliza Fay may have found the animals' suffering painful, but not so much that she was prepared to inconvenience herself to save them. Of the three dogs that set out with them, not one survived. One of these, a beautiful Italian greyhound ('he cost seven guineas at Venice'), had caught her special attention, appearing from the first to be in excruciating pain from the heat. The dog's condition quickly dete-riorated, until 'he was in the most frightful state, his tongue hanging out of his mouth, his eyes wildly staring, and altogether presenting the idea of madness'. At this point the owner, the same Mr Taylor, asked Mrs Fay if she might give the dying dog a place in her litter. She refused. 'I hope no person will accuse me of inhumanity for refusing to receive an animal in that condition,' she wrote disingenuously, 'self-preservation forbade my compliance.' It was shortly after this that the dog dropped down on to the burning sand, unable to go any further; but even before he had breathed his last he was 'brutally' cut to pieces by one of the Arabs before his master's eyes. 'You may judge from this incident, what wretches we were cast amongst,' Eliza Fay wrote, failing to appreciate that this was an act of tough-minded mercy far greater than her own.

Amazingly, the Fays arrived safely in Suez and boarded their ship, the *Nathalia*, with no further mishaps. Mrs Fay seems to have enjoyed the passage across the Indian Ocean, as it gave her plenty of time to observe the other passengers, most of whom soon fell foul of her unforgiving pen. There was one other Englishwoman on the voyage, Mrs Tulloh, and although at first Mrs Fay was delighted to think that she would have female company for a change, this pleasant thought did not last long.

Mrs Tulloh, who was, as will be remembered, 'one of the very lowest creatures taken off the streets of London', gave herself too many airs for Mrs Fay's liking. The 'consequence' of her husband, whom 'nobody chooses to offend', gave 'Madam' full scope to exercise her mischievous talents, 'wherein he never controuls her'. Mrs Tulloh was given to swearing and other 'indecent behaviour' – for which Mrs Fay, nobly, and 'for the Honour of the Sex', ticked her off – and she was surprised when Mrs Tulloh, 'that vile woman', was determined to triumph over her.

Mrs Fay, in her turn, was not much better behaved.

'It is a common expression of the lady: Lord bless you, if I did such, or such a thing, Tulloh would make no more to do, but knock me down like an ox.' Exactly what she had done to deserve this punishment is not recorded.

It was not a happy ship. Before long the passengers were divided into two camps: those for the Tullohs, and those for the Fays. Too afraid to voice her dissatisfaction directly, Mrs Fay amused herself 'by examining their countenances, where ill nature has fixed her Empire so firmly, that I scarcely believe either of them ever smiled maliciously', and writing it all down. On paper, at least, she could vent her feelings freely.

In addition to the Tullohs there were four other Englishmen – either too young or too generally cowed by the combined efforts of Mrs Fay and Mrs Tulloh to put up much of a fight. Eliza Fay's description of them presents us with a fairly typical cross-section of the kind of English people now making their way to India. There was the amiable but melancholy merchant Mr Taylor (the same one who had nearly died in the desert); Mr Mansety, a fresh-faced EIC writer still in his teens; Mr Moreau, a musician, hoping to find employment among the fleshpots of Calcutta; and Mr Fuller, a middle-aged bankrupt, who had apparently fallen prey to 'sharpers' back home and was travelling to India (as so many did) 'as a last resort'. All were 'very civil and attentive' to her, she noted approvingly, even Mr Fuller, who despite the fact that he had gone over into the Tulloh 'camp' was in her eyes the product of 'genteel society', so she forgave him. 'How different *his* manners from those of Hare!'

John Hare, Esq., Barrister at Law, came in for special vituperation. 'I want to make you see him,' she wrote. 'Figure to yourself a little mortal, his body constantly bent in a rhetorical attitude, as if addressing the Court, and his face covered with scorbutic blotches. Happily from an affectation of singularity, he always wore spectacles. I say happily, as they serve to conceal the most odious pair of little white eyes I ever beheld.' Even though John Hare passed himself off as a man of fashion who 'would faint at the thought of any thing Plebian', Eliza Fay was determined that his origins must be in 'Trade'. He affects not to care for Quadrille,* 'as it is only the wives and daughters of Tradesmen, in country towns who play it. He will only buy his swords from the very best Bond Street shops.' His real crime, one suspects, was to spot that Mrs Fay herself was more

---

*A card game popular in the 1700s, played by four people with a deck of forty cards. Not to be confused with the dance of the same name.

than a little 'Plebian' (and probably enjoyed a game of quadrille, too).

Everyone quarrelled, even the captain, an overbearing, insolent 'Jack in Office . . . who everyone detests'. While insisting on the best of everything for himself – cutlery, chairs, drinking vessels – he half-starved his passengers. The roundhouse at mealtimes became the locus of some unedifying scenes.

'During the first fortnight of our voyage,' Eliza Fay wrote, 'my foolish complaisance stood in my way at table; but I soon learnt our genteel maxim "catch as catch can," the longest arm fared best; and you cannot imagine what a good scrambler I have become – a dish once seized, it is my care to make use of such good fortune: and now provisions are running very short we are grown quite savages; two or three of us perhaps fighting for a bone . . . ' If they did not reach their destination soon, she lamented, 'what must be the consequence, Heaven knows'.

Little did Eliza realise that when she reached India at last, a far worse fate awaited her than petty squabbles over a few bones.

The *Nathalia* finally reached the ancient Hindu city of Calicut, on the Malabar Coast, on 5 November 1779. Unbeknown to the Fays, the Nawab, Hyder Ali, was on the brink of war with the British.

The first thing to strike the passengers on board the *Nathalia* as strange was that there was no British flag flying – it would turn out later that the EIC factor had already fled the city in panic – but since the *Nathalia* was a Danish ship, and its captain a Frenchman, at first no one was particularly worried.

The next day Mr Hare went on shore to reconnoitre, and came back with the information that they would all be safe in the Danish factory, on condition that they should pass themselves off as Danes. While the other passengers resolved to do this, the Fays decided to bide their time and remained on board. On the afternoon of the third day, when Mrs Fay was sitting sewing peacefully in the round house, she saw an ominous sight: a large boat had come alongside the *Nathalia* containing more than twenty armed men. To her amazement one of these was an Englishman, Captain Ayres,* a former highwayman turned mercenary, and now in the pay of Hyder Ali.

The news Ayres brought might have been comical if their situation had not been so dangerous. Their fellow countrymen, now safely holed up in the Danish factory and passing themselves off as Danes, were not only quarrelling but fighting duels with one another over the division of the spoils that remained on board the *Nathalia*, and the Danish factor had been obliged to call his guards to separate them. On hearing that their ship was without an owner (he had been one of the six who had died in the desert), the Governor, Suder Khan – Hyder Ali's brother-in-law – had decided to impound the ship for himself. While Ayres claimed that he had no personal designs on the merchandise, Mrs Fay later heard him tell his sergeant that orders had come to imprison the ship's officers and plunder its contents.

Still grimmer news followed: an attack on Calicut by the British was expected imminently, and the French captain of the *Nathalia* had offered his services to Hyder Ali to help defeat them. That night a hundred and fifty sepoys (soldiers) were to come on board to 'defend' the *Nathalia*.

Playing for time, the Fays bolted themselves into their cabin, but they both knew that there was no escape. Mrs Fay had never felt more alone. Despite the fact that her husband was with her, as the only woman on board the captured ship, and an enemy Englishwoman, she was doubly vulnerable. She was so traumatised by this turn of events that it made her physically ill. 'The fright had disordered me so much that a violent retching came on, succeeded by a strong fever, which occasioned dreadful pains in my limbs.

---

*Ayres is an extraordinary figure in Anglo-Indian history. Born in London and apprenticed at an early age to a saddler, he soon became bored with such a lowly profession and turned to highway robbery. After several years of successful looting he was caught and sentenced to death, but later pardoned on condition of life transportation. He enlisted as a soldier with the East India Company (which gives us some idea of the standard among its troops), but allegedly managed to continue his former profession nonetheless. When the pickings proved less lucrative than he had thought, he deserted the army and offered his services to Hyder Ali, who promoted him to the rank of captain.

'Can anything be imagined more distressing, than my situation without the means of relief – no possibility of obtaining advice, and no female to whom I could look for succour or assistance?'

Even the despised Mrs Tulloh would have been better than no one.

At two o'clock in the morning the soldiers eventually came for them. At first all she could hear was a breaking and tearing sound outside her door. Then shouting, and demands were made that they must come out, or they would be murdered. Anthony Fay did his best, pulling out his sword and 'swearing solemnly that he would run the first man through the body, who should presume to enter his wife's apartment', but one inexperienced swordsman was no match for a hundred and fifty sepoys brandishing scimitars.

There was nothing to be done but to give themselves up. Mrs Fay tried to rouse herself but was still so weak with fever that she could hardly stand. She would recollect later that it took her about an hour to dress. Anticipating (correctly) that they would be thoroughly searched, her husband hid some of their valuables, and what little money they had, about her person. Ingeniously, he concealed their three watches in her hair, having first stuck pins in them to stop them ticking.

Together, the Fays staggered on to the deck to find a terrible scene awaiting them, one that 'would have appalled the stoutest heart'. All was lost: the *Nathalia* was completely overrun. 'The poor sailors were so distracted that many of them could scarcely be restrained from jumping over board to escape slavery – sometimes crying for their wages, and asking the Officers to pay them; who incapable of affording any consolation, walked about like men bereft of reason: no wonder, since this fatal event would, to say the least, occasion them the loss of twelve months pay, exclusive of their private ventures.'

Forced to abandon all their possessions other than the clothes they stood up in, the Fays were ordered into the boat which would convey them to the shore. By now it was raining in torrents, and the surf was so high that they had to transfer to a canoe, 'scarcely bigger than a butcher's tray', and half full of water, to get them to shore. Not only was Mrs Fay soaked to the bone, she was also tormented by the 'blue lights'* that the sepoys tossed into the canoe behind them: 'the rancid oil and abominable rags used in their composition' almost suffocated her.

She had reached India at last, but how different it was from the one she had imagined in 'the many cheerful and flattering conversations' she had had with her family at home. 'Little did I imagine that any power on the Continent, however independent, would have dared to treat *English* subjects with such cruelty,' she wrote.

Unceremoniously tossed on to the beach in her dripping wet clothes, Eliza Fay was then compelled to march more than a mile through heavy sand to the town, surrounded all the while by the mob of Calicut, 'who seemed to take pleasure in beholding the distress of white people, those constant objects of their envy and detestation'. They were then detained nearly an hour in the town square, 'till the Governor's pleasure should be known'.

Bedraggled and exhausted, the little party stood in the rain in front of Suder Khan, the Governor of Calicut, who sat smoking his hookah for nearly an hour 'feasting his eyes' on the prisoners. Just as she thought that things could not get any worse, Mrs Fay noticed a horrible tickling sensation on her scalp. A pin that her husband had stuck in one of their watches had come loose. 'Never shall I forget what a terrible sensation the ticking of the watch caused! I think had it continued long I must completely have lost my senses; for I dared not remove it, from fear of worse consequences.'

Eventually the Governor gave the order that the Fays should be taken to the English factory, and confined there under guard. 'How I dragged my weary limbs I know not,' she wrote plaintively; but arriving there afforded her no relief. They found the house completely abandoned (the factor having taken all his possessions with him when he fled, including the furniture), and Mrs Fay was now convinced that they meant to strip and murder them: 'for why else were we sent to an empty house?'

*A 'blue light' would have been the signal that the craft heading for the shore was a friendly one.

'These were my heart-breaking reflections, as I threw myself in despair on a window seat, worn out with fatigue and want of nourishment; without means of procuring even a draught of water to assuage my thirst, which grew excessive,' she wrote. Even the offer of a bribe would have been dangerous.

Hearing of their plight, the Danish Consul, Mr Passavant, sent them a dinner, although Mrs Fay was so exhausted that she could not eat it. She found an old lumber-room in which she could lie down to sleep for a few hours (which later was found to be infested with venomous snakes and scorpions). Mr Fay, meanwhile, rescued the watches from his wife's hair, and together with the small amount of money that they had also managed to secrete around her person, concealed them inside one of his gloves on the veranda.

Bad decision. In the night there was 'a dreadful hurricane of rain and wind' and when they woke up the next morning they found to their consternation that their little treasure, 'to which alone we could look for the means of escape', had blown away. Mr Fay was in despair. Happily, his wife still had her wits about her. Noting which way the wind was still blowing, she worked out that if she could find her way to a little enclosure at the back of the house she might find their possessions there.

I did not tell Mr Fay my scheme, as there was nothing he opposed so strongly as the appearance of seeking to escape; but when he was completely absorbed in contemplating this new misfortune, I stole to the back door. There was a large lock and key inside, and to my surprise, when I had turned this, my passage was clear to the stairs leading to this enclosure; and not a soul in sight. The grass was excessively high and wet, but I struggled to make my way through it and waded about, determined at least not to leave an inch unexplored. Imagine my joy, when in the midst of a deep tuft I found the old glove, with its contents safe and uninjured. What a treasure it seemed! How many are there who never felt so much true delight on receiving a magnificent fortune, as we experienced in again beholding this sheet anchor of our hopes, thus unexpectedly restored.

This little incident was one of the few to enliven the monotony of their days in captivity. That, and the unwelcome visits from some of the other English passengers, who came round occasionally to visit them and, as Mrs Fay thought, to gloat.

The relative freedom of the Tullohs, Mr Hare and the rest of the English party did not last. In an attempt to frighten Suder Khan into releasing them they had pretended to be people of good fortune and good connections, but their boasting backfired. The Governor grew suspicious, and 'determined to frighten them into the payment of a large sum of money'. When they could not deliver, he ordered that they be imprisoned with the Fays at the English factory.

Mrs Fay tried – and failed – to conceal her glee at their comeuppance. 'God forbid that I should, generally speaking, be capable of rejoicing in the miseries of my fellow creatures, even when they merit punishment,' she wrote, 'but I must own (blame me if you will) that for a short time I *did* feel satisfaction in this stroke of retributive justice.'

It was certainly a curious sight to behold them, after all their airs of superiority, reduced to take up their residence with us, whose situation, while singular, was the object of their ridicule and contempt. The scene was however now changed; although *they*, like many others in the world, were able to support their neighbours misfortunes, with stoical firmness, and even render them a source of amusement, each readily discovered when personally attacked by a similar calamity, that close imprisonment is by no means a proper subject on which to exercise wit, and that people when in distress are not precisely in the humour for relishing the pleasantry of others on their troubles.

Eliza Fay's satisfaction at this turn of events was not to last. Hostilities between the British and Hyder Ali had now begun in earnest, and Mrs Tulloh stole her teapot and tea 'catty' (in terms of importance to Mrs Fay, not necessarily in this order). Sepoys could no longer be spared to guard them all at the factory, so they had to be moved.

'I have now a lamentable tale to relate,' she recorded. 'We were this morning hurried away at a moments warning to the fort, crowded together in a horrid dark place scarcely twenty feet square, swarming with rats and almost suffocating for want of air.' Mr and Mrs Tulloh (of course) were sharp-elbowed enough to bag a small room to themselves, but the luckless Fays had to pass the night with the rest of the group in the miserable, rodent-infested room. The gnawing of rats on the feet of her couch, and their perpetual squeaking, kept her awake all night long.

Once again, it was Eliza's sharp wits that came to their rescue. 'Luckily discovered a trap-door, or rather lofts, where no human foot had trod for many *many* years,' reads her diary entry for 1 December 1779. It turned out that these had been Angria's storerooms and were full of broken chairs, tables, looking glasses and books: 'even a spinnet was among the articles, but beyond all repair, and vast quantities of broken bottles, which had been filled with liquors of all kinds: but the rats in their gambols had made havoc among them'.

In this strange room, accessible only by a rickety ladder which they had great difficulty in climbing, the Fays made themselves a makeshift camp. It was disgustingly dirty, but it was private, and they thought themselves lucky to have secured it. Mrs Fay made up a bed on an old sofa for herself, and some bolts of canvas were rescued to make up a mattress for Mr Fay. 'Here we lay down, comparatively happy in the hope of enjoying a tolerable night's rest, my husband being provided with a long pole to keep off the rats.'

No sooner had they extinguished their lamp, however, than they heard a fluttering sound accompanied at intervals by high-pitched squeakings – 'by degrees it approached the beds, and we felt that several creatures were hovering over us ... sometimes their wings swept our faces, seeming to fly heavily – then again they would remove farther off, but still continually squeaking – Good God! What horrors I felt. Mr F— protested that whole legions of evil spirits had taken possession of our apartment.' The creatures persisted in their assaults until dawn, 'when what should we find had caused this disturbance, but a parcel of poor harmless bats … We cannot help laughing very heartily at it ourselves now, and you are at full liberty to do the same.'

Eventually, after more than a month in captivity, their gaolers seem to have lost interest in them and the prisoners were given permission to go their various ways. The Tulloh party was the first to go, but for reasons that were not clear to them the Fays were kept behind. The Lieutenant-Governor (Suder Khan was away at the war) offered Anthony Fay a position in Hyder Ali's army, which in addition to Ayres could already boast several English mercenaries: to his rage, Fay refused. Again and again their release was promised, their licence to travel and even their transport arranged, but each time it all came to nothing.

The anxiety made Mrs Fay ill again. She became convinced that some 'dark design' was at hand, and that they would be sent 'up country' to be either massacred or enslaved.

The suspense took its toll on Anthony Fay too. One day he came running into her room like a madman, 'uttering a thousand extravagant expressions': 'we are betrayed, ruined, utterly undone,' he shouted at his wife; 'you must leave this place instantly, or you may be made a prisoner here for ever'. It turned out that on yet another attempt to petition the Lieutenant-Governor, Fay had lost his head completely. Rushing up to the *musnud* (throne) of the Lieutenant-Governor he had seized him by the throat, 'peremptorily insisting on the immediate fulfilment of his promise'. Happily, and perhaps rightly, everyone present could see that 'grief and vexation had literally turned his brain', and Fay survived a loss of control which under other circumstances would have led to instant death.

After more than a month of uncertainty and delays, the Fays decided that their only hope now was to escape. A Portuguese officer in Hyder Ali's service, Pereira, had become friendly with Mr Fay, and offered his services to help them. Eliza Fay was dubious – she did not much like the man – but had no choice but to trust him. Another Portuguese in the unlikely form of Father Ricardo, a priest attached to a local convent, was said to be able to produce the necessary travel documents.

At first all went smoothly.

'A License of Passport is procured for us as two Frenchmen going to Mahey,'* reads her diary entry for 13 January 1780. 'We have paid twenty rupees boat-hire to a smuggler; they are commonly very courageous men; which is some comfort to me ... His house is admirably situated for our purpose, close by the seaside; this is to be our place of *rendez-vous*. The precise time is not yet fixed upon: the intervening hours how anxiously they will pass!'

In the end, their escape was fixed for the next day, 14 January, at six in the evening. As soon as it grew dark they put on their disguises.

'Mr F— put on a sailor's dress and I equipped myself with a nankeen jacket – a pair of long striped trowsers – a man's night cap, and over that a *mighty* smart hat – with a pair of Mr F—'s shoes tied on my feet, and a stick in my hand. In this dress Mr F— declared that I was the very image of my dear father, which highly gratified me. I had tied the clothes we took off in a handkerchief; with that in one hand and brandishing my stick in another, I boldly sallied forth ... '

Father Ricardo met them at the smugglers' rendezvous, and was paid the agreed fee of twenty rupees. 'When this was settled nothing remained, as we supposed, but to step into the boat – when behold! news was brought that the sailors had made their escape, no one knew whither!'

For two whole hours they waited for the smugglers to return, but in vain. Eventually, the Fays had no choice but to trudge back to their

---

*Mahé, on the Coromandel Coast just south of Madras. In their operations against the French, the British had occupied the port, which Hyder Ali thought should have been under his 'protection'.

prison, still wearing their French disguises and 'raving in all the folly of angry disappointment'.

And so matters continued.

17th January, 1780

Had all arranged for our escape last night but so many people were about us, that we dared not make the attempt.

19th January, 1780

Father Ricardo has once more arranged all things for tonight – we must give more money, but that is no object. Once free and we shall doubtless find means of proceeding on our journey.

Three weeks later they were still waiting.

5th February, 1780

Every day has this wicked priest contrived some scheme, to amuse us with false hopes of escaping; every *night* have we lain down in the full persuasion that it was the last we should pass in confinement; and as constantly have we awoke to meet bitter disappointment ...

The suspense must have been unbearable. The Fays had been very thoroughly duped: not only by the smugglers, but also by Father Ricardo, and most of all by Pereira, the man they had once thought their friend, who in the end went to Ayres himself, betraying them utterly by relating their escape plans. (They were only saved because he got the date wrong. The night Pereira gave as the one of their attempted escape, Mr Fay had been with Ayres, helping him celebrate his birthday.)

In the end the Fays left Calicut quite undramatically, in a sloop belonging to a local merchant, 'Isaac the Jew', which took them to Cochin, and from there to Madras and finally Calcutta. An introduction to this man had been given to the Fays when they were still in Cairo, and now he went out of his way to help them, persuading Suder Khan to release them and furnish them with the right travel documents. Mrs Fay's travails were over at last. The stress of her three-month-long captivity in Calicut was to take a considerable toll on her health, but as it turned out her predicament was never so bad as that of the detested Mrs Tulloh.

Later on in her diary we learn that the Tulloh party had taken fifteen days to travel to Seringapatam, Hyder Ali's capital. There they had been held in a kind of shed for twelve days, 'half starved to death' as no one was permitted to assist them except with the coarsest food in small quantities. For once, Mrs Fay had the good grace not to gloat. Her only comment was one that could quite as easily have been applied to herself. 'Mrs Tulloh has now seen enough, poor woman,' she wrote sombrely, 'to satisfy her taste for adventure.'

# CHAPTER 8

It was not only the fear of warfare, rebellion, rioting and piracy that contributed to women's sense of the fragility of life in India. Sickness and disease struck with terrifying rapidity. The saying that a person could be perfectly well at breakfast and dead by dinnertime was literally true. Cholera, typhoid and malaria were rife, but there was little knowledge of the distinction between them, even less of how to treat them. They were simply 'agues' or 'fevers'.

'The illness of which most people die is what is called here a Puker [pukka] Fever, which frequently carries a person off in a few hours,' wrote Jemima Kindersley in her letters published in 1777, 'but some have more lingering illness, such as bile in the stomach, which indeed is a disorder very few are entirely exempt from in these cases; the intense heat relaxes the coats of the stomach so as to prevent digestion, which occasions much illness and oft times death.'

The harshness of the climate was often thought to be to blame. 'The baneful influence of the sun is a melancholy reflection,' Mrs Kindersley went on; 'the number of sudden deaths among the English, and the caution they are obliged to use to preserve life, makes this season [the summer] very uncomfortable, and when it happens, as it sometimes does, that the rains are late before they set in, the mortality exceeds belief.'[1]

In the eighteenth century, far from being the weaker sex, women were generally regarded as hardier than their men when it came to preserving their health. The climate 'never kills English ladies', Mrs Kindersley declared, nor did they die so often of 'violent fevers' – the reason being, she believed, that women exposed themselves less often to the heat of the day, and in general tended to live more temperately than men – which given the eye-popping quantities of alcohol most men imbibed at that period was not hard to do.

Women suffered in other ways. They were afflicted by weak nerves, 'slow' fevers and bile. 'The disorders I have mentioned and the continual perspiration, soon destroys the roses on the cheeks of the young and beautiful and gives them a pale yellow complexion.'

There were few remedies. Patients who tried them tended to recover in spite of, not because of, them. Alcohol in large quantities, when it was not destroying their livers, was thought to have a highly beneficial effect. When Charlotte Hickey nearly succumbed to a fever on board the *Raynha de Portugal*, the only recourse was to pour a stimulating glass of red wine down her throat every ten minutes, until the poor woman had imbibed a bottle and a half of claret. Not surprisingly, she soon passed out into a profound sleep. The next morning, however, her fever had broken.

Others were not so lucky. Should they be fortunate enough to survive their 'fever', the sufferers were almost always condemned to a long and weary convalescence. One woman took five months to recover from one illness, but she was luckier than her husband, who was struck down by cholera regularly at full moon and nearly died each time. The same woman also recalled one of her soldier husband's postings in Dacca, known for its insalubrious climate. They arrived to find all six hundred of the troops remaining there either dead or dying of fever. Their families had been struck down too. 'It was sad to see the little children suffer,' she wrote, 'for none escaped.'[2]

Reminders of the deadliness of climate and disease were everywhere, not only in the ever-expanding graveyards but in the faces and demeanour of the people themselves. One of Charlotte Hickey's first experiences on setting foot in India was the sight of an English gentleman 'having more the appearance of a corpse than a living creature'.

The patient had been confined to bed for many weeks with 'a jungle fever' which had brought him 'to the brink of the grave'. He had survived, but even in convalescence was so debilitated that he could barely stand, and when he tried to rise from his seat he 'tottered from extreme weakness'.[3]

Death, that 'remorseless tyrant' as Hickey puts it, was ever present. One visitor to a Madras tavern was horrified to learn that in the previous five weeks no fewer than seven unfortunates had died in his bed, which had not been aired in all that time. On enquiring after another room, he discovered that in one a man had died of 'putrid fever' only two days earlier, and that the others were commonly known as the Tavern Sepulchres. Prudently, he chose to sleep that night on the billiard table.

Charlotte Hickey may have recovered from her fever on board the *Raynha de Portugal*, but only a few months after settling down in Calcutta she once again became ill. Seeing her grow slowly weaker and weaker, Hickey was alarmed enough to call in two medics, Dr Sark and Dr Wilson, who could find nothing wrong with her and agreed that she might benefit from a change of air.

On 7 December 1783 they took a boat upriver to visit a friend, Major Mestayer, where Mrs Hickey seemed briefly to revive. Quite soon after that, however, she 'rapidly fell off' again, and after less than a week, at her request, Hickey took her home, where she seemed if anything still weaker than when she had left it, 'in every respect worse'. Dr Stark and Dr Wilson were called in again, but still they did not think her to be in danger.

Mrs Hickey continued to sink, and her despairing husband could do nothing but sit by her bedside and watch as his darling grew steadily worse. The next day, 19 December, the useless Dr Stark was called in yet again, who told him that his patient 'was in extreme danger, that so alarming a change for the worse had taken place in the preceding night he saw no hope left, and her death, even in a few hours would not surprise him!'

Hickey was in despair. 'I could not attempt to describe the grief with which [these tidings] overwhelmed me,' he wrote. That night he did not leave Charlotte's bedside for a moment, despite her urgings that he should get some rest. But so long as she was in danger, sleep was wholly out of the question.

The next day he was forced to go out of the house on urgent business. 'Oh! What a morning did I pass,' he lamented. 'I scarcely knew what I said or did, and was in a constant tremor from the momentary expectation of the fatal event being announced.'

When he finally arrived home it was to find Charlotte no worse than before, and he was briefly comforted. 'On entering the room she languidly smiled, held out her emaciated hand, saying she was in not quite so great pain.' But Hickey knew that she only said this to comfort him. She continued in the same way for another four agonising days.

By Christmas Day it was clear that there was no hope of recovery. Large doses of laudanum had sent her into a brief, fitful sleep, but when she awoke at last to see William hanging over her 'in an agony of grief', she cast him a mournful look, 'then raised her poor arms and, drawing me towards her, kissed me with her almost clay-cold lips – such a kiss as I never can forget! ... In a faint and scarcely audible voice she bid me be comforted and submit to the fiat of the Almighty.'

After a long pause she spoke again, urging him to accept what was now clearly unavoidable. 'God bless you, my dearest William, God bless you! Oh, leave me, leave me!' she whispered, and fainted.

'The physicians entered at that moment,' Hickey recalled, 'when Doctor Wilson exclaimed, "'Tis all over. She's gone." This was the last I saw of her.'

Hickey was bundled from the room, and out of the house. It was only later that he was told that Charlotte had continued to breathe for some time after he left, but 'without any other signs of existence', until ten o'clock that night, when, 'with a gentle sigh', she died.

Unlike the heartless Bob Pott, who barely stopped to mourn his courtesan mistress, William Hickey was heartbroken at the loss of his Charlotte. 'It is only those who have truly loved and survived to mourn the loss of all they held dear upon earth that can conceive the agonies I endured,' he wrote of her death. Theirs had been a true love affair. 'Safely may I say I truly, fondly loved her, loved her with an affection that every new day, if possible, strengthened. Our tastes were similar, our foundation of happiness depended upon one another; kindred feeling was the standard of both, and we were perfectly satisfied with one another.'

Given the extreme fragility of life in India, it was not surprising that there was a certain feverishness to the way the British lived. 'The life was gay but it was the forced gaiety of people to whom the presence of death and sickness was a constant reality. Husbands saw their wives and wives their husbands, slowly wasting away before their eyes and were helpless to save them.'[4] They ate and drank, danced and gambled – and the women partied every bit as hard as the men.

Eliza Fay's description of her genteel evenings, peacefully sipping a dish of tea and playing whist, does not do justice to the grander social life which was now taking place at the Presidencies. The idea that the East India Company was more than merely a trading organisation, that it had an 'Empire' to protect, was beginning to take hold.

By the second half of the eighteenth century, the British were already giving themselves viceregal airs. On the King's birthday every year, the entire community gathered together to celebrate (a tradition still carried out in embassies and high commissions around the world). A public dinner was given at Government House for all the gentlemen of the Presidency, followed by a ball and a supper for the women. The formal clothes that they were expected to wear on these occasions – elaborately decorated headdresses and immense hooped skirts – were ludicrously unsuited to the Indian climate. George III's birthday fell in June, one of the hottest months of the year. In the crush and the stultifying heat, women fainted, and some were taken seriously ill. In consequence the festivities were moved to 8 December, when the weather was cooler.

In the lead-up to Christmas the festivities were particularly frenetic.

In November, the subscription assemblies had begun. On Christmas Day itself there was another public dinner, and another supper and ball for the ladies. A third was held at New Year. English traditions were adapted to suit the Indian climate. Large plantains were decorated and placed at the entrance of each house, the gates and pillars ornamented with wreaths of flowers. Everyone gave presents, even servants, who brought gifts of fish and fruit to honour the *burrah din* (great day).

The hot-weather months were the time for outdoor entertainments. Despite the best efforts of the Court of Directors, who inveighed strenuously against the new fashion for building country houses, complaining that they were a wicked extravagance and quite unsuited to their employees' station in life, many people in Calcutta had built themselves garden houses. One particularly memorable *fête champêtre* was given at Garden Reach just outside Calcutta by 'a gentleman high in the Civil Service', Mr Edward Fenwick, the elaborate plans for which 'entirely engaged the public attention and conversation during the greater part of the month of May'.

> The gardens were to be brilliantly illuminated with many thousand coloured lamps: an eminent operator in fireworks had been brought down from Lucknow to display his talents ... Ranges of tents were fixed in different parts of the gardens wherein tables were covered with all the dainties the best French cooks could produce, for the accommodation of three hundred persons ... Different bands of martial music were stationed in several parts of the gardens, and also in the house, with appropriate and distinct performers for the dancers. The last two miles of the road were lighted up with a double row of lamps on each side, making every object as clear as day. In short nothing could exceed the splendour of this rural entertainment.[5]

As well as garden parties, masquerades were a hugely popular feature of eighteenth-century social life, and enormous amounts of time and energy went into organising suitable costumes for them. In 1783,

Sophia Plowden attended a masquerade with a group of friends all dressed as 'Cashmerian' singers, a disguise, she proudly relates, which 'had never been attempted before'. In a letter to her sister in England she described her costume for the occasion in detail. She wore long drawers or 'Pie-jammas' which were of dark green silk with small gold flowers on them, a shift, and a habit or shirt over them, all 'perfectly decent'. On her feet she wore gold and silver embroidered slippers and on her head a turban, 'fastened in a point with a clasp of jewels composed of rubies, diamonds, and emeralds'. Her hands were hennaed red 'as is the custom among eastern ladies'.

'My hair was of course out of powder and plaited in a broad plait which came up loosely on one side of the turban ... Gold earrings, on my neck a locket of jewels ... With a prodigious long string of gold beads that went over my shoulders and hung down below my waist in tassels, the same behind fastn'd with a clasp of jewels at the breast and arms, the same on my wrists; a ring on every finger and on my thumb ... As the singing and dancing ladies who are in any high state always smoke and chew betel leaf,' she added proudly, 'we were also amply provided.'

Sophia Plowden's costume was a brilliant success. Indeed, her group was 'so admirably drap'd that many people insisted on us being really Industanis', she recorded. 'I rec'd an infinite number of fine compliments on my appearance and after wearing my mask about two hours I was glad to take it off and speak my own language.'[6]

If Englishwomen could not mix with 'Industani' women themselves, then they could at least emulate them and adopt their dress – although this was considered respectable only when it was donned as a form of fancy dress.

Sophia Plowden had an interest in the singers, or *nautch* women, that went far beyond that of merely wanting to dress up in their clothes. A talented musician herself, she became fascinated by the *nautches*, or musical parties, that feature so prominently in many European accounts of this time. These were intimate occasions on which women sang, danced and recited poetry; they appeared in front of men as well as women, and were well known for their wit. *Nautches* provided one of the few one of the few occasions at which Englishwomen could encounter Indian women on anything other than a mistress-servant basis.

The status of the *nautch* women is an interesting one: they are often described as courtesans, but their role seems to be much more akin to that of the Japanese geisha, in that they had a recognised, and highly respected, cultural role in Indian society. Some of them were indeed of very 'high state'. One in particular, the Kashmiri musician Khanum Jan, was a celebrated diva in her day. Sophia Plowden records her first meeting with this musical celebrity in December 1787, when she and her husband were living in Lucknow. At Khanum Jan's performances Mrs Plowden was sufficiently skilful to be able to write down the songs, both Persian and Hindustani, in European notation. She also made a collection of the lyrics that went with them, written out in Urdu on exquisitely decorated cards, and preserved today in the Fitzwilliam museum.* Not only did Sophia Plowden go on to perform these pieces herself, but her notations were later transposed into a collection of songs for the harpsicord by William Hamilton Bird. These 'Hindustani Airs' became all the rage in British drawing rooms in the last decade of the eighteenth century. The encounter between Sophia Plowden and the Lucknow musicians seems to have been one of great mutual respect and enjoyment, for Mrs Plowden was created a begum by Shah Alam II, the exquisitely decorated and gilded *ferman* for which is still held in the British Library.

Balls and masquerades, concerts and *nautches*, were not the only form of entertainment available. As early as 1721, the directors of the East India Company had cause, in yet another of their directives, to lament 'the itch of gaming' which had spread throughout the English

---

*I am grateful to Dr Katherine Butler Schofield for her scholarly detective work, which has reunited many of these verse folios – previously catalogued as a set of miniature paintings – together with their music, for the first time in two hundred years. See her blog, *When an Englishwoman visited Mughal Courts and transcribed their music in Western-style notation*.

settlements, complaining particularly that 'even the gentlewomen play for great sums. Discountenance it in all our covenant servants ... And civilly acquaint the gentlewomen we desire they will put a stop to all high gambling.'

It did no good. The vast distances between Leadenhall Street, where the Company had its headquarters, and their employees in India had at least some advantages. To both receive and reply to any letter could take anything up to three years. As with their directives against the luxury of garden houses, no one paid them any attention.

More than fifty years later, gambling was still in high fashion. Lady Rumbold, wife of the Governor of Madras Sir Thomas Rumbold, became famous for the 'immense' parties at which she frequently entertained the English inhabitants. A hardened gambler herself, she obliged her guests to follow suit or risk offending her, as William Hickey found to his cost.

On his first visit to India in 1769, he was invited to dinner with the Rumbolds, 'according to the etiquette of the place', and on his arrival his hostess gave him the choice between dancing and playing cards. When he demurred, saying that he was not fond of either, she declared that this was impossible, one or the other he must choose.

'As the lesser evil therefore I chose cards, and was placed at her Ladyship's table, she observing loo was their game, and that they played very *low*, only for Fanams *unlimited*, at which *low* rate I, in about two hours, notwithstanding the utmost caution, found myself minus upwards of six hundred pagodas.'*

Appalled that he could have lost so much, so quickly, Hickey leaped to his feet as though to leave the table; but Lady Rumbold was having none of it. '"Oh my dear Mr Hickey! You cannot think of giving up already. Pray don't leave the party!" To which I answered in a somewhat peremptory tone, "Your Ladyship must excuse me. I shall certainly stop now, for were I to continue a few hours longer at the same rate, instead of pursuing my purposed voyage to England,

*About £300. *Fanams* and *pagodas* were forms of Indian currency in the eighteenth century.

I should be compelled to return to Bengal, there to refurnish my empty purse.'"[7]

Theatrical productions were also popular during the cooler weather in spite of, or in some cases because of, the appalling performances of the amateur actors. 'One of the chief inconveniences in establishments of this kind, is that the performers being independent of any controul will sometimes persist in taking parts to which their abilities are by no means adequate; this throws an air of ridicule over the whole, as the spectators are too apt to indulge their mirth on the least opening of that kind: in fact, many go to see a tragedy for the express purpose of enjoying a laugh . . . '[8]

Despite this, it was not unknown for duels to be fought over the best parts. Ladies did not perform – it would have been indelicate in the extreme to expose themselves to such public scrutiny – but by the 1780s professional actresses were beginning to be imported from England to take the female leads.

A surprising number of careers and business ventures were open to women in eighteenth-century India. As well as actresses, professional portrait painters such as Sarah Baxter and Catherine Read, and miniaturists Martha Isaacs and Diana Hill, plied their trade with great success. In 1780, Mrs Hodges opened the first school for girls in Calcutta, and by the turn of the century there were twelve all-female seminaries. After her husband had left her for another woman, Eliza Fay was made a 'very eligible' proposal by a woman of her acquaintance to go into business with her, but declined it on health grounds – a decision she later regretted.

Women were also active as shopkeepers. They ran bakeries, confectionery shops, boarding houses and dressmaking and millinery establishments. Eliza Fay, once again, for a time managed one of the latter, together with another friend, Miss Hicks, and learned double-entry book-keeping in order to do so, 'which afterwards proved very advantageous in the prosecution of my concerns'.[9]

From the very earliest times many of them had also attempted to trade, either in partnership with their husbands or independently, often very successfully. The Minutes of the East India Company from the seventeenth century contain frequent references to requests from women to import and export goods. In February 1614, three years before Mrs Hudson took her £100 to Surat to trade in indigo, an entry reads 'Permission to Mr Stockley's widow to adventure £1,200'[10] – an immense sum in those days. In Bombay in the 1770s, Mary Cross traded regularly with Persia; while other women, such as Elizabeth Marsh's great friend the wealthy Calcutta widow Johanna Ross, made money by lending capital through their *sarkars* (Indian bankers). At the same period, in Madras, one commentator described how the presence of she-merchants was considered completely normal. What is more, they 'drove as large a trade as men, and with no less judgement. Nay ... some are so forward as to have invoyces, accounts current etc, in their own names, though their husbands are in being.'

Many others travelled to India as female attendants and maids. On the Company's very first attempt to entice settlers to India in 1668, the Minutes record that John Brodnax was to serve at Bombay for three years, 'and he is to be permitted to take with him his wife, his child, and one or two maid servants'. Increasingly as the century progressed there was a demand for more superior, and educated, governesses and music and drawing teachers. Since the days when Mrs Hudson and Frances Webb had accompanied Mrs Towerson to India, female companions were also in demand. In her later years, having resolved never to travel on her own again, Eliza Fay employed a Miss Tripler to accompany her on her last voyage to India in 1791, engaging her for two years at the tidy sum of £30 per annum. But of all the opportunities that India opened up, marriage would always be the principal one.

From the seventeenth century onwards, when the soon-to-be married Frances Webb set off to India on board the *New Year's Gift*, it was an acknowledged fact that women came to India to look for husbands. In 1668, as part of the push to attract settlers to their new territory in

India, the Company had made specific provision for this eventuality in their Minutes: '[single] women and maidservants going to Bombay are not obliged to remain with their employers within the said year from the time of arrival, and, if they marry an Englishman within the said year, with the consent of the Governor and Council, they are to have their liberty and their husband is not to give their employer any consideration for that time'.[11]

A hundred years later there was an assumption that most, if not all, women travelling to India did so in order to find a man. 'By this time I reckon you are able to give one an account of the new-arrived angels,' wrote a friend to Robert Clive in 1752. 'By God, it would be a good joke if your countenance were to smite one of them and you was to commit matrimony . . . '[12]

Much has been written about the 'fishing fleet' – the trail of young women travelling to India to find husbands – but by the early eighteenth century there were enough Britons born and bred in India for them to marry frequently among themselves.

The story of Eliza Draper (née Sclater) is a typical one. Both she and her husband, Daniel Draper, were from well-known Anglo-Indian* clans that had been among the earliest settlers on the subcontinent (her grandparents had arrived in Bombay in 1715, making her a third-generation addition to the family: it was her grandmother, Mrs Whitehall, who was said to have been captured by the 'pirate' Angria, but whose story did not make it into the East India Company annals). In 1758, when Eliza Sclater married her husband, she was just fourteen. He was thirty-four, twenty years her senior, an arrangement that, although not approved of by everyone, was not unusual for its time.

At first the young Mrs Draper seemed happy enough with the match, although the birth of two children in quick succession seemed to sap both her health and her spirits. On 26 September 1762, she wrote to her cousin Elizabeth back in England: 'I really, my dear

---

*In the eighteenth century the term 'Anglo-Indian' meant a British person born in India. It was only later that it came to mean someone of mixed Indian and British descent.

Cousin, am so much altered with breeding and suckling and other dangerous illnesses that I appear ten years older than I am, nor do I believe you will know me again if I return to England. When I left London [she had been sent home to school] I was fat and rosy but now I am quite the reverse, yet my spirits are good as ever, and till they subside, I shall not give myself up for lost.'[13]

Cracks were already beginning to appear in the marriage, as the cynical tone creeping in to some of her letters shows. In one such, she meditates on the fate of another cousin, Bess, offering to give her 'assylum' in her own household after her mother dies, 'tho' I've no hopes of fixing her advantageously in India', she wrote, 'sensible and good girl though she is, as in the first place she is too old [it is not known how 'old' Bess then was]. The men here like green trash better than wholesome fruit.' Nor was Bess 'sufficiently versed in the little Coquetries to engage the Merchant or seduce the Nabob; but I shall be glad to see her for all that'.

Whatever feelings Eliza Draper may have had – if any – for her husband, a few years were enough to disillusion her completely. He was 'by nature cool, phlegmatic, and not adorned by Education with any of those pleasing Acquirements which help to fill up the Vacuums of time agreeably'.

It was no surprise, then, that when Mrs Draper returned to England briefly to find schools for her children, she would be highly vulnerable to 'gallantry' of various kinds. She was still young, high-spirited – and unaccompanied by her husband. A portrait of the day shows her wearing one of the 'balloon' hats then fashionable (and so coveted by the fashionistas of Calcutta), her chin resting pensively against one hand. She is not a beauty, but her expression beneath her heavy, dark brows is quizzical, amused and highly intelligent. She had, if not the best education (something she would always regret), then at least a depth of imagination and feeling – qualities held in high regard in the eighteenth century – which made her stand out from other young women of her age.

The Irish novelist and clergyman Laurence Sterne certainly thought so. 'I'm half in love with you . . . ' he wrote after first meeting her in London in 1767, 'I ought to be wholly so – for I never valued (or saw more good qualities to value) . . . or thought more of one of Yr Sex than you.'

Before long, Sterne was much more than half in love with her. Despite the unseemly age difference – almost thirty years – he was soon in the grip of a helpless, obsessive passion. If she were ever to be widowed, he declared, his intention was to marry her. His own wife 'cannot live long', he observed callously: 'And I know not the woman I should like so well for her substitute as yourself.' When this was clearly not going to happen, he tried to persuade her at least to let him visit her when she was ill in bed. 'Remember, my dear, that a friend has the same right as a physician,' he wrote creepily. 'The etiquette of this town (you'll say) otherwise – No matter! Delicacy and propriety do not always consist in observing their frigid doctrines.'

He pressed her to sit by him for just two hours a day while he wrote *A Sentimental Journey*, and was even prepared to pay her husband £500 for the inconvenience of parting with her (ruining this apparent munificence by observing 'I am sure the work would sell so much the better for it that I should be reimbursed the sum more than seven times told'), but none of it did any good.

What Eliza Draper herself felt towards the elderly, gargoyle-faced Sterne, or what her thoughts were about being traded like a commodity between two old men, is hard to ascertain. Certainly she was flattered by his attention, for Sterne was a literary celebrity in his day, but despite his efforts to persuade her that she should stay in England another year (he offered to pay for this too) she decided to return to India, and be a good wife. '[My husband's] humour, I am now resolved to study, and if possible to conform to him, if the most punctilious attention can render me necessary to his happiness, it shall be so. Honour, prudence, and the interest of my beloved children demand the necessary sacrifice and *I will make it*. Opposing his Will, will not do. Let me now try if the conforming to it, in every particular will better my condition.'

Sterne was devastated.

It cannot have been easy for Eliza Draper either. Leaving her children behind her in the care of her maternal grandparents, she returned to India alone, and to a loveless marriage. 'A fortnight more I am my own Mistress, then Controulled all my Life after,' she wrote home to her cousin and chief confidant, James Sclater. 'Pray for me, that the State may be more pleasing than one of Freedom.'

Of some consolation, perhaps, was the fact that British society in Bombay now afforded similar amusements to those enjoyed in Calcutta and Madras. The population there had doubled in Eliza Draper's own lifetime from 70,000 to 140,000. There were all the usual balls, receptions and King's birthday celebrations. There was even a recently created spa town at Dasgaon, near Fort Victoria, some sixty miles south of the Presidency, where bilious Britons could go to drink the waters, much as they might have done at Buxton or Bath. But even these distractions could not make up for her increasing disillusionment with her marriage. As she wrote to her cousin James: 'it is Evident to the whole of our Acquaintance, that our Minds are not pair'd'.

The Drapers did not remain in Bombay long. By order of the directors of the East India Company, in October 1768 they were posted south to the small but important outpost of Tellicherry, on the Malabar Coast. Eliza Draper submitted to her exile with as good a grace as she could muster.

As it turned out, Tellicherry was not at all what she had expected. After the social whirl of Bombay, she now found herself the first lady in a small 'family' of about thirty English residents. It seemed to suit her mood. 'The way of life I'm now in is quite new to me, but not utterly unpleasant,' she wrote. 'I'm by turns the Wife of a Merchant, Soldier, and Inn-Keeper, for in such different capacities is the Chief of Tellicherry destined to act.'

The Company's servants all lived within the walls of the fort, which was strongly garrisoned by a large number of British troops. The house where the Drapers would reside was 'not only large, but a superb building . . . situated on the same mount as the adjoining castle, and overlooks and commands the seashore'. There were two gardens: a private one adjoining the house, 'well stocked with flowers', and another public one, where 'the gentlemen of the Factory sometimes pass a little time in walking in the evening'.[14] Since the late seventeenth century, a pack of twenty hounds had been kept at Tellicherry at the Company's expense (the dogs were allowed two pounds of rice each a day), so perhaps Mrs Draper included hunting as one of her leisure pursuits. Her others were riding, sea bathing, reading and filling 'Reams of Paper with my scribble'.

The hostilities with Hyder Ali, in which Eliza Fay was later to be caught up, were just beginning, and would much affect the pepper and cardamom trade for which Tellicherry was principally noted. Nonetheless, Mrs Draper's energies were now almost entirely focused on her husband's business. 'The war is a great bar to Commerce, yet I do a great deal of work in the Mercantile way as my Husband's Amanuensis,' she wrote: 'you know his inability to use the pen; and he has lost his Clerke and Accountant, without any prospects of acquiring others'.

It must have been grindingly dull work, but she made the best of it. 'I am necessitated to pass the greatest part of my time in his office, and am content to do so, as it gives me consequence and him pleasure,' she wrote. In another letter she was more specific: 'if I was not capable of assisting and maintaining his correspondence for him I know not what he would do at this juncture'.

The cracks continued to show. So much time spent in the company of Laurence Sterne could not but bring the contrast between him and her husband into cruel relief. 'Art had put me out of my Course, by rendering me the property of Mr D, for that nature designed for me an Actress, or the wife of a very feeling Poet or Philosopher,' she confided, 'rather than to a Gentleman of Independence and general Talents.' But there was no way round it: she was now 'absolutely necessary to Mr D's business, if not his happiness'.

Slowly, her high spirits were quelled; even her health began to suffer in this 'hated country'. From Tellicherry, the Drapers moved to Surat, and after a brief stay there took up residence in Bombay again, but even the social life there had lost its charms. 'No Wit, Beauty, Sense, Merit have We – nor yet Taste, Humour, Amusements or Social Converse.' She found the women insipid and silly, their only topics of conversation fashion and scandal. Even Tellicherry, with its small 'family' of English residents, was preferable.

Mrs Draper was now third or fourth on the Governor's 'list', and could imagine herself queen of society there, but for all her youth, good looks and intelligence, the fact was that her status was entirely an artefact of her marriage. Without her husband, she was nothing. Always small and claustrophobic, English society in India was becoming even more brutally hierarchical than it was back in England.

Eliza Draper would hardly be the first or the last young woman in India to repent of her choice of husband. Through her letters, however, she is one of the very few to whose innermost thoughts and feelings on the subject we are party. In India, where matches were frequently made with almost indecent haste, and often when women were not much more than children, she was not alone in her regrets. To her cousin James Sclater (with whom one suspects she was always a little in love), Eliza Draper wrote eloquently and movingly about the moral jeopardy which faced women in her predicament.

How wretched must that Woman's Fate be, my dear James, who loving Home and having a taste for the Acquirements both Useful and Agreeable can find nothing congenial in her Partners senti- ments – Nothing Companionable, nothing engagingly domestic, in his manner, to endear his Presence ... Sad! sad state!, my James, and woe! to the feeling heart so circumscribed. A Woman who might have been a valuable Member of Society, is by this disunion either a mere blank – or liable to every disgrace resulting from Infamy – if finely organised – Grief and Disappointment, may render useless all her Mental Faculties – if cheerful by nature and calculated to struggle with trying difficulties, in Hopes of surmounting them, these very excellences are so many snares to her as to excite Envy, Malice and Detraction – for who is just enough to acknowledge, that an amiable sensible Woman, has fund sufficient in her own mind, to be a perpetual Resource to her in all Calamities and Exigencies – on the Contrary, who does not Insinuate, that when such a character is unhappily pair'd, & maintains her cheerfulness, secret pleasures make her Amends for public Penances?

By January 1773, the estrangement between husband and wife was complete. To her humiliation, Mrs Draper had discovered that her husband was having an affair with one of her English maids, Leeds; he, in turn, accused her of an improper relationship with Sir John Clerke, commander of HMS *Prudent*, which was then anchored in the bay. A terrible altercation ensued. A few days later, Eliza Draper did the unthinkable: she eloped.

There are several versions of her elopement, the most colourful of which has her climbing down a rope from her bedroom window into a waiting skiff which then spirited her on to the waiting (and ill-named under the circumstances) *Prudent*. She remained there for some time under Sir John's protection.

Eliza Draper's anguished letter to her husband after the event shows just how desperate her state of mind must have been to make her take this irrevocable step. Nonetheless, she was at pains to point out that she had been the instigator of the scheme, not Sir John. Until the day of her elopement her relationship with him had been entirely innocent, she swore, no matter what her maid Leeds might have accused her of to the contrary. It was her husband, and he alone, who had driven her to such 'serious extremities' by his behaviour. 'But for the conversation on Monday last, he had nothing to hope for, or you to fear.' All the disgrace and infamy that she had predicted in her letter to her cousin James Sclater would now be hers. 'Lost to reputation, and all hopes of living with my dearest girl on peaceable or creditable terms, urged by a despair of gaining any one point with you, and resenting, strongly resenting, I own it, your avowed preference of Leeds to myself, I myself proposed the scheme of leaving you thus abruptly ... A conduct that will so utterly disgrace me with all I love.'

But the deed was done. There was no going back.

# PART THREE

# FIRST HALF OF THE NINETEENTH CENTURY

*In which the East India Company, bolstered by its ever-expanding armies, continues to seize new territories, and when its charter is renewed in 1813 provision is made for Christian missionaries to enter the country for the first time – by mid-century the Company has direct rule over two thirds of the subcontinent, while the remaining Princely States all recognise Britain as the paramount power – Dalhousie's 'Doctrine of Lapse' enables the EIC to bring yet more territories under its aegis, even in peacetime, and forces the Kingdom of Oudh (Awad) to submit to British control – and the Indian elements within the East India Company armies become ripe for revolt.*

Territories of the British
East India Company, 1805

KASHMIR

PUNJAB
Amritsar •
• Ferozepur
• Karnal
DELHI •

RAJPUT                    OUDH
SIND
• Nasirabad

MARATHA                        BENGAL
                                      Dacca •
TERRITORY              Ichapur •
                              CALCUTTA •

BOMBAY •        NIZAM

                Hyderabad •
                Rajahmundry •

Arabian Sea                              Bay of Bengal

MYSORE
                MADRAS
Bangalore •
Mysore •
                Nilgiri Hills
Coimbatore •
                Trichy • Tanjore

Himalayas

Malabar Coast

Coromandel Coast

CARNATIC

Indian Ocean

British
Hindu
Muslim

# CHAPTER 9

Eliza Draper should have been a ruined woman.

In Britain, the disgrace involved in absconding from the marital home was so absolute that it was very rare indeed for a woman in her situation to be taken in by family or friends should her relationship with a lover or protector come to an end. With no independent means of her own, Mrs Draper was now completely dependent on the whims of her protector. In a letter written some months previously she had claimed to have too much 'worldly wisdom' to leave her husband's house without a proper settlement, but sheer desperation had forced her to do so (or, as seems likely, he had refused to give her one).

A life of poverty or, worse, prostitution would have been almost inevitable now. As it was, it was the circumstance of her living in India that would save her from this unhappy fate.

When we next hear of her, she is living with her maternal uncle, John Whitehall, who was Company chief in Masulipatam (Machilipatnam)*, an important administrative centre north of Madras. Mrs Draper kept house for him there, and seems to have been visited by all of English society, both men and women. Her fellow countrywoman Elizabeth Marsh, who travelled extensively in southern India in the same period, was accorded 'a very polite reception' when she met her there in 1775, and much enjoyed the 'continual parties and

---

*This was the first British trading post in Bengal, founded in 1611. From 1686 to 1759 it was held by the French and the Dutch before finally passing into British hands again.

engagements'[1] that Eliza Draper, still something of a society queen, presided over. Since Elizabeth Marsh's own moral character – she was travelling with a man who was not her husband and almost certainly her lover (of which more later) – is somewhat ambiguous, perhaps she felt a more than usual sympathy with her hostess.

In general, sexual adventures were enjoyed with far greater frequency by Englishmen in India than by their women. Eliza Draper's uncle, to whose house she fled after she left the protection of Sir John Clerke, is a good example. John Whitehall was an eccentric character whose life was even more irregular than his niece's. Not only did he have at least one, if not more, Indian concubines, he also seems to have had a taste for young men.

When his niece first went to live with him, he was involved in a passionate affair with another man, Mr Sulivan, a 'sweet Character' of whom Whitehall was inordinately jealous. 'My Uncle doats on him with all the Extravagances of violent passion,' Eliza Draper wrote to her cousin at home. 'He cannot live without Him. He cannot even bear Him out of his Sight. He cannot like to have him sleep in any apartment but his own.' But there was no moralising about his male lover, nor about the brood of natural children he had produced with his *bibis*.*

In the eighteenth century, so many Englishmen took Indian mistresses that it was barely cause for comment. A study of the wills of Company servants in Bengal from 1780 to 1785, preserved in the India Office, found that no fewer than one in every three contains a bequest of some kind to an Indian *bibi*, or companion, and their natural children. One Company man was reputed to have no fewer than sixteen concubines. When asked how he managed them all, he replied airily, 'Oh I just give them a little rice and let them run around.'[2]

'The practice became so common that the Urdu poets in Lucknow

*English law, which after 1730 recognised the natural-born children of men living abroad as British subjects, made no such provision for the offspring of British women. 'Indeed, it is indicative of contemporary expectations that, before 1791, Parliament declined to legislate about what should happen if a British woman abroad gave birth to a child by an "alien" of any kind.' See Colley, *The Ordeal of Elizabeth Marsh*.

began abandoning the old time-honoured formula of Hindustani romantic poetry – Muslim boy meets Hindu girl with fatal consequences – and began composing *masnavi* [Persian or Urdu love poetry] where Hindu girls fell for English men, though with the same time-honoured denouement.'[3] In *White Mughals*, his account of the cross-race love affair between James Achilles Kirkpatrick and the young Mughal princess Khair un-Nissa, the historian William Dalrymple quotes from Rajab Ali Beg Suroor's *The Story of Wonders*: 'The love-struck Englishman ("a handsome youth of noble lineage and high rank; in his head the ardour of love; in his heart the fire of passion . . . ") falls so deeply in love with the beautiful daughter of a Hindu shopkeeper that he lapses into love-induced insanity before dying of heartbreak when the girl's parents forbid the romance ("he dropped on the bed of dust, crying in anguish . . . "). The story ends with a scene reminiscent of a modern Bollywood movie when his Hindu lady-love throws herself on to his coffin from a second-floor window as the funeral procession winds its way past her door, leaving her mortally injured. Suroor concludes: "The attraction of passionate love united the separated ones. All who had witnessed this scene shuddered in awe and the more compassionate ones fainted. Rumours about the misfortune spread through the city. The girl's parents were so grief-stricken that they soon died. This is what Love the troublemaker has done: it laid to rest, side by side in the dust, the victims of separation as well as those responsible for it. People in their thousands would come to look at the tomb . . . "'[4]

Inevitably such close contact with Indian women meant that some of their habits and customs were bound to rub off. Many British men, particularly those living away from the highly anglicised Presidencies, took to wearing Indian clothes; they smoked hookahs and washed more frequently; some became vegetarian, and occasionally even had themselves circumcised. Others were even rumoured to be religious converts. They built their houses to accommodate their women. In a later period, the separate guest-houses that were such a notable feature of English residences in Madras had all once been women's *zenanas* (secluded women's quarters). But this did not mean that society, as a European might understand it, had become mixed. Indian mistresses and wives, even when they were of high or even noble rank, were only ever an amenity to be enjoyed in private. They were never seen in company by other English men,* and nor did English women, except in rare cases, either visit or entertain them. But already, by the start of the nineteenth century, these liaisons were beginning to seem not only eccentric but undesirable.

What is far less well known, or documented, are the occasional liaisons between English women and Indian men. At least two women of British descent joined the ranks of the Oudh (Awadhi) *zenana*. One was Mary Short, who arrived with her brother Joseph in Lucknow in 1817, where she married the ruler of Oudh, Ghaziuddin Haider, and lived with him there as Sultan Mariam Begum Sahiba.[5] The other was a Miss Walters, about whom nothing is known except that she is said to have had a mosque built in her name.[6]

A group of British women, invited to visit the King of Oudh's *zenana* in Lucknow in 1823, encountered a begum (Muslim woman of high rank) of British descent, although since her name – either English or Indian – is not mentioned, it is impossible to know if she was one of the above or another woman altogether. As one of the guests observed in a letter to a friend, the begum was 'nearly *European*, but not a whit fairer than Tajmahul [the new favourite]. She is, in my opinion, plain, but is considered by the native ladies very handsome; and she was the king's favourite until he saw Tajmahul.

'She was more splendidly dressed than even Tajmahul; her headdress was a coronet of diamonds, with a fine crescent and plume of the same. She is the daughter of a European merchant, and is accomplished for an inhabitant of the *zenana*, as she writes and speaks

*There were some exceptions. After Charlotte Hickey's death, William acquired an Indian mistress called Jemdanee, 'a lovely Hindustanee girl ... who was very lively and clever'. She was notable for the highly unusual fact that 'unlike the women in general in Asia she never secluded herself from the sight of strangers; on the contrary she delighted in joining my male parties, cordially joining in the mirth which prevailed, though she never touched wine or spirits of any kind' (Hickey, *Memoirs*, Vol. 3).

Persian fluently, as well as Hindustani, and it is said that she is teaching the king *English*; though when we spoke to her in English she said she had forgotten it, and could not reply.' Her correspondent added: '*On dit* [they say] the English *begum* was the daughter of a half-caste and an English officer; her mother afterwards married a native *baniya* [shopkeeper]. She had a sister ... They were both very plain; nevertheless, one of them sent her picture to his majesty who, charmed with the portrait, married the lady.' As a royal begum, she was now said to have money 'in profusion' at her command, and – so the gossip went – had made her father-in-law treasurer, and pensioned her mother and sister. 'Poor thing,' the first woman had ended her letter, 'I felt ashamed of the circumstance, when I saw her chewing *pan* with all the gusto of a regular Hindustani.'[7]

The occasion of her visit to the court had been a ceremony to mark the anniversary of the King of Oudh's coronation, but the real highlight of the day had come when the group of British women were allowed to visit the Queen Mother afterwards, 'when the whole of the wives, aunts, cousins etc were assembled in state to greet us'. None of them had ever visited a *zenana* before, nor seen so many women assembled together all at once – 'I suppose from first to last we saw some thousands' – and they were amazed to find that women filled all the roles that outside the confines of the *zenana* usually devolved on men. '*Women bearers* carried our *tanjans* [litters], and a regiment of female gold and silver-sticks, dressed in male costume, were drawn up before the entrance.'[8]

Neither Miss Walters nor Miss Short left any record of their experiences, but another English woman, Biddy Timms, did. Miss Timms had met her Muslim husband, Meer Hassan Ali, when he was employed for several years as an assistant teacher at Addiscombe, the Company's military college. Before her marriage in 1817, Miss Timms had been a milliner, employed in the household of Princess Augusta, George III's sixth child and second daughter. She travelled to Lucknow with her new husband, where she spent more than a decade living in his *zenana*. Her book, entitled *Observations on the*

*Mussulmans of India, Descriptive of their Manners, Customs, Habits and Religious Opinions. Made during a 12 year Residence In their Immediate Society*, was printed by private subscription in 1832. Its dedicatee was Princess Augusta, her former employer.

Englishwomen's fascination with life behind the purdah screens had remained undimmed since Jane Smart first described her visit to the Nawab's lady in mid-eighteenth-century Madras. They often found the experience less than edifying. Some pronounced the women dirty and their rooms horribly cramped and airless. A frequent, disappointed, observation was that the women lived in conditions more like those in a convent than the bejewelled eastern luxury they had been led to expect. 'Some were handsome but still nothing like the beauties in the Arabian Nights nor no pearls like pigeon's eggs.'[9]

On her epic thousand-mile journey through the Carnatic in 1800, Henrietta Clive, the daughter-in-law of Robert Clive, and her two daughters visited a number of different *zenanas*, most memorably those of the many wives of the now deceased Hyder Ali and his son Tipu Sultan (the latter recently killed by the British during the Mysore Wars). Tipu's four sons, including the royal princes, Futteh Haidar and Adbul Khaliq, were then living under house arrest under British 'protection'. '[Futteh Haidar's] habitation is divided by a high wall from those of Abdul Khaliq, and there was lately a serious engagement between these *zenanas*,' she wrote in a letter to her husband. 'His elder wives overheard something impertinent said of them by the young ones of Abdul Khaliq, and resented it; stones were presently thrown from each party till the stones were exhausted. They then sent their old female attendants out into the street to collect more. A message came to Colonel Doveton to inform him of this civil war, and he sent them word that unless peace was immediately established, that he should be under the necessity of sending in a guard which would disgrace them for ever. This quieted the fury of the combatants.'[10]

For all her amusement at the '*zenana* wars', Henrietta Clive had a good deal of sympathy for the women she encountered, all of whom were in mourning for Tipu Sultan, 'the Tiger of Mysore' and Hyder Ali's son, who had been defeated and killed the previous year by the British. Maria Graham, whose *Journal of a Residence in India* was published to critical acclaim in 1813, found only disappointment. Despite the fact that she herself came from an intellectual background, and while in India could boast of having 'the good fortune to be acquainted with many individuals distinguished for oriental learning and research', her views are already discoloured by assumptions of racial and cultural superiority that by the turn of the century were slowly creeping in. 'Prepared as I was to expect very little from Mussulman ladies,' she wrote, 'I could not help being shocked to find them so totally void of culture as I found them. They mutter their prayers, and some of them read the Koran, but not one in a thousand understands it. Still fewer can read their own language, or write at all, and the only work they do is a little embroidery'[11] was her dusty view. She was further disappointed to find that there was nothing they could do – hardly surprisingly – to persuade their hostess to let 'any of the gentlemen of our family' visit with them.

The truth is that neither Henrietta Clive nor Maria Graham was equipped with either the language or the cultural understanding to make sense of what they saw. Mrs Meer Hassan Ali, on the other hand, had both in abundance. Her account is a fascinating first-hand riposte to these accounts. After twelve years of living among her husband's female relatives her voice has an authority that the others, with their too-short visits and lack of a common tongue, cannot equal.

In her *Observations*, Mrs Meer confesses that at first she had pitied the sheer monotony of women's lives spent secluded in the *zenana*, but that the longer she had spent in their company, the more sympathetic she had become to their way of life. 'They are happy in their confinement, and never having felt the sweets of liberty, would not know how to use the boon if it were to be granted to them,' she wrote. 'As the bird from the nest is immured in a cage, and is both cheerful and contented, so are these females. They have not, it is true, many intellectual resources, but they have naturally good understandings, and having learned their duty they strive to fulfil it ... they strive to be obedient wives, dutiful daughters, affectionate mothers, kind mistresses, sincere friends, and liberal benefactresses to the distressed poor.'

Their situation was helped by the fact that the women in her husband's *zenana* had been accustomed from infancy to their confinement. She also noted that they had many 'employments and amusements' to fill up their time. Even though these would not be to the taste of English women, 'nor suited to our mode of education, they are not the less relished by those for whom they were invented'. She goes on to speculate about what Indian women might make of European women's choices when filling up their time, and fancies that Indian women, equally, might think their energies better spent: '[they] appear always happy, contented, and satisfied with the seclusion to which they were born; they desire no other, and I have ceased to regret they cannot be made partakers of that freedom of intercourse with the world, we deem so essential to our happiness ... besides which,' she added, 'they would think it disgraceful in the highest degree to mix indiscriminately with men who are not relations'.[12]

Fanny Parkes, who travelled extensively around India in the 1830s, and counted many Indian women among her friends, elaborated on this point. 'The conduct that shocked them was our dining with men not our relations, and that too with uncovered faces. A lady going out on horseback is monstrous. They could not comprehend my galloping about on that great English horse just where I pleased, with one or two gentlemen and the coachman as my attendants. My not being afraid to sleep in the dark without having half a dozen slave girls snoring around me surprised them. My remaining *alone* in my own room: in not being unhappy when I was alone – in fact, they looked upon me as a very odd creature.'[13] Mrs Parkes was alive to the smallest nuance. If she dined in mixed company, and a special dish was sent to her from a friend in the *zenana*, she noted that the servants merely said 'it comes from within'. It would have been considered indelicate in the extreme even to mention the lady's name.

There were, however, no limits at all to the amount of female company *zenana* women could enjoy, and of this they were 'extravagantly fond'. To be alone was considered 'a calamity', Mrs Meer noted, but was happily a trial 'to which they are seldom exposed ... every lady having companions among her dependants – between two and ten, depending on rank'.

Wealthy Indian women also had large numbers of servants and slaves to wait on them, sometimes several hundred. In very noble or rich families there were eunuchs too, the ultimate sign of superior status. Often both servants and slaves were as superbly dressed as their mistresses, 'richly adorned with precious metals, in armlets, bangles, chains etc – the lady thus adding to her own consequence by the display of her attendant slaves'. Sometimes, on visits from one *zenana* to another, the procession of women and their female attendants could take more than half an hour to pass by. Even when Mrs Meer Hassan Ali went on her own to pay a visit to another harem, she always took at least two or three of her own slaves with her, 'as no-one expects someone else's slaves to wait on them'. Such visits always lasted three days and three nights.

Her days passed peacefully enough, with visits, daily 'shampooing' (by which she means bathing and massage) and reading Urdu poetry, which her husband translated for her. The *zenana* ladies may not have been able to read or write (skills which were not considered especially necessary, since these were the work of lowly scribes) but they enjoyed a rich and complex oral tradition. Storytelling was a favourite pastime, and women often employed a companion whose sole occupation was to recount stories and fables while her mistress was preparing to sleep – 'one story begetting another, Arabian Nights style'.[14]

There were times, however, when even Mrs Meer's sympathies were stretched. On discovering that one of her friends had never seen a river or a bridge, she undertook to try to get permission from either her husband or her father to take her to see one. The scheme was not well received. 'They did not approve of the lady being gratified and I was vexed to be obliged to convey the disappointment to my friend – But she answered mildly: "I was much to blame to request what I knew was improper for me to be indulged in. I hope my husband's family will not be displeased with me for my childish wish ... I shall be ashamed to speak on the subject when we meet.'"[15]

This was not to say that Indian women were without power. A common misconception among Europeans was that because the vast majority of Indian women lived in seclusion all their lives, they had no agency in the outside world. Nothing could have been further from the truth. In the early seventeenth century, Nur Jahan, wife of the Mughal Emperor Jahangir, traded in indigo and embroidered cloth, and coins were minted bearing her name. As Sir Thomas Roe would observe, on special feast days men wishing to curry favour at court sent presents to the Emperor's *zenana*, hoping to gain influence with his women. Ladies from wealthy families were also notable as philanthropists, collectors, and patrons of art, architecture and gardens. Some founded libraries; others were skilled as calligraphers and poets; and there is speculation that others may have become painters. Those born or married into the families of the elite were also politically influential in ways that, had they but realised it, would have confounded British women.

Lena Login was one of the few who came to realise this during her years living in Lucknow. 'These *purdah*-women exercise an influence and power that is only slowly being realised by Europeans,' she observed wisely, 'and as the *zenana* is the actual source of all the intrigues that constitute Oriental diplomacy, I learnt to be of real use to my husband in his political work.'

Lena Login's *Recollections*, written in old age for her children, contain an introduction by one of her sons. 'Although few of those who saw her in her later years could fail to recognise in her a strong personality, a wonderfully clear judgement and a keen insight into character, coupled with immense force of will and vitality, I doubt if the majority of her acquaintances realised the varied scenes through which my mother had passed in her long life,' he wrote. 'She was not one to speak of these things in general society, and knew, as do the wives of most Indian officials, how to keep her own counsel, and that of those who trusted her with their confidence.'

He goes on to paint a charming picture of Lady Login in her old age, immersed in her garden, her poultry-yard and livestock, 'clad in the oldest and shabbiest of garments, tending her bees, superintending indoor and outdoor work in the fashion learnt from her thrifty and capable Highland mother, and with her own hands doing odd jobs of rough carpentry'. Little would anyone have ever dreamed, he added, 'that in other days she had been equally at home, and happy, in the atmosphere of courts, and the daily duties of official life'.[16] What he does not mention – but what comes across abundantly in her *Recollections* – is what fun she must have been.

Lena Login was born a Campbell of Argyllshire. After the early death of both her parents, in 1840 she travelled to India to visit her brother, a soldier (later a general) who was then posted at Cawnpore (Kanpur) in the North-Western Provinces. She travelled out with her sister Maggie, who was engaged to be married to an EIC official, and was met at Calcutta by a third, already married sibling. 'Those were curious days in India,' she would later write. Even in the 1840s 'ladies were scarce, and unmarried girls few and far between'. Lena Login did not even get as far as Cawnpore. En route she stopped at Lucknow, where she met her future husband, and very soon after that married him.

Login, as she always refers to him, served for many years in the post of Residency-Surgeon at Lucknow under two successive Kings of Oudh. One of several other appointments that he held there was that of Physician to the Court, which gave his wife unusually good opportunities for meeting Indian women. Her husband's many friends among the Nawabs (the King's deputies) meant that she had the chance 'of seeing native ladies, and their children, in a social intercourse very unusual in those days between the two races'.

It was the numerous princesses and begums of the Oudh royal family, however, who showed her the greatest friendliness, from the Queen Mother downwards. Her special friend was Malika Geytee, the

King's favourite wife. Even after the Logins had left Lucknow, she kept up a correspondence with them, and her letters, in exquisite Persian script, would reach them long after they had retired to England.

'Many of the Princesses were women of great intelligence as well as high lineage,' Lady Login recalled, 'and we used to discuss all sorts of subjects, though not often religious matters, unless they specially questioned me, for my husband had a great dislike of any attempt to teach Christianity except with the husband's permission; but their curiosity was great concerning European clothes and customs.'[17]

On the birth of each of her children, she was presented with two complete sets of 'native dresses' which the princesses had sewn themselves as a mark of their favour, one for herself and one for the baby, each exquisitely embroidered in gold and silver thread. 'These I still possess,' she wrote, 'as evidence that these native ladies do not all pass their lives in complete idleness as is commonly supposed.'

After more than seven years living on intimate terms with these ladies of high rank, Lena Login came to speak Urdu, the court language, fluently,* and was often present when her husband was called on to attend one of the King's women. 'Of course he was never permitted to have a full view of her face! Instead, he had the fleeting vision of a *hand*, or a *tongue*, without visible means of support, waggling through a hole cut in the curtain, by which to judge of her general condition!'

But I was privileged to view, at close quarter, the comedy that was being enacted behind the *purdah* – the solemnity of the eunuchs supporting their mistress, while they assisted her to open her mouth and thrust her tongue through the orifice! The shouts of laughter

*Many years later, during the time of the Indian Uprisings, when she was living back in England, Lena Login found herself to be one of the only women in the country who was an Urdu speaker, and to her horror was asked to be the translator for 'the old Queen' of Oudh, who had come to plead the case of her son with Queen Victoria. 'I much feared I should have to undertake the office, as Her Majesty approved of the idea, for having had such constant kindness from the poor old lady, it would have been terrible to have been the instrument of making plain to her that her mission was in vain.' In the end, an Indian official was placed behind a screen in the room at Windsor Castle where the interview took place.

from the entire *zenana*, present *en masse* at the proceedings, the hysterical giggles and fidgeting of the patient, not at all averse (if good-looking) to making use of an opportunity to view eye-to-eye, and unveiled, such a popular Englishman. Undoubtedly, most of the Begums, and especially my friend, Malika Geytee, thoroughly entered into the humour of the situation, once their minds were relieved of the dread lest my jealousy might be aroused by the undoubted attractiveness of many of these patients.

Occasionally, she took over the doctoring herself, and once, in the case of the Wuzeer's (Prime Minister's) only child, saved a life. The little girl was in the last stages of consumption when Lady Login first examined her, discovering 'that the unfortunate child was slowly pining away, owing to the fact that her skin was encrusted with a hard shell, formed by the succession of ointments she had been plastered with, since to wash a patient in illness is regarded as fatal in native medical science!'

Her prescription of a warm bath was received with 'indignant horror' by the child's mother, the Begum, and it was only after much persuasion that she agreed to it, and then only on condition that the 'Mem-Sahib' herself would come and see it carried out. 'So I and my ayah arrived at the *zenana*, armed with a supply of soft towels, scented soap and sponges, and it was the interest and excitement aroused by the first sight of the latter that finally overbore all the opposition. Never in their lives had the Begum and her attendants beheld a sponge, or the European scented soap for that matter.' The sponges, in particular, caused a sensation. 'At first their alarm was great when the unknown marine monster swelled in the water, and they shrieked when we held it towards the child, for fear it should bite her! But, once reassured on that score, they regarded it as a piece of magic, and were enraptured at being presented with it on my departure. They amused themselves with it for hours, filling and squeezing it, and throwing it at each other, accompanied by peals of laughter!'

The little girl's treatment, however – 'a long and delicate process of softening the poor little mite's coat of armour' – was no laughing matter. When her ordeal was finally over, the child was so emaciated and weak that it was 'pitiful to behold', and even then Lena Login did not hold out much hope of saving her. If she could be removed to the cantonment where the Logins lived, where her continued treatment could be closely supervised, she might stand a chance. Amazingly, this was agreed to, and a bungalow was taken for her next to the Logins' own.

Slowly, and after many months, the child began to recuperate, becoming an object of intense interest to the English children of the cantonment, for every morning and evening the 'chota Begum' ('little Begum'), Wuzeeroolniza, would be taken out for a drive in an extraordinary chariot, 'shaped to represent a peacock, the outspread tail forming a sort of canopy, beneath which she sat, attended by her *zenana* guards'. Much later, when her recovery was complete, her grateful parents presented this 'fairy coach' to Lady Login's children, to the envy of all their friends.

Wuzeeroolniza and Lena Login became very close. During the child's recovery she would go to see her friend every day for English lessons, and by the end addressed her as 'Mother'. Like Malika Geytee, this adopted 'daughter' continued to write to them for many years, even after the Uprisings of 1857* had all but destroyed their former home, the beautiful city of Lucknow itself. Lena Login had a letter in her possession, dated Lucknow, 25 February 1859 – two years after the Uprisings had ended – addressed to her husband at Church House in Kew. It commenced 'Worthy Pappa' and ended 'Your most affectionate daughter, Wuzeeroolniza Begum'.[18]

For the majority of British memsahibs, however, Indian women remained an enigma. Their apparent absence from all aspects of public life – such a puzzle to Englishwomen from the very beginning of their involvement in India – remained so well into the nineteenth century.

---

*The Indian Uprisings of 1857, often called the First War of Independence, were referred to by the British as the Mutiny.

It is a telling fact that even that independent-minded traveller Fanny Parkes, whose journals describe her travels 'up country' over more than two decades (1822 to 1846), and who would later be on intimate terms with many *zenana* ladies, lived in India for more than four years before she met a single Indian woman, with the exception of 'those in attendance as servants in European families, the low caste wives of petty shopkeepers and *nautch,* or dancing, women'.[19]

# CHAPTER 10

From the beginning of the nineteenth century, British women were already experiencing India in a very different way from how they had done in the days of Mrs Draper and Mrs Fay. However hard it remained for the majority of them to penetrate the world of the *zenana*, their contact with India in general had expanded greatly. Although they still vastly outnumbered by men, the slow trickle of women brave enough to venture there was becoming a steady stream. Despite the fact that they still had to gain permission from the East India Company to travel to India, no one now questioned their right to be there.

For a start, the journey had become (relatively) far easier. In 1821, the three young daughters* of Peter Cherry, the Company's Collector in Madras, set sail to join their father. Although the traditional perils of the long sea voyage – storms, piracy, shipwrecks – were largely unchanged, the journey itself now took only a fraction of the time that it had done in previous centuries.

While in the latter part of the nineteenth century there would be guidebooks and instruction manuals galore to advise women what to expect – from what kind of tea-gown would be acceptable attire at breakfast on the voyage, to advice on how best to pack their kid gloves

*Georgiana Cherry, who kept a journal of her voyage, was fifteen. The names and ages of the other two sisters are unknown, although since the letter (see below) was addressed to Georgiana, they are likely to have been younger. Small wonder their father was anxious.

(they should be well-aired, wrapped in several layers of tissue paper, and then inserted into special stoppered glass bottles) – in 1821, the year of George IV's coronation, no such thing existed. So Mr Cherry wrote his own.

His epistle – the manuscript of which runs to fourteen pages, and amounts to nearly four thousand words – covers, quite literally, a multitude of sins, including everything from what his daughters should take with them on the voyage, to the etiquette of walking on deck with a young man, should one be forward enough to offer her his arm (they were instructed to keep the conversation general, change the young man as often as possible, and make sure that another sister was with them at all times).

Despite the increased speed of the voyage, preparations for it in the early nineteenth century were not very different from those in the seventeenth and eighteenth. Passengers might hire a cabin, or a portion of the round house, but what they were paying for was an empty shell. They were entirely responsible for fitting it out themselves, often employing a carpenter on site to carry this out (as William Hickey had done on the *Raynha de Portugal*). So Mr Cherry begins his enormous letter by enumerating the cabin furniture his daughters should take with them. It includes not only luxuries such as a piano and a harp, but bureaus with bookshelves and sofas that could be converted into beds, hanging lamps, a good supply of candles, 'pewter gurglets' and, last but not least, a foot tub.

Although the Cherry sisters did not take any pets with them, a great many women did, and these too had to be suitably provided for. On her return to England from Madras in 1801, Henrietta Clive made arrangements to transport her entire menagerie, including at least two horses, a cow, a bull and an aviary of different birds including their particular favourite, Cockatoo. She and her daughters Charly (Charlotte) and Harry (Henrietta) were disappointed to learn that a baby elephant could not also accompany them, since it was discovered that the creature required fourteen gallons of drinking water a day.

It was an unpalatable fact that in rough weather these animals were even more vulnerable than their owners, particularly those that were housed on deck. In 1848, one thirteen-year-old recalled the ferocious tempest that almost destroyed the Indiaman taking her home. She was particularly moved by the suffering of the livestock. 'On deck it was a dreadful sight,' she wrote, surveying the destruction afterwards, 'the sheep which were penned up in the long boat on deck were by now almost dead, a great many of them *were* dead, some with their legs off and others frightfully torn to pieces.' In addition, 'one of the cows, for there were two, fell down the hatchway, and was killed, and the butcher got drunk and upset the pail of milk so there was no milk; but how curious, an old sow on board lay down in a corner and gave birth to 12 piglets ... '[1]

Half a century earlier, fourteen-year-old Charly Clive, hearing 'an uncommon uproar' from the cuddy, where the gentlemen were enjoying their dinner, ran to see what the commotion was about. 'The sheep for our consumption had been secured on the poop and their pen giving way, it broke through the skylight, and the sheep came tumbling upon the guests and dinner table,' she wrote in her journal. 'I, of course, went to the door to see the confusion, glasses and plates were scattered and such a smell of sheep!'[2]

The dangers of hurricanes and flying sheep were the last thing on Mr Cherry's mind when he wrote his long missive – and just about the only eventualities he did not cover.

Even though he had arranged for his daughters to be provided with a cabin to themselves, their safety preyed much on his mind. Not only were they to block off the porthole of their cabin with wooden bars, but the inner windows were also to be similarly secured, 'to prevent you from falling out, or thieves coming in'.

On the whole, though, it is clear that it was not so much their physical safety as their moral conduct that was uppermost in Mr Cherry's mind. 'That my anxiety is great for your safety and protection on board ship you will naturally suppose,' he begins, 'and will not consequently be surprised at my deeming it necessary to lay down certain regulations and to offer certain advice for your conduct during the voyage ... more especially of consequence when it is considered that you will meet persons whose character, morals, and behaviour you are unacquainted with.'[3]

How times had changed from the days of Charlotte Hickey and Emily Pott.

'Neither is anything more severely censured than loud talking, dancing over the heads of those in the great cabin under you, or any unusual noises against the bulk-head, thus indelicately attracting the attention of persons in the next cabin or cuddy,' he went on, adding, 'nothing is so indelicate or indecent as from the windows of ladies' cabins to see anything towing overboard, or hanging out to dry'.

Mr Cherry followed this with precise instructions as to how his daughters were to pass their days. They should begin each morning by making their beds: 'neatly folding up your night clothes and putting them in one fixed place'. After that they were to wash themselves, 'cleanliness in every way being highly conducive to the health and nowhere more so than on Board Ship'.

Prayers were to follow the washing and dressing rituals, 'commencing with the prayers for Grace in the Morning Service ... And the collect for the first Sunday in Advent'. At the same time they were to confess any sin 'committed in thought, word or deed the preceding day'. After prayers, they must make sure their books had been safely stored away, 'otherwise by the rolling of the ship they may be injured or by falling against you may hurt and maim you'. No detail was too small for Mr Cherry.

At last the girls were to be allowed to breakfast, preferably in their cabin, but even then, no cosy pyjama-party would be permissible. They must be fully attired, 'as if you had been going out into Company; it is one of the most pleasing parts of an English Lady's Education that she is always properly dressed to see visitors and can never be surprised in an undress'.

Their mornings were not to be frittered away, but spent usefully, 'in a course of musical practice, drawing and reading, avoiding as much as possible (however oppressive you may find the heat of the weather or the cabin) lying down. Do not let even the example of your Lady passengers induce you to this enervating practice.' As was the custom in Georgian England, their dinners were not to be eaten until three o'clock in the afternoon, so at noon they were allowed to eat 'a biscuit' and drink 'a little weak Port Wine and water'. Even the increased appetite likely to be caused by the bracing sea air was to be 'indulged with much caution, taking little exercise to assist digestion, you will be otherwise liable to many little indispositions'.

After a long, dull confinement in their cabin, dinnertime came at last. For this meal they were finally allowed out, but only when 'dressed in a neat and becoming manner avoiding with the utmost exactness all appearance of finery'. Keeping as near as possible to their own cabin door, the sisters were instructed to eat only 'plain roast and boiled meats and vegetables, a moderate portion of pastry'. Unless specifically required to do so under doctor's orders, or by a medical regime, they were never to exceed a regulation two glasses of wine, and when they drank beer, never to mix it with wine at all. 'You will naturally, and agreeably to the custom of the World, be asked to drink wine by the Gentlemen near you.' This could be avoided by 'keeping a little wine in your glass, so as never to exceed the quantity above-mentioned'. No Mr Woodhouse could have been more solicitous of their constitutions.

The Cherry sisters' recreation hours were similarly regulated. After dinner they were forbidden to play cards, or backgammon, or even to do needlework in the cuddy, and 'on no account' were they to go out to supper. Above all, he enjoined, 'On no account from the day you enter the ship until the day you quit it ever dance either up on the Quarter Deck or in the Cuddy: never go to the Poop whatever you may see other ladies do.' With any hope of simple entertainments quashed, a long and equally dull evening awaited them back in their cabin, with yet more lessons, psalms and prayer.

The thought of his daughters taking any exercise or fresh air was yet another vexed question for their father. 'I have not yet touched

upon Exercise up on Deck, and I confess this gives me much distress.'
It would not do to go there before breakfast, he mused, as the decks
would be too wet. After breakfast they would be too hot. After dinner,
the young men on board would be too drunk to engage in the 'chaste
conversation' suitable for young ladies.*

Poor Mr Cherry. The idea that his girls should walk about alone on
the decks he deemed highly improper, but what was the alternative?
'From the motion of the Ship the arm of a gentleman is necessary,
the Captain, under whose care you may be placed, may have others
to attend in the same way, may be ill, a thousand things may occur to
prevent his fulfilling his promise . . . besides there will be three of you,
a laborious charge to walk with daily.'

The prospect of his daughters going on shore when the opportunities arose was beset with evils. These would have been possible at
Madeira, the Cape and Mauritius, but the sisters were forbidden from
any such excursions, 'for landing on a strange beach is attended with
much inconvenience and exposure'. They would be 'in an unprotected
situation, surrounded with difficulties and dangers in a Lodging
House with passengers, male and female, leading you into unnecessary extravagances and idleness'. In fact, now he came to think of it,
it would be best not even to look out of the windows when they came
into harbour, and they were not to 'run to the windows of the Cabin
or Cuddy door, as it has an unseemly appearance in young ladies and
the object attained is not worth the exposure it subjects you to'.

Although one can sympathise a good deal with Mr Cherry's anxieties for his young and unchaperoned daughters, sometimes his advice
borders on the mildly hysterical, such as what to do in the event of

---

*One such drunk young man, a Mr Traherne, accosted Harriet Tytler (of whom much more later)
on her return voyage to India in 1845. Observing that he had come over 'rather queer' after drinking too much champagne, and in an attempt to get rid of him without hurting his feelings, she
introduced him to her travelling companion, Miss Moresby, who just hours later 'whispered to me
that she was engaged to the handsomest man on board. On asking who that could be, she replied,
"Mr Traherne!" "Why," I exclaimed, "you never knew him before!" "No," she answered, "but he
proposed to me and I have accepted him."' Alas for Miss Moresby, she waited for her young man to
reappear in vain. After three days 'he met her on the stairs and passed on as if they had never met
before. Poor girl, I can imagine her mortification.' Perhaps Mr Cherry knew a thing or two after all.

sharks: 'as not infrequently sharks are caught over the stern, avoid going too near the windows of your cabin, as well to prevent accident as any appearance of interfering in what no way concerns you'.

It is odd, then, that his advice for what to do when they arrived at Madras, and prepared to breach its terrifying surf, is feeble to say the least. The thorough dowsing they were likely to get in waves and the naked, slippery fishermen on whose backs they would be carried ashore are barely even hinted at. Perhaps he thought that ignorance was bliss. 'In landing let your dress be plain and neat . . .' went his only instructions. 'As is possible, tho' not probable, you may receive a little of the spray of the surf on reaching the beach, wear a bonnet and certainly a veil, not to conceal anything it has pleased God to give you, but to prevent and check that idle gaze all ladies are subject to on landing.'

It is tempting to imagine the Cherry sisters rising up as one in revolt against their father's strictures, but apparently they did not. Georgiana, who wrote a journal of her experiences on the journey, records that she spent her time copying out sermons for the captain and reading mind-numbingly improving books such as Hervey's gloomy *Meditations among the Tombs*, Watt's *Improvement of the Mind* and Hannah More's *Sacred Dramas*. It was two weeks before they even dared to emerge from their cabin at all, a state of purdah that would have pleased the strictest Brahmin, and no doubt their father as well.

But perhaps Georgiana Cherry did not remain such a slave to her father's caveats for the entire journey. On 16 May, after eighty-two days at sea, she records a cheerful meal in the cuddy, flanked on one side by a young Mr Fruse, and on the other by his sister. 'I have fine fun at dinner such as laughing etc,' she wrote to her father, 'I long to hear your opinion of this subject.'[4] Luckily she was in no danger of Mr Cherry's opinions on the matter for at least another month.

'Fine Fun at Dinner' would be a good title for the experiences of another young woman making the voyage to India in the first half of the nineteenth century. Caroline Baker, fourteenth of the sixteen children of Sir Robert and Lady Baker of Montague Place, was a very different character altogether, travelling to India under very different conditions. She made the voyage in 1831, a decade after the Cherry sisters, accompanying her brother, Captain Baker of the Madras Native Infantry, and his wife Barbara. Although the first steamer had made its maiden voyage between Suez and Bombay the previous year, Caroline Baker made her voyage the traditional way, on a sailing ship, the *Alfred*, from Portsmouth to Madras.

While Georgiana Cherry barely mentions food (we get the impression that it was one of the many things of which her father did not really approve), Caroline Baker's diary contains little else. Gone were the days when, as Eliza Fay had found on board the *Nathalia*, the food provided was in such short supply that passengers had to become good 'scramblers', jumping into the fray with sharpened elbows to get their share.

On board the *Alfred*, Caroline Baker's breakfast alone amounted to a substantial feast. 'You may see on the table two great dishes of Hot Rolls, Bread baskets of Biscuit, Mashed and Roast Potatoes, Boiled Rice, Cold Fowl and Ham, Pork or anything that may be left from the previous dinner which it resembles more than a breakfast. Coffee, Green and Black Tea and butter running away.'[5]

Whereas the frugal Cherry sisters were rationed to a single biscuit at noon, Miss Baker feasted on 'Sago or Arrowroot Biscuit, Cold Plum Pudding, cakes and buns occasionally, any wine you please – Pea Soup and Mulligatawny in cold weather'. On hot days they were provided with 'hot plum pudding, Biscuits, Jam and Port Wine'.

Dinner might start with any number of different soups, from pea to mock-turtle, followed by mutton, pork, fowl of various kinds, goose, duck, salt fish and bacon. These were followed by tarts, rice pudding and 'maccarone' and cheese, washed down with a choice of white wine, bottled beer, claret, sherry and port.

By the 1830s this meal was sufficiently formal for the passengers to change beforehand. Caroline Baker, whose journal was written for the private entertainment of her many sisters back home and by her own admission might 'contain any nonsense that comes uppermost', recorded her changes of evening dress for them assiduously. They included a pink and white French gingham, gowns made of batiste (a fine, light, cambric-like fabric) and chintz, a blue muslin, a brown silk, a shot silk, a pink palmarine and her sister-in-law Barbara's 'low black body'.

Tea – or hot water with milk in it, when the supplies of tea ran out – was served later in the afternoon. Passengers, if not completely floored by their gargantuan dinner, could also partake of a supper which was produced last thing at night, consisting of 'Brandy, Rum, Sherry and Port, Cheese and Biscuits'. Occasionally 'Hot Negus', a drink consisting of port or sherry mixed with hot water, sugar and spices, was also served.

With only a brother and sister-in-law to chaperone her, Caroline Baker was able to have a much more cheerful time on her long sea voyage than the Cherry sisters. She played chess and cards – whist and *écarte* – read vast amounts of Walter Scott, practised music and danced on deck under the moonlight almost every night: reels, gavottes, quadrilles and minuets. The band, as had been traditional since at least the sixteenth century, was provided by various members of the crew. Singing was also a popular pastime among the women, their repertoire including 'The Wreath', 'Flow On', 'Rise Gentle Moon', 'Ye Banks and Braes' and 'The Canadian Boat Song'. She also assisted the gentlemen to prepare performances of *She Stoops to Conquer* and *The Rivals*, but did not act in them herself. Even in the 1830s it would have been considered highly improper for a young lady to perform in public.

Caroline Baker's other occupations were killing cockroaches and flirting, not necessarily in that order. 'Killed about a dozen cockroaches,' she wrote on 18 October, 'am getting quite expert in that art and can even look at them now with the greatest complacency.' Another entry reads: 'Had mince pies for dinner and took Wine with *nine* gents who I thought had a design upon me.' Another records: 'Fowler in the sulks because I did not honour him' – presumably either by dancing with him, or allowing him to sit next to her at meals.

One young man of particular interest to Caroline was Captain Legatt, whom she later went on to marry, undeterred by the fact that in rough weather she could hear him being loudly seasick in the adjoining cabin. (Perhaps it was this sort of thing that Mr Cherry had in mind when he advised his daughters against making 'unusual noises' in their room.)

The experiences of Georgiana Cherry and Caroline Baker, however different they may at first seem, precisely mirror the changes that were taking place in the British attitude to India since the turn of the nineteenth century.

On the one hand a new morality was creeping in to both public and private life, putting new strictures on women's behaviour; on the other was a new and unspoken confidence in a British right to make the journey at all. As is the case with Eliza Fay's companions on board the *Nathalia* in 1779, Caroline Baker's fellow passengers are a neat paradigm of the kinds of people now making their way out to India. On the table plan that she provides in her diary are listed eight officers of the Madras Native Infantry and five of their wives, a cornet (cavalry officer) of the 13th Light Dragoons, two surgeons, a Scottish minister and his wife (not much liked), two writers, five cadets and four unmarried young women.

In addition to the surprising number of women on the voyage (eleven), what is most noticeable is the increased numbers of military men: fourteen in total, as opposed to only two EIC writers. By the beginning of the nineteenth century, British influence now extended over a vastly increased area, and the East India Company Army* had grown massively in response. By mid-century it is estimated that almost every family in Britain had some relation or connection with either the EIC's civil or military service.

The greatest change of all, however, was to the British mind-set. Until the late eighteenth century the Company attitude to India had

*By mid-century there would be an estimated 40,000 British soldiers in India, and 230,000 native troops. See David Gilmour's *The Ruling Caste*.

been quite straightforwardly self-serving. Pioneering factors such as Job Charnock, the founder of Calcutta, and his like had been grateful for any scraps of trade that came their way. In the wake of their huge political and military successes, their successors in the EIC came to believe it their right – their duty, almost – to tax and plunder the land as they saw fit. While it is true that many 'White Mughals', both men and women, would come to have a profound respect for Indian culture and learning, most paid them no heed at all. It did not occur to anyone to try to interfere. Not only was God not yet an Englishman; at this point, God did not come into it at all.

All this was about to change. It is an amazing fact that it was the East India Company that, until after the Uprisings in the mid-century, exerted absolute control over every man, woman and child who came and went to the subcontinent. In this respect nothing had changed from the days of Mistresses Towerson, Hudson and Steele. Back in England, however, public unease at the Company's growing power had resulted in several Parliamentary efforts to check the worst of its abuses. The most important of these, Pitt's East India Act of 1784, had established a Board of Control, which for the first time gave the British government in London some powers to oversee the Company's business. The impeachment of the Governor-General, Warren Hastings, for corruption, a trial that convulsed the country for seven long years (but after which he was eventually acquitted), followed four years later. These, together with other pieces of legislation, put paid to the rampant corruption of fortune hunters such as Bob Pott and his like. Nonetheless, the Company, with its own army, administrators and judiciary, continued to rule over its ever-expanding territories like a private fiefdom. The only difference was that from now on 'solid advancement' would take the place of 'the glittering prospects of the past'.[6]

From its outset, the East India Company had taken a dim view of any activity that might be thought to interfere with the culture or religion of the people in the territories it now controlled. Company chaplains were explicitly forbidden from preaching to Indians, and missionaries were banned altogether. The care of Indian souls was not what the Company was about – and in any case, it was likely to be bad for business.* The rise of the Evangelical movement in England would profoundly change this outlook.

The movement, which began in one church, Holy Trinity, Clapham, in the 1780s, had extremely fast-growing roots. The 'Clapham Sect', as it became known, with William Wilberforce† among its number, also included Charles Grant, a former East India Company director, who, after a riotously spent youth, had experienced a religious conversion. When the Company's charter came up for renewal in 1813, it was Grant, an EIC insider, who spearheaded the campaign to put a stop to these prohibitions.

'Is it not necessary,' he wrote, 'to conclude that ... our Asiatic Territories ... were given to us, not merely that we might draw an annual profit from them, but that we might diffuse among their inhabitants, long sunk in darkness, vice and misery, the light and benign influences of Truth?'[7]

The directors of the EIC protested, but there was not much they could do in the face of the carefully orchestrated public campaign that followed, in which nearly half a million people signed petitions urging an end to the ban on missionaries. When the new East India Charter was finally granted, it not only allowed missionaries access to India,‡ it also made provision for the appointment of a bishop and three archdeacons.

---

*'We are very far from being adverse to the introduction of Christianity into India,' wrote Robert Dundas, the President of the Board of Control, to Lord Minto, the Governor-General, in 1808, '... but nothing could be more unwise than any imprudent or injudicious attempt to induce it by means which should irritate and alarm their religious prejudices ... Our paramount power imposes upon us the necessity to protect the native inhabitants in the free and undisturbed possession of their religious opinions.' Others, such as Thomas Munro, Governor of Madras in 1813, went further still. 'If civilization is ever to become an article of trade between [Britain and India], I am convinced that this country will gain by the import cargo.' Besides, as the historian Niall Ferguson has noted, since by the 1830s and 1840s 'the total value of Indian exports took the form of opium, there was not a great deal of room for high-mindedness in the boardroom'.

†Wilberforce believed that the conversion of India was even more important than the abolition of slavery. See Gilmour, *The Ruling Caste*.

‡Just twenty years later there were fifty-eight Church Missionary Society preachers and their wives active in India. See Niall Ferguson, *Empire: How Britain Made the Modern World*.

Secular thought was not far behind. In her *Journal of a Residence in India*, written between 1809 and 1811, Maria Graham's tone is already verging on the proselytising. She begins by hoping that her observations 'may contribute, in some instances ... to the means of improving [the Indian's] moral and intellectual conditions, as well as securing them from political or civil injuries'.[8] By the 1830s the gambling, drunkenness and debauchery so characteristic of the eighteenth century had all but died out. 'Methodism is gaining ground very fast in Cawnpore,' wrote one observer, with perhaps a tinge of disappointment; 'young ladies sometimes profess to believe it highly incorrect to go to balls, plays, races, or to any party where it is possible there may be a quadrille.'[9]

From now on the Nabobs, in all their delightful sartorial vulgarity, had been replaced by men in frock coats who wished 'to emphasise their Britishness and to demonstrate the moral and cultural superiority of their civilization. They had come not to revel in the Orient but to improve it – and in the process to limit its revelry.'[10]

# CHAPTER 11

Happily, revelry of various kinds was never entirely absent from Anglo-Indian life. Nor did the new mores change everyone's attitudes all at once – and in some cases, not at all. Women, particularly new-comers to India, were mostly too bound up with the practicalities of their own lives to worry much about anyone else's.

One of the things almost all of them were most forcibly struck by on arriving in India was the enormous numbers of servants that would be required to run their households. When the wife of the Governor of Madras arrived there in 1798, the lack of privacy that this entailed worried her a great deal:

> It is impossible to be invisible a moment without going round and shutting fifty Venetian blinds in every direction. All is perfectly open which annoyed me terribly at first. At every moment the first night I saw a black face and a turban through the blinds. It was sometime before I could express that I did not want such *faithful* attendants. I am now more at my ease and only find six or seven upon every staircase. Women with parasols appear the moment I go outdoors that no entreaty can get rid of them despite all my acts and ingenuities. I have tried everything but getting out of a window to escape. They are certainly the most attentive servants I ever met with and I am growing to like them extremely.[1]

Even outside the sophisticated Presidencies, living or travelling about in the *mofussil* (countryside), there was no end to the numbers of servants required. Another newcomer to Madras some thirty years later considered herself very economical when she employed a mere twenty-seven, a number that was 'reckoned very few' by her contemporaries. This skeleton household included one butler, one dress-boy or valet, one *matee* (who cleaned the silver, washed china and lit candles), two ayahs, one amah (wet nurse), one cook, one *tunnicutchy* (housemaid), two gardeners, six bearers, one water-carrier, two horse-keepers, two grass-cutters, one dog-boy, one poultry-man, one washerman, one tailor, one hunter (whose sole job was to shoot game for their dinners when they went travelling) and one amah's cook.

The 'whims' of her wet nurse, in particular, were especially hard for an inexperienced young housekeeper. As a 'caste woman', the nurse could not eat any food unless it was prepared by someone of her own caste. A special hut made out of coconut leaves had to be constructed for her in the garden, where her meals could be specially cooked, but even then 'she will sometimes starve all day if she fancies anybody else has been near it'. Her employer was also obliged to keep a separate nurse for the amah's own baby, 'and see after it regularly myself, because they are so careless about their own children when they are nursing other people's, that she and her husband would let the poor little creature die from neglect, and then curse us as the cause of it'.[2] When they thought no one was about, the amah's family were found smuggling in generous supplies of arak and opium for her to drink and smoke.

In addition to these immediate household servants there were nine peons that 'John Company' (the East India Company) allowed them 'to look grand with'. Their business was 'to stand about, go on messages etc.', she explained vaguely in a letter home. Most of the time, however, 'I have nothing on earth for them to do.' She was astonished to find that even their horses had servants, two each, a man and a maid. 'I enquired whether the cat had any servants,' she added mischievously, 'but I found she was allowed to wait upon herself.'

A more usual number of servants for a private family was estimated by to be between fifty and sixty persons. The childless wife of a junior army official in Allahabad compiled this list of her personal domestics, complete with their salaries, in monthly rupees – fifty-seven in total, costing them 290 rupees per month, which she estimated as about £290 per annum:

A *khansaman* or head man: a Musalman servant who purchases the provisions, makes the confectionary, and superintends the table: Rs 12

The *abdar*, or water-cooler; cools the water, ices the wines, and attends with them at table: Rs 8

The head *khidmatgar*: he takes charge of the plate chest, and waits at table: Rs 7

A second *khidmatgar*, who waits at table: Rs 6

A *bawarchi*, or cook: Rs 12

A mate *bawarchi*: Rs 4

*Mashalchi*: dishwasher and torchbearer: Rs 4

*Dhobee*: washerman: Rs 8

*Istree wala*: washerman for ironing

A *darzee*, or tailor: Rs 8

A second tailor: Rs 6

An *ayah*, or lady's maid: Rs 10

An underwoman: Rs 4

A *doriya*: a sweeper, who also attends to the dogs

A Sirdar-bearer, a Hindu servant, the head of the bearers, and the keeper of the sahib's wardrobe; the keys of which are always carried in his cummerbund, the folds of cloth around his waist: Rs 8

The mate-bearer; assists as valet and attends to the lamps: Rs 6

Six bearers to pull the punkahs, dust the furniture etc at 4 Rs each: 24 Rs

A *gwala*, or cowherd: Rs 4

A *bher-i-wala*, or shepherd: Rs 5

A *murgh-i-wallah*, to take care of the fowls, wild-ducks, quail, rabbits, guinea-fowls and pigeons: Rs 4

A *malee*, or gardener: Rs 5

A mate *malee:* Rs 3

Another mate, or a
    *cooly:* Rs 2

A *gram*-grinder, generally a
    woman who grinds the
    *chana* for the horses: Rs 2

A coachman: Rs 10

Eight *sa'ices*, or grooms,
    at Rs 5 each for eight
    horses: Rs 40

Eight grass cutters, at Rs 3
    each, for the above: Rs 24

A *bhishti*, or water-
    carrier: Rs 5

A mate *bhishti* Rs 4

A *Barha'I mistree*, a
    carpenter: Rs 8

Another carpenter: Rs 7

Two coolies, to throw water
    on the *tattis*, at Rs 2
    each: Rs 4

Two *chaukidars*, or
    watchmen, at Rs 4
    each: Rs 8

A *darwan*, or
    gatekeeper: Rs 4

Two *chaprasis*, or running
    footmen, to carry notes,
    and be in attendance
    in the veranda, at Rs 5
    each: Rs 10[3]

What might at first appear as the trappings of a luxurious existence was not always so in reality. 'I am afraid they will be very poor,' one woman observed after attending the wedding of a young friend. 'It seems to me that in this country a small income must be wretched indeed, for what would be luxuries in England, such as a large airy house, carriages, plenty of servants etc are here necessaries, indispensable to the preservation of health ... The real luxury here, and for which one would gladly pay any price, would be the power of doing without such matters.'[4]

Sometimes even the servants had servants. One woman recorded how her English maid had her own *kitmatgar*, or footman, and he in turn 'has an old man to attend upon him, who dresses his dinner, etc, and so on'. It was particularly noticeable when a long journey was contemplated. 'All our servants took their wives, and those of higher caste their slaves to prepare their meals, which do not give great trouble, as they only eat boiled rice and curry ... which they never vary, and only drink water.'[5]

In the previous century, slavery was still a normal part of Anglo-Indian life, and many Englishwomen had also owned slaves. Elizabeth Marsh had three female slaves to attend her on her journey through southern India in 1775, and Eliza Fay caused a scandal when she abandoned her slave woman, Kitty Johnson, on the island of St Helena on one of her journeys back to England. She gave Kitty to a friend, Miss Betty Mason, who sold her on for £10, despite the fact that no papers had been exchanged. Kitty denounced her, and Mrs Fay was apprehended when she returned to St Helena in 1791, and made to pay £60, for Kitty's passage back home to Bengal and the maintenance of her two babies.* Charlotte Hickey also owned a slave, a little boy named Nabob, who had acted as William's page boy on his voyages to and from London in the 1780s (although very little mention is made of him in Hickey's account of that time, and we do not know what he thought or felt during the great hurricane that almost destroyed the *Raynha de Portugal*). Nabob 'had never been the least use to me as a servant', Hickey wrote, although apparently he had looked very fine dressed as a Hussar, and as a fashion accessory had been a great pet among the fashionable London ladies.

Indian servants were, naturally, very different from their British counterparts. Most women found them extremely puzzling, at least to begin with. 'The servants provide for themselves in the most curious way,' wrote one. 'They seem to me to sleep no-where and eat nothing – They have mats on the steps and live upon rice. But they do very little, and everyone has his separate work.' Even speaking to them was something of a problem. 'The jargon that the English speak to the natives is most absurd. I call it "John Company's English" . . . it seems so silly and childish, that I really cannot yet bring myself to make use of it; but I fancy I must in time for the servants seem unable to understand the commonest direction till it is translated into gibberish.'[6]

---

*The case caused a flurry of correspondence between the Governor and the East India Company, as a result of which new regulations were passed concerning the owners of slaves. They were required to teach them a useful profession and to make them attend church at least once a fortnight (India Office Records, St Helena, 57).

Their written English could be even more testing. Here are some examples: 'One beef of rump for biled'; 'one mutton of line beef for *almoor estoo*', meaning *a-la-mode* stew; 'one mutton for curry pups' (puffs); 'durkey for stups' (stuffing for turkey); 'eggs for saps, sobs, tips, and pups' (chops, snipes, tipsycake and puffs); 'mediation [medicine] for ducks'; and at the end 'ghirand totell' (grand total), and 'howl balance'.

Other would-be servants simply hung around the gates 'to keep themselves in remembrance in case of an appointment falling vacant'. There was one in particular who called on a Madras couple regularly, twice a week, when the same conversation invariably took place:

Visitor: – Salam, great chief!

[Her husband] A: – Salam to you.

Visitor: – Your Excellency is my father and my mother!

A: – I am much obliged to you.

Visitor: – Sar, I am come to behold your honourable face.

A: – Thank you. Have you anything to say to me?

Visitor: – Nothing, great chief!

A: – Neither have I anything to say, so good morning; enough for today.

Visitor: – Enough; good morning, sar: great chief, salam!

'One has to dismiss one's own visitors, as they generally think it an impoliteness to go away of their own accord,' the 'great chief's' wife explained. 'We are obliged to appoint a particular hour at which they may come else they would be hindering us the whole day.'[7]

For all their numbers – perhaps because of them – the dilatoriness of Indian servants was a very frequent lament. It took a good deal of getting used to. 'They are *dreadfully* slow,' sighed one Anglo-Indian housewife in her early days. 'I often tire myself with doing things for myself rather than wait for their dawdling; but Mrs Staunton laughs at me, and calls me a "griffin" [newcomer] and says I must learn to have patience and save my strength.'

For others it was the sounds of their household that they would always remember. 'The noises of an Indian house! The echoing of every sound through the gaping, yawning, staring dark rooms and corridors! The reverberation of *Qui hai*? [Who's there?] in every direction and the annoyance of servants sitting all about to shout out *hasir*!, ready!, or the greater annoyance of their having gone outside to smoke and talk, so that you may *Qui hai*? till you are black in the face ... '[8] Sometimes, she lamented, it took three servants to fetch a bottle of soda water.

In the very grandest households these situations were taken to the extreme. At the very beginning of the century, Maria Nugent found herself presiding over a household comprising more than a hundred staff. On her arrival in Calcutta in 1811, where her husband Sir George Nugent had been posted as Commander-in-Chief of the East India Company Army, she found all of them lined up to greet her. 'The yard in front of the house, called a compound, was filled with servants, with a *Sukar* and a *Khanasomah* at their head ... The footmen are called *Kitmatgars* – we dress ours in white, with scarlet sashes, or rather white and scarlet mixed or twisted together – scarlet bands to their turbans – silver crescents in front – this dress is really very pretty,' she recorded in her journal. 'The servants were all drawn up in order, and when we got out of the carriage they all made salaams down to the ground.'

Even for a British aristocrat, and one quite used to a household of servants, it was a formality that threatened to overwhelm her. On her first morning – after a sleepless night, and 'half dead with mosquitoes' – Lady Nugent asked for tea to be brought to her. 'I sat leaning on the table, expecting a cup of tea and biscuit on a waiter,' she wrote, 'when the folding doors were thrown open, and the huge butler, or *khanasomah*, looking like the great Mughal himself, marched up towards me, followed by eight men, one with a cup of tea, another with milk, a third with sugar, and so on – one man with a *chowrie*, or silver stick, with a white cow's tail to keep off the flies, etc. I begged to be left alone, and at last, by signs, made them understand me;

however, the Mughal would not leave me, he placed the others outside the door, and then stood behind my chair . . . '9

In the corridors, and on the staircase, there were always at least twelve people. At dinner it was worse, with three or four servants always standing behind her chair. 'In the hot weather, the dining table crowded with large joints of meat, etc and three times as many servants as the company consists of, you may conceive what kind of a stew we must be in.'*

The men with silver sticks proved particularly troublesome. Even if Maria Nugent had tried, as the Governor's wife in Madras had joked, to jump out of the window to escape them, there were always several more waiting for her outside, attending on her when she went for a walk in the garden. Moreover, she wrote, 'We are both sadly annoyed by the number of salaams that are made, whenever we move from one room to another. The house really is full of these people.'

It was not only the house that was crowded. Yet more staff were attached to the stables and grounds. Each of her horses had its own *syce*, or groom, whose duty it was to run beside the horse as it trotted along. 'The establishment in the stables is, besides, a postillion to each horse, a groom and a grass cutter to each,' she recorded. That is, four servants to each horse. In addition, the Nugents had a *derangar*, or chief coachman, who came gloriously attired in silk and gold trimming, with a turban made from silver tissue. As far as Maria could make out, his only duty was to usher them in and out of their coach. They also had squads of *bhishtis*, or water-carriers, whose job was to water their drive; and *massalgies*, or linkmen, whose duty it was to meet them when they drove out at night and light their way home. Even though their carriage had lamps affixed to it, and the moon was often very bright, they always had at least six *massalgies* running before them with flaming torches. It must have been quite a sight.

Like all new arrivals, Maria Nugent was particularly struck by the

---

*Later, on her journey 'up country' by boat, on one of the hottest days she had ever experienced, Maria proposed that they should in future have only one servant behind their chairs, and that the others should wait on deck: 'but the customs of the country would not permit of my plan'.

absence of women in her household. Apart from her personal maid, Johnstone, whom she had brought with her from England, in her entire household there were only two: her ayah, and a sad-sounding *materannee*, or chambermaid, called Malmah. 'This poor outcast ... has nothing to do but to bring and take away water from the bedrooms – that is from mine and Johnstone's,' Lady Nugent recorded. Although she does not specify, this would have included emptying their chamber pots. 'She never makes an appearance, unless called for by the ayah, but sits squatting like a cat on the backstairs, with a long veil, which covers not only her head, face and shoulders, but her whole person – her dress is a coarse petticoat, very full, and plaited round her, like a Dutch woman's, and so long that it covers her feet – then the veil I have just mentioned covers the rest of her dress, concealing almost everything but her eyes.'

For Maria Nugent, and very probably for all women, trying to understand the inner workings of her household brought her sharply up against the strictures of India's caste system. Malmah the chambermaid was an outcast because she was an Untouchable, or Dalit, and therefore 'held in the greatest contempt by all the natives'. On her first morning, eating her breakfast under the watchful gaze of her huge *khanasomah*, Maria had tentatively mentioned Malmah, observing that she seemed like a good woman. 'You would have thought I had mentioned some odious reptile,' she wrote; 'he shrunk back and said "bad, very bad! Eat anybody dinner!" This is a most severe reproach, I understand, and it is the greatest mark of contempt to give that character of anyone.'

Lady Nugent was born Maria Skinner in 1771, in colonial New Jersey. Her grandfather, a Jacobite, had settled there after fleeing Scotland in 1717. Her father, a loyalist during the American War of Independence, was to flee back again with his enormous family (Maria was one of ten) when the war ended in 1783, forced to abandon his estates and most of his other assets. The Anglo-Irish George Nugent (his grandfather was the 1st Earl Nugent), whom Maria married in 1797, was similarly impoverished but well connected. Both families had turned to the military, and to Britain's ever-expanding empire, to restore their family fortunes.*

Maria and George were no exception. With four children to provide for, the youngest of whom was born in India, Lady Nugent makes it clear in her journals that their reasons for accepting the post in India were entirely pecuniary. While the worst excesses of the Nabobs were now a thing of the past, curbed by legislation in the 1780s, in 1811 a senior post in either the military or the administration could still be exceptionally lucrative. The Nugents are said to have amassed a considerable fortune in the four years they were away.

Nonetheless, there was a huge price to pay. Having left all three of her children in England, including a six-week-old baby, Maria Nugent found herself not only profoundly depressed by her separation from her children, but struggling to make sense of an enormous, claustrophobic new household. Furthermore, since Sir George's appointment as Commander-in-Chief was second in importance only to that of the Governor-General, Lord Minto, whether she liked it or not, she now found herself with a public role to play.

Mostly, she did not like it at all. She and her husband were hardly ever alone. It was not only their servants who filled their house, but large numbers of visitors, both military and civilian. Her first few weeks in Calcutta were 'completely occupied in receiving and returning visits, receiving and giving dinners etc'. On the evening of 20 January 1811, for example, her journal reads: 'in the evening we attended the great ball at the government house, in honour of the Queen's birthday.† We had silver sticks etc etc, all in great state. The house is really a very fine one, and the marble hall beautiful. The crowd was very great and the figures were extraordinary. The men wore black caps and aprons and the women had towers on their heads, ornamented with all sorts of jewels and precious stones in abundance.

*As the historian Maya Jasanoff has noted, 'India particularly appealed to ambitious but somewhat marginalized individuals, like down-at-heel gentry, Scots, Irish Protestants – and American loyalist refugees.' See Jasanoff, *Liberty's Exiles*.
†Queen Charlotte, the wife of George III.

We supped at half past 12 or 1 o'clock and Sir George and I came away immediately after. I pass over many descriptions of people, dresses, buildings etc etc as I intend to get drawings of everything, and my time is now so occupied, and I am so unwell, that I cannot write much or distinctly.'

Even a month later, there was little let-up. On 19 February she wrote: 'On 16th we gave a large dinner to Lord Minto and the principal people of Calcutta; on the 18th (last night), we gave a ball to the whole Presidency, which went off extremely well. Our house was not quite quiet till after 4 o'clock, and today we feel a little worse for our exertions.' On the 26th, she records 'a very large dinner party – wished not to go down, as there were only gentlemen, but Sir George made it a point I should'.

And so their life flowed on. When they were invited to dinners or entertainments away from home, they took their own servants with them.

The custom here is, for your *kitmatgars* to enquire where you dine; they then all precede you, and are ready when you arrive. I have four footmen, Sir George has the same number, and a *chowrie* man each – the *jamindar* and the silver sticks go with us. The *jamindar*'s business is, to take Sir George's hat and sword, and to give orders to the other servants; he wears a short sword in his sash; the head silver stick wears a sword also, and he is a Brahmin – he is fond of his caste, and has always a white mark from his turban to nearly the tip of his nose, with a vermilion spot between his eyes. The *jamindar* wears a finer muslin than the other servants, and a shawl, put on like a Scotsman's plaid.

Religious scruples kept the Nugents from accepting or receiving any social visits on a Sunday, or indeed on any other holy day. Lady Nugent was quite struck, as well she might be, by the general lack of reverence among the British community. 'I cannot ... avoid remarking ... how much upon one's guard one ought to be, respecting religious observances, at this distance from home,' she observed only a week after her arrival. She was particularly disconcerted to have been invited to 'a great entertainment' at the house of Mrs Lumsden, the wife of one of the members of Council, on Ash Wednesday. 'No one seemed to remember it was the first day of Lent,' was her shocked response, 'and no service was performed in church.' Moreover, since Mrs Lumsden was a senior figure in Calcutta society, and 'a very particular person', Lady Nugent felt she could not refuse her invitation. 'We could not begin society with a discussion,' she concluded.

In her view, even such church services as there were in Calcutta left much to be desired. On Sundays, divine service was 'pretty well attended', but she suspected that people went there as a 'place of public entertainment' rather than from any more elevated religious feelings. 'The women are all dressed very fine,' she noted, and the clergymen had a habit of discussing 'party business' rather than preaching the more spiritually sustaining parts of the Gospel. And as if this were not enough, she found that the continual up-and-down motion of the punkahs hung all around the church made her feel seasick – a frequent complaint among other women too.

'I see how necessary it is to keep up, in one's own mind, the remembrance of those days set apart by our church, as well as to keep a vigilant watch upon our minds and hearts: for at any age we are but too apt to be negligent of duties that we are not in some degree reminded of, by the example of others,' was her pious conclusion.

Whereas Maria Nugent thought it her duty to be at her husband's side at all times, not only to entertain for him but also to set a high moral tone for the rest of the British community, and 'give the Young Ladies a chance of Husbands', her contemporary, Henrietta Clive, thought it all a terrible bore. Arriving in Madras in 1798 as the wife of the new Governor of Madras, Lady Clive took one look at what passed for 'society' there and headed, quite literally, for the hills.

Although separated in age by a mere thirteen years, and in time on the subcontinent by less than ten, Maria Nugent and Henrietta Clive had radically different experiences of India. While both came from similarly aristocratic backgrounds, Henrietta seems a child of the eighteenth century, Maria a harbinger of the new. Whereas for Maria Nugent, a devout Evangelist, God was a constant presence, and her Anglicanism a prism through which she interpreted much of what she saw, in the latter's letters there is almost no mention of God or of her religious faith at all.

Far from seeing the necessity of helping the young ladies of Madras to catch husbands, Henrietta Clive seems to have rather disapproved of them. 'Many women have come out to Madras to marry,' she wrote in a letter home shortly after her arrival. 'I really think I never saw so many females that had quite forgot what beauty *might* be. I have no idea of so many people assembled without one that would be thought tolerable in London.'[10]

Apart from their reprehensible ugliness, the sheer quantity of English women now living at Madras vastly increased the number of return visits Henrietta would be required to pay – 'a troublesome ceremony from their houses being so dispersed'. She was perhaps the very last woman to describe a version of the Setting Up Ceremony, which seems still to have existed in Madras at that time. For the aristocratic Lady Clive, it was almost ludicrously old-fashioned. 'I sat perched upon a chair at the end of a large room during three hours for three successive nights – when they all came and curtsied – till every bone ached.'[11]

Born in 1758, Henrietta Clive was the daughter of Henry Herbert, 1st Earl of Powis. At twenty-six, she had married Lord Edward Clive, the son of 'Clive of India', the hero of Plassey. Lord Edward's acceptance of the appointment as Governor of Madras (1798–1803) came as a surprise to everyone. Unlike George Nugent, he was wealthy enough not to need the money, had no previous government experience, and was considered to be almost entirely lacking in the charisma and ambition that had so characterised his father. Nonetheless, as his wife's affectionate letters to him show, the marriage seems to have been a happy one. Of their four children, the two girls, Charly and Harry, aged eleven and twelve, travelled to India with them – their mother under the mistaken apprehension that 'the climate is wholesome and cannot do them injury. On the contrary, it is said to be remarkably otherwise at their age.' Their two boys, Edward and Robert, remained at school in England in the care of their uncle.

A portrait of Henrietta Clive by Sir Joshua Reynolds, for whom she sat in 1777, shows an elegant eighteenth-century figure with a mass of powdered hair beneath a large, coquettishly angled bonnet (possibly the first and last things that were ever coquettish about her). Her black eyes meet the observer with a cool and determined expression that seems to suggest that she did not suffer fools gladly: a presage, perhaps, of things to come.

If Calcutta was the biggest and most important of the Presidencies, Madras was reputed to be the healthiest and most beautiful of the three. Jemima Kindersley, whose description of it was written in 1765, at the very beginning of the reign of George III, thought it 'without exception the prettiest place I ever saw'. She describes a town laid out in orderly streets and squares, the houses 'neat and pretty', with large, airy rooms leading off one another, each one fronted by a 'varendar', which not only gave a 'handsome appearance to the houses on the outside, [but] are of great use – keeping the sun out by day and in the evenings are pleasant to sit in'. She was struck too, as were all visitors to Madras, by the glistening white decoration of the houses, all of which were plastered, inside and out, with 'channam' – a kind of stucco made from crushed oyster shells, egg white and milk – which gave the buildings a shining, marble-like appearance. As with Calcutta, Madras had grown up originally in and around a fortification, Fort St George, but, as usual, the British were soon building themselves garden houses along the coast.

When Henrietta Clive arrived there, over a quarter of a century after Jemima Kindersley, Madras had grown considerably, but it still maintained something of its country town air. The town itself was divided into two parts: the European half, and the 'Black Town' where the 'natives' lived. Mrs Kindersley, who came from a modest

Norfolk family and was married to a low-ranking officer in the Bengal Lancers, was rather impressed by the inhabitants of Madras. 'I can hardly believe myself among English people,' she wrote; '... they are expensive in horses, carriages, palangeens [palanquins], and numbers of servants; are fond of entertainments, dress and pleasure, sociable with each other, hospitable and civil to strangers.'

For Henrietta Clive, coming to them from a very different viewpoint, most of them were irredeemably vulgar, a great number of them being 'in trade'. 'I am terribly inclined to believe the fair sexes in this country are not too agreeable,' she wrote to her most trusted friend, Lady Douglas. 'If I dared, I would tell what my Ladies and Gentlemen are like. It will be difficult and I hope my evil genius is not now looking over me and going to publish my observations on them.' A few lines later, however, she cracks. 'There are a few with good manners and sensible,' she confessed, 'but for the greatest part are as much otherwise as any body can invent. As you see, I am none too happy with the level of entertainment in Madras, equating Madras society with that of Ludlow in Shropshire.' It was not meant as a compliment.

Henrietta Clive's peers thought very well of her. As one of her acquaintances observed, Lady Clive 'had a mind open to receive pleasure from everything, to please as far as she can, is incapable of offending and will not tire, I am sure, of any situation she is placed in'.[12] But the women of Madras were clearly daunted by her aristocratic demeanour.

A year later, she was still puzzling over her fellow countrywomen, who were clearly giving her a wide berth. 'The people here are in general not much enlightened,' she wrote to Lady Douglas. 'There are a few women that are good and many clever men ... I believe the women are afraid of *me*. I do not know why,' she protested, 'as I am most *outrageously* civil but they are alarmed. I live a great deal with my girls.' And again, to her brother George Herbert, 2nd Earl of Powis, she wrote, on 3 July 1799, 'There is an idea spread about that we do not like company and therefore nobody comes near us except at my dull assemblies and [Lord Clive's] dinners. I believe they dislike me a good deal from Mrs White, a Salop [Shropshire] lady having written a long history of my pride and formality, which makes people avoid me, though nobody was ever so civil to them before.'

When she was not alarming her fellow countrywomen with her aristocratic ways, Lady Clive found plenty to keep her occupied. 'I cannot sit by and be idle nor can I bear to have visits from people I do not care for by way of something do, so . . . I am beginning Persian and hope in all due time to be able to read Hafiz and all the learned books. Then I shall be romantic and so extremely flowery in my discourse that I suppose I shall not be able to give a rational answer to a common question.'

Not for her, even for a moment, were the idleness and ennui that were reputed to afflict all European women. In addition to learning Persian, Henrietta took classes in 'Hindustanee' ('I must do something to make me understand and be understood'); supervised her girls at their lessons (aided by their governess, Signora Anna Tonelli,* who had travelled out with them from England); and was an avid, and extremely knowledgeable, collector of both botanical and mineral specimens. One of the first things she did on her arrival in Madras was to build a special room for them in the garden, 'and a laboratory for all sorts of odd rocks and works', as well as the occasional reptile, such as the snake caught in their gardens, then killed and bottled.

Henrietta Clive took an interest in everything. She took her daughters to visit temples and to observe the local festivals, and had soon amassed a large menagerie, which included two miniature bulls and a cow, a hog deer, an antelope, a cockatoo, a canary, a mynah bird and some avadavats (tiny weaverbirds). Their terrier, Friskey, gave birth to seven puppies. Dutifully, she went through the motions of giving assemblies and, as was now customary, balls for both the King and the Queen's birthday celebrations. She attended theatrical performances (*Henry IV* was a particular success), visited the newly built Pantheon

---

*Signora Tonelli was an extremely gifted artist, who would later exhibit her paintings at the Royal Academy of Arts, a rare distinction for a woman. Her husband was a violinist from the famed Tonelli family, renowned for their musical skills in and around Florence.

(a replica of the one in London) and took her daughters to see the jugglers at the theatre. Even so, none of this was enough to use up her super-abundant energies. 'It is impossible to imagine the sameness and dullness of this place,' she wrote to her mother-in-law, the dowager Lady Clive. To her brother she lamented, 'the solitude, the confinement and the heat make me at times so low that I can scarcely support it'.

What she really yearned to do was travel. This 'indescribable wish' had been her dream since she first heard of her husband's appointment. In this she had been thwarted, for the whole of her first year in Madras, by the threat of Tipu Sultan and his army, with whom the British were then still at war. Their final campaign against him – which ended in his overthrow and death on 4 May 1799, at Seringapatam – would change all this.

The following year, Henrietta Clive and her two daughters set off on a journey around southern India that would take them more than seven months, and cover more than a thousand miles.

# CHAPTER 12

'Neither you nor myself believed it *prophetic* when you called me a *bird of passage*, which I really am in preparing to take a very long flight,' Henrietta Clive had written to her friend Lady Douglas in 1797 on first hearing that she was to accompany her husband to India. 'I look forward to all sorts of things – like the Arabian Nights – and put away every idea of other places as much as possible.'[1] The same was true now. On 7 March 1800, after months of preparation, she set off on her journey, 'not with seven leagued boots, but with elephants and camels like an eastern damsel with all possible dignity'.

Although she may not have found anything to equal the Arabian Nights of her imagination, the manner of her travelling was every bit as exotic as she could have wished for. In addition to fourteen elephants to carry their tents – as well as, bizarrely, Harry's harp (she was to become an accomplished musician) and Charly's pianoforte – there were a hundred bullocks to pull the enormous provision carts, a one-horse *bandy* (small carriage) that Lady Clive liked to drive herself in, and two racing camels for the express delivery of messages and letters. Following behind came an enormous retinue of over seven hundred and fifty people. It included a bodyguard of sixty-six infantry, 'cooks, *palanquin* bearers, maids, hangers on, and her Persian teacher'.[2]

The depression and homesickness that had threatened to overwhelm her in the heat and isolation of Madras did not disappear overnight.

The arrival of letters from friends and family, particularly from her brother George Herbert, to whom she was exceptionally close, would always be bittersweet reminders of home. Just six weeks before her departure, she wrote to her mother-in-law, the dowager Lady Clive: 'At this horrible distance every little circumstance is very interesting, and it is *many* months since I had a word from you. I cannot help thinking of a good fire and the little worktable near it where I used to sit at Oakley Park, with nieces and children at another table, with great envy, and had rather see one of the old oaks than the finest Banyan Tree in India.'[3]

In the first days of their journey, it was not only letters arriving from England that reminded her of home. Within a week of setting off from Madras they had stopped at both Vellore and Arcot, both of special interest to the family as the sites of two of the young Robert Clive's earliest victories in India, half a century previously.

On 15 March they stopped at Vellore. 'We went in the evening to see the fort,' Lady Clive wrote to her husband in Madras. 'It is a sad, ruinous place. The mud walls are still remaining sufficiently to show the extent of the fort ... [which is] most extremely narrow, populous and dirty: everybody looking poorer. All is desolate.' She was particularly struck by 'the breaches made in the wall by your father. It was late and soon grew dark, but I was determined to see as much as I could for a place so remarkable in the annals of this family. The dust and heat were prodigious.'[4]

At first, memories of England continued to be the measure by which she judged much of what she saw. On 11 March she wrote in her journal, 'The country is beautiful and put me very much in mind of Maidenhead.' Later, when riding through a 'country of fine cultivation', it seemed to her 'like large fields in the Vale of Evesham'. A few months on, at Rangherry, she wrote to Lord Clive describing the views: 'The hills near the villages were so much covered with wood that it put me in mind of those in Berkshire, which I think a great compliment to it.'[5] In another letter, she describes the countryside around Bangalore, and wishes that her husband could be there to see it with her. 'I am sorry to find there does not seem any prospect of seeing you here in this place so like *England* and *Paradise* that I would give anything to see you here.'[6]

Not surprisingly given the size of their entourage, their progress was leisurely, so there was plenty of time for letter writing. Henrietta Clive's letters to her husband are affectionate and domestic. She wrote to tell him how much she missed him – 'I am very sorry that you say that obstacles increase to prevent your coming here because though we are all well here I feel uncomfortable the distance we are from each other and the length of time'[7] – and chided him gently when his replies to her letters did not come frequently enough: 'pray come in from the garden a little sooner and take a pen and write to me'. She also filled him in with news of their two daughters, whose health pre-occupied her greatly throughout the time she was away. On the whole Harry and Charly, now thirteen and twelve, thrived throughout the seven-month journey ('the girls are very merry and desire their love to you'), although Charly, who had begun her menses ('last night there was an unexpected change in her constitution which I had rather had not happened this twelfth month'), proved the more delicate of the two. Their doctor, Dr Hausman, was very attentive to her, 'but I do not think he has been much used to females', she wrote to Lord Clive in October, 'and I am particularly anxious about Charlotte if this time does or does not come on again, as it ought to do'.[8] Throughout this time, the two girls continued their music and other lessons with Signora Tonelli.

For his part, Lord Clive sent his family gifts of fruit (his pineapples were particularly popular) and details of his plans for the refurbishment of their garden house at Madras. 'I shall be very glad to see the plan and to know when it will be finished,' his wife wrote back to him in April. 'If the girls have what you then proposed by the *music room*, may it be as much out of my hearing as it can because here I enjoy it so much that I shall be glad to have a little cessation now and then. There are discordant sounds and a little scolding of Signora Anna, which altogether *is not amusing*.'[9]

Little by little, the freedom from formality and restraint worked on her spirits. The physical exercise that she was now able to take – scrambling up rocks and through woods, driving herself whenever possible in her *bandy* – clearly had beneficial effects as well. From being 'weak, low and nervous', there is a sense of her energy returning – a fact that could make her seem eccentric. 'I believe I am thought a strange, restless animal. A black woman never moves and the white ones in this country are not much more active. Besides, I descend from my dignity and walk upon my own feet at every place where I take up my abode.'

England, and English concerns, were not exactly forgotten, but they occupied her thoughts and feelings far less than they had done, although she was not above exulting in the fact that she had escaped the stultifying social life at Madras. 'There are, I hear, a great importation of ladies,' she wrote with satisfaction to her brother George, 'which I escape, being at Bangalore.'

The sheer beauty of the countryside she travelled through soon drew her in. The comparisons with loved places in England became less frequent. Gradually, she was able to allow India to be just India. On 24 September their party arrived in Kumbakonam near Tanjore (Thanjavur). 'Here we arrived this morning through the most glorious country I ever saw,' she wrote in a letter to Lord Clive. 'We left Tanjore in the evening and found *pandals* [pavilions] erected by [their host] Mr Harris ready for us. Yesterday we had one that was beautiful and today I am writing in a house of cocoanut leaves where there is a gallery, which beats the great room at the Garden House ... It is impossible to describe the luxuriance of the trees and the cultivation. It really is beyond anything I recollect in England. We are still by the riverside, which supplies all this immense vegetation without any tanks except for the pagodas. In short it is perfection.'[10]

At every opportunity Henrietta Clive stopped to hunt for new and rare botanical and geological specimens for her collection. Plants of all kinds were a particular passion that she shared with her husband, and her letters to him are full of references to them. On 15 May 1800, she wrote: 'I have got two trees of sandalwood, about six feet long and one diameter. They are fresh and just cut down. Would you like to have any more as the *havildar* [sergeant] can get more if you wish it from Saverdroog. I shall try to get some young plants if possible to send you.'

'I am very glad your garden goes on well,' she wrote to him a month later, 'I think I shall make some additions to it that you will like.' In another letter she added, 'You say nothing of white roses, but I mean to send you some.' When they were ready to send she included precise instructions: 'Pray take care of the roses and seeds. I should like to see a hyacinth once more. They should be planted with a *great deal* of sand and a little mould.' On other occasions she sent him peaches, specimens from cardamom, pepper and cinnamon trees, wild limes ('pray let great care be taken of the Malabar names (*tied to them*) when they are planted'), 'a very fine cabbage', four jungle fools (a species of bird) and 'a very curious sort of mistletoe with a beautiful flower' ('pray have it grafted directly upon a tamarind tree. It *will not grow* in the ground and is really well worth preserving'). In return she asked him to send her some common garden seeds so that they could grow their own vegetables while at Bangalore: 'radishes, turnips, or anything; ours are nearly at an end'.

In Bangalore, where the party holed up for two months during the hottest part of the summer, quarters were made for them in Hyder Ali's old palace. Henrietta was charmed by it. Despite its air of general neglect, the interiors were magnificently painted with gold, scarlet and green, the open-air galleries and verandas more delightful than anything she had ever come across at Madras. Altogether it was Henrietta's 'complete idea of an eastern palace', and 'the only thing like *India* I have ever seen'.

Best of all was the garden, where the air was sweet and cool, and where she could write her letters beneath the shade of an avenue of immense cypress trees, perfumed with the scent of 'the only sweet roses in India'. The rest of the garden, however, was now much neglected, and she took upon herself its restoration. She planted myrtles, and found some very old and neglected orange trees, from which she sent graftings back to Madras.

By the end of the summer they were back on the road again. She continued her collecting with renewed energy. 'I have been at Coimbatoor [Coimbatore] and in unfrequented woods in search of teak and other strange trees,' she wrote to Lady Douglas. 'Many I have discovered that are quite *new descriptions*. I shall have some seeds. When I return to Madras I think I shall be able to send you some pretty creepers for the little hot house. When I meet with a beauty, the Collector or somebody promises to get the seeds. I have really found one or two plants that are very sweet and not known.'[11]

Her interests extended not just to plants, but to almost anything that could be bottled, stuffed or catalogued. 'I try to collect any little things I can to show you ... and my natural history is, I hope, likely to be in a good way,' she wrote to Lord Clive. 'I want to have all I can of Mysore and have birds stuffed and insects bottled by Dr Hausman. Dr Hyzer is in hopes of producing some very curious stones from his tour, which are to be given to the Governor and Council, I suppose, and a little heap to me.'*

She sought out everyone she could who shared in her enthusiasm for collecting. On 30 September, her journal reads: 'After breakfast I went to see Dr John's collection of shells, fishes, and a very handsome Macaw. He showed me several books of shells, fishes and animals, the titles of which he is to give me, and some of his drawings of new fishes. I have many more shells than he has,' she noted triumphantly, 'and duplicates of his most valuable ones. Afterwards I went to Dr Rotthem to see his herbarium, which contains 4,000 specimens of plants ... in the evening I went to Dr Rotthem's gardens where there are very many curious plants and trees, but they are dispersed under the cocoanut trees and it was so late that it was scarcely possible to see them.' The following day she added:

---

*Henrietta Clive's mineral collection eventually comprised over a thousand specimens. Her collection, including a meticulous catalogue in two exquisitely handwritten volumes, was donated to the Amgueddfa Cymru (the National Museum of Wales) in 1929, and is considered to be one of the most important of its kind. Lady Clive purchased and exchanged minerals with many other prominent collectors and dealers, including another woman, the Countess of Aylesford.

I went to see Dr John's collection of butterflies, which are very beautiful. Some of them, which I had never seen, had wings of the brightest purple. His insects are also very good ... Dr Klein's birds are not so curious as I expected nor dried in a more complete manner than those hastily done by Dr Hyzer and sent to Ryacottha ... Dr Rotthem thinks the plants and cinnamon etc that I brought from Daraporam country will not be any use either there or in the Carnatic. He disliked most of those I brought from the Annamalee Woods. I have desired him to get me a collection of insects, butterflies and birds packed properly to be sent to England.

Henrietta Clive was travelling at a particular moment in history – the aftermath of the Second Mysore War. During this time Tipu Sultan, by far the most formidable enemy the EIC had faced in southern India, had been defeated and killed. Under the Treaty of Seringapatam of 1799, the south Indian territories formerly controlled by Tipu were divided up among the British and their allies. Some were restored to the Nizam of Hyderabad, others to the Raja of Mysore, while the rest – the provinces of Malabar, the Barahmahal, and Salem, in other words almost all of the southern tip of India and its eastern coastal regions – now came under the control of the East India Company. It was mainly through these vastly increased Company territories that Henrietta Clive travelled.

It never occurred to her to question the rightness of these British conquests. 'Before this time you have heard of the taking of Seringapatam,' she had written to her brother in England shortly after Tipu's assassination. 'What a wonderful people we are really, having the command of the whole world. It makes me very proud of being an Englishwoman.' Nor did she question the division of Tipu's spoils among the English:

The plunder of Seringapatam is immense. General Harris will get between £150,000 and £200,000. Two of the privates of the 74th have got £10,000 in jewels and money. The riches are quite extraordinary. Lord Clive has got a very beautiful blunderbuss that was Tipu's and much else at Seringapatam. Some of the soldiers have got 20,000 pagodas; some have 10,000 pagodas, and one a large box of pearls ... There was a throne of gold, which I am sorry to say they are breaking into pieces and selling by parts. Lord Mornington has presented me with one of the jewelled tygers from the throne.[12]

Evidence of the recently concluded hostilities was everywhere. At Vellore, in addition to visiting the fort, they were visited by the four sons of Tipu Sultan, who were being held there under house arrest. Two of them, Moyen Uddeen and Mousa Uddeen, although now grown men, had been brought to Madras by Lord Cornwallis as children, where they were looked after by the wife of the then Governor. 'I have heard that Lady Oakley was very kind and attentive to both the hostages,' Lady Clive observed; 'she said (through the Interpreter) to the youngest, that she would teach him English, and that he must teach her his language; he answered her, that she might teach him English, but she was too old to learn his language.'

At Seringapatam, scene of the final 'Storm' against Tipu, Colonel Wellesley lent her his house, the Doulat Baugh, until recently the residence of the Sultan himself. From there she was able to inspect 'all the marks and horror of the siege', including the blood stains still visible on the walls where Tipu had been killed. She was also taken to meet both Hyder's and Tipu's surviving wives and daughters. Hyder Ali alone had between thirty and forty women in his *zenana*. 'Some of [them] have fine features and are light brown. His daughters were dressed with jewels and pearls. Their eyes were large and there is a great degree of family likeness between them all.'

All the women cried when the English visitors were brought in to see them, but Lady Clive claimed not to see any real tears, except in the case of Tipu Sultan's principal wife. 'She was old, rather large, and not handsome,' she recorded in her journal on 12 August. 'She met me on the step of the veranda and cried so much that it was really painful to see her. She was in more state than the rest and had a carpet of scarlet and gold to sit on supported by cushions. I was really glad to quit her. She was really distressed to a great degree.'

Their visit to Mysore a few days later proved altogether more soothing to her nerves. There the Clive women were received in state, as liberators. They met the newly restored Raja of Mysore, a little boy of six, and the only male member of his dynasty who had been allowed to survive under Tipu's rule. The British, she claimed, did not even know of his existence until he was discovered after the siege of Seringapatam, imprisoned in the palace stables under the care of his old grandmother.

The Rani, in Henrietta Clive's opinion, had 'a very sensible countenance', but was also 'one of the fattest and most battered women I almost ever saw'. It was her young grandson who interested her the most. 'The Rajah was sitting on an ivory throne that belonged to the ancient Rajas and is seven hundred years old . . . [He] is a very fine boy, six years old. He was dressed very magnificently in a silver dress with many ornaments, some very fine diamonds and fine pearls hanging to the ornament on his neck with several hanging on his shoulders . . . He asked several questions and seemed very much inclined to be merry if his dignity would have allowed him.'[13]

During her visit, which lasted two hours, there was a violent downpour of rain, which luckily was interpreted by her hosts as a highly auspicious sign. 'It was impossible not to see with pleasure an unfortunate family restored to the life of which they had been cruelly deprived,' she wrote with satisfaction. 'I shall always think of the two days that I passed in Mysore and care more about the affairs of India than I ever did from having beheld these two persons.'[14]

# CHAPTER 13

Throughout Britain's centuries-long involvement in India, women would always take to the road, even if it made them seem perverse, eccentric, or even dangerously unconventional to do so.

In the same way that the subcontinent had opened up women's opportunities for economic survival, so it also gave them unlooked-for opportunities for travelling. Usually this was done to accompany their husbands, for administrative, military or trading reasons, as Jemima Kindersley had done as early as 1767 when she travelled five hundred miles, by budgerow and palanquin, from Calcutta to Allahabad with her soldier husband, a journey of more than three months.

Occasionally, however, as had been the case with Henrietta Clive, they did it for themselves, just for the adventure of it. One of the first women to do this was Elizabeth Marsh, who in 1774 had embarked upon a journey through southern India that was lengthier, more dangerous and a great deal more scandalous than Henrietta Clive's plant-collecting progress.

'My extreme ill health *obliged* me to undertake a journey to the coast,' she wrote, perhaps not entirely truthfully, at the beginning of her Indian Journal. The unofficial reason was a man named George Smith, who was very probably her lover, and would become her insep-arable companion on her eighteen-month journey.

Besides travelling with a man who was not her husband, there was much else about Elizabeth Marsh that was extremely unusual. Even by today's standards, she was already a phenomenally experienced traveller. Born in 1735, she was conceived in Jamaica but born in Portsmouth, the daughter of an English master-shipwright and his Jamaican-born wife (it is this fact that has given rise to the theory that she may have been of mixed-race parentage). The *Portrait of a Lady said to be Miss Marsh*, attributed to Allan Ramsay, which was painted around the same time as Henrietta Clive sat for Joshua Reynolds, shows her to be an altogether different kind of woman from her aristocratic successor. She wears a plain, low-cut dress; her hat, while fashionably angled, is about a third of the size of Henrietta Clive's; her dark hair is unpowdered. The impression is of a neat, busy, curious person, of what historians are fond of calling 'the middling sort'. But there any claims to normalcy end.

This 'remarkable but barely known woman, travelled farther and more dangerously by sea and in four continents than any female contemporary for whom records survive'.[1] The stories she lived to tell about her adventures, both on land and at sea, were even more absurdly picaresque than the novels so fashionable at the time.

Throughout her lifetime Elizabeth Marsh travelled: she crossed the Atlantic from Kingston to London (albeit *in utero*), lived for extended periods in Menorca and Gibraltar, and undertook the arduous voyage to India not once, but twice, visiting Brazil and the Cape en route. More remarkable still were her North African experiences.

In 1756, as an unmarried young woman of twenty-one, she took the brave – some would say rash – decision to travel from Gibraltar back to England. It was the beginning of the Seven Years' War, and the entire Mediterranean was overrun with French warships under orders to 'take, sink, burn or otherwise destroy' British vessels. Nonetheless, against her parents' wishes, Elizabeth Marsh took a passage aboard the *Ann*, a 'battered, unarmed, 150-ton merchantman, loaded with casks of brandy, and with only ten crewmen', to Lisbon. Despite the fact that she would be the only woman on board, she was determined to go.

For safety's sake, the *Ann* travelled at first in convoy with fourteen other merchant vessels, but almost immediately became separated from the rest of the fleet, lost in thick fog. When the ship finally emerged, it was to find an enemy ship bearing down on her: not a French vessel, but a twenty-gun Moroccan cruiser with more than 130 armed men on board.

Along with three English merchants, Elizabeth Marsh was taken first to Salé on the Atlantic coast of Morocco, and from there on a forced caravan march on mules to Marrakech, a journey of six or seven days. Eight miles outside the city she was made to dismount and dress in her finest clothes. She was then placed not on her own mule but in front of one of the other prisoners, a merchant named James Crisp. To an audience of jeering, shouting onlookers they were then paraded, bare-headed in the burning sun, through the streets of Marrakech.

At this point it would have been the assumption of all the prisoners that they had been taken to Marrakech to be sold as slaves. For centuries Barbary corsairs had been terrorising both the Mediterranean and the Atlantic shores in search of human prizes, and had been known to raid villages as far north as Devon and Cornwall. Salé, or 'Sally' as it is often referred to by the English of this period, was one of the great slave trading centres of the time.* If this were not enough to persuade Elizabeth Marsh of her probable fate, on the journey their caravan had passed some Bedouin tribesmen, who were 'inclined to be rude', upon which her guard had shouted out, or so she was told, that 'I was going as a present to [the Sultan] Sidi Muhammad'.

In the end, Elizabeth Marsh was not enslaved in the Moroccan Sultan's harem, but only by the narrowest of shaves. Instead, the acting Sultan of Morocco, Sidi Muhammad, a highly cultivated and intelligent man, went on to use his prisoners as bargaining chips. His aim was to 'persuade' the British to appoint a Consul in Marrakech, to further his country's international trading and commercial interests. (One of Elizabeth Marsh's fellow captives, Joseph Popham, was indeed later sent to take up this post.)

---

*In the seventeenth century there are thought to have been more Europeans sold into slavery throughout the Ottoman Empire, and on the Barbary Coast, than there were West Africans enslaved by Europeans. See Linda Colley's *Captives*.

Nonetheless, as a young, unprotected female, she soon attracted the Sultan's special attention. Unlike the other prisoners, kept in seclusion in a broken-down house in the city's Jewish quarter, she was twice taken, alone, to the palace, where she was received by the Sultan and a number of his women. Her second invitation to attend the Sultan was preceded by gifts of fruit and flowers, and a young French slave boy to act as her interpreter.

Escorted through elaborate gardens to the palace, she found the Sultan waiting for her. Sidi Muhammad was 'tall, finely shaped, of a good complexion ... Dressed in a loose robe of fine muslin, with a train of at least two yards on the floor, and under that was a pink satin vest, buttoned with diamonds'. On his head he wore a cap that was also decorated with diamonds. There were bracelets on his arms, and slippers of gold filigree on his feet. 'His figure, altogether, was rather agreeable, and his address polite and easy.'[2] She refused anything to eat or drink, afraid that it might be drugged, but accepted a gift of some silver bracelets.

All this time, in order to protect herself, Elizabeth Marsh had claimed to be married to her fellow prisoner James Crisp. Clearly not believing her story, the Sultan questioned her about her lack of a wedding ring, but she told him that she had packed it away to keep it safe during her travels. It was not until some of the women tried to speak with her that the situation became dangerous. One of them encouraged her to repeat certain words in 'Moorish', which, thinking that they were merely pleasantries, she duly did. These words were '*La ilaha illa Allah wa-Muhammad rasul Allah*' – the Islamic affirmation that there is no god but God, and that Muhammad is His Prophet. On speaking them, the atmosphere in the room instantly changed: 'the palace was in the utmost confusion, and there was every sign of joy in all faces'.

After this – her apparent conversion – it was only with the utmost difficulty that she was able to explain away her mistake, and extricate herself from the palace. 'Having hurried, as far as possible to the gates, [I] found it no easy matter to pass a great crowd which had assembled there,' she wrote in her account of these adventures, *The Female Captive*. 'My worthy friend [James Crisp] was on the other side, with his hair all loose, and a distracted countenance, demanding me as his wife; but the inhuman guards beat him down for striving to get in, and the *black* women holding me down and hallooing out – No Christian, but a Moor – tore all the plaits out of my clothes, and my hair hung down about my ears. After a number of arguments, my friend prevailed; and, having forced me from the women, took me in his arms, and, with all possible expedition, got out of their sight.'[3]

It was this 'worthy friend' and pretended husband, James Crisp, who was to become Elizabeth Marsh's real-life husband. He was therefore the man whom nearly twenty years later she would leave behind in Dacca (Dhaka) while she went travelling through southern India with her lover, Captain George Smith.

Elizabeth Marsh's flight proved to be even more scandalous than Eliza Draper's had turned out. Having married James Crisp, an entrepreneurial salt and textile merchant and small-time East India Company official, she had followed him to the Mughal city of Dacca, in present-day Bangladesh, in the early 1770s. In 1775, leaving her husband and young son behind, she embarked on a journey round southern India, moving between different settlements in what is now Tamil Nadu and Andhra Pradesh, that would take her away from her home for over eighteen months. Her travelling companion was an unmarried military man. Although she refers to George Smith as her 'cousin', in the eighteenth century this was a loose term, and did not necessarily mean that they were related. Even if they had been, to have travelled so long and so far, and in such close proximity to a man who was not her husband – their palanquins were placed next to one another at night, and at one stage they openly shared a house together – would have been considered scandalously improper back in England.

But in India, in those days at least, apparently not so.

The first half of Elizabeth Marsh's travel journal consists largely of accounts of the vigorous social life she was able to enjoy; one that, as a woman of modest background (her father was a shipwright), was far grander than anything she could have been party to at home. The fact that she may also have been of mixed race only adds to Elizabeth's unusual story.

On board the *Goodwill*, on which the couple sailed from Dacca down the coast to Madras, she was paid visits of courtesy by many naval officers, one of whom was Sir John Clerke, Eliza Draper's protector. As another of her contemporaries, Eliza Fay, had done, Elizabeth Marsh always had her tea caddy and best china to hand, in order to entertain her frequent visitors on board. She dressed for dinner every evening; and the Commodore of the Royal Navy's East India squadron himself once sent her a polite note, and 'a number of refreshments', including, bizarrely, three dozen bottles of English spa water, 'warm and stale in its glass'.[4]

Elizabeth Marsh's society was not only tolerated but, if she herself is to be believed, eagerly courted by both men and women. Outside the three Presidencies, in the smattering of smaller settlements along the Coromandel Coast where the British had congregated, either for trading or administrative purposes, she would have come into contact with a closely knit group of Europeans comprising not only fellow Britons but also Portuguese, Danish, Dutch, Swiss and Germans. If anyone was scandalised by her behaviour in travelling with a man who was not her husband, she certainly did not record it.

In fact, rather the opposite seems to have been true. Of her time in Masulipatam, Elizabeth records with intense satisfaction how 'My company was daily solicited ... my tea table was the resort of all the sensible and polite, and crowded every evening.' In Ichapur, she dined 'with a very large company all cheerful and well-bred'. In other settlements there was also music, when she was often prevailed upon to sing, and dancing. In Ganjam, not one but two dances were given 'in compliment' to her, which she opened on both occasions with a minuet: 'all the company ready for me to open the Ball, which I did'.[5]

Although much of the early part of Elizabeth Marsh's Indian Journal is spent cataloguing the various Anglo-Indian entertainments to which she was invited along the way, the longer she spent away from home in Dacca, the greater her interest in India itself – in its people, customs and religions – became; the more vigorous, too, the style and tone of her writing.

In the spring of 1776, when she had already been away for over a year, instead of travelling back to Dacca by sea, she took the highly unusual decision of returning overland, a route that would eventually take her beyond the confines of the EIC territories, and one which, as she proudly notes, 'no European lady had ever undertaken before'.

En route to Aska, where George Smith had military business, they stopped off in Srikakulam where she climbed the tower of what she called 'a famous mosque' (it is more likely to have been a Hindu temple): 'I ventured (where no woman ever had) to the top,' she wrote proudly. They also stopped off in Puri, a famous site of Hindu pilgrimage with its towering twelfth-century temple to Vishnu in his avatar Jagannath, the Lord of the World. Although they did not seem to realise that the great chariot festival of Ratha Yatra was shortly to be celebrated, and were not themselves allowed to see the deity, Elizabeth was amazed and moved by the sheer numbers of pilgrims, some of whom had walked a thousand miles or more to take part in the festival.

As Henrietta Clive was to do a generation later, Elizabeth Marsh responded with particular intensity to the beauty of the landscape she passed through. 'As we drew near to Aska, it was all enchantment,' she wrote, 'so delicious a country, stately trees, fine pasture, rising hills, fertile vales, winding rivers, that I never beheld any prospect so heavenly. To sleep was impossible, as the eye (through moonlight) was constantly engaged by a new object.'[6]

But it was not always and only enchantment. When travelling through Orissa, at that time still substantially under Maratha control, the travellers found themselves contending with open hostility. A famine was raging through the land, and it proved impossible to buy enough rice to feed their large retinue, most of whom they were obliged to send home. Even with a reduced party of just sixty people

(Elizabeth and George were the only Europeans among them) it was sometimes hard to find any food at all, and they spent many days on a diet of damp water biscuits. Later on she records an altercation with a group of Maratha horsemen, who refused them room at a local *choultry*. When George Smith and his remaining sepoys were forced to back down, their own coolies, following the example of the Marathas, became 'distressingly insolent', refusing to carry their baggage onwards unless their pay was doubled.

Towards the end of their journey, arriving in Cuttack, the principal city of Orissa, the simmering hostility they had encountered in the villages turned to open aggression. First they were refused entry to the city; later it proved equally hard to extract themselves. 'The palanquins could hardly be squeezed through the crowd of men and boys, each with a drawn scimitar or knife in his hand, loading us with every abuse.' Did she remember the moment when she was paraded with 'shouts and hallooings' through a hostile crowd in Marrakech all those years ago? Her experiences there must have stood her in good stead.

Her parting from her 'dear cousin' cast a shadow over the last weeks of their journey, and she struggled to reconcile herself 'to that common event in life, parting with those we esteem and admire'. The 'dreadful hour of separation' finally came on 13 June. 'I parted from my dear, dear cousin – he for Ganjam, and I for Calcutta,' Elizabeth Marsh wrote, and for 'some hours my whole soul was absorbed in grief'.

# CHAPTER 14

Just fifty years after Elizabeth Marsh's palanquin was jostled and jeered through the streets of Cuttack, there was little left of India that was not either directly or indirectly under the control of the East India Company.

After the Third Mysore War against Hyder Ali, which ended in 1792, portions of the Kingdom of Mysore had been annexed to the Madras Presidency; and in 1799, after the defeat of his son Tipu Sultan at Seringapatam (the Fourth Anglo-Mysore War), still more of his former territories in southern India were taken over by the Company.

The British congratulated themselves on restoring the rightful ruler – the little six-year-old Raja so admired by Henrietta Clive – to his ancient throne, but from now on this much-reduced kingdom, while notionally independent, was in fact firmly under the control of the British. The same applied to the vast province of Hyderabad, where a British Resident had been attached to the Nizam's court since 1798.

Elsewhere, in central and northern India, the British had fought three wars against the Hindu Marathas, a loose confederation of warrior tribes whose vast reach had come to extend over most of the former Mughal Empire, stretching from Delhi to Madras. Delhi was conquered in 1803, during the Second Anglo-Maratha War, while the Third Anglo-Maratha War, which ended in 1818, finally brought an end altogether to the once powerful empire, and the EIC was able to bring large swathes of northern and central India under its control.

The British were now unquestionably the paramount power in the subcontinent.

The further the tentacles of British influence extended into the subcontinent, the greater the numbers of women who found themselves not only travelling but also living 'up country', even if their numbers were still relatively tiny. According to one estimate, at the turn of the century there were only around two hundred and fifty European women in the entire subcontinent. In 1800, Henrietta Clive, her two daughters and their governess were four out of only seven women that one man they met on their travels, Major Macleod, had spoken to in twelve years. Even in the Presidencies they were still hugely outnumbered.

In the *mofussil*, European women were rarer still. Despite this, there were many women who found life in the countryside a welcome relief from the anglicised hothouses of the Presidencies. Not only did it often bring them great personal fulfilment – through collecting, learning Indian languages, music and mythology, sometimes teaching, and frequently writing about their experiences – but their travels also had the effect of opening their eyes to India in a way that rarely happened in the more firmly entrenched British enclaves.

When large groups of British people gathered together, it was inevitable that they would bring their own culture with them. This they managed with amazing rapidity. It was in this period, for example, that the first British hill stations were created, lampooned by many as perfect reconstructions of English middle-class suburbia. Other already existing towns, such as Bangalore in central India, with its delightfully cool climate, were about to suffer the same fate.

When Henrietta Clive stayed there in 1800, she described its pleasingly melancholy avenues of cypress trees and the forgotten rose gardens of Hyder Ali's ruined palace. By the time Julia Maitland, the wife of a Company judge, arrived there nearly forty years later, it was a fully-fledged watering hole with 'an English church ... botanical garden, public ball-rooms, Dissenting meeting-house, circulating library, English shops and Parsee merchants, all within sight of each other'.

The air was cool, clear and bright, and the early mornings especially were as pleasant as anything she could imagine, with all the sweetness and freshness of an English summer. Mrs Maitland was charmed by it. 'The air smells of hay and flower, instead of ditches, dust, fried oil, curry, and onions, which are the *best* of the Madras smells.' Everyone had fireplaces in their houses.

Instead of the tuberoses and pomegranates she had been used to seeing, Mrs Maitland found 'superb dahlias growing in the gardens and today I saw a real staring full-blown hollyhock, which was like meeting an old friend from England'. The fruit available included apples, pears and peaches, and 'the boys bring baskets of raspberries for sale, which are very like blackberries'. Most noticeable of all was how healthy the children looked, 'quite fat and rosy' – and, most remarkable of all, they wore shoes and stockings.

Not so much could be said for the adults. The women went about 'dressed to every pitch of distraction they can invent, with long curls which the heat would not allow for an hour elsewhere, and warm close bonnets with flowers hanging in and out of them like queens of the May'. She was amused, too, by the evening promenade, 'where people take a good brisk walk at an English pace, and chirp like English sparrows, while a band of blackies play "God Save the Queen"* and call it the "General Salute"'.

Hyder Ali's fort, known as the Pettah, was still there, although it is impossible to ascertain what had happened to the garden that Henrietta Clive had tried to restore. The fort, so the English ladies of Bangalore told Julia Maitland, was 'a horrid place – quite native!' and they advised her never to go into it; 'so I went the next day, of course,' was her instant response, 'and found it most curious'.

The fort was so crammed with people, bustling and humming 'like bees in a beehive', that at first her bearers could scarcely make their way through the crowds of men, women, children and monkeys that thronged the streets. She was fascinated, and recorded what she saw with delight:

*The eighteen-year-old Queen Victoria had inherited the throne the previous year.

The ground was covered with shops all spread out in the dirt; the monkeys were scrambling about in all directions, jumping, chattering, and climbing all over the roofs of the houses, and up and down the doorposts – hundreds of them; the children quarrelling, screaming, laughing, and rolling in the dust – hundreds of *them* too – in good imitation of the monkeys; the men smoking, quarrelling, chatting, and bargaining; the women covered with jewels, gossiping at their doors ... and one or two that were very industrious, painting their door-steps instead of sweeping them; and native music to crown the whole. Such confusion was never seen![1]

Life in the rural provinces suited some women very well. Julia Maitland had been delighted to hear of their appointment to Rajahmundry, in the Northern Circars, some four hundred miles from Madras, where her husband (she refers to him only as 'A') had been appointed District Judge. The place enjoyed at least two months of 'really cool weather' every year – she had heard that the thermometer sometimes dropped as low as 58°F! It was cheaper than Madras, and much closer to the 'real' India that she longed to discover. 'I continue to like "up country", as they call it, far better than the Presidency; it is much more amusing,' she wrote. 'Of course, everybody tried to make Madras as English as they could, though without much success, except doing away with everything curious; but this place is real India, and I am every day seeing something new and foreign.'

Julia Maitland had arrived in India in 1836, the last full year of the reign of William IV. Initially she had been delighted by Madras, with its glittering white buildings and healthy sea breezes, but she very quickly found its society every bit as oppressive as Henrietta Clive had done a generation earlier. The ordeal of the Setting Up Ceremony was now a thing of the past; instead, there were dinner parties, each one as 'grand, dull and silent' as the next. The company was made up of women who were 'young and wizen' and gentlemen who were 'old and wizen', and everyone generally tired out with the heat. 'They assemble at 7pm, when the houses are generally infested by musquitos which are in themselves enough to lower one's spirits and stop conversation . . . After dinner the company all sit round in the middle of the great gallery-like rooms, talk in whispers, and scratch their mosquito bites.'[2]

It was the 'real' Anglo-Indian women who came in for her particular scrutiny. If they so much as dropped a handkerchief, she remarked, they 'just lower their voices and say, "Boy!" in a very gentle tone, and then creeps in, perhaps, some old wizen skinny brownie, looking like a superannuated thread-paper, who twiddles after them for a little while, and then creeps out again as softly as a black cat, and sits down cross-legged in the veranda'.

Women's complete lack of engagement with anything outside the anglicised little world they had created for themselves was dismaying to her. 'It is wonderful how little interested most of the English ladies seem by all the strange habits and ways of the natives; and it is not merely that they have grown used to it all, but that, by their own accounts, they never cared more about what goes on around them than they do now. I can only suppose they have forgotten their first impressions.' Innocently, she asked one woman what she had seen of the country or the natives since she had been in India. '"Oh nothing!" said she. "Thank goodness, I know nothing at all about them, nor I don't wish to: really I think the less one sees and knows of them the better!"'

Mrs Maitland was made of different stuff: 'this only makes me wish to try and see everything that I can while the bloom of my Orientalism is fresh upon me', she wrote. Blessed with a practical nature and a wicked wit (her great-aunt, the novelist Fanny Burney, with whom she was a great favourite, remarked on her 'very good sense and truly blithe juvenile love of humour'), she loved Rajahmundry from the start, enjoying its fresh, sweet country air (unlike Madras, which she pronounced 'like England in a perspiration'), and its lack of 'troublesome company' (by which she meant her fellow English). The view from their windows was said to be one of the most beautiful in India. She set herself to create a garden, make her own butter, and, like Henrietta Clive, to catch and bottle as many insects as possible. Later, she and her husband would start a successful school and a lending library for Indian children, and vigorously championed the education of girls.

For all the time she was in India, Julia Maitland wrote about her Indian neighbours with gentle good humour. One day they had a visit from one of the local rajas, all of whom were 'very sociable and fond of paying us visits'. They thought it 'a great incivility' to come without a gift of some kind, which usually took the form of 'limes, oranges, yams, etc.' since according to the new Company regulations the Maitlands were not allowed to accept any gifts of value. On this particular occasion 'we heard a kind of twanging and piping, like a whistle and a Jew's-harp. This was the Raja's music, played before his palanquin: then came his guards – men with halberds; then his chief officer, carrying a silver mace; then his principal courtiers running by the side of his palanquin to keep him "pleasant company". When they all arrived, the halberdiers grounded their arms, and the whole cortege stopped at the military word of command, "*Halt! Present! Fire!*" but the *firing* consisted of the old gentleman's getting out of his palanquin and quietly shuffling into the house, between two rows of his own servants and ours, salaaming him at every step.'

There was only one other Englishwoman for company, Mrs Price, the wife of the commanding officer, who came to call on her soon after her arrival. Mrs Maitland had been sitting on the floor unpacking her books when the visitor arrived, fully kitted out in her best clothes, 'worked muslin and yellow gloves'. 'I thought the only way to prevent her being ashamed of me was to make her as dirty and dusty as myself,' she recalled; 'therefore, under pretence that it would be so nice for her to have some new books to read, I made her sit down by me and look them over too, and we got on very well. She is very young, pretty, and unaffected, and I like the thoughts of having her for a neighbour.'

Other visitors were not so welcome. Rajahmundry, while being a relatively small outpost, was positioned on the main north–south Madras road. As Eliza Draper had found in Tellicherry in the previous century, Julia Maitland was expected to entertain all British travellers who passed their way. 'I fancy the civilians all expect to come to us on their journey,' she wrote, 'and the militaries go to Captain Price: and whichever of us receives the visitor must make a dinner party.' As time went on, she became altogether blunter in her views. 'Our house is a complete hotel for people we do not care to see,' she complained, 'and I know of no greater bore than "Indian hospitality" as it is called by travellers.'

As English society in India expanded, it both solidified and fractured. At the beginning of the nineteenth century, in the days of Maria Nugent and Henrietta Clive, the most highly sought-after (and lucrative) postings had been gained through an old-fashioned system of patronage. Lady Nugent's husband, for example, had acquired his post through his family connection with Lord Greville; he in turn took two of his nephews to India with him as aides-de-camp. By mid-century, in addition to its own military and judicial systems, the EIC would create a much larger, more formal Civil Service to administer to the Company's vast territories, based on talent rather than connections.* But even before then, new hierarchies and rivalries had been quick to appear. The British in India did not only look down on the 'natives' but, whenever possible, on each other.

Julia Maitland was half amused, half appalled by what she found. After the visit of an entire regiment, when she had been obliged to dine all the officers and their wives, she noted:

I perceive the officers' ladies are curiously different from the civilians. The civil ladies are generally very quiet, rather languid, speaking in almost a whisper, simply dressed, almost always lady-like and *comme il faut*, not pretty, but pleasant and nice-looking, rather dull, and give one very hard work in pumping for conversations. They talk of 'the Governor', 'the Presidency', the 'Overland', and 'girls' schools at home', and have daughters of about thirteen

*The first exams were sat in 1855.

in England for education. The military ladies, on the contrary, are almost always quite young, pretty, noisy, affected, showily dressed, with a great many ornaments, and chatter incessantly from the moment they enter the house. When they are alone with me after dinner, they talk about suckling their babies, the disadvantages of scandal, 'the Officers', and 'the Regiment'; and when the gentlemen come into the drawing-room, they invariably flirt with them most furiously.

In her experience, the military and the civilians did not get on with each other at all.

There is a great deal of foolish envy and jealousy between them, and they are often downright ill-bred to each other, though in general the civilians are much the best of the two. One day an officer who was dining here said to me, 'Now I know very well, Mrs —, you despise us all from the bottom of your heart; you think no-one worth speaking to in reality but the Civil Service. Whatever people may really be, you just class them all as civil and military – civil and military; and you know no other distinction. Is it not so?' I could not resist saying, 'No; I sometimes class them as civil and uncivil.' He has made no more rude speeches to me since.

Although Julia Maitland was closer to Maria Nugent than to Henrietta Clive in her religious convictions – she was a staunch believer in missionary activity, for instance, and would always defend the decision to teach from the Bible in their school, despite protests that it was 'a dangerous interference with Native feelings' – her enthusiasm and curiosity for all things Indian leap from her every page. Even for the most open-minded, however, an enormous cultural gulf still yawned between the two nations.

On a domestic level, the Indians and the British remained remarkably ignorant about one another. It was a situation that cut both ways, as one especially poignant anecdote in Julia Maitland's *Letters* shows.

While they were still living in Madras, an 'extremely rich native' who was also a protégé of her husband's invited them and another couple, Mr and Mrs Staunton, to attend a feast in their home. 'I was extremely glad, for I was longing to get into one of the native houses,' Mrs Maitland wrote, while at the same time being somewhat surprised that the Stauntons, despite having lived in India a great deal longer than the Maitlands, had never experienced anything of the kind. It was, by her own admission, 'a most curious entertainment', including cooks, musicians, *nautch* girls and a conjuror, all borrowed from the local Nawab for the occasion.

One of the conjuror's most extraordinary tricks was to make a huge cobra and six or seven live scorpions – 'not little things like Italian scorpions, but formidable animals, almost as long as my hand' – appear and disappear. Since the man was naked from the waist up, and there seemed no possible place for him to have hidden them, Julia thought it 'quite beyond my comprehension'. Another of the highlights proved to be a man whose talent was to imitate the notes of various birds: 'this sounded promising, but unfortunately the Madras birds are screaming, and not singing, birds; and my ears were assailed by screech-owls, crows, parrots, peacocks etc, so well imitated that I was again obliged to beg relief from such torture'.

While some of the entertainments were clearly more successful than others, no one could possibly have found fault with the enormous thought that had gone into receiving foreigners among them, particularly the two women. After supper, their host made Julia a speech informing her 'that he was aware that Hindoos did not know how to treat ladies: that he had therefore been that morning to consult an English friend of his, Mr Tracey, concerning the proper mode of showing me the respect that was my due; and that Mr Tracey had informed him that English ladies were accustomed to exactly the same respect as if they were gentlemen, and that he had better behave to me accordingly. He begged I would consider that, if there had been any deficiency, it was owing to ignorance, and not to want of affection; for that he looked upon me as his mother! Then he perfumed us all with attar of roses, and we came away after thanking him very cordially for his hospitality and all the amusement he had given us.'

The picture presented here is of two worlds that even after well over two hundred years of co-habitation remained almost entirely sealed off from one another. It is striking that despite the unusual presence of two foreign ladies in their midst, the women of the host family were nowhere to be seen, nor were the English memsahibs invited to visit them in their quarters. Julia Maitland described how she 'peeped about' trying to see the ladies of the family, but in vain: 'and I did descry some black eyes and white dresses through one of the half-open doors, but I could not see them distinctly'.[3]

The ever-increasing numbers of women arriving in India in the nineteenth century have been universally blamed for the widening social gulf, and the increased racism, between the two peoples. The late eighteenth and very early nineteenth centuries – when there were even fewer women, and many more interracial liaisons between English men and Indian women – have been hailed as a time of far greater sexual, cultural and racial tolerance: 'an attractively multi-cultural world', in the words of the historian William Dalrymple, that would soon vanish altogether. The commonly held and extraordinarily persistent perception is that it was the arrival of so many Englishwomen that somehow brought this about. In fact there were a wide range of factors in play, and difficulties on both sides.

The rise of the Evangelical Christian movement, when 'natives' came to be seen no longer as inheritors of some of the most exquisitely sophisticated art and philosophy the world has ever seen but as idol-worshipping heathens, mired in ignorance and ripe for conversion, was one. The other was a marked escalation in imperial arrogance as British-controlled territories expanded, and Indians were increasingly seen as a conquered people. It was in this period, too, that ideas about racial purity and ethnic hierarchies first began to be developed. All of these would combine together in India in a single toxic brew. While it is true that this newly evolved mind-set coincided with an increased influx of Englishwomen, the moral turpitude that was so often displayed by the British towards Indians was every bit as true for men as it was for women, if not more so.

Women had no political power. Their snobbery and racism – and there was plenty of it – was generally confined to the domestic sphere. It was men who devised the laws that kept Indians, and those of mixed race, in a state of subjugation in their own country. As early as 1786, a series of laws were passed which excluded the offspring of British men who had Indian wives from Company employment. They also banned the Anglo-Indian children of British soldiers from travelling to England to be educated, and thus from qualifying for applying for jobs in the military. A further edict, in 1795, was still more specific: only those with European parents on both sides might serve in any capacity in the Company's armies except as the most lowly sepoys, 'pipers, drummers, bandsmen and farriers'.* Anglo-Indians – the term now came to mean those of mixed descent – were also prohibited from owning land. All of these short-sighted and unjust measures would turn out to have grave repercussions in the not-too-distant future.

For all their many prejudices, many women were nonetheless an ameliorating influence on their men, and were not afraid to speak their minds. 'These people must have been so very magnificent in what they did before we Europeans came here with our bad money-making ways,' wrote Fanny Eden, the sister of the Governor-General, Lord Auckland, in 1837. 'We have made it impossible for them to do more, and have let all they accomplished go to ruin. All our excuse is, that we do not oppress the natives so much as they oppress each other – a fact about which I have my suspicions.'[4] Her more conservative sister, Emily, was inclined to agree. In the hill station at Simla, where they would spend the summer months, 'where twenty years before no European had ever been, and all this in the face of those high hills,

---

*Lord Cornwallis, the instigator of these new laws, had arrived as Governor-General of India still smarting from his defeat by George Washington at Yorktown, and was 'determined to make sure that a settled colonial class never emerged in India to undermine British rule as it had done, to his own humiliation, in America'. See Dalrymple, *The Last Mughal*.

some of which have remained untrodden since the creation', she wondered about '105 Europeans, being surrounded by 3,000 mountaineers, who, wrapped up in hill blankets, looked on at what we call our polite amusements, and bowed to the ground if a European came near them. I sometimes wonder they do not cut all our heads off, and say nothing more about it.'[5]

Newcomers were especially struck by the way the old India hands treated their servants, whose behaviour towards their 'masters' appalled them. 'The servility of these people is beyond anything I ever saw,' Maria Nugent wrote in 1812, 'it is indeed quite melancholy to see human nature so degraded.' Julia Maitland agreed. 'The natives are a cringing set, and behave to us English as if they were dirt under our feet; and indeed we give them reason to suppose we consider them as such,' she observed during her early days in Madras; 'the rudeness and contempt with which the English treat them are quite painful to witness. Civility to servants sees a complete characteristic of *griffinage*.'

More painful still was to witness British treatment of the higher classes. 'The other day an old Brahmin of high caste called on us while the Prices were in the house,' Mrs Maitland wrote. 'Captain Price, hearing his voice, sauntered out of the next room with his hands in his waistcoat-pockets, and planted himself directly before the poor old creature, without taking any other notice of his salaams and compliments than, "Well, old fellow, where are you going?" in a loud rude voice. The Brahmin answered with the utmost apparent respect, but I saw *such* an angry scowl pass over his face. A little politeness pleases them very much, and they have a good right to it. The upper classes are exceedingly well bred, and many of them are descendants of native princes, and ought not to be treated like dirt.'[6]

At the time of this particular episode, the Maitlands were reading Shore's *Notes on Indian Affairs* in which the writer also criticised British 'incivility to natives'. Mr Maitland said that he thought the point was exaggerated; his wife vehemently disagreed. 'I quite agree with [Shore],' she wrote, 'it is a great shame.'

Sometimes women went so far as to publish their thoughts on the matter. In her 'Advice for Young Men', written in 1841, Eliza Clemons, the wife of a major in the Madras Army, spoke out forcefully against what she regarded as the shameful treatment of Indian soldiers by the British. 'There are many young men who, on their first entering the service, treat the native officers in an unbecoming and disrespectful manner, call them black fellows and many opprobrious names, and consider them unworthy of even common civility,' she wrote. 'Never be prejudiced against their colour; there are as brave hearts, as honourable feelings, and as high-spirited behaviour in these men, as in the heart, and feelings, and conduct of any European ... Never ask them to do what is unbecoming,' she cautioned, 'or which may interfere in any way with their religion. On this subject I cannot too much put you on your guard.

'We should naturally rebel against those by violence and opposition endeavoured to undermine our religious faith, and interrupt us in the discharge of our religious duties ... Your duty as a soldier of the EIC is to conciliate the native soldiery, pay attention to their prejudices and respect their forms of worship, at least as far as not ridiculing or making yourself obnoxious to them by interference. No good will you ever effect by so doing; on the contrary, the greatest harm.'[7]

British women may have had no political power, but they did have enormous influence in their own homes. They soon found that the social life they enjoyed was organised along completely different lines from its Indian counterpart. Whereas the latter, centred largely around weddings and religious festivals, was entirely segregated, the British, wherever possible, enjoyed eating, drinking and dancing in mixed company.

Even when British women wanted to mix with 'well bred' Indians they soon found that a multitude of customs and caste restrictions militated against it. Indian women rarely, if ever, left their *zenanas* except to visit other *zenanas*; their men were frequently prevented by their caste from accepting invitations. Food – what, where, by whom it was prepared, and in whose presence it was eaten – was subject to particularly strict rules, and so the dinners, luncheons, picnics and breakfasts so beloved by the British were, in most instances, insuperable obstacles when it came to entertaining Indian guests. Writing in the 1820s and 1830s, the traveller Fanny Parkes, who in her day spent more time than perhaps any other Englishwoman visiting her Indian women friends, observed that even though an English gentleman might marry a Muslim lady 'she will not permit him to be present during the time of meals'.[8]

Misunderstandings and perplexities occurred on both sides. Music in particular, whether singing or playing an instrument, considered such an accomplishment in British women, was held in very different regard by Indians. Mrs Parkes reflected frequently on these cultural differences. 'Music is considered disgraceful for a lady of rank, dancing the same – such things are left to *nautch* women,' she observed on visiting Mulka Begum, one of the nieces of the Mughal Emperor, Akbar Shah. On one occasion the princess had made enquiries concerning the education of young ladies in England, 'and on hearing how many hours were devoted to the piano, singing, and dancing, she expressed her surprise, considering such *nautch*-like accomplishments degrading'.[9]

Given this fact, even when Indian men did attend British entertainments in mixed company, it could make for some uncomfortable moments. In 1827, when the King of Oudh visited the British Resident at Lucknow, the Englishwomen present were not allowed to dance while His Majesty was present, 'as on one occasion [the King] said, "that will do, let them leave off": thinking the ladies were quadrilling for his amusement, like *nautch* women'.[10] The view that 'ladies are not treated by natives with the reverence they receive at home' was echoed by many, and was thought to expose Englishwomen to 'inappropriate behaviour', such as the occasion, at a charity bazaar in Cawnpore in the 1830s, when the Nawab and his friends simply threw their money down on the counters, causing great indignation among the respectable ladies serving behind them.

Even those who were less ready to take offence could see the difficulties. In 1837, Emily Eden described a ball given by her brother, the Governor-General Lord Auckland, at which there were a number of rajas present, in splendid dresses and jewels; 'some of them had never seen an English ball before. They think the ladies who dance are utterly good for nothing, but seemed rather pleased to see so much vice.'[11]

English women, well aware of this disagreeable fact, increasingly took matters into their own hands. During the Edens' sojourn in Simla, Miss R— reported to Fanny Eden that all the ladies at the hill station had settled among themselves that they would not dance at a ball at which some Sikh envoys were expected to attend, 'and they had no idea of dancing before natives'. Fanny Eden was scathing: 'Considering that we ask forty natives to every dance we give in Calcutta, and that no-body ever cares, it was too late to make any objection.' Her acquaintance, Miss R—, agreed, and announced that, despite being in deep mourning, she would dance every quadrille 'just to show what she thought of their nonsense'.

In the end, only three ladies did not attend on the evening, so there were plenty of partners for everyone. Even so, when some of the dancers asked for a waltz, a new and extremely risqué dance* 'which is seldom accomplished even in Calcutta', even Miss Eden's tolerance was stretched. 'I was afraid the Sikhs might have been just a little astonished,' she wrote; 'and I think Govind Jus gave Glolaub Singh a slight nudge as General K— whisked past with his daughter; but I dare say they thought it very pretty.'[12]

---

*The waltz caused a sensation when it was first introduced into London society in 1813. Unlike other dances which were popular in India, such as the quadrille, which were danced in a group, the waltz was the first in which partners danced together, the man's arm clasped around his partner's waist. It was considered greatly daring by everyone, 'riotous and indecent' by many.

# CHAPTER 15

Life in the Presidencies had changed a good deal since the days of Eliza Fay and Charlotte Hickey.

Calcutta, for instance, had grown hugely in size. There was very little in the way of European commodities that could not be acquired to make life both comfortable and familiar. Whereas in the past most imported goods were brought in by enterprising individuals, to be sold off in job lots at auction, by now there was a wide variety of 'Europe shops' from which virtually anything could be bought – for a price. 'The most beautiful French furniture was to be bought in Calcutta of M. de Bast, at whose shop marble tables, fine mirrors, and luxurious couches were in abundance.' For those who could not afford the originals, 'very excellent furniture' was also to be had, 'expertly copied by native workmen under the superintendence of European cabinet and furniture makers'.[1]

A much greater variety of English foodstuffs was available now, too, some of them better than others. English vegetables, for example, such as 'peas, asparagus, turnips etc' could all be bought at market but were likely to be completely tasteless. 'Pines [pineapples] were stringy, oranges tough and dry, and mangoes tasted like turpentine.'[2] On the other hand 'all kinds of preserves, jams and dried fruits' could be sourced, tins of smoked salmon and sardines, as well as 'sauces, potted meat and fish, cheese and biscuits. Soda water – called Balatee Panee, or "English water" – was also to be had.' Ice, that luxury of luxuries in a hot climate, was now readily available, for a price, since it was sometimes imported from as far away as America.

In the *mofussil*, of course, English supplies were more difficult to come by – but by no means impossible. In the 1820s and 1830s an enterprising travelling salesman called Myers used to import English goods, and then bring them by boat as far as the rivers were navigable, stopping at every station along the way. 'Everybody, on hearing of Myers's arrival, used to go as quickly as possible to him to get the first choice of these antiquated articles, but which were of course quite modern to us.'[3]

On one memorable occasion, Myers brought his boat as far as Agra. One woman remembered her delirious joy – 'so great that it knew no bounds' – at being bought a real English doll, 'a beauty, so I thought, all dressed in the fashion of the day'. Until now her only doll had been a plank of wood with a bit of cloth tied round it for an apron (her father, apparently, did not approve of shop-bought toys, Myers's doll being an improbable exception). On the whole, though, the general opinion was that India was at least fifty years behind England in most fashions.

It was unheard of for women to do their own shopping, and those who tried to go against this custom and do it for themselves invariably regretted it. The picture which Maria Nugent presents of herself with her *sircars* (stewards), sitting on a chair in 'a loosed dressing-gown, distributing rupees to them squatting on the floor', is one that can be seen in many paintings and sketches of Anglo-Indian women of the time. Fanny Parkes, too, had a *sircar* who attended her house each morning to receive her orders: 'he then proceeds to the bazaars, or to the Europe shops, and brings back for inspection and approval, furniture, books, dresses, or whatever may have been ordered: his profit is a heavy percentage on all he purchases for the family'.

Despite the necessity of shopping in local bazaars, many Indian products, customs, food and clothing, so much of which had been happily adopted by the British in the eighteenth century, were increasingly looked down on. Curries were no longer regarded as suitable food for public occasions, giving way to enormous, unsuitable, cuts of meat. 'I never before saw so many large joints of so many large beasts upon one table,' wrote Fanny Eden after attending one of her Governor-General brother's 'great dinners'. 'I am certain they served up a baked shoulder of elephant and called it a shoulder of mutton.'[4]

The fashion for smoking hookahs, an almost universal custom during the eighteenth and early nineteenth centuries, would soon go the same way. Maria Nugent found the custom abhorrent. After one of her dinner parties she wrote: 'a great many hookhas today; and, for the first time, a lady brought hers, a Mrs Palmer ... Her hookah was a particularly gay one, with a gold mouth-piece, and her hookah-bedar (the person who has the particular charge of her hookah), had a most picturesque dress. I tried to smoke it, as she assured me it was only a composition of spices, but I did it awkwardly, swallowing the smoke, and the consequence was I coughed all night.'[5] Although Lady Nugent held no sway over the old India hands who, even in 1812, were accustomed to taking theirs with them wherever they went, even to grand dinners at Government House, she lost no time in forbidding her husband's young aides-de-camp from taking it up.

Clothing, too, was a sticking point. Loose, comfortable Indian clothes, perfectly suited to the hot climate, had long been popular with European men. These included 'long drawers, a banian coat, and slippers', which they wore not only at home but in public too, even at the racecourse and in church.

Women had always been more conservative when it came to adopting Indian attire. A survey of Madras will-books in the second half of the eighteenth century has shown that the inventories of men's possessions frequently included items of Indian clothing. The few inventories that were found detailing the contents of women's wardrobes contain no reference to them,* although exquisitely embroidered

---

*Mrs Cope, for example, left 'a silk brocade gown and petticoat, a white satin sack half trimmed with gold, a checked lute-string nightgown, a pink satin quilted petticoat, 4 gowns of white morees, 20 coarse dimity petticoats, 14 ditto bedgowns, and 24 shifts'. Mrs Bromley left, among numerous shifts and petticoats, '2 chip hats, a gauze dress hat, and 3 muslin silver-flowered dresses'. See Dodwell, *The Nabobs of Madras*.

cashmere shawls were always eagerly sought-after. On her journey through Orissa, Elizabeth Marsh had experimented during the monsoon season by wrapping some long rolls of muslin around her in what seems to have been a rudimentary sari, but, like so much else about her, this was highly unusual. At the same period there seems to have been a growing fashion for turbans among the women in Madras – 'caps, Hats, etc etc, all are now given away for this more convenient Asiatic head dress'[6] – but this may have had something to do with the great difficulty and expense of acquiring fashionable English millinery.

The blazingly vivid colours and textures worn the previous century – think of William Hickey's scarlet and gold spangled coats, or Margaret Fowke's lilac, blue and bright pink ostrich feathers – gradually gave way to an altogether more muted world. In 1830, the EIC passed an edict forbidding its employees from wearing Indian clothes in public, but the desire to do so was fading anyway. *Pajamas* and *banian* coats became items to be worn in private, or in the bedchamber, only.

For women, it was not only the clothes they wore but even the fabrics they used that were indicative of the new mind-set. Exquisite Indian muslins, all the rage in England at this time, were never worn in India itself, where it was considered 'the extremity of bad taste' to appear in anything of Indian manufacture, although Fanny and Emily Eden would make a point of wearing both Indian and Chinese fabrics.

For the most part British women clung to their familiar modes of dressing in a way that sometimes seems perverse given the climate. To go without stays, for example, was considered almost indecent, and is perhaps one reason why to dress in Indian women's apparel (other than as a fancy-dress) was never really an option.* There was also the perennial fear that they would end up looking like *nautch* girls. To be dressed correctly became not just an issue of comfort and practicality, but an indicator of superior moral standing.

*In England, even the most destitute of women, including those who ended up in the poorhouse, were provided with a set of stays.

Augusta Becher, a soldier's wife who lived in India in the mid-century, was shocked and disgusted to find the wife of Colonel N— 'without corsets, in loose white garments of old fashion; often no shoes; children barefoot, with only one garment ... No doubt the natives preferred and understood these households better than the more civilized style of ours now coming into vogue.' As if to prove her point, she observed dryly that Colonel N— had taken to drink, and as for the corset-less Mrs N—, 'I daresay [she] did as well as she could, but her soul did not soar above her surroundings.'[7]

While Fanny Parkes noted that at an Indian wedding she attended in 1835, the party of English gentlemen who were also present 'were all attired in native dress', she makes no comment about her own, or that of another British woman, Mrs B—, who also attended, which she surely would have if they had been similarly dressed.

Instead, Mrs Parkes describes the attire of her Indian women friends in loving detail, considering it 'the most becoming attire imaginable'. Her friend, the great Indian beauty Mulka Begum, came in for her special appreciation. First came the *angiya*, or bodice, made of silk gauze and profusely ornamented; second the *kurti*, a loose sleeveless body falling to the hips, made of net, crepe or gauze, and also highly ornamented; thirdly the *pajamas*, voluminous trousers made from gold or crimson brocade. And fourthly, the *dupatta*, 'which is the most graceful and purely feminine attire in the world; it is of white transparent gauze, embroidered with gold and trimmed with gold at the ends, which also have a deep fringe of gold and silver'.

'This *dupatta* is so transparent it hides not; it merely veils the form, adding beauty to the beautiful by its soft and cloudlike folds,' Fanny Parkes enthused. 'The jewellery sparkles beneath it; and the outline of its drapery is continually changing according to the movements or coquetry of the wearer.

'Mulka walks very gracefully,' she continued, 'and is as straight as an arrow. In Europe how rarely does a woman walk gracefully! Bound up in stays, the body is as stiff as a lobster in its shell; that snake-like undulating movement – the poetry of motion – is lost, destroyed by the stiffness of the waist and hip, which impedes the free movement of the limbs. A lady in European attire gives me the idea of a German manikin; an Asiatic, in her flowing drapery, recalls the statues of antiquity.'

Reading these descriptions it is perhaps a little easier to understand why an early Victorian memsahib might have had doubts as to her ability to pull off such a costume, let alone walk about in it in public – and if she *had* managed it, why it would have proved 'highly detrimental to her reputation'.[8]

Fanny Parkes had been fortunate enough to be allowed to meet Mulka Begum, a niece of the Mughal Emperor, because she was the daughter-in-law of her great friend Colonel Gardner. William Linnaeus Gardner (he was a godson of the famous botanist Carl Linnaeus) was an English mercenary, and one of a group of thoroughly Indianised Englishmen whose hybrid lifestyle was coming to look increasingly old-fashioned. His story was so romantic that even within his own lifetime he was considered something of a national treasure. In addition to numerous episodes of soldierly derring-do, as a young man he had caught a fleeting glimpse of a young Indian princess through a purdah screen, and successfully demanded her hand in marriage.

Fanny Parkes gives an affectionate portrait of him in his later years, when she went to visit him at his remote country residence at Khasganj, sixty miles from Agra. 'On our arrival, we found our dear friend seated on the steps in front of his house with many gentlemen, both English and native, around him. I thought I had never seen so dignified and graceful a person; he was dressed in a red-figured *lubada*, or Indian shawl, the rest of his dress was English, but the style of the *lubada* was particularly good and suited to an old man.'

In the eighteenth century no one had given a second thought to the fact that many men took Indian wives and mistresses; but by the time Fanny Parkes was writing, the custom was already outmoded.*

---

*Between 1780 and 1785 bequests to *bibis* appear in one in three wills; between 1805 and 1810 they appear in one in four; by 1830 it is only one in six; and by mid-century such bequests had all but died out. See Dalrymple, *White Mughals*.

White Mughals such as James Achilles Kirkpatrick and Sir David Ochterlony, the British Residents at Hyderabad and Delhi respectively, with their 'Asiatic' clothes and their tremendous whiskery beards, their Mughal titles, their many consorts (Ochterlony was reputed to have thirteen, all of whom rode behind him on elephants to take the air each evening) and their well-stocked and closely guarded purdah-quarters, had by now become part of Anglo-Indian mythology: not so much shocking as interesting relics of a bygone era.

Colonel Gardner had fallen in love with his wife when she was just thirteen. As a young man, he had been sent on a mission to negotiate an important treaty with one of the native princes of Cambay, but was distracted one day during an endless durbar when he noticed one of the purdah curtains being gently moved aside. 'And I saw, as I thought, the most beautiful black eyes in the world,' he told Mrs Parkes. 'It was impossible to think of the treaty; those bright and piercing glances, those piercing dark eyes, completely bewildered me.

'I felt flattered that a creature so lovely as she of those deep black, loving eyes must be, should venture to gaze upon me; to what danger might not her veiled beauty be exposed, should the movement of the *parda* be seen by any of those at the durbar. On quitting the assembly I discovered that the bright-eyed beauty was the daughter of the Prince. At the next durbar, my agitation and anxiety was extreme again to behold the bright eyes that had haunted my dreams by night, and my thoughts by day! The *parda* again was gently moved, and my fate was decided.'

When he demanded the princess's hand in marriage, he was at first indignantly refused by her relatives; but he would not be put off. Her family deliberated again, and on mature reflection found that 'the ambassador was considered too influential a person to have a request denied and the hand of the young princess was promised'.

Preparations for the wedding went ahead. '"Remember," said I, "it will be useless to attempt to deceive me; I shall know those eyes again, nor will I marry any other."

'On the day of the marriage I raised the veil from the countenance of the bride, and in the mirror that was placed between us beheld the bright eyes that had bewildered me; I smiled – the young Begum smiled also.'[9]

A handful of Englishmen made famously happy marriages to their Indian wives. For the most part these were the so-called 'White Mughals', high-ranking administrators or soldiers who tended to live far away from the main British centres, and had become thoroughly 'Indianised' in every aspect of their lives. Colonel Gardner was one such. He once confided to Fanny Parkes his fear that after he was gone his wife – her full title was Nawab Matmunzilool Nissa Begum – would not long outlive him, and so it proved. When he died, aged just sixty-five, his Begum pined away and died just over a month later.

Colonel Gardner's circumstances were exceptional. Not only had he married an Indian princess, he had also allowed his daughters to be brought up as Muslims, 'and in the strict observance of all the restrictions prescribed to Asiatic females of rank ... and in the same profound seclusion – points seldom conceded by a European father'. Under the terms of his marriage contract, his sons were brought up Christians. As a result, his children and grandchildren were eligible to be married into the Indian elite – and many of them did.

His son, James Gardner, had married Fanny Parkes's friend Mulka Begum, the niece of the Mughal Emperor, and it had been his granddaughter Susan's* marriage to Mulka's half-brother, the Emperor's nephew, that Mrs Parkes had been invited to attend in 1835. (She was, incidentally, inordinately proud of having been distinguished in this way: 'I know of no European lady but myself, with the exception of one, who has ever had an opportunity of becoming intimate with native ladies of rank,' she wrote. Her invitation to the wedding was equally rare.)

Few liaisons between English men and Indian women ran their

---

*In the *zenana*, Susan was known as Shubbeah Begum. At the request of Colonel Gardner's wife, his granddaughters had all been brought up as Christians.

course quite so harmoniously. For a start there was always speculation, on the part of the British, as to the legitimacy of such 'marriages'. Aristocratic or wealthy Indian women had families who arranged proper marriage contracts for them, but not many women enjoyed these protections. This was particularly true for those at the lower end of the social scale. Too often these women were duped into believing that they were legally married, only to be callously abandoned, together with their children, when the man either moved or went home.

Soldiers were particularly resourceful when it came to providing their women with fake marriage 'certificates' – a practice that would continue until well into the twentieth century. Just before the First World War, one army officer described the scene of chaos when he asked to be shown the women's documents before organising their passage home with the rest of the regiment. 'The storm that burst around me was such as I never want to experience again,' he wrote. 'The most extraordinary pieces of paper were put before me, which quickly showed up the whole tragic affair. For every legal document there were a dozen which were just scraps of paper of no value whatsoever ... on coloured or printed paper such as beer-bottle labels or labels from tinned food.'[10]

It was what to do with the offspring of such unions that would become the really intractable problem. The British may have thoroughly enjoyed looking down on one another, but when it came to those of mixed race, they brought their prejudice to new heights. These people were despised by everyone.

At the turn of the century, Maria Nugent had been gently surprised by the number of 'half-caste' women who appeared on social occasions in Calcutta, many of whom still had the *entrée* to her own and other grand British establishments. By mid-century they had been banned altogether from attending at Government House, and according to Emily Eden, were not even allowed to sit down in the presence of Europeans. It was a development that thoroughly disgusted her. 'The "uncovenanted service" [junior members of the

Indian Civil Service] is just one of our choicest Indianisms, accompanied by our very worst Indian feelings,' Emily Eden wrote in a letter home. 'We say the words just as you talk of "poor chimney-sweepers", or "those wretched scavengers" – the uncovenanted being, in fact, clerks in public offices. Very well-educated, quiet men, and many of them very highly paid; but as many of them are half-castes, we, with our pure Norman, or Saxon blood, cannot really think contemptuously enough of them.' Others would make the same observation, with the caveat that the prejudice worked both ways. 'The half-caste population ... are coming into more notice ... They are held in the greatest contempt by the natives, except as they may possess money or influence, and the European prejudice is very strong against them, so they are much to be pitied.'[11]

At a fancy sale that Emily Eden organised during her stay in Simla, she made the suggestion that the wives of these uncovenanted clerks should be allowed to send in contributions. 'This was rather a shock to the aristocracy of Simla, and they did suggest that some of the wives were very black. That I met by the argument that the black would not come off on their works.'

However humble and unsuited to their talents, employment was usually available for the young men; young women of mixed-race parentage had far fewer options. Even in the generally more tolerant eighteenth century, men with a brood of natural children had no illusions about their status. Eliza Draper's uncle, Mr Whitehall, declared to her 'that he never would give them more than five thousand rupees each, because he never would tempt any Gentleman to Marry them for the sake of Money, and had rather dispose of them to [husbands] of their own Colour – than to Europeans'.[12]

From the late eighteenth century onwards, a number of orphanages had been set up to cater for these children – 'orphan' being a well-understood euphemism for 'illegitimate'. The Kidderpore Orphanage in Calcutta, which catered exclusively for the daughters of officers, held monthly balls at which it was hoped that some of their inmates, who were 'renowned for their gaiety', would find husbands. At the

Byculla School in Bombay they preferred to entertain prospective suitors over cups of tea. 'A suitable candidate having been chosen beforehand, the proposal was expected the day after the tea-party, and the orphan, unless she was very strong-minded, did not refuse.'[13]

A story told by Fanny Eden gives an insight into how the system worked. 'My new ayah, Mary O'Neil, is a very attractive person, a half-caste; she was brought up at the Military Orphan school – was married at twelve years old to a man forty years older than herself who came and *chose* her from the school as was then the custom – she is little more than twenty now. He went home to England leaving her here. She had six sisters who all married in the same way, most of them happily. She is very highly spoken of herself and takes my fancy.'[14]

Tea parties and dances later gave way to more formal interviews, but either way it was a peculiarly bloodless system. Maria Nugent was horrified by it. Very soon after her arrival in India, she discovered that by virtue of her rank as the second most senior lady of Calcutta she was automatically the patroness of the Orphan School. When she attended one of their balls she was shocked to see 'so many young officers dancing and flirting with these dark complexioned young ladies. It is really laying a snare for them, and cruel to their families, to arrange such meetings.'

Lady Nugent decided, early on in her Indian career, to give assemblies rather than the dinners that until now had been customary, and was soon sending out her cards accordingly. The reason for this was, as her husband put it, 'to give the young Ladies a Chance of Husbands', but the thinking behind it was more subtle. By doing so, she was able to keep careful control over who was invited, and who was not.

Her husband, Sir George, thoroughly agreed with her decision. 'The Subaltern part of the Army are I am sorry to say marrying fast, those of the half caste Race, commonly called Mulattoes in the West Indies. When this happens to anyone with good Connections at Home, it is pitiable, as neither their Wives nor Brats can be *presentable* to Society in England.'[15]

The reason for this had as much to do with class as with race, and everything to do with the legality of their parents' marriages. Colonel Gardner's offspring may have gone on to make glittering alliances, but by his own account this was as much to do with his wife's ties to the Mughal Emperor as with anything else. As his haste to refute even the smallest hint that he was not properly married to his Begum suggests, in the majority of cases these interracial 'marriages' were not legitimate at all, and therefore neither were their offspring. Even without the question of race, this fact alone put them well outside the pale. Gone were the days when adventuresses and courtesans could pass themselves off as 'respectable'. By the nineteenth century, a mistress of any shape or hue, with or without children, was completely inadmissible in mixed society.

As the century progressed, it was as much the saving of the souls of these 'orphans' as their marriage prospects which were uppermost in people's minds. The first duty of the orphanage establishments was to make good little Christians out of them. Mrs Wilson's Orphan Refuge, eight miles from Calcutta on the Hooghly River, was renowned for doing exactly this. The girls, aged between three and twelve, were arranged in rows 'all dressed exactly alike and exquisitely clean, and not being disfigured with earrings and nose-rings, looked simple and child-like' in their matching white saris, one visitor noted approvingly. When questioned on the Gospel, the girls answered 'readily and intelligently', and later sung her a hymn in Bengalee, it being 'very sweet to hear a hundred young voices join in its simple music, especially when one thought from what they had been rescued.'[16]

By mid-century, God was indeed an Englishman.

Tolerant and open-minded voices, such as those of Julia Maitland, Emily Eden and Fanny Parkes, were becoming increasingly rare. Mrs Parkes, in particular, took a deeply cynical view of the increasingly vigorous presence of missionaries in her adopted country. 'People think of nothing but converting the Hindus; and religion is often used as a cloak by the greatest schemers after good appointments.

Religious meetings are held continually in Calcutta, frequented by people to pray themselves into high salaries, who never thought of praying before.'

Fanny Parkes had no time for this sort of thing. Arriving in India in 1822, just two years into the reign of George IV, she was married to a junior official in charge of ice making, based for the most part in Allahabad. In much the same way as Elizabeth Marsh had used her illness as an excuse to set off on her travels, so Mrs Parkes used her husband's (he suffered from some kind of mental instability) as hers. Although it took her a few years to transform herself from *griffin* memsahib into the 'Independent Woman' she would later claim to be, from the beginning of her time in India she was entranced by it. 'I thought India a most delightful country, and could I have gathered around me the dear ones I had left in England, my happiness would have been complete,' she wrote shortly after her arrival in Calcutta.

She did not so much resist the prejudices and foibles of her countrymen as ignore them, serenely devoting her time instead to travelling and visiting her Indian friends. 'With the Neapolitan saying "Vedi Napoli, e poi mori" ['see Naples, and die'], I beg leave to differ entirely, and would rather offer *this* advice – "See the Taj Mahal, and then – see the Ruins of Delhi",' she wrote. 'How much there is to delight the eye in this bright and beautiful world! Roaming about with a good tent and a good Arab, one might be happy for ever . . . Oh, the pleasure of vagabondizing through India.'

On 19 January 1835, Mrs Parkes came to a city she calls Betaizor. She wrote in her journal: 'The Raja Buddun Sing built his *ghat* here and very beautiful it is; a perfect crowd of beautiful Hindu temples clustered together, each a picture in itself, the whole reflected in the bright blue waters of the Jumna. I stopped there for an hour to sketch the *ghat*, and walked on the sands opposite, charmed with the scene – the high cliffs, the trees; no Europeans are there – a place is spoiled by European residence.'

When she did come across her fellow Britons, she was frequently disgusted by their philistine ways. When visiting the Taj Mahal at Agra – a sacred place, in her view, and one that instilled in her only the deepest feeling of devotion – she was shocked by the behaviour of a party that had come there before her. 'Can you imagine anything so detestable?' she wrote furiously. 'European ladies and gentlemen have the band to play on the marble terrace, and dance quadrilles in front of the tomb! ... I could no more jest or indulge in levity beneath the dome of the Taj than I could in my prayers.'

The general impression on reading Mrs Parkes's journals is that (although she was not without her criticisms), she was in love with all things Indian, and refreshingly quick to see life from an Indian point of view. She learned Indian languages, took to eating opium, and as the years went by began to enjoy Indian food (which she learned to eat with her fingers) far more than European fare, and was delighted when her friend Colonel Gardner banned the latter from his table.

It is hard to imagine any other Englishwoman of the period submitting herself so cheerfully to the care of Colonel Gardner's *zenana* when she fell ill. His women put her immediately into a steam bath, where they 'shampooed, mulled and half-boiled' her; 'cracked every joint after the most approved fashion, took me out, laid me on a golden-footed bed, gave me sherbet to drink, shampooed me to sleep and, by the time the shooting party had returned from the Ganges, I had perfectly recovered'.

She even learned to play the sitar, to the mingled amusement and, one suspects, horror of her English friends. When she left Khasganj, Colonel Gardner's residence sixty miles from Agra, armed with her new talent, she rashly favoured some of them with a few Hindustani airs on the sitar, 'which I could not persuade them to admire'. A harp was hastily found for her to play on instead, and the sitar quietly removed.

Perhaps most crucial to her development, however, was her bravery in daring to travel frequently, and alone, with only her servants to accompany her. No wonder her contemporaries thought her eccentric.

'An acquaintance, the Hon. Mrs R——, has just arrived in Allahabad from England,' she wrote on 17 January 1835; 'nothing could exceed her astonishment when she heard I had gone up the Jumna alone, on a pilgrimage of perhaps two months or more to see the Taj, not forced to make the voyage from necessity. I have books and employments of various sorts to beguile the loneliness; and the adventures I meet with give variety and interest to the monotony of life on the river.'[17]

Mrs Parkes was perhaps at her happiest when visiting her Indian friends, and was stung to learn that she had been criticised for visiting one of the royal princesses, Hyat-ool-Nissa Begum, an aunt of the Emperor's, in Delhi in 1838, 'it being supposed that I went for the sake of presents'. With her genuine love for Indians, and her long, painstaking study of their customs and culture, she knew that it was a result of their lack of knowledge. Nonetheless, 'I felt it hard to be judged by people who were ignorant of my being a friend of the relatives* of those whom I visited in the *zenana*,' she wrote. 'People who themselves had, perhaps, no curiosity respecting native life and manners and who, even if they had the curiosity, might have been utterly unable to gratify it unless by an introduction which they were probably unable to obtain.'

After she had greeted the princess and conversed with her a while (a difficult undertaking due to the Begum's having no teeth), Mrs Parkes was shown around the *zenana* quarters, a strangely depleted, melancholy place, rather dirty and wet in places, where a few old women sat around on *charpoys* (bedsteads) and stagnant black drain water collected on the marble floors and in the once glistening marble fountains. She was shown the bastion where the Emperor slept, but soon crept away lest the laughing of the children who accompanied her should wake him.

When Mrs Parkes finally came to take her leave from the princess, she was presented with a garland of freshly gathered white jasmine. 'In former times strings of pearls and valuable jewels were placed on the necks of parting visitors,' she observed, but their present poverty had

*James Gardner, the son of Colonel Gardner, was the princess's adopted son.

long ago put an end to such munificence. Nonetheless, Mrs Parkes bent her head to receive the necklace of flowers 'with as much respect as if [the princess] had been queen of the universe. Others may look upon these people with contempt, I cannot,' she added: 'look at what they are, at what they have been!'

Fanny Parkes remains perhaps the closest Britain ever came to producing a female White Mughal. To her dying day she would wear the names of three hundred Hindu gods interwoven in silk and gold on a cord around her neck. Whatever her contemporaries may have thought about her, she was not someone they ever forgot.

# CHAPTER 16

'We are rather oppressed just now by a lady, Mrs Parkes, who insists on belonging to our camp,' wrote another Fanny, Fanny Eden, when the two women first encountered one another in the Upper Provinces in January 1838. 'She has a husband who always goes mad in the cold season, so she says it is her duty to herself to leave him and travel about. She has been a beauty and has remains of it, and is abundantly fat and lively. At Benares, where we fell in with her she informed us she was an Independent Woman and was going to travel to Simla by herself – which sounded very independent indeed.'[1]

The Honourable Frances Eden was a traveller of a very different kind from the eccentric and indefatigable Fanny Parkes. She and her sister Emily had accompanied their brother, the unmarried Lord Auckland, when he was appointed Governor-General in 1835. Emily Eden, the elder of the two, was an admired and energetic society hostess in intellectual Whig circles back in England. Although she regarded her time in India as one of exile, counting the days until she could return home, her waspish but acutely observed account of her time in India, published as *Up the Country* in 1866, became an instant best-seller, and has rarely been out of print.

It is her less well-known sister, however, who emerges as the more imaginative and adventurous traveller. Together, their experiences are an extraordinary and intimate account of what it was like to travel at the height of British imperialism before the Uprisings of 1857. As

Emily Eden herself wrote many years later to her nephew, William Osborne, who had accompanied them on their travels and to whom she gifted her letters, 'Now that India has fallen under the curse of railways ... the splendour of a Governor-General's progress is at an end ... The Kootub [the Qutub Minar in Delhi] will probably become a railway station; the Taj, of course, under the sway of an Agra Company (limited, except for destruction), be bought up for a monster hotel; and the Governor-General will dwindle down into a first-class passenger with a carpet-bag.'[2] In the meantime, theirs was travel on a scale of such magnificence that its like would never be seen again.

Unlike Mrs Parkes, who prided herself on the simplicity of her arrangements, the Edens were travelling, as befitted their exalted status as India's First Ladies, in an entourage a good deal bigger than most of the villages they passed through. Their immense juggernaut of a caravan was made up of twelve thousand camp followers, which stretched over twenty miles at its fullest extent. Their tour of northern India, which took them in state from Calcutta, through Allahabad and Delhi, to Simla, and on a selection of steamers, barges, carriages, palanquins, sedan chairs, horses and elephants, took eighteen months to complete.

This was travelling in India at its grandest and most luxurious, in a style that deliberately emulated the Mughal emperors of old. Their vast entourage was as much a political statement, designed to dazzle and intimidate, as it was for their personal comfort. Emily Eden was not impressed. 'Everyone keeps saying "What a magnificent camp!"; and I thought I had never seen such squalid, melancholy discomfort,' she complained. It felt altogether too '*open-airish* and unsafe' for her liking. George (Lord Auckland) called his tent 'Foully Palace'. She named hers 'Misery Hall', and was astonished when her sister observed that hers 'was like a fairy palace'. She consoled herself by reading Charles Dickens's *Pickwick Papers*, which made her laugh till she cried.

The three siblings each had a private tent, while a fourth one, making up a square, was used as their private sitting room. Each tent was further divided into a bedroom, dressing room and sitting room.

But there was no pleasing Emily. 'They have covered us up in every direction, just as if we were native women,' she wrote; 'there is a wall of red cloth, eight feet high, drawn all around our enclosure, so that, even going out of the tent you see nothing but a crimson wall ... They say that everybody begins by hating their tents and ends by loving them, but at present I am much prepossessed in favour of a house.'

Their private enclosure covered two acres of ground. The maze of crimson corridors that were necessary to link the different parts were particularly disorientating. '[George] was sitting in my tent in the evening, when all the purdahs are all down, and all the outlets to the tents are so alike that he could not find which *crevice* led to his abode; and he said at last, "Well! It is a hard case; they talk of the luxury in which the Governor General travels, but I cannot even find a covered passage from Misery Hall to Foully Palace."'

Fanny Eden, who had experienced camp life once before on a trip to Rajmahal Hills, may have liked her own tent well enough, but privately she thought the rest of it very 'grand and dull' compared to the smaller but more cheerfully decorated ones she had used on her previous travels. Cordoned off in splendid isolation, she bemoaned the lack of 'picturesque' scenes to sketch – 'not an elephant or camel or cooking fire to be seen' – threatening to take out her penknife and cut a hole in the canvas if necessary. 'Nothing shall induce me to let them make a Government House of this,' she wrote.

But it was not to be. A Government House in transit was exactly the effect that Lord Auckland and his aides-de-camp wished to create. In addition to the Edens' private quarters, their camp within a camp included a durbar tent that had two enormous rooms within it, one for a drawing room, the other for dining in. When they ate their dinners in the 'dining room' it was, somewhat bizarrely, to the accompaniment of a band playing tunes at full throttle in the background.\*

---

\*Half a century later, their successor, Lady Dufferin, would write about the 'tent-palace' that was set up for the viceregal entourage one summer at Rawalpindi. It included such modern conveniences as telephones and its own post-office. The sleeping quarters were fitted with every luxury including lavender water, ink, paper, pins and scissors.

It was into this holy of holies that Fanny Parkes now tried to insert herself. For all her insistence that the beauty of India was often spoiled by the presence of Europeans, and her disapproval of their sometimes high-handed or philistine behaviour, she had no compunction about attaching herself to their number when it suited her to do so – whether they wanted her there or not. In the case of the Edens, they did not.

First, Mrs Parkes had applied to Captain Codrington, who was in charge of organising their sites, to allow her to pitch her tent among them, but 'the sacredness of the Governor-General's street of tents is such that . . . of course it was refused', Fanny Eden observed in a letter to her friend Eleanor Grosvenor. Mrs Parkes, however, was not so easily deterred. If the Governor-General's camp would not have her, then one of the others within the entourage would do just as well.

It was the custom during these progresses for the magistrate of each station to travel on with the Governor-General as far as the next. 'To each of these Magistrates she has severally attached herself, every one declaring they will have nothing to do with her,' Fanny Eden elaborated, 'upon which George observes with much complacency, "Now we have got rid of our Mrs Parkes . . ."' – but they had reckoned without her persistence. The next day, there she would be again, large as life, 'her fresh victim driving her in a tilbury – and her tent pitched close to his'.*

It is one of the many splendid aspects of Fanny Parkes's character that the social gulf between herself, the wife of a junior EIC official, and the aristocratic Eden sisters did not seem to impinge upon her at all. Perhaps, in her various wanderings through India, during which she had become intimate with several Indian princesses, she somehow came to imagine that British class distinctions no longer applied to her. The Edens, being somewhat behind her in this view, spent a good deal of time trying to shake her off, without much success.

---

*It was nearly too much for one magistrate, the 'thin, unhappy-looking' Mr Bose, who begged Captain Codrington 'to conceal where his tent is to be pitched as he is very much worn out attending to Mrs Parkes'.

Fanny and Emily Eden's nephew William Osborne,* who was also Lord Auckland's military secretary, had come to know her a little from his time in Calcutta. To Mrs Parkes he was a useful acquaintance of whom she took full advantage, plying him constantly with notes and small presents. The sisters, at a loss to know how to deal with her, found themselves 'longing for the day when we shall find him conducting her on the march'.

No sooner were these unkind thoughts set down when, to their fascination, who should pop up again but the very same Mrs Parkes. 'You will be very glad to know that when George and I were walking to warm ourselves after our ride we came upon a little tent just outside the line of sentinels. We wondered who it was and about twenty voices answered: "Bibi Parkes!" This has been a heavy blow.'[3]

The very next day the siblings were returning from visiting some nearby ruins when George turned to Fanny with a puzzled expression. '"There comes Macintosh and Colvin† on an elephant. How fat Colvin grows," he exclaimed. "Colvin" turned into Mrs Parkes in a man's hat and riding habit. She had met Captain Macintosh and as far as we can make out had climbed up the elephant's tail into his howdah when least expected. She will certainly be the death of us all.'

At the very least, Fanny Parkes would provide them with some light relief from the rigours of their journey. For all the grandeur of their entourage, travelling through the *mofussil* was not without its difficulties. Bandits were everywhere, and there were frequent robberies. One of the English women in their entourage, Mrs A, had woken up in the middle of the night to find a man on his knees creeping through her tent, 'but she called out, and he ran away without taking anything'. Mr B told Emily Eden that on one occasion when he and his wife had been encamped on the same spot they lost everything, 'even the shawl that was on the bed and the clothes Mrs B had left out for the morning wear, and he had to sew her up into a blanket, and drive her to Benares for fresh things'.[4]

---

*Later Lord William Osborne; in 1859 his brother became Duke of Leeds.
†One of Lord Auckland's aides-de-camp and his private secretary.

Roads in northern India were still few and far between, and when they did exist were so rudimentary as to be almost impassable. 'The roads grow worse every morning, and the names of the places we stop at more unpronounceable,' Fanny Eden recorded on 31 January 1838. 'Captain Codrington goes on every night to pitch the camp and sends back an account of the road written by his sergeant, that we may arrange our travelling plans. Every day his view of our prospects grows more gloomy. This is tomorrow's: "1st mile – ruff and dusty (he evidently thinks ruff a more emphatic mode of spelling) 2nd, 3rd and 4th mile rugged and sandy, 5th mile a brute no water, very bad passage – better go to the left of it; and 6th 7th and 8th miles, very rugged and heavy, 9th, 10th, 11th miles, better but ruff and dusty. Camp 11 miles distant by perambulator – encamping ground dusty and not good."' And so it went on.

Their days followed a regular pattern. At five thirty in the morning the bugle would sound, and they were off by six, often still in their nightclothes, to take advantage of the cool. Camp etiquette dictated that no one might go ahead of Lord Auckland and his sisters, so they missed most of the dust created by the vast cavalcade. Emily Eden thought that this setting off was by far the most amusing part of the day, and gave this pen-portrait of their camp on the move:

Besides the odd native groups, our friends catch us up in their *deshabillé* – Mrs. A. carrying the baby in an open carriage; Mrs C with hers fast asleep in a *tonjaun* [litter]; Miss H. on top of an elephant pacifying the big boy of the A's; Captain D. riding on in a suit of dust-coloured canvas, with a coal heaver's hat, going as hard as he can, to see that the tent is ready for his wife; Mrs B. carrying Mr B's pet cat in her palanquin carriage, with her ayah opposite guarding the parroquet from the cat. Then Giles comes bounding by, in fact, run away with, but apologises for passing us when we arrive, by saying he was going on to take care that tea was ready for us. Then we overtake Captain D's dogs, all walking with red great coats on – our dogs all wear coats in the morning; then Chance's [one of their pet dogs] servant stalking along, with a great stick in one hand, a shawl draped over his livery, and Chance's nose peeping from under the shawl. F[anny]'s pets travel in her cart. We each have a cart, but I can never find anything to put in mine.[5]

At times the state of the roads was nothing compared to the state of the country and the people as they passed through. In 1837 a famine had gripped certain parts of the Upper Provinces, leaving thousands of people either dead or dying by the side of the road. It was a spectacle that shook them all.

'My dearest, I am sick at heart with all this starvation we see about us,' Fanny Eden wrote to Eleanor Grosvenor on 3 January from Cawnpore. 'Now we are only upon the outskirts of the country where famine is raging but we are among those who have only wandered from it to die, and even here some of the villages are depopulated, the crops dying fast from want of rain.' Despite the fact that there were funds available to all the civil stations for distributing food, every day they saw fresh horrors: mothers offering to sell their 'skeletons of babies' for a rupee, and children looking scarcely human with hardly enough strength to swallow, even when they were given food. 'Already I feel as if we were only giving a few more days of misery to those we feed, for they must all die of hunger at last,' she wrote. 'Three or four days must take us away from all this suffering but I am sure I will never forget it.'[6] She was particularly sickened by having to sit down to dinner each night 'with the band playing and all the pomp and circumstances of life about us, which is just as much kept up in a tent as anywhere else' while the cries of starving children could be heard outside.

Famine or no famine, the show of government business had to go on. In Benares, Lord Auckland paid a courtesy visit to 'the old Delhi Ranee'. They set off in state. Although the sisters would have places of honour in the procession, they were not allowed to ride on the same elephant as their brother. Fanny Eden described the scene: 'There was George in his cocked-hat and dress coat, persuaded by the united mental force of all the aide-de-camps . . . to mount his elephant alone, for a woman by his side would detract immensely from his dignity.' The trappings of the two state elephants were magnificent. George rode with a gold umbrella held aloft over his head, 'his peacock feather and chouries,* and his long train of silver sticks preceding him', Fanny Eden wrote. 'Emily and I were on the other state elephant, with crimson and velvet umbrellas held over us and peacock feathers and silver sticks according to rule'.

As custom required, the two women were provided with gifts for the Rani. Emily was to present her with an emerald ring, large but full of flaws, while Fanny was provided with a gold chain 'remarkably light and frittery'. It was the etiquette to give something they were wearing, she noted, 'and these are the kind of handsome things the Company provide', she added with heavy irony.

The Rani herself proved to be 'a little old woman with magnificent eyes', but 'most absurdly dressed in a pair of tight white trousers and net jacket quite tight, and a little white muslin draped over that'. Behind her sat her son's wife and her own married daughter, 'melancholy looking and not pretty', wrapped up in shawls. The Rani shook hands with them and the presents were given and received. The Rani gave them a number of 'great diamond rings' and necklaces made of silver filigree, together with several trays of shawls and jewels, which, as they had been instructed to do, they 'looked at as if we did not see them or think them worth thanking for'.[†] Emily thought this system absurd. 'It is a stupid etiquette that we are not to appear to see these presents,' she wrote. 'It is a *tribute*, and the superior is too grand to see what the inferior offers.'[7]

They were greatly entertained, however, by the courtly language which was always used on these occasions. When Lord Auckland spoke to the Rani from behind the purdah curtain, his aide-de-camp Macnaughten translated, poker-faced: 'The Rani, my Lord, says that

---

*A yak's tail set in a handle and used as a fly whisk – a Mughal symbol indicating very high status.
†Due to the EIC regulations about accepting gifts, they were not allowed to keep any of these, but had to turn them over immediately to the Company coffers.

it is utterly impossible for her to express how inconceivably well she feels that your Lordship has entered her dwelling.' And when the sisters took their leave from the *zenana*, Macnaughten, translating once again for the Rani, assured them that she felt 'like a locust in the presence of an elephant'. The instant the door had been shut behind them, however, he swiftly took possession of the diamond rings they had just been given, 'which made me feel like a locust too', Fanny Eden added ruefully.

Less amusing altogether was having attar of roses poured on to their hands when they rose to leave. This was a custom that took place everywhere, and was written about by English women in every century. Although it was meant to honour the departing guests, the oil was often so strong that at times they were almost overpowered by it. This time it was not the faint-inducing perfume that was offensive. 'The daughters took a fit of fun and instead of quietly pouring attar over our hands took to smearing our gowns all over with it, laughing vehemently at the utter ruin they were perpetrating.'[8] (Perhaps the *zenana* ladies agreed with Isabella Fane, the daughter of Sir Henry Fane, the British Commander-in-Chief in Bengal at that time, who observed on meeting the Edens that 'both are great talkers ... both ugly, and both s***k like polecats'.[9] On the other hand, since Miss Fane also described her fellow memsahibs variously as fools, pigs, nasty creatures, 'looking ninety and undistinguishable from a corpse', and 'surrounded by hordes of pasty children looking like maggots', perhaps they got off lightly.)

In April the Governor-General's cavalcade reached Simla, in the eastern foothills of the Himalayas, where they took refuge from the burning summer heat. In the autumn of the same year they set off again, on one of the most important legs of their journey: to make a strategically crucial state visit to the independent Sikh Kingdom of Ranjit Singh.

After the fall of Napoleon in 1815, the threat of French incursions into British territories in India, such a huge preoccupation of the second half of the eighteenth century, was at an end; but the Company was increasingly worried about another enemy, Russia, which had already swallowed up all the Persian territories south of the Caucasus. Now Russian influence was steadily seeping into Afghanistan, the neighbouring kingdom to the west of the Punjab.

The latest intelligence from Kabul had revealed that the Russians were building themselves a fort between the Caspian and Khiva, in present-day Uzbekistan. As Auckland's predecessor, Lord William Bentinck, had written in a memo: 'This is the best line of their operation against India, but it can only be considered a very distant speculation.'

The East India Company continued to hope that Russian designs on India would remain a distant speculation, but they could not be too sure. Before he left London, Auckland had received specific instructions to build a buffer of friendly states around the North-West Provinces of British India. The most important of these was the Sikh Kingdom of Ranjit Singh, 'Lion of the Punjab'.

For all the many splendours of their own viceregal life, the visit was an experience none of them would ever forget. They arrived in Amritsar, the Sikh capital, to find the regiments of Ranjit Singh's soldiers lined up in their honour. Fanny Eden wrote home to Eleanor Grosvenor, describing the scene:

My dearest, if you could but have seen the splendour of the sight we saw this morning, you would simply have died of it . . . I think that the entrance to the camp this morning was the finest thing I ever saw anywhere. There were altogether four miles of Runjeets soldiers drawn up in lines. We passed through a mile and a half of them – his bodyguard. A great number of these are uniformly dressed in bright orange turbans, tunics and trousers, the others provide their own dresses for which they have an enormous allowance. They are all of the same form, made of 'kincob' – gold and silver [embroidered] cloth of every possible shade of colour. They have long black and white beards half down to their waists and a large expenditure of shawls and scarves disposed in drapery, about them. Their matchlocks are inlaid with gold or steel or silver, and some of them with bows and arrows, some with long spears, and all the chief ones with ... black heron's plumes. Everything about them is showy and glittering – their horses with the gold or silver hangings, their powder flasks embroidered with gold.[10]

Not all the Edens' official work was so exalted. Part of it entailed entertaining British subjects wherever they found them – something of a trial to both sisters. 'My dear, the process of eating dinner!' moaned Fanny Eden. 'The manual labour lasts "in the Mofussil" two whole hours, consequently for at least an hour and a half mine is purely a mental feast, chiefly shared with the Colonel or Brigadier of the prevailing regiment. I am erudite about cantonments and military hospitals and I wonder and re-wonder why the government does not allow *verandahs* to some barracks, and *choppahs* [thatched roofs] to another ... '

It was not only the military men whose conversation and manners were found wanting. When they made a Sunday halt in Fatehgunj, in present-day Gujarat, Emily Eden wrote: 'A great many of the men here have lived in the jungles for years, and their poor dear manners are utterly gone – jungled out of them.' Luckily, she added, the band played all through dinner, drowning out most of the conversation. 'The thing they like best is a band,' she explained, 'and it was an excellent idea that, of making it play from five to six.'

Isolated postings were hard on everyone. On another occasion the sisters came across a family acquaintance, Mr Lushington, who had been sent off to a station in India where there were only three other Europeans, and not a single woman among them for him to talk to. 'This is what happens to half the young writers,' Emily Eden wrote; 'some are quite alone, no other European within reach – and in a climate where for some months they can hardly get out of the house, and why they do not go melancholy mad I cannot conceive. Some do come back to Calcutta in a frightfully nervous state of health.'[11]

Another young writer, whom they had known in Calcutta, a

sophisticated young man who had been brought up in Naples and Rome and who cared for nothing but 'society and Victor Hugo's novels and that sort of thing', had found himself posted to a remote station (she refers to it only as 'B') consisting of only five bungalows. There were three married women there: 'one lady has bad spirits (small blame to her), and she has never been seen; another has weak eyes, and wears a large shade about the size of a common veranda; and the other has bad health, and has had her head shaved. A tour [wig] is not to be had here for love or money, so she wears a brown silk cushion with a cap pinned to the top of it.'[12]

At least the sisters had each other to talk to. For Fanny Eden, it was the only female resident of a station of thirty Company men who was most deserving of their sympathy. 'She was evidently so glad to see two other women that she would not cease talking. The more we told her we had got up at five in the morning and were fast asleep, the more she said "No wonder" and talked on.'[13]

Some women lived in places so remote that fashion was but a distant memory. 'Mrs V— appeared in a turban made I think of stamped tin moulded into two fans, from which descended a long *pleureuse* [weeping] feather floating over some very full sleeves' – a fashion from at least a generation previously. Then there was Mrs C—, who was past fifty, 'some say near sixty', but who still wore 'a light-coloured wig with very long curls floating down her back, and a gold wreath to keep it on', and a gown cut very low at the front – a fashion which seems to date from even earlier than Mrs V—'s turban. Worst of the lot was Mrs T—, who had nobly travelled over forty miles to attend a dinner with the Edens, but who wore long thick thread mittens with black velvet bracelets over them. 'She may have great genius, and many good qualities,' Emily Eden wrote, 'but, you know, it is impossible to look for them under those mittens.'[14]

One woman in particular had been 'in perfect ecstacies' with the band music at one of the viceregal entertainments. At first Emily longed to go and talk to her, guessing that the woman, who was said to be the wife of an indigo planter, would not have met another

Englishwoman for many months. A moment's reflection made her think again: 'but then, you know, she might not have been his wife, or anybody's wife, or he might not have been an indigo planter. In short, my dear Mrs D., you know what a world it is – impossible to be too careful ...'

But come they did, suitable or unsuitable, fashionable or frowsy, sometimes travelling many scores of miles, often across difficult terrain, for the chance to be present at one of the Governor-General's entertainments. Emily Eden would always remember a Miss T—, who in her eagerness had ridden for forty-two miles up the mountains to Simla. She had made the punishing journey, without stopping once, through the heat of the day, and as a result 'the sun had literally burnt all the skin off her shoulders, through her habit'. She lent Miss T— a blonde shawl, but it could not conceal the state of things. 'I never can understand the extraordinary exertion that women sometimes make – and without dying of it, too.'

Where there was music and dancing to be had, no Himalayan peak was too high for the British, and the scarcity of women no impediment. 'There were great doubts whether a ball could be made out, as the want of ladies in the Mofussil makes dancing rather difficult,' Emily Eden wrote from Gazipur. But there was nothing British ladies loved more than a ball. 'I wish you could have seen the dancers. A Mrs —, something like Mrs Glover the actress, only much fatter, with a gown two inches shorter than her petticoat, *bounding* through every quadrille, with her three grown-up sons dancing round her. She is an exemplary mother, and has been a widow many years, and a grandmother many more, but she never misses a dance!'[15]

There was another person, they would soon discover, who did not miss a dance either. 'How odd of me not to have told you that the very first person I saw at the very first ball at Meerut was Mrs Parkes,' Fanny Eden wrote to Eleanor Grosvenor. 'How she got there nobody knows and nobody ever will know. The day after we got here they got up a morning review for us – blew up mines and took a fort, and not only a fort, but Mrs Parkes, for as the smoke blew off she was discovered riding. If she were not so fat I should say she was something supernatural. My spirit is almost broke about her. I dare say we shall find her settled in our home at Simla and shall not have strength to turn her out.'[16]

# CHAPTER 17

It is not known who the exemplary mother and grandmother was, *bounding* round the dance floor in Emily Eden's description. All that we know about 'Mrs —', except for her too-long petticoats, is that she was accompanied by her three grown-up sons. Not many mothers in India could claim such happiness. According to one estimate,[1] women could expect to lose from a quarter to a third of their entire family, as the sad little headstones that exist to this day in graveyards all over India can attest.

The ferocious, often deadly illnesses that struck down so many were no respecter of age. Children were as vulnerable as their parents, if not more so. Henrietta Clive was almost alone in believing – surely under a misapprehension – that Madras would be a healthy place in which to bring up her two young daughters. Usually parents took every possible precaution to protect their children, which in practical terms meant either leaving them behind or, if they were born in the country, sending them home as soon as possible. It was, in Julia Maitland's phrase, 'the grand Indian sorrow'.

Maria Nugent had become almost unhinged by her decision to leave her three children in England when she set sail for Calcutta in 1810. Her youngest was a tiny baby, born just six weeks previously. It was a bittersweet moment when, on their first attempt to leave, adverse winds sent them temporarily back into harbour, and she was able to snatch an extra week with them. 'My feelings mixed and various,' she wrote in her journal; '– sometimes quite happy with my children, and seeing the dear little baby thriving so well – then again, almost in despair at the idea of parting with them.' When that dreadful moment finally came, she wrote: 'I wish to forget all that I felt that day.'

The six months that she spent on the voyage out, and her first months in Calcutta, were marred by deep depression. She developed an infection in both her eyes that left her almost blind, said by her doctor to have been brought about by 'nerves'. For all the grandeur of her household, dinners and assemblies, Maria Nugent's diaries reveal both her psychological torment at losing her children, and the intense inner struggle she waged to try to overcome it. 'My dear Nugent suffers as much as I do,' she wrote, 'but he does not indulge his grief, and I must endeavour to follow his example. My greatest, my only consolation, is in prayer, and I find myself able to put on a calm appearance often, when my heart is nearly breaking.'[2]

Letters from home, especially those from her great friend Lady Buckingham, who acted as her children's guardian while they were abroad, sent her into a state of near collapse. She became so agitated by the first batch of correspondence to arrive that she was unable to go down for dinner. It was almost as hard for her husband. 'It would be quite impossible to describe to you, my dearest good and kind Lady Buckingham, the Sensations with which your Letter was received,' Maria Nugent wrote. 'For my part I could not read more than the first Line. General N— undertook to go on with it, but he was interrupted a dozen Times at least by his Tears and when yet finished it he said it was not only the very best Letter, but the *finest piece of eloquence* he had ever read in his Life.'[3] Two little enclosures from the eldest children, George and Louisa, were 'almost too much for me', she admitted. But the letters brought the good news that the children were all in good health and flourishing – a great relief to her, 'for had I the anxiety of thinking they might not be well taken care of added to what I have already gone through, I must have sunk under it'.[4]

For all the pain it caused, no one was in any doubt about the absolute necessity of sending children home. The threat to their health was by far the greatest consideration, but there were other factors in play. In Jamaica, where her husband had been posted as Governor before taking up his position as Commander-in-Chief in Calcutta, Maria Nugent had been quick to notice the adverse effect of the tropical climate. 'The children here are fat but deadly pale and sallow,' she observed, not mincing her words. 'Very few of them speak a word of English and I should imagine the indolent Habits and suspect ideas instilled in them here would be very difficult to get the better of in England.'

Increasingly throughout the nineteenth century, parents worried about the 'Indianisation' of their children, most particularly – as Maria Nugent put it – 'their little funny talk', or what would later become known as a *chi-chi* accent (originally spelled *chee-chee*, from the Hindi word for 'dirty').

Prejudice against the adverse effect of Indian servants on children grew in line with all the others that were now gaining traction. 'The greatest stress should be laid on their not understanding any language which their parents do not: when they comprehend the quarrels of the lower classes, which, I am told, are literally untranslatable, as our own English has not words to express their grossness, there is no guarantee that they are not falling into the depths indeed'5 was the extreme advice given by the anonymous author of *The Englishwoman in India*. It was considered 'a rare accomplishment' for any small children brought up in the country to speak English at all.

Either way, most people seemed to agree that British children brought up by ayahs were not only sallow and unhealthy, but also downright badly behaved. It rarely occurred to anyone that the parents might also be to blame.

In 1783, Sophia Plowden sent all four of her children, ranging in age from seven to eighteen months, back to England into the care of her sister. The eldest, Edward, was 'a sad riotous fellow', with a propensity for 'idle tricks' which he indulged in the moment he boarded the ship by throwing his ball out of the window 'and seeing it did not sink as he had expected he disposed of half a box of turnips, which a gentleman had preserved in sand for the voyage'. As all men were 'fond of encouraging this disposition', his mother added mildly, 'I suppose he will be a perfect monkey by the time he arrives in England'. She goes on to imagine him visiting another sister in her room as she is dressing. Apparently Edward had acquired 'a vast fondness' for powder, 'and I'll answer for it will [seize] the stuff to powder himself the moment he casts his eye on it, and should she dispute the point will most probably throw the powder box at her'. Loweringly for the new family, the second child Harriette was described by her mother as having almost as great a propensity for mischief as her brother, 'and is the most complete romp you ever saw'.

It is easier to forgive Mrs Plowden's indulgence when it comes to her description of her third child, also named Sophia, who seems to have contracted polio, or a similar crippling disease, which had left her unable to lift or move her head properly. Much of her long letter concerns the medical attention her parents required for her, but more striking still is her understandable wish that this child, in particular, should be protected by something as near to her own mother's love as possible.

With what anxious expectation shall I wait for the accounts of their safe arrival, and to hear from you the state of our sweet little Sophia's health. Sh'd you have no little girl of your own, mine will I am sure be in high favour, you must love her she resembles *you* so strongly. I hope you will be particular in telling me what she said and how she looked on her first [glance?] of devotion to you. That she will think she has some acquaintance with you & be puzzled to make out who you are – in short I think there is that look of resemblance in our voice and [manner?] that when she looks at you & hears you speak she will think of her poor mother, & if she does it will produce a smile & the sort of look I describe she will be half inclined to run into your arms – but having a doubt of you being her mother will stick close by Colonel Cormac & watch to see what he has to say on the subject.[6]

Occasionally a mother, such as the Mrs Rishel mentioned by Emily Eden, became so distraught at the thought of being parted from her family that she simply rebelled: 'the poor woman is just arrived, half broken hearted at leaving four children at home under the care of strangers. She was to have left the fifth but when the ship was at the point of sailing she could not part with it and smuggled it aboard.'[7]

Not all women were as lucky as Maria Nugent and Sophia Plowden, both of whom had close relatives with safe, comfortable homes for their children to go to. Many more endured the torment of never really knowing if their children were being well taken care of or not, during a separation that usually lasted for many years. Sometimes it could take more than a year 'before we could hear of our children's safe arrival in England, or get a reply to a letter'.[8] In the nineteenth and twentieth centuries, seven was the average age at which children were sent home, but often they were much younger, some little more than babies.

In the eighteenth century, Eliza Fay had considered seven 'rather late', but the opportunities for children to travel home were, in those days, very infrequent. Sometimes, as in the case of the seven-year-old son of Mrs Fay's friends Sir Robert and Lady Chambers, they were put in charge of acquaintances who were also travelling. At other times, a job lot, so to speak, would be sent off together. In the early nineteenth century, the kindly Captain Hopkins of the *Seringapatam* became known as 'the Bengal Ayah' because so many unaccompanied children were sent home in his charge.

The system had been in place for some time, with varying results. Eliza Fay records a sad crocodile of some thirteen little children all gathered under 'the immediate protection' of one sea captain. Who knows what became of them. I would like to think that they did not suffer the fate of Elizabeth Marsh's nine-year-old son Burrish, who travelled alone to join his parents in Madras in 1772, again under the 'protection' of the ship's chief mate. Despite the money and presents that had been given to the mate in an effort to encourage his kind treatment of their little son, their 'manly, beautiful boy' was so neglected and abused during the year-long voyage that his parents discovered him in the hold, 'almost destroyed with vermin and filth'.[9]

Very occasionally, children left their own record of their experiences. The East India Company archives in the British Library contain the fragile fragments of two letters written by Emily Royal and George Dawson, two thirteen-year-olds who in 1848 took a passage home, from Madras to London, aboard the ill-fated East Indiaman *Sutlej*.

George Dawson's mother, originally a Miss Wood, had gone out to India early in the century as governess to an English family. After her marriage, this enterprising woman had bought 'a very large boarding hotel' and several other houses to rent out in Ootacamund, or Ooty, in the Nilgiri Hills, southern India's first hill station. George was subsequently born there in 1835. Not so much is known about Emily Royal, although she too seems to have been brought up in the Nilgiris, where their families became friends.

Rounding the Cape of Good Hope, their ship encountered 'a terrific hurricane'. The first the children knew about it was when they were awoken by the 'dreadful rolling and lurching of the ship, so that we were in great danger of falling', George wrote in his account. 'Papa was sitting at our bedside, and told us that there was a dreadful hurricane ... When Emily and May rose from their beds to come into our cabin the ship gave a terrific lurch and a heavy chest of drawers of which the lashings gave way, fell forward and crushed poor Miss Butler's chest ... we heard a frightful crash followed by a deathlike silence for some seconds, and then Miss Butler screamed ...'

Seconds later, the storm porthole in their cabin gave way with a crash, and water rushed in. 'Papa, with great presence of mind seized the bedding and attempted to stuff it in the hole, but it was soon washed out and the water poured in dreadfully.'

They were removed to another, supposedly safer cabin, but even then all the ladies and children were up to their knees in water with nothing but their nightdresses on; the gentlemen stripped down to their shirts and 'sleeping drawers'. Between them they had not a single dry piece of clothing to put on, and the contents of every single piece of their luggage were ruined. Above them on deck they heard the terrible sound of the cannons giving way from their lashings, rolling about to the great danger of those who passed to and fro. Three of these cannon were eventually thrown overboard to lighten the load.

Emily Royal took up the story. 'I remember Miss Ottley telling me about the mountainous seas,' she wrote. 'Papa took us all on deck to see the sea ... and it looked exactly like the Nilgiris, or immense hills and valleys, and no-one could help crying when we first looked out of the cuddy door and not a piece of timber to be seen and to hear the crying of the few poor sheep, pigs and poultry that was left ... Thousands of wild birds were flying about, seeming to enjoy our misery.'

The children were eventually moved again, to the steward's cabin this time, where they holed up, six of them in one bed, subsisting on biscuits and beer. They survived like this for ten days before the hurricane finally subsided and the sea became, once again, 'beautiful and calm and the sun shone out in all its brightness'.[10]

Whatever the dangers and discomforts of the voyage home, the expense of it, let alone paying for a boarding school when they got there, was beyond the reach of many. British schools had existed in India since the eighteenth century, but in the early days their standards were not high. The main difficulty was in finding a teacher – any teacher – with sufficient qualifications. The Bombay Council wrote home to Leadenhall Street complaining that 'they had often endeavoured to appoint a schoolmaster, but without success for want of a person qualified',[11] and implored the directors to send one out from England.

A number of establishments based on the British boarding school model were now opening to cater for the less affluent. On her progress through northern India in the mid-century, Emily Eden's sharp eyes had been quick to notice a little girl among the 'hangers on' in their entourage who appeared to have no one but bearers to look after her. She had surmised, correctly, that she was being sent to the school in

Mussoorie,* a hill station in the foothills of the Himalayas, 'where parents who are too poor to send children home now send them'.[12] Whatever insulting things the author of *The Englishwoman in India* may have had to say about the servant classes, the fact that parents were prepared to put such an extraordinary amount of trust in their bearers tells a very different story.

Emily Eden, who had no family of her own, was astonished by the way in which even very small children travelled long distances around the country without their parents, an apparently haphazard system which those with more hands-on experience of India seem to have had no hesitation in adopting. It was described to her in detail by Mr T, one of the magistrates she met along the way.

> He said a palanquin was brought to his house containing three little children, a little girl nine years old and two smaller brothers. They were going up to Mussoorie, had been travelling three days, and had about a week's more journey. They had not even their names written on a piece of paper, or a note to the magistrates of the district, but were just passed on from one set of bearers to the other ... The bearers who brought these children to Mr T's said they thought the children were tired, and so they brought them to a European house for a rest. Mr T had them washed and dressed, and fed them and kept them half a day, when he was obliged to send them away for fear they should lose their *dak* [an arrangement for travelling in relays]. He said they were very shy, and would hardly speak, but he made out their names and gave them notes to other magistrates, and some months afterwards he saw them at school in Mussoorie; but it is an odd way of sending children to school.

Sending children home to school remained the ideal. Augusta Becher and Harriet Tytler both of whom were born in India (in 1830

---

*They were just outside Delhi at the time. Mussoorie was nearly two hundred miles away.

and 1828 respectively), and would go back to live all their adult lives there as army wives, were sent back to England to school. Augusta, who came from a well-known Anglo-Indian family, the Princeps, was relatively old when she was sent aged eight, but she was still four years younger than any other of the twenty girls at Miss Connell's, 3 York Place, Regent's Park. 'I remember myself in a little narrow-striped red and white Belgian cotton frock made abroad, quite plain and different to all the other children, and a grey silk pelisse with little bows all down the front and then a small cape. I am sure it was very pretty, but then very French, and picture to yourself a poor small thing four years younger than any in the house, a doll in arms, launched into a London schoolroom of 20 girls!'

The school had been chosen because her cousin, Anna, had been there, and another cousin, Georgie, a girl of sixteen, still was. 'But Georgie took no notice of me, she was silly and conceited, and her charity to me was to promote all the bullying possible by announcing me as a vixen and a spoiled brat ... So for the first year I was very miserable.' Little Augusta also had such bad chilblains she could hardly use her hands at all. Mrs Glen, the principal, sent for a doctor who wound leather plasters of red mercurial around each finger, and then sealed her hands up 'in bags made of white rag, not to be opened. Imagine the misery; how they sweated and burned.' When she eventually rebelled and took them off, 'each poor finger was one long white blister.'[13]

Harriet Tytler, who also suffered from chilblains, wrote an equally graphic account of what it was like to endure them during the harsh English winters. Although every finger was covered with them, she was still expected to practise the piano in her aunt's freezing drawing room. 'What torture I went through!' she remembered. 'My first hour at the piano was devoted to chords and scales. The first chord I struck always caused the chilblains at the root of the fingers to burst and bleed, when I had to bring out my handkerchief and wipe off the blood from the keys before continuing my practice.'[14*]

---

*When I was first at boarding school, in the early 1970s, I remember a friend from Malaysia who also suffered terribly from chilblains. Thankfully, you never hear about them now.

Many people have read and wept over Rudyard Kipling's short story *Baa Baa Black Sheep*, about the neglect and trauma suffered by two small children sent 'Home' to school, but even Kipling's account (said to be largely autobiographical) cannot compare to the sadistic cruelty of the aunt into whose care Harriet Tytler and her younger sister Emily were entrusted. 'My aunt, one of the old school, was thirty years of age and had married at sixteen to spite another lover,' Mrs Tytler remembered, and spite continued to govern her every interaction with her two little nieces.

The couple, Mr and Mrs Raine, had had six children, all of whom had died at birth, but this seems to have had no ameliorating effect. 'My aunt was horribly strict with us and really cruel in many ways,' Mrs Tytler wrote. 'For a start we were never allowed a fire through the whole winter.' She was expected to attend piano practice in the frigid drawing room every morning, summer and winter, at six o'clock, 'clad in a low-necked short-sleeved print dress all the year round. The only difference in the winter was that we were allowed to wear a small plaid shawl round our shoulders. This was all we had, whether out of doors or indoors, but after all both were about the same temperature. I was allowed no candle to practice by, although it is pitch dark at that hour nearly six months in the year as far north as Birmingham.'

Every day followed the same relentless routine. Their breakfast consisted of bread and water, the bread sometimes too hard to bite into. Taking their plates outside, they began their morning run: fifty rounds of the garden, a distance Mrs Tytler calculated to be four and a half miles. 'As soon as we finished one hunk [of bread], we dived down whilst running, like an eagle on its prey, and picked up another.' In the bitter, frosty weather, they would sometimes shrug up their shoulders under their shawls, hoping to get a little more warmth, 'when my aunt would tap from one of the windows, to signify that we had been caught in the very act of so heinous an offence, and down went our poor shoulders again'.

They were never allowed to talk to their servants, except to say 'good morning' and 'thank you', even though they passed through the kitchen many times in one day to reach their schoolroom. Summer and winter followed the same pattern, with a half-holiday granted them on Saturdays only, when they mended their stockings. They were made to go to bed at eight o'clock. 'In the winter we had to break the ice in our jug to wash our faces with our unfortunate chilblainy hands. Poor wretched children ... but on Saturday nights we were allowed a hot bath, a real treat.'

Another treat was a two-week visit from their brother Edward, 'the only holiday we ever had, and the only time we met'. This brother had saved up his money and one day went out and bought his sisters 'a quantity of cakes and tartlets – enough to have lasted us for ever so many days'. But the aunt found them out. 'She never made a remark, but took the whole lot into her room, and we never saw them again.'

By her own account, Harriet was blessed with a 'passionate' nature, and stood up to the sadistic Aunt Raine as often as she could, but little Emily, having a more timid nature, was completely crushed by her. 'We often used to lock ourselves in each other's arms and sob ourselves to sleep.'

Eventually, when Harriet turned seventeen, she was sent back to India to be reunited with her parents, leaving the wretched Emily behind. Her travails were not yet ended. During the voyage she learned that her father had unexpectedly died, and when she was reunited with her mother at long last, it was only to be told that she was intending to return to England with the two younger children almost immediately. Harriet could not go with them, as she would lose her pension if she left India again so soon.

She implored her mother, on her knees, to take her with them, but to no avail. 'Poor me,' she wrote, 'who had looked forward to the one happiness of my life all the miserable years I had spent with my aunt, was doomed to meet with disappointment akin to sorrow.'

Giving birth and bringing up small children in India was in itself beset with difficulties and heartache. For army wives, such as Augusta

Becher and Honoria Lawrence, these difficulties were hugely exacerbated by the fact that they were constantly on the move. Harriet Tytler's mother, Mrs Earle, had been forced to set off on the long march from Secrora in Oudh to Nasirabad, with her husband's regiment, the 9th Native Infantry, when Harriet was just thirteen days old. Mrs Earle had three other small children with her, as well as her newborn infant. Every day they rose between two and three o'clock in the morning to begin the day's journey: the children of course slept soundly in their palanquins, 'but not so the poor mothers, who had little rest I fear, day or night'.

At least all her children survived the experience. For first-time mothers, with no experience of labour or childbirth to help them through the ordeal, it must have been terrifying. Their babies were particularly vulnerable. Augusta Becher's eldest child died of dysentery on his first birthday. Honoria Lawrence was luckier in that hers, Aleck, survived into adulthood, but the miserable conditions she endured at the birth, which occurred during a journey to accompany her soldier husband Henry who was joining his regiment at Karnal, was something she never forgot. It would have been a difficult confinement even under the best of circumstances, but she also suffered from postnatal depression. In her journals she describes her utter despair at being expected to continue on the march, in the hot weather, when her baby was just three weeks old: 'the whole journey seemed to me like a funeral procession', she recalled, 'baby very ill and me sinking fast, yet obliged to push on that we might get a nurse for baby and advice for me'.[15]

One night, as Henry was riding ahead, she gave way completely to her despair. Sending one of the bearers ahead to fetch her husband back, she climbed out of the *dhoolie* (covered litter) in which she was travelling. 'Oh, the anguish of that hour!' she wrote. 'I carried my babe till I almost fainted. At last I laid him on my cloak by the roadside, but he cried so piteously that I at once took him up again, I thought I would die there and then; and I was so weak that I had no self-control to sustain me. Just as I got back into the *dhoolie*, Henry rode up. The bearer had never gone near him. He had only turned back from surprise at my not appearing.' They carried on to Cawnpore, but by then both mother and baby were so ill that they had to stay there a whole week before it was possible to journey on.

# CHAPTER 18

The marriage of Honoria and Henry Lawrence is one of the great love stories of British India.

Henry Lawrence, who at the beginning of their marriage was a relatively humble surveyor would later become a famous and much lionised figure in Anglo-India, distinguishing himself in both the Sikh and Afghan Wars and later during the Uprising in Lucknow. Their contemporaries thought just as highly of his wife. Lady Login, who counted her as an intimate friend, and made her a godmother to one of her children, wrote: 'I have never met a woman quite like Honoria, never a wife who more entirely shared in, and helped her husband in his work, yet without in any way bringing that fact to the knowledge of the world at large.'[1]

A miniature of Honoria, painted just before her marriage, portrays her as a conventionally pretty young woman, her hair framing her face in the hideous clusters of ringlets that were fashionable in the early decades of the century. In real life there was something altogether more energetic and unusual about her that no portrait was ever able to convey. Like her husband, she was famously badly dressed, and by her own admission could be brusque, even sometimes prickly, in character. An acquaintance, who knew her as a young woman, would later write: 'Well do I remember, after so many years, the impression made on our circle by those fine features and the still more striking figure; the freshness, almost wildness, of that natural

grace; the frank, unencumbered demeanour, and the step of an hunt-
ress Diana.'[2]

Honoria Lawrence was born on Christmas Day 1806, near Malin
Head, the northernmost tip of Ireland. She was the twelfth of a family
of fifteen. Henry, her cousin, was brought up in the same part of
Ireland, although they never met as children. He too was from a large
family, and all five of the surviving Lawrence brothers went to India
to make their fortunes. Henry, who joined the Bengal Artillery, was
just sixteen when he first made the voyage, and apart from two visits
home, would remain in India his whole life.

The story of their falling in love and eventual marriage is beset
with so many vicissitudes that it reads more like the plot of an early
Victorian novel than a real-life love affair. They first met in August
1827, when Henry was sent home to recuperate from a long illness, and
the bond between them seems to have been instantaneous, cemented
on a long rambling walk down the Thames. Before declaring himself
to his future wife, however, Henry decided he needed to ask for permission from her family, and in the absence of her father, went to an
older female relative, Angel Heath, instead. He was quickly rebuffed.
As a young army officer he simply did not have the means to support
a wife, and a disappointed Henry returned to India later that year
without a bride. Neither had spoken a single word to the other about
their feelings.

Honoria Lawrence never forgot her cousin. Knowing that her
chances of ever seeing him again were almost non-existent, she now
decided, against her family's wishes, to train as a governess (she is
said to have taught herself French, Italian and enough ancient Greek
to read the New Testament). A long, severe illness put paid to these
plans, and during the two years that it took her to recover fully, she
met and became engaged to a clergyman, Mr Briggs. Meanwhile,
at almost exactly the same time and on the other side of the world,
Henry had received a promotion. He had been seconded from the
army to a civilian job as a revenue officer. The increased salary would
be enough for him to marry his cousin at last.

All this time, both Honoria and Henry had confided their feelings about one another to one of Henry's sisters, Letitia. In July 1833, six years after they had first met, Henry wrote to his sister, telling her of his intention to propose to his cousin at last. 'Really I think I shall be mad enough to tell her my story; try to make her believe that I have loved her for five years and said nothing of my love. The thing seems incredible, but it is true.'

His letter crossed, mid-ocean, with Letitia's, in which she had written to tell him of Honoria's engagement.

Henry was devastated. 'Had I but tried, as one in his senses would have done, to gain her heart, matters might have been managed. If anyone is to blame, I am the culprit, as I am the sufferer. The chances are now very many against my ever being married. This I say, not as a boy of seventeen, but as one – though unattractive in himself – not easily captivated,' he wrote back. And then: 'Tell me always where and how she is,' he enjoined. 'Keep up your correspondence with her.'

Letitia was as good as her word. When Honoria made the decision to break off her engagement to the Rev. Briggs, taking a post as a teacher at Prior Park School, Ashby-de-la-Zouch, Letitia decided she should break her silence. She told Honoria of Henry's love for her. In March 1836, almost nine years after they had first met, Honoria wrote to Henry for the first time, telling him that she would marry him. His ecstatic letter in reply did not reach her until the autumn. After so many cruel delays, it was decided that she should set off for India on the first available passage after February the following year, and she wrote asking him to meet her either in Madras or Calcutta. Once again his letter crossed mid-ocean, this time with Honoria herself, who had been obliged to take up her passage to India before Henry's reply could reach her.

Although highly conventional in her religious views, Honoria Lawrence was sufficiently unconventional in other ways to take very readily to the peripatetic life that was ahead of her. From the beginning she relished the adventure, and was thoroughly energised by the journey. Whereas other women occupied their time with sewing, music or reading copious quantities of Scott and Dickens, Honoria amused herself by finding likenesses between people at the table and the dishes on it: 'Captain Cobb is the image of a shoulder of mutton. Captain Davis is like a dried reindeer's tongue, and Mr B., who sits near me, is exactly like a crispy, brown roast pork. These odd notions dance before my eyes very often, and I find myself on the verge of laughing out loud at my own whimsies.'

She also spent much of her time writing her journal, addressed to her husband-to-be – and in which, after their marriage, he would also write – a habit which she kept up all her life. 'You say you have nothing to offer me but unbounded love' is one of her first entries – 'And what more, dearest can mortal give to mortal? . . . We were formed, as Coleridge says, "to find in another being the complement of our own".'

Nonetheless, she must have been apprehensive at the thought of travelling to the other side of the world to marry a man she had neither seen nor spoken to for almost a decade. She wonders whether he likes to smoke (she hopes not, as she detests the habit); and how he would like her to dress (Letitia reassures her that Henry will admire her in anything, 'even that hideous red gown' that she wore in London). She tells him not to buy her jewellery or 'trinkets', especially earrings which she considers 'barbarous things'; and as for 'billing and cooing', or any demonstrations of affection in public, they are 'perfectly intolerable and indelicate'.

For all these questions, she seems to have had no doubts about her choice of husband. She had never met a man who could enter into a woman's feelings in the way he did, she told him. 'But your letters convince me that you are strung so that the chords of your mind will respond to that which wakens mine,' she wrote. 'Surely there will not be less of this when we are face to face, than there was while sea and land divided us.'

Her composure only failed her when her boat finally arrived in Madras at the end of June. Would Henry be there to claim her? Or would he at least have sent her a letter confirming a rendezvous? To her acute disappointment there was no Henry, and no letter. 'It is a very great blessing to me that I do not habitually fear,' she wrote in her journal, 'though my heart sinks when I reflect that my latest news of you was in January ... ' She sailed on to Calcutta, and there her apprehension reached fever pitch. 'Every brig, barge, that comes in sight, I set the glass to, for I think you may be on board,' she wrote on 6 July.

A few days later, there was still no news. 'It seems like a century, since I last opened this,' she wrote in her journal on 9 July. 'Such a variety of feeling has passed through my mind. I continued every moment to expect you as we went up the river. I paced about my cabin like one demented.'

Finally, when no Henry arrived to claim her and she was left almost alone on board the *Reliant*, she went on shore to a hotel, 'and then when I got into the room alone I did give way to the poignant disappointment'. Still Henry did not come. Over the next few weeks, her nerves were almost at breaking point, not helped by the arrival of several men whom she was convinced must be Henry. On one occasion, a 'Sahib Lawrence' was even announced, but it turned out to be Henry's brother, Richard, ratcheting up the tension still further.

Henry finally arrived on 17 August, nearly six weeks after Honoria had first landed in India. They were married very quietly just a few days later, and almost immediately set off on the long journey to Gorakhpur (in present-day Uttar Pradesh, near the Nepalese border), a large military station from where Henry's work would take place.

For the new Mrs Lawrence it was her first taste of the ritual of packing up, travelling and following her husband over long, long distances, which would characterise the whole of the rest of her life.

The kind of travelling that Honoria Lawrence experienced at her husband's side was very different from either the cheerful 'vagabondizing' of Fanny Parkes or the imperial glamping of the Eden sisters. This was small-scale, business-like camp life of the kind experienced by countless women in this period, particularly soldiers' wives, who travelled frequently, often over extraordinarily long distances, to accompany their husbands. Unlike Mrs Parkes, or the Misses Eden, all of whom were childless, they often had the added complication of having babies and young children in tow.

Blissfully married to Henry at last, and as yet unencumbered by a family, Honoria took to her new life at once. On the journey to Gorakhpur, the first part of which was accomplished by river, she was entranced from the very beginning. 'I should like our voyage to last for months,' she wrote to Henry in her journal, 'it is so free from care, so unshackled, so independent of any enjoyment beyond what we have in each other's society, intellectual pursuits and the fair face of nature.'

The pinnace they travelled in was 'fifty five feet long but not drawing above two feet of water, with two masts, and rigging somewhat like a yacht. It has sixteen oars, but we proceed chiefly by sailing and tacking.' The poop contained two cabins, 'venetianed all round, having a *purdah* or curtain let down from the outside during the heat of the day'.

In a letter to a friend she described their daily routine. 'We get up about daylight and after a cup of coffee go on deck, where we sit till the sun drives us in. We then dress and are ready for breakfast at nine o'clock. During the day we read, write and otherwise occupy ourselves till towards five o'clock, when we dine, and afterwards go on deck. When the pinnace comes to, we land and ramble or sit on the shore till eight o'clock. Then we have tea, and busy ourselves till ten o'clock.'

She was entranced by everything she saw, especially the abundant plant life, the bell-like flowers of the *datura*, bright blue convolvulus, and purple, white and red balsams, the blossoms of which were laid as offerings at the various shrines they passed, 'and are afterwards thrown in the river, which I have seen quite enamelled with them'. Even the grasses by the banks of the river, the feathery heads of which 'presented in places a surface so unbroken, so unspotted as to look like a heavy fall of snow', were things of wonder, while the peculiar mode of growth of certain palm trees, which appeared to shoot, fully formed, from the ground, reminded her 'of Milton's idea of the fully formed animals rising out of the earth at their creation'.

She also proved to be surprisingly tough, soon making up her mind that the prevailing western views of 'the horrors of India' were vastly exaggerated, despite grappling with cockroaches, scorpions and even a huge centipede that hid itself in her slipper. Even Henry, a seasoned traveller, was impressed by his wife's resilience. 'At 11pm while you are snoring like a young rhinoceros, I again take up the book to testify how good a traveller you are, how courageous by land and water, and how gentle and forbearing to your cross husband,' he wrote in her journal on 13 October, one of the many playful, loving messages he would leave there for her to find.

After that blissful honeymoon journey, life in Gorakhpur, which they reached towards the end of October, seemed enervatingly dull, 'worse than a county town at home'. It became the new Mrs Lawrence's habit to accompany her husband on his surveying trips into the *mofussil* as often as she could. 'Every mile we advanced into the jungle I felt my spirits rise' reads her very first journal entry after leaving Gorakhpur on 1 November. 'All our annoyances seemed left behind, and my mind regained that tranquil elasticity which "in the crowd and bustle of resort" is much impaired. No mode of life could fill in with my tastes better than this does ... I would willingly take the inconveniences of a wandering life in consideration of its pleasures.'

This being India, the inconveniences were of course relative, and the Lawrences travelled with the usual complement of bearers and domestic servants, including their own smith, carpenter and bookbinder. India, she declared, was 'the land of lands for domestic enjoyment'. Camp life taught her how many so-called civilised things they could do without, including 'all scandal, all censure, all the deteriorating gossip which one despises, yet is led to join in' when living in a society, however small. There was, in addition, 'the fullest enjoyment of nature, perpetual change of air and scene'.

Over the next sixteen years Honoria was to follow Henry loyally. From Gorakhpur they were transferred to Allahabad, and then in 1839 on the eve of the First Afghan War to Ferozepur, on the border between British India and the Sikh Kingdom of Ranjit Singh, the still independent lands visited so recently by George Auckland and his sisters. In 1844 she accompanied Henry to Nepal, where he had been appointed British Resident, and in 1850 to Kashmir, both times becoming the first white woman ever to have travelled to those lands. She also lived for a time in Lucknow, where Henry was appointed Resident after the First Sikh War, and a few years later they moved yet again, to 'Rajputana' in present-day Rajasthan. As well as helping Henry with his work, and writing numerous articles and papers, during this time she gave birth to four children, one of whom died, and endured the anguish of sending off her eldest son Aleck – whose birth on one of their many moves had reduced her almost to despair – to live with relatives in England.

Although she was to live in various cities during her time in India, it was always in their more rural postings that she was happiest, and where their daily routine could be easily adapted to suit the punishing climate. One of her most vivid diary entries describes a typical day:

At 4 am the house is stirring. The children are called and before 5 they are washed, dressed, tea-ed, and out of doors. On the elephant go Honey, Mona, Billy and Marianne [her English neighbour's children], with *dhai* [nurse] and a *chaprassi* [running footman]. Harry and John go out for a ride if they like. Otherwise they play in our own grounds, harnessing a goat to a little carriage, working in the garden, visiting the stable or anything they like. After 6 they are confined to the western side where the tall house casts a shadow for many yards, where they play, but must be in the house before 7 ... At 8 Bell comes to teach the children, and lessons go on, interrupted by prayers and breakfast to 2. By 1, Harry's lessons are ended, and he too lies down for a siesta. One by one the children's attendants drop off, so that about 2 or 3 there is a lull over the house. After 3 little voices are heard again. 4 o'clock dinner. Then play till nearly 6 – go out again as in the morning – home soon after 7, tea and to bed. And the seniors do not sit up much later.[3]

The constant upheaval of transporting herself, her young family and all their possessions became a leitmotif of Honoria's life in India, as it would for many other women like her. The preparations for their journey to Kathmandu in 1844 involved a month of 'hurry skurry, bustle bustle', as she put it. '*This* we must take, *that* no-body would buy. What *shall we do* with these?'

Usually, it was easier to travel as lightly as possible, which meant selling most of their possessions, except for their clothes. 'Buying things dear because we must have them, selling them cheap because we must get rid of them ... and then trying to carry about some few household goods, the vexation of their arriving smashed, cracked, rubbed, bruised, drenched after jolting on miserable *hackeries* over unutterably bad roads, being dragged through streams of all imaginable depths and regaled with alternate showers of dust and rain. Such are the luxuries of Indian life.'[4]

Augusta Becher would have sympathised. She too spent long months on the road with her husband Septimus and his regiment, the Bengal Staff Corps, and would later calculate that in all her many years in India she had never lived for more than a year in any one place. In the *Personal Reminiscences* that she wrote in her old age at the request of her daughter Bess, she described the system in detail. 'The compulsory sale of one's goods and chattels were hard things on staff officers. The juniors, of course, felt it most. The things must go, and therefore prices had to be fixed far below their value, and the usual custom was to make the lists oneself, and send them round the station to every house by a *chuprassee*, and everyone put their names against articles they chose to purchase, and probably sent for it in a day or two, sending the money at the same time.'[5] Harriet Tytler, too, remembered the dispiritingly low prices. On one of their many moves they sold all their possessions in a similar auction. 'They were sold for nothing – my *palkee gharee* [palanquin] for five shillings, a child's pony for a shilling; my mother-in-law's antiquated carriage and a pair of horses also went for almost nothing.'[6]

The pinnace that was Honoria Lawrence's first introduction to travelling in India was a luxury compared to most of the other forms of travel then available. Travelling overland, particularly in mountainous regions, was always a much tougher proposition. As well as horses and elephants, together with a variety of carriages and buggies, other modes of transport considered suitable for women and small children included the *dhoolie*, a covered litter, and the *dandee*, a kind of hammock slung across a pole and carried by two men. Honoria Lawrence's first experience of this 'uncouth but most comfortable conveyance' was on her journey to Nepal in 1844. 'At first I felt rather as though I had been sewed up in a sack to be thrown into the Bosphorous,' she wrote, 'but I soon found how very easy a conveyance I was in.'

In 1851, Augusta Becher marched for three months from Lahore to Peshawar on the Afghan border with her husband's regiment, having given birth only a month previously. Even this was only possible by covering between twelve and sixteen miles a day. Mrs Becher, who was always an excellent traveller – 'A stirring life, and so happy!' – did not find it too much, 'but for the camels and numberless servants, and others who walked', including the foot soldiers, it was exhausting, since they rested only on Sundays, and at the large stations along the way.

For much of this time she and her tiny baby travelled in a palanquin or *palkee*, a long box-like contraption (some thought it alarmingly like a coffin) on poles, about six feet long and three feet wide, lined and stuffed with a mattress and pillows. It had sliding doors on each side, and little windows at either end. Eight bearers were required to carry each *palkee*. They worked in shifts, four at a time, each shift covering a distance of about ten miles (about three hours of travelling time). As they moved further north, the weather became colder, and Augusta Becher lined the palanquin with a sturdy felt called *numda*, and most nights took her baby to sleep with her, wrapped up in a thick quilt.

On top of the *palkee*, travellers provided themselves with a flat tin box containing everything they would need for the journey. Typically, these might include 'a change of clothes with all the dressing apparatus ... a box of tea, canister of sugar, ditto sago, teapot, plate, cup, saucer, knife, fork and spoon. A loaf of bread, cold fowl, pepper and salt, two pints of beer, a cork screw and metal tumbler, a candlestick and some wax candles.'

'Take care you have the medicine chest inside,' was Mrs Lawrence's advice. 'Oh, and don't forget to tie on the pole your little tin kettle, your brass *chilumchee,* or large basin, to wash in, your *lota,* or small brass cup, and, as you are not strong, you had better add a small *mora,* or light bamboo stool. Now are the *banghies* ready? Those tin boxes with pyramid shaped lids and wax cloth covers, which are slung in pairs at each end of a long bamboo that a man carries across his shoulders. Yes, all right ... Then just tie that roll of string to the palkee in case you want it, and now goodbye. But stop! You have left behind your little writing case. Well put it under the pillow, and now you are ready for a start.'[7]

On the Grand Trunk Road, the great artery that had connected Bengal to the Upper Provinces since ancient times, there were now '*dak* bungalows' positioned along the way, at a distance of ten miles (or one march) apart. These were kept up at the expense of the government for the convenience of European travellers. Here, for a rupee, you could lay up for twenty-four hours; or, for half that sum, take a three-hour rest in the middle of the day. Food was extra. 'There was not much choice,' remembered Harriet Tytler. 'A moorgee (fowl), or "sudden death" as they were called, was cooked either as a curry, grilled, or roasted. This, with rice kedgeree, dahl, boiled eggs or an omelette, constituted a dak bungalow menu.' She added: 'Bye the by, an omelette is never cooked to such perfection anywhere as by an Indian cook.'[8]

In the remoter areas, where no such *dak* bungalows existed, obtaining food could be a real problem. Harriet Tytler remembered one terrible forced march of fourteen days across Bengal in the heat of the summer, with her husband's regiment. They were obliged to cross three huge rivers, 'like seas', in one day. 'No one can conceive the difficulty of that march,' she wrote. 'The inhabitants of the villages, who had never seen a soldier, still less a white man, all ran away, leaving their villages deserted and empty, so that we had the greatest difficulty getting food en route.'⁹

Elsewhere on the subcontinent, where the roads were still almost non-existent, no amount of mattresses or cushions could make the journeys comfortable. 'Fancy yourself in a sieve shaken to try to send you through it, and occasionally receiving a smart jog to facilitate the process,' Honoria Lawrence wrote. 'Had it been possible to be ground small enough first, I am sure I should have been sifted out on the road at the first stage.' Whether they were travelling with their families, or alone, none of these women ever questioned their duty.

The absolute safety of this mode of travel was so well tried and tested, the trust in the bearers who carried them along so absolute, that no one doubted that even an unprotected woman could travel safely from one end of India to another. On first arriving back in India, and devastated to find herself a virtual orphan, eighteen-year-old Harriet Tytler's health broke down, and she was sent up to the hills for her health. At first she was chaperoned by a Mr Neave – 'a cranky old fellow' – but when her *palkee* pole broke (hoping to save on the cost of an extra bearer for her luggage, she had packed the litter too full) she persuaded him to go on without her. 'I was delighted with such freedom, for I was left entirely to my own devices,' she wrote later, 'but knowing the world as I do now, I have often wondered how my friends could have allowed me, a girl of 18, to travel a journey of 900 miles alone. It was an awful risk, but in those days the peasants of India would no more have thought of harming an Englishwoman than of flying.'¹⁰

It was not surprising that women felt so safe. To safeguard the security of their empire, by the mid-nineteenth century the East India Company had no fewer than three separate armies at its command, one for each Presidency. Each of these was made up of a mixture of troops: those raised and funded by the Company itself, and those making up regiments belonging to the British Army but now stationed in India.

By this time the Company had direct rule over about two thirds of the subcontinent (although, following Pitt's India Act of 1784, technically they did so as agents of the British government). The remaining third was ruled over by the Indian princes, but all of these had recognised Britain as the paramount power. They were advised by British Residents, political representatives of the Company, and their armies, many of which had been raised by the Company, were still commanded by its officers.

By this time the contradiction between the Company's dual role as ruler and trader had finally been removed. In 1833 the Act of Parliament that had renewed the East India Company charter had ordered the Company to cease all commercial transactions (in return for a sizeable annuity).

By far the greatest accumulation of territories had occurred during the late eighteenth and early nineteenth centuries, chiefly as the result of the many battles fought against the Maratha and Mysore Kingdoms. Since then, a number of wars fought by British India against their more bellicose neighbouring states had resulted in yet more acquisitions. Assam, Arracan and Tenasserim were acquired in 1824; Sind in 1843; the Punjab (the former Sikh Kingdom of Ranjit Singh) in 1849; and Pegu in 1853.

Yet more territories had been gathered together under the British yoke without resorting to actual war. This was done under the so-called 'Doctrine of Lapse', a questionable piece of pseudo-legalese dreamed up to prevent rulers of hitherto independent states from adopting an heir, should they have no 'heirs of the body' to succeed them. Without an heir, so the thinking went, the take-over of the state in question would be fully justified. The Doctrine of Lapse was used to great effect to justify the annexing of the state of Satara, the original Maratha principality in western India, in 1848; Sambhalpur in 1849; and Jhansi and Nagpur in 1854. The then Governor-General, Lord Dalhousie, revealed the 'cynical thinking behind such appropriations when he told a family friend that the huge state of Nagpur, with its annual revenue of £400,000 a year, was "too good a 'plum' not to pick out of the Christmas pie"'.[11] It was a system that would have cata-strophic consequences for the British.

At the time, however, Britain's occupying grip on the subcontinent seemed unassailable. With the expansion of their territories, the Company's Armies had grown accordingly. By 1857 their strength totalled 45,000 European and 232,000 Indian soldiers.

It was safe in the knowledge of this formidable fighting force that Augusta Becher, her two small children and her new baby made their way to Simla in the spring of 1857.

Mrs Becher had been a soldier's wife in India for eight years. She had a large acquaintance among her husband's military friends and their wives, and each year, like scores of other families, she took her children to Simla, in the foothills of the Himalayas, to escape the summer heat. It was a moment to be relished. 'How delicious again is the fresh air from the snow, and the sough and smell of those glorious pines' was her fond recollection, even a quarter of a century later.

If she had heard reports of the rumbling disquiet among the Indian troops over the introduction of the new Enfield rifle, and the rumours circulating that the cartridges had been greased with a mixture of pork and beef fat – one anathema to Muslims, the other anathema to Hindus – she paid them no heed. Just a month earlier, two hundred miles south in the British station at Meerut, there had been rather more than just rumblings.

Meerut had been established in 1803, forty miles from Delhi. It was a key military post, being the headquarters of the Bengal Artillery. The large cantonment there, which covered four miles of burning plains to the north of the city, was nonetheless known for its pretty bungalows, flower-filled gardens and healthy climate. As well as the usual barracks and parade grounds it included the Artillery School of Instruction, known as the Damdammah, at which the troops were instructed in the use of the new Enfield rifles.

In April that year there had been an incident in which a group of Indian sepoys had refused to fire the controversial new cartridges with which they had been issued, despite every assurance that they had not been greased with anything that could be objectionable either to Muslims or to Hindus. Eighty-five men were subsequently tried, found guilty and sentenced to ten years' hard labour.

The sentence was carried out on the morning of Saturday 9 May. The guilty sepoys were forced to stand in the blazing sun, in front of all the troops, while iron shackles were slowly and methodically hammered around their ankles – an operation that lasted two hours, 'each in turn loudly calling on his comrades for help, and abusing, in fierce language, now their colonel, now the officers who composed the court-martial, now the Government'.[12] 'They could not have hit upon a more severe punishment,' wrote Cornet McNabb to his mother, 'as it is much worse to them than death. It is in fact 10 years of living death. They will never see their wives and families, they are degraded, and one poor old man, who has been 40 years in the regiment, and would have got his pension, is now thrown back the *whole* of his service.'[13]

If Augusta Becher ever heard word of this incident, she does not mention it in her memoir. Instead her thoughts were full of the long summer holidays ahead, in the blissful cool of the mountains, picnicking with her friends in the beautiful Annandale valley nearby, attending concerts, amateur dramatics and gymkhanas with her friends.

Perhaps no single other place in India reflected the absolute confidence of the British in India at this time than Simla. Perhaps nowhere else were English life and English tastes so perfectly recreated. The first European house had been built there in 1819, and was first visited by a Governor-General in 1827. Soon after, the regular retreat into the hills had come to be considered a necessity during the summer months, and Simla became the government's principal summer seat. Just twenty years earlier, Emily Eden had written a description of a 'fancy fair' over which she and her sister had presided in the summer of 1838. It was, she wrote, 'more English than anything I have seen in this country' – almost more English, one feels reading it now, than anything in England itself.

The fete took place in the nearby valley of Annandale. Here, a long booth had been constructed for all the ladies who kept stalls, each one decorated with different mottoes or devices. 'The Bower of Eden' – so named in compliment to two First Ladies – was at the centre.

Before we came to the booth, there was a turnpike gate with a canvas cottage and an immense board, 'the Auckland toll bar,' and Captain P. dressed up as an old woman who kept the gate. On one side there was the Red Cow, kept by some of the uncovenanted, who spoke excellent Irish, and whose jokes and brogue were really very good. There was a large tent opposite the booth for G[eorge], and in every part of the valley were the private tents sent by careful mothers for their ayahs and children. There were roundabouts for the natives. W[illiam] O[sborne] and three of the aides-de-camp kept a skittle-ground, with sticks to throw at, and a wheel of fortune, and a lucky bag, which had great success. G[eorge] and F[anny] came soon after eleven, and the selling went off with great rapidity.

After a light luncheon there were organised games.

Captain D. was dressed up like an old woman, and Captain P. exactly like a thimble-rigger at Greenwich, and they kept everybody, even Sir G.R., in roars of laughter. It was very amusing to see the grave, pompous people, like R—, taking three rows for a rupee, and quite delighted if they knocked off a tin snuffbox or a patent stay-lace. Then we had pony races, which ended in Colonel F— riding his old pony against a fat Captain D—, and coming in conqueror with universal applause. And then, the sports having lasted from eleven to five, and everybody in a good humour, we all came home.[14]

1857, however, was very different from other years. At the beginning of May, when Augusta Becher arrived, there were already whispers that something was wrong. The bazaars were full of rumours: 'it was "in the air" as the natives said, and they all knew it'. But Mrs Becher was too busy with a sick child, Phil, from whose birth she was still recovering, and too delighted to be back in the cool of the hills to pay any of it much heed.

In 1857, Simla remained an almost ludicrously English enclave. That year the Bechers had taken 'Garden House' and many of their friends were staying nearby. 'We had the Chesters in the big house above us ("Strawberry Hill"). The Keith Youngs were in "Ellerslie" immediately above that. The Goughs had left India, and Colonel Congreve occupied their later house close by, and in our immediate group of "Garden Houses" were the Normans, Mrs Brind, and Mrs Olpherts.' 'Barnes Court', always reserved for the Commander-in-Chief of India, at this time General George Anson, was just above the Mall, about a mile away.

On 12 May the General gave a dinner to which Augusta and Septimus were invited, a party of about twenty people. For two days there had been 'great anxiety', she recalled, but no particular news had been forthcoming, and the dinner went ahead as planned. The guests had almost finished eating when a telegram was brought in. Augusta noticed that the General read it and then immediately put it under his plate. 'All felt there was something grave,' she would recall of that moment, 'and as soon as possible the ladies withdrew and waited in suspense while those left discussed the event.'

The telegram announced that the Native Cavalry at Meerut had 'broken out' on parade two days before, killing most of their officers. They had proceeded to the gaol and released the eighty-five prisoners from the sentencing on 9 May, before embarking on a killing spree in which many women and children had been attacked and brutally murdered. They then rode all night for Delhi, 'when on arriving at the city by daybreak they were joined by the city and other mutineers and massacred every living Christian in the town'.

The Indian Uprisings – known to the British as the Mutiny – had begun.

# PART FOUR

# THE UPRISINGS:

## 'Nothing has ever happened in the world like this'

*In which uprisings convulse the north of India, and the British pay the price.*

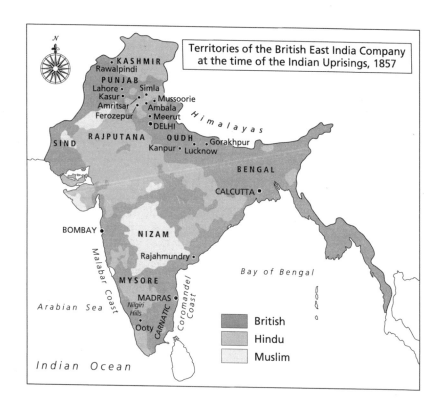

Territories of the British East India Company at the time of the Indian Uprisings, 1857

N

KASHMIR
• Rawalpindi
PUNJAB
Lahore •     • Simla
Kasur •     • Mussoorie
Amritsar •  • Ambala
Ferozepur  • Meerut
           • DELHI

RAJPUTANA    OUDH
                  • Gorakhpur
SIND         Kanpur • Lucknow

Himalayas

BENGAL

CALCUTTA •

BOMBAY •

NIZAM

Rajahmundry •

Malabar Coast

MYSORE

Arabian Sea

MADRAS •
Nilgiri Hills
• Ooty

CARNATIC

Coromandel Coast

Bay of Bengal

Indian Ocean

British
Hindu
Muslim

# CHAPTER 19

The next morning General Anson* ordered every man to rejoin his regiment immediately, and set off with them to the military garrison at Ambala. Over a thousand 'women, ladies and clerks' wives and numberless children' were left behind to shift for themselves: in Augusta Becher's words, 'a most helpless colony'.

The handful of men who remained, which included her husband Septimus, who had been left in charge of the Adjutant-General and Quartermaster-General's offices, were otherwise mostly tradesmen, clerks, and those who were too sick to move. Two safe houses were quickly organised, and for the following two nights the upper rooms of these houses were crammed with women and children. In the lower rooms the men, arming themselves against possible attack, kept watch. Although reports reached them that the bazaar was 'most unquiet', nothing happened. 'I went for one night,' Mrs Becher remembered, 'but the thing seemed so absurd I did not go again.'

If she had had any idea at all of the horrors that were going on elsewhere, she would not have been so sanguine. One of the orders Septimus had been given was to organise his own regiment, stationed at nearby Jutog, to join General Anson at Ambala. There seemed to be some inexplicable delays about getting them going, and so on the 15th he sent a messenger to Jutog to find out what was happening. The

*He died soon afterwards of cholera, although some, including Harriet Tytler, were convinced he had been poisoned.

messenger came back quickly 'in quite a fright', with the intelligence that the sepoys had seized their arms, imprisoned their officers, and were about to march on Simla. 'This, which of course was public news, was enough to light the smouldering fears of the last three days!'

That same day, her wedding anniversary, Augusta Becher was quietly finishing her lunch with her friends the Chesters when Septimus came in with a slip of paper from the regimental Colonel: 'They are looting the Bazaar; go!' There was no time to lose. Scooping up a handful of rupees, and some hats for the two children, she called to her ayahs and *jampannes* (litter bearers) and they fled the house at once. They were joined by their friends Mrs Olpherts, a bedridden invalid, and her sister Isabella, walking on foot beside her.

When they reached the banks of a nearby river, the ayahs, who had left their shoes behind, sat down and cried, and so they sent them back. But for Augusta and her three children, one of them a small baby, no turning back was possible. Wearing only the clothes she had been lunching in, the thinnest of muslin dresses ('with flounces!'), she was forced to cross and re-cross the river, until she was soaked to the waist, and her thin boots were almost destroyed. Septimus had his horse, but no saddle (which had been left behind in the scramble to get away), and sometimes she rode this astride, but for the most part she walked. All the while, from the first sounding of the alarm, they had the unnerving sight of groups of local Indians passing them, laden with everything they could carry – and running fast. It did not bode well.

The little party carried on up the narrow gorge of the river until it was too dark to carry on, so they lay down for a few hours to rest. In the middle of the night their messenger, Ganesh, who had been put on watch, came to them and whispered that he could see lights and a crowd of people heading their way. 'For the few moments that the alarm lasted,' Augusta wrote, 'I knew the feeling of having to face the possibility of death.' All she could do was sit still over her baby, her heart in her mouth. Apart from her fear that the infant's cries might alert the enemy, she could only think of one thing: 'to entreat

[Septimus] to keep one barrel of his little gun for me'. As it turned out, the 'enemy' was nothing more sinister than a 'great crowd of coolies' carrying one of their neighbours, Mrs Brind, and her family.

Elsewhere, the situation was far more serious.

On Sunday 10 May, two days before General Anson had received his telegram, it had been business as usual in the European parts of the Meerut cantonment, despite the stifling early summer heat. Few gave even a thought to the cruel fate of the eighty-five sepoys who had been sentenced the previous day. Eliza Greathead, the commissioner's wife, had told her fellow guests at a dinner the night before that she had heard rumours of placards being posted round the bazaar 'calling on all Mussulman's to rise and slaughter the English', but the news was received with 'indignant disbelief' and no more was said about it. Instead the conversation turned to the favourite topic of the day – the onset of the burning winds that presaged the arrival of summer.

For eighteen-year-old Kate Moore, whose brother was serving as the post-master at Meerut, the first intimations came from the clear agitation, amounting almost to panic, of their household servants. In the account that she later wrote, she remembered how their cook had begged her mother to keep the younger children inside that morning. Later that day, when they were preparing to go to the evening service at the cantonment church, St John's, the same man tried yet again to persuade the family to stay at home, but his entreaties were ignored. It was not until they were halfway to the church, to be met by an ashen-faced individual screaming at them to turn back, that it dawned on them that something was seriously wrong.

A mixture of confusion and disbelief greeted the first few hours of the Meerut Uprising. Mrs Dunbar Douglas Muter, the wife of a captain in the King's Royal Rifles, had already driven to church and was sitting unsuspectingly in her pony-carriage outside the door. The evening service was habitually preceded by a military parade – the parade ground was right next to the church – and Mrs Muter was expecting at any moment to hear 'the sound of a gay march which so strangely heralds the approach of a body of soldiers'. She listened in vain.

Instead, 'a dull sound, very different from that I expected, came over the stillness of Nature around'. At first she thought it was the sound of 'holiday-making' in the bazaars. It was only when the clock struck seven, and she realised that none of the rest of the congregation had arrived, that she gave the order for home. 'Up to this, I was seated with my back to the cantonment,' she wrote, 'but the moment the horses' heads were turned I saw the Native lines in a blaze, and, in some alarm, but not the least understanding the gravity of the position, I gave the order to hasten home.'[1]

As it very soon became clear, it was the gravest possible situation. Fifty *sowars* (mounted soldiers) from the 3rd Native Cavalry, together with an angry rabble of civilians from the bazaars, were marching together towards the European quarters to the north of the cantonment. The lull of that blisteringly hot afternoon turned into a scene of utter mayhem. 'Frightened people were running to and fro, and sounds of firing distinctly heard in the direction of the Sudder Bazaar (Sadar Bazaar) and native lines. Englishmen and ladies drove past for life, lashing their horses with fury.'[2]

Many of the Indian soldiers, already mounted on horseback, were 'careering wildly about, shouting and brandishing their swords, firing carbines and pistols into the air, or forming themselves into excited groups'. Others, on foot, were intent on setting fire to everything in their path. 'Burning bungalows sent their horrid brightness far up. Cattle sheds and Godown's Commissariat were blazing away ... Cattle were flying wildly about – torches, held by demon hands, lighted up the work of destruction and swords reeking with the blood of Europeans were flourished aloft by fiends, and shouts never before heard out of hell, rent the air. "Allah-I-Allah. Mare Feringhee!" [By the help of God, let us kill the Christians!]'[3] The mutineers had broken open the bells-of-arms, and seized as many weapons as they could carry.

Mrs Craigie and her friend Miss Mackenzie had been trotting down the road in the direction of the church when a furious, howling mob appeared on the road in front of them. A young English soldier was coming towards them just ahead of the crowd, running, as they soon realised, for his life. With incredible presence of mind they managed to haul him into the safety of their carriage (the crowd close enough to beat against it with their *tulwars*, some of these curved swords piercing right through the carriage roof) before turning it round and fleeing for home. Mrs Courtnay, the wife of the hotel keeper, was not so fortunate. She was later found in her carriage, hacked to death.

Some people, such as Eliza Greathead and her husband, had given way to their servants' entreaties and hidden themselves on their rooftop terrace. Mrs Craigie and Miss Mackenzie, having made it home to safety, were also protected by their servants. Their next-door neighbour, Charlotte Chambers, the beautiful and heavily pregnant young wife of an army adjutant,* who had only recently arrived in India, was not so lucky. Mrs Craigie could only watch in horror as the mob reached the Chambers bungalow and set fire to it. The stables, full of screaming horses, were the first to burn down, and soon the flames were leaping up the walls of the house too. Charlotte Chambers, 'delirious with fear', was trapped inside. Mrs Craigie ordered her servants to climb over their garden wall and get her out through the back veranda, but they arrived too late. The young mother-to-be was already dead, butchered with a meat cleaver: her throat had been cut and her unborn child ripped out of her belly and placed on her chest.

The Craigie bungalow, which at this point was the only one not on fire, was clearly next in line to be torched. Inside, the two women prepared themselves for what they were sure was a similar fate. They found Captain Craigie's three double-barrelled shotguns, and were trying with trembling hands to load them (the young dragoon they had rescued was in a 'state of nervous collapse' and unable to help them) when the same servants, with incredible tenacity, rushed through the gardens towards the mob, 'waving their arms and yelling

*Harriet Tytler, who came to know him during the siege of Delhi, reported that he was so devastated that he later 'went out of his mind' with grief.

at them to remember what sort of man was their master' ('the people's friend', they called him).*4

The new Enfield rifles were only ever the spark that would ignite the Uprisings. Rumours about the offensively greased cartridges – and for the most part they were only rumours, since in many places the cartridges were never issued – were manipulated to make it seem part of a British conspiracy to deprive the Bengal regiments of their religion and caste. In fact, the Indian troops had reached a tipping point long before. Disgruntled elements within the army had a long list of legitimate grievances, including pitifully poor pay, poor leadership, almost nugatory career prospects, and dangerously high levels of absenteeism from the British officers being among them.

By the spring of 1857 the Bengal Army† was ripe for rebellion. Among them was a group of conspirators – there were thought to be cabals within each regiment – who seized upon the issue of the cartridges as a way of inflaming these disgruntled elements into open revolt. 'Its infantry regiments, in particular, contained a significant proportion of malcontents who were seeking an end to British rule.'5 It was with this in mind that the Meerut soldiers now rode to the court of Bahadur Shah Zafar, the King of Delhi,‡ with the avowed aim of ousting the British, and restoring him as Emperor in their place.

On the morning of Monday 11 May, Harriet Tytler was sitting peacefully at home with her family in Delhi, little suspecting the events that were about to unfold. By this time she had been married to Captain Robert Tytler of the 38th Native Infantry for ten years. She had met him when she was just nineteen, very shortly after she

*Craigie's regiment remained loyal to him, as did many others. A dozen of his *sowars* who had volunteered to guard the two women arrived soon after and, throwing themselves off their horses like madmen, 'prostrated themselves before the ladies, seizing their feet, and placing them on their heads, as they vowed with tears and sobs to protect their lives with their own'.
†The rebellion was mostly confined to parts of northern and central India over which the Bengal Army had sway.
‡'King of Delhi' was the title conferred on the former Mughal emperors by the British in 1803.

had arrived back in India. Robert was ten years older than her, a widower with two small sons. Mrs Tytler would later claim that she had only married him because she felt so sorry for him. She was not in love with him (and was, in fact, in love with another man at the time) and he had proposed to her several times before she accepted. Fortunately, his persistence paid off and their marriage turned out to be an extremely happy one. 'Thank God I did, for he proved the dearest of husbands and my love for him grew day by day into earnest devotion.'

Despite her miserable childhood at the mercy of a sadistic aunt, Harriet Tytler had grown into an extraordinarily gentle and sympathetic young woman. She had become known as 'the angel of the regiment, and also the mother of it – I suppose the former from my love for the children and the latter because the young fellows used to come to me and beg of me to ask their young women to lunch, along with the boys, to give them a better opportunity of carrying on their little flirtations', she wrote in her memoir. 'Several of them did win their wives this way, but oh! how many of those are dead and gone.' She went on to have three children of her own with Robert (one died), and that May was expecting a fourth.

At the time that the Uprisings spread to Delhi, Harriet Tytler was nearly eight months pregnant. She and her family were living in the military cantonment to the north-west of the city, on the far side of a spine of rocks overlooking the city itself, known as the Ridge.

'The early morning was as usual,' she later recalled, 'every door being as one may say hermetically sealed to keep out the raging hot wind. Tattees* were fixed to the outer doors and watered.' The children had all been bathed, and had taken their breakfast with their French nanny, Marie. At about eight o'clock the couple sat down to their own breakfast. Their tailor was sitting at his work on the veranda nearby, and everything seemed quiet and peaceful. They were just finishing their last course (she would remember this detail vividly: it was

---

*Grass screens. When watered they were thought to lower the temperature by as much as 20°F.

melons) when the door flew open and the tailor 'rushed in with his hands clasped and in a most excited manner said, "Sahib, Sahib, the *fauj* [army] has come."'[6]

Robert set off immediately to see his Brigadier. His wife, who did not know what '*fauj*' meant, asked what the matter was. 'Oh! nothing,' he replied. 'Only those fellows from Meerut have come over and I suppose are kicking up a row in the city. There is nothing to be frightened about, our men will be sent to coerce them and all will soon be over.' In consequence, Harriet Tytler would remember being 'not much frightened', and remained unsuspectingly at home.

Her peace of mind did not last long. Later that morning her husband looked in on her briefly, telling her again that there was nothing to be frightened about, but soon after that it became clear that there was something very wrong. 'Servants running about in a wild way, guns tearing down the main street as fast as the oxen could be made to go', and, most alarmingly of all, 'Mrs Hutchinson, the judge's wife, without a hat on her head and her hair flowing down loosely on her shoulders, with a child in her arms and the bearer carrying another, walking hastily in an opposite direction to the guns. What could it mean?'

The person who had known immediately what it meant was Marie. When Mrs Tytler called her to see to the children, she found her 'shutting up under lock and key everything she could lay her hands on – even the clean clothes the washerman had brought in that morning were all locked up'.

'Madame,' she said, 'this is a *revolution*, I know what a revolution is.'

The same blind panic that had reigned in the streets of Meerut the day before now descended on Delhi. An order arrived from the Brigadier instructing all women and children to take shelter at Flagstaff Tower on the Ridge. Immediately there was a mad scramble for the carriages. As Augusta Becher would do several days later, Harriet Tytler fled from home in just the clothes she stood up in. Not only did she forget to order her carriage neither did she remember any hats or umbrellas with which to shelter either herself or her children, then aged four and two, from the burning sun.* With the help of friends she nonetheless reached the Tower, although 'the long caval-cade resembled more a funeral cortege than the living flying for their lives, but to some it was indeed a funeral march as they never saw the light of another day'.

Inside the Flagstaff Tower they were safe for a while, but the condi-tions there were so appalling it seemed like 'a Black Hole in miniature'. Temperatures that day are recorded as having reached 38°C (60°C in full sun). The tiny room, which measured just eighteen feet in diameter, was soon crammed with terrified women, children and their servants, making the already furnace-like conditions unbearable.† 'Many ladies were in a fainting condition from extreme heat and ner-vous excitement, and all wore that expression of anxiety so close to despair ... And oh! *how* hot,' Harriet Tytler later wrote, 'but we bore it all, believing as we did that it could not be for long.'

They were quickly disabused. The news soon reached them that in the city below a full-scale massacre of Christians – men, women, chil-dren, even babies – was taking place. 'My little boy Frank, only four years old, who evidently had heard the servants on the other side of the Tower were talking of how the rebels had killed the little children ... came to me crying bitterly, saying "Mamma, will these naughty sepoys kill my papa and will they kill me too?" He was a very blue-eyed, fair child. I gazed at his little white throat and said to myself, "My poor child, that little throat of yours will be cut ere long, without any power on my part to save you."'

Expecting an attack on the Tower any moment, the women helped pass arms and ammunition up to the soldiers now taking up their positions at the top of the Tower, but as they were doing so they heard 'a most sudden and awful explosion'. When they looked out, they saw a large white cloud billowing across the city below them, 'looking like

*The British in India were completely paranoid about the sun, which was as deadly as any disease. People regularly died from sunstroke.
†Their number included Brigadier Graves, and a large number of troops. The Brigadier's fatal delay in ordering a retreat was later severely criticised. 'By doing so he would have saved many a life that was lost, even of those in the Flag Staff Tower', Harriet Tytler observed.

a very long sheet, which gradually turned into a thick brown mass'. The magazine containing all the city's ammunition had been blown up. 'As you may imagine our hearts were filled more than ever with hopeless dismay and, at the smallest noise, my children would clasp me all the tighter and I myself felt, as I am sure everyone else did, that our last moment had come.'*

Quite soon after that Captain Tytler appeared, and a conversation ensued with his Brigadier, who seemed quite at a loss to know how to proceed. With only two guns, no water and no food, their chances of surviving there were nil. At that moment a bullock cart appeared: in it were the butchered bodies of all the officers of their regiment. Whether the corpses had been brought there out of kindness, or to intimidate them, Harriet Tytler said she never knew (she suspected the latter), but there was now a stampede, 'everyone rushing to their carriages to see who could get off the first'. The bullock cart with the bodies would remain at the Flagstaff Tower for several months, by which time only the skeletons of the murdered officers remained.

Only those who had carriages or horses stood any chance of surviving the retreat. One soldier who had neither was the severely injured Colonel Ripley, who was in any case too sick to move. 'I can never forget his poor death-stricken face,' Harriet wrote, 'and could realize his feelings of despair at coming to be with his comrades and then being left by them to his sad fate.' Those with no means of conveyance 'almost to a man met their deaths on the way.'

The plan of retreat that was eventually embarked upon would send the Tytlers first to Baghput, and from there to Meerut, the nearest military station to Delhi. It was a scene of utter confusion. The road before them was like 'a large fair that had suddenly broken up, carriages, horses, men running and screeching to each other in sad and awful confusion'. At one point they looked back, only to see that every bungalow in the cantonment behind them was on fire. 'It was a sickening sight,' Mrs Tytler wrote, 'knowing all we valued most was lost to

---

*In fact it had been blown up by the British, in an attempt to stop the rebels from getting their hands on its contents.

us forever, things that no money could ever purchase.' She would later estimate that they lost some £20,000 in money and goods, in those days a small fortune, 'but one absorbing thought of flying for our lives soon made us forget that which at any other time would have been an inconsolable trial'. Among the things whose loss she would most mourn was a lock of her dead child's hair.*

Compared to many of the other testimonies that were later written by fleeing Britons, Harriet Tytler's experiences were relatively bloodless. Nonetheless, her account of their escape – they made it eventually not to Meerut but to Ambala, a hundred and fifty miles away – reads like a thriller. When their overloaded carriage simply collapsed beneath the weight of too many passengers, and Captain Tytler's horse almost died of exhaustion, they walked, carrying the two children as they went. On another occasion, they narrowly avoided being duped and murdered by a band of armed men. For long periods the only water they could find to drink was 'greeny mire' from roadside pools, water so stagnant that Harriet Tytler had to close her eyes and hold her nose in order to drink it. Her husband became so footsore that eventually he simply threw his shoes away and walked in bare feet. Amazingly, they all survived.

Stories about those who had not managed to flee the city, almost all of whom were brutally slaughtered, would haunt the Delhi survivors for ever after. One particularly gruesome tale involved a group of forty women and children who were caught trying to make their escape. At first, having been promised their lives, they were imprisoned in the Red Fort, but a week later were brought out and threatened with a firing squad. One of the women, who had given birth just the night before, pleaded with the Nawab, the eldest son of the old King, for mercy.

'The Nawab said, "Let her speak,"' Harriet Tytler recounted. 'Poor thing, with her baby in her arms, she implored for all their lives saying,

---

*Small details such as this one make particularly poignant reading. Another woman, Mrs Wood, who was also robbed of everything she possessed, remembered seeing one of the looters wearing a pair of her white kid gloves.

"Oh Nawab Sahib, such a thing as killing poor helpless women and children was never heard of as being done by brave men." Upon hearing these words, the Nawab said, "Is that all she has to say," and gave the signal, but not before one of the soldiers had speared the new-born baby and thrown it up into the air, before slaughtering it in front of its mother's eyes. The rest were then immediately executed by firing squad.'

Having against all the odds made it to safety, less than a month later the Tytlers and their children were back on the Ridge again, this time with an army behind them.

With the arrival of the Delhi Field Force, as the army that now advanced on the city was called, many other refugees, in hiding until now, began to return to the city. Orders were given for the women and children among them to be escorted to Meerut, away from the fighting, by pad elephants.* Mrs Tytler, who was by now within days of her confinement, greeted the news with despair: in her advanced state of pregnancy she was sure that the journey would mean certain death for both herself and the baby. Her husband put the case to the new Commander-in-Chief, General Barnard,† and he agreed to let her stay (although her presence there during the subsequent siege was later much criticised).

Two days later, on 21 June, her baby was born on the back of the same bullock cart in which she had returned to Delhi. It was a dire situation: the infant was born with dysentery, and was not expected to live. Amazingly, he did. 'When out of immediate danger, the dear old doctor said, "Now Mrs Tytler, you may think of giving him a name."‡ Poor child, his advent into this troublesome world, a pauper to begin with, was not a very promising one. There he lay near the opening in the cart with only a small square piece of flannel thrown over him, with the setting moon shining brightly on him, with nothing but the sound of the alarm call and shot and shell for music to his ears for the rest of the siege.'

---

*These had straw mattresses thrown across their backs, rather than the more comfortable howdahs.
†He, too, died soon after, of dysentery.
‡She called him Stanley.

As if her situation was not already desperate enough, a week later the monsoon broke. At first Harriet thought the thatched roof of the cart might keep the water out, 'but instead it leaked like a sieve and in a few minutes we were drenched, baby and all, to the skin'. Fortunately her husband located nearby an empty bell of arms (a small circular building in which rifles were stored), and into this she was moved. Some straw was found to make some bedding for herself and the infant. 'I walked bare-footed with a wet sheet wrapped around my baby and went into the bell of arms,' she would recall, fully expecting that both she and the infant would die: 'But through God's mercy, we were none the worse.'

Mrs Tytler, her three children and the ever-pragmatic Marie now settled in to wait out the siege. Fortunately she was able to feed the newborn herself, but it was only with the greatest difficulty that she was able to find some material with which to make him a few crude petticoats. Clothes for herself and her two other children were impossible to obtain. Since they still had only the garments they had fled in more than a month previously, her life was now given over chiefly to darning, 'from morning to night, the little we possessed, to keep them from going to pieces'. When her petticoat was being washed, she would wrap herself in a sheet* until it dried.

A greater nuisance altogether were the flies, the numbers of which had doubled or even trebled in number 'from all the carcasses of animals and dead bodies lying about everywhere'. Their numbers drove everyone mad, so much so that the officers used to amuse themselves by laying a trail of gunpowder over one of the mess tables on which they had poured some sugar. They would then wait for the 'enemy' and when the whole table was swarming with flies would blow them up. 'The game [was] repeated, but it didn't seem to lessen the flies.'

Another pressing problem was how to keep her two older children occupied. It proved impossible to keep Frank, the four-year-old, in either the bell of arms or the bullock cart during the day, but the

---

*Captain Tytler had bought this luxury from the sale of a dead officer's property.

soldiers often played with him and kept him busy. Two-year-old Edith, who was delicate and given to fainting fits, and could not be allowed to run around in the sun, proved a much greater trial. 'At last a bright idea entered my head. It was rather a unique one, which was to scratch holes in my feet and tell her she must be my doctor and stop their bleeding. This process went on daily for hours. No sooner did my wounds heal, when she used to make them bleed again for the simple pleasure of stopping the blood with my handkerchief. But it had the desired effect of amusing her for hours.'

Although Harriet Tytler herself witnessed direct fighting on only one occasion, she and her children became quickly inured to the sound of battle below, even the little baby: 'If he had lain on a feather bed in a palace he couldn't have slept more soundly.' On one occasion a relative of her husband's, Captain Frank Willcock, came to join the force on the Ridge. He was paying a visit to Mrs Tytler in her bullock cart when a shell came over Flagstaff Tower, 'whizzing as it came along', until it fell behind the sepoy lines very close to where they were sitting. 'Poor Mr Willcock jumped up saying, "My God, what was that?" I replied calmly, "Oh! it's only a shell." He was so astounded at the indifferent way I took it that he repeated it at the mess, after which it became a byword in the camp. "Oh! it's only a shell."'

Although Harriet Tytler would later become famous as the only 'lady' to have been present during the siege of Delhi,* she was joined at one point by a Mrs Leeson, whose story was even more harrowing than her own. This woman had been smuggled into the camp by two Afghans, her rescuers, and was herself disguised as an Afghan boy, dressed in khaki clothes, when she arrived.

Mrs Leeson was a teacher who ran a small school in the city. During the massacre she had witnessed the murder of all her children, both her own and her pupils. Some of the King of Delhi's guards had

---

*Although it would always be referred to as the siege of Delhi, the events witnessed by Harriet Tytler did not amount to a true siege. From their camp on the Ridge, the Delhi Force controlled only the north-west perimeter of the city. The south-eastern approaches to the city remained open, and the mutineers inside the walls had access to supplies and reinforcements throughout.

shot at her as she was trying to escape, and she had fallen unconscious on to the ground. The same bullet that had wounded her also struck the baby she was holding, and he had been thrown from her arms. When she came to, it was to hear her aunt, Mrs White, calling out to her daughter, 'Kneel down my child and say your prayers before you die.' Then followed the retort of shot after shot, until the whole party was killed.

While this was happening, her little son of six and her daughter of three both crept over and cowered next to her on the ground. 'After [the soldiers] had butchered the rest of the family they came up to the little boy and cut his throat,' Harriet Tytler recalled. '[Mrs Leeson] told me she was quite sure he, being a highly nervous child, must have died of fright before the sword ever touched his poor little throat, as she never felt him even tremble.' They then took the little girl and cut her from ear to ear through her mouth. 'That poor child was some six hours before she died, all the time writhing away, in her agony, further and further from her mother till she heard one piercing shriek and then no more, so the mother supposed somebody must have killed her outright.' The baby, too, lay on the ground beside her 'moaning pitifully' until he died. Mrs Leeson, who had been left for dead, was conscious enough to witness the slaughter of her children but had been unable to move a muscle to help them.

# CHAPTER 20

Two hundred and fifty miles away, in Lucknow, another siege was now taking place, only this time it was the British who were trapped inside the city walls.

Lucknow, the capital of the recently annexed Kingdom of Oudh, was the jewel in the crown of British India. Almost everyone who went there fell under its spell. It was an enchanted city of 'palaces, minars, domes azure and golden ... long facades of fair perspective in pillar and column, terraced roofs – all rising up amid a calm, still ocean of the brightest verdure. Look for miles and miles away, and still the ocean spreads, and the towers of the fairy-city gleam in its midst. Spires of gold glitter in the sun. Turrets and gilded spheres shine like constellations.'[1] Even Honoria Lawrence, the least romantic observer of Indian life, had been entranced. It was, she wrote, 'a city of pleasures'. She described taking part in the festivities that had been organised to celebrate the arrival of the new Resident. The assembled company had sailed down a canal 'of exquisitely pure water' in a 'fairy ship that glides between hedges of roses'. It was as near as anything she had ever seen 'to realise my dreams of Arabian Nights and Lala Rookh'.

By 1857, however, the city was ripe for revolt. The annexation of the kingdom the previous year, made possible by Dalhousie's hated 'Doctrine of Lapse', had created 'an ocean of discontent' throughout the province. The fact that this was accomplished in peacetime – Oudh had always been loyal to the Company and had accepted a

British Resident there since the late eighteenth century – was particularly inflammatory and, while by no means the only cause of the Uprisings, was to play a major part in the events that were now unfolding.*

In May that year, Lucknow was swarming with hundreds of new British administrators, both military and civilian. Among them was Sir Henry Lawrence (he had been knighted in 1848), who had been made Chief Commissioner. His wife had not lived to see her husband's latest appointment, having died of rheumatic fever three years before. She had been expecting their fifth child. Henry, it was said, never really recovered from their loss.

Henry Lawrence knew that Lucknow was especially vulnerable to revolt. In addition to the iniquitous annexation, a significant proportion of the Bengal Army – as many as three quarters of all sepoys, according to one authority – were recruited from Oudh.'[2]

The Uprising in Lucknow broke out at precisely nine o'clock on the morning of 30 May. Five days earlier Sir Henry had given orders that all women and children living in the cantonments should take shelter at the Residency. This was the name given not just to the official dwelling of the former British Residents to Oudh, a magnificently colonnaded three-storeyed building dating back to 1780, but also to the compound attached to it. This contained a variety of buildings including a banqueting hall, treasury, hospital, church, storerooms and various other dwelling places spread over some sixty acres of ground. The entire complex had been built on raised ground overlooking the River Gumti, and was entered by a brick archway known as the Baillie Guard Gate.

The women had been prepared for such an eventuality for some time, keeping a set of 'necessaries' at hand. But they arrived at the Residency, after a short and fairly sedate journey in a series of carriages and buggies, to find a scene of utter confusion.

*As one Indian witness, Sitaram Pandy, would later admit, the 'seizing of Oudh filled the minds of the sepoys with distrust and led them to plot against the Government'. See Saul David, *The Indian Mutiny*.

It soon became clear that 'everything was being prepared within the Residency walls to sustain a siege', wrote Julia Inglis, 'cartloads of provision and grain, ammunition etc coming in continuously'. Outside the walls there was an unnervingly war-like scene: 'guns pointed in all directions, barricades and European troops everywhere'. Families who had arrived before them were already crammed into every available space. To add to her uneasiness they were told 'not to crowd too much together as the building was not very strong, and it was feared would not stand so great a pressure'.[3]

For all the war-like atmosphere around them, social hierarchies among the women were still preserved. As one of the 'burra mems' (*burrah* or 'great' memsahibs), Julia, later Lady Inglis, was given one of the better billetings at the Residency. Her husband, Lieutenant-Colonel (later Brigadier) John Inglis, commanded the 32nd Regiment. Even so the conditions were so oppressively hot and crowded that she soon took to sleeping on the roof with her children.

For a few days nothing much happened. The women settled in as best they could, and for a while were able to keep up a very British pretence of normality. 'Our party here is a very agreeable one,' wrote Maria Germon, the wife of a Captain in the 13th Bengal Native Infantry. 'We meet at *chota hazree* [early morning snack] and then after dressing, breakfast at ten – then have working, reading and music, (there are some good performers amongst our party), *tiffin* [luncheon] at two, dine at half past seven, and then the Padre [Mr Harris] reads a chapter and prayers and we retire.'[4] Several husbands visited their families, and some of the women were brave enough to venture out in the early mornings to check on their houses.

At the beginning of the siege, those who had fled to the Residency compound were relatively well provisioned, despite the rationing of essentials such as beef, mutton, flour, rice and salt, which were issued according to a fixed scale. These rations were then supplemented by whatever extras they had had the foresight to smuggle in with them. Henry Lawrence's financial commissioner, Mr Gubbins, and his wife, whose home was already within the Residency complex, were better supplied than most. Although even they were soon obliged to cut down their regular meals from three to two a day – 'A cold luncheon only was served, and we made an early dinner at four' – they were still cooked and served up by the usual battalion of servants.

Their well-stocked storeroom even provided the correct drinks. 'One glass of sherry and two of champagne or of claret was served to the gentlemen, and less to the ladies, at dinner. One glass of light wine, Sauterne, was provided at luncheon.' In addition to alcohol, they also had 'a few cannisters of preserved salmon, and a few of carrots, which were produced whenever we invited a friend from any of the other garrisons* to dinner'. At dinner, the chief luxury was rice puddings, 'of which two daily appeared on the table. The eggs for these were derived from a few poultry which we had managed to preserve; and the milk from goats and two cows belonging to our guests, which were half starved during the siege.' One cup of tea was made for each person at six in the morning, 'our English maid, Chivers, presiding at the tea table'.[5]

From the beginning of June, accounts of murder and mayhem in the surrounding localities began to arrive with awful regularity. On 3 June, Julia Inglis wrote: 'We received the sad news today that Captain Hayes, Mr Barber, and Mr Frayer, brother to Dr Frayer, have been murdered by their own escort. Mr Gubbins communicated the dreadful intelligence to Mrs Hayes; and in the evening, finding that Mrs Barber was still in ignorance of what had occurred I asked Mr Polehampton [the chaplain] to break it to her. She had only been married three months. Captain Hayes left 5 children. This was a very, very sad day.'

On 8 June, news came from Cawnpore (Kanpur) describing the garrison there as being in great distress. 'We felt deeply anxious about them,' Julia Inglis wrote. 'There were three officers in Lucknow whose wives were in Cawnpore. One, Captain Evans, was in our house and his wretched face used quite to haunt me. He seldom spoke.' The horrifying events that would take place there later that summer were, as yet, an undreamed-of nightmare.

*Each building within the Residency compound was considered a separate garrison during the siege, each with its own share of fighting men and arms.

Of more immediate concern was the plight of the large numbers of fugitives from elsewhere who were now arriving on an almost daily basis. Many of them were injured, or suffering from heat stroke; others, who often had only the clothes they stood up in, were simply traumatised by the events they had witnessed. Throughout there was a sense of utter shock that 'their' troops should have betrayed them.

One of these refugees was Kate Bartrum, a twenty-three-year-old Somerset girl, the wife of Assistant Surgeon Robert Bartrum. She and her little boy Bobbie, and her friend Mrs Clark, had made their way from the remote station of Gonda, near the Nepalese border, to Lucknow. They had travelled the perilous seventy miles by elephant, seeking refuge in Lucknow on 7 June. They were shown to a tiny little room which they would share with thirteen other fugitives. Mrs Clark, who was shortly expecting her confinement, joined her there a few days later, with her eldest child, a little boy called Teddie.

Kate Bartrum watched the health of the two children anxiously. Within a matter of a few weeks she observed that Teddie was beginning to look sickly; her own child, Bobbie, was still healthy, but the lack of food was beginning to tell. Unlike the Inglises and the Gubbins, with their relatively plentiful supplies, not only did Mrs Bartrum and her party lack food, but also any means to cook the little they did have. Within a short time their servants had all deserted them. 'Our little ones used to be so hungry,' She wrote; 'many a time did Baby look up in my face and say "dinner, Mama", when I had no dinner to give, or food of any kind, that was fit to give him.'[6]

As it had been for Harriet Tytler on the Ridge in Delhi, one of the most intractable problems for Julia Inglis was the sheer boredom of waiting out the siege. 'Our life was a most wearisome one; the heat was very great. It was impossible to read much; but we occupied our time in making clothes for the refugees, and this employment was a comfort to us.' Sometimes she and her friend, Mrs Case, the wife of Colonel Case, visited the sick or injured, and on more than one occasion had to break the news to some poor woman that her husband had been killed. Mrs Case was noted for her 'sanguine and cheery'

Portrait of Henrietta Clive by Sir Joshua Reynolds, 1777. Leaving her husband, the Governor, behind her in Madras, in 1800 Lady Clive embarked on a journey of over a thousand miles around southern India. Her entourage comprised more than 750 people, including her two daughters, their Italian music teacher, a piano and a harp. Henrietta Clive was an avid collector of plants, seeds, minerals and even insects, some of which are preserved to this day in the National Museum Wales.

Madras Landing, 1837, engraved by C. Hunt after a drawing by J. B. East. The terror of navigating the surf when landing at Madras was commented on by many women, who were obliged to be carried to shore on the back of 'a wet, slippery, and half-naked fisherman' – a double trauma for some new arrivals. Although this painting shows a scene of relative calm, during rough weather when the 'black surf' was up, people were regularly injured, sometimes even killed, by the force of the waves.

By the early nineteenth century there was little in the way of British luxuries that could not be bought in the new 'Europe Shops' that were to be found in the three Presidencies of Calcutta, Madras and Bombay.

Portrait of Warren and Marian Hastings, by Johann Zoffany, c.1784. The German-born Anna Maria Apollonia Chapuset was the second wife of the first British Governor General of Bengal. As a divorcee, the 'Lady Governess' was considered something of an adventuress by the hypocritical British – many of whom at this period were busy making vast fortunes through corruption and embezzlement – largely on account of her flamboyant wardrobe and expensive jewellery. One satin riding habit, trimmed with diamonds and pearls, was alleged to be worth £30,000.

The Impey Family in India, by Johann Zoffany, 1783. As well as being a patron of the arts, Maria Impey was a talented natural historian. She kept extensive notes about the habitat and behaviour of Indian birds and animals, many of which were housed in the menagerie she created in the grounds of her house in Calcutta. Shown here with three of the four children she bore while in India, she had been forced to leave her four older children behind in England when she accompanied her husband, Sir Elijah Impey, to Bengal: a common practice which nonetheless caused some women to become profoundly depressed.

In Britain, the profession of milliner had long been synonymous with that of prostitute, as the lascivious look in this customer's eyes suggests. In India, however, a variety of economic opportunities opened up for women of all classes. As well as successful (and genuine) milliners, they worked as bakers, confectioners, actresses, boarding house keepers, portrait painters, teachers, governesses, ladies' maids, female companions, doctors, nurses, and even traders and merchants. By the late eighteenth century, 16 per cent of EIC shares were owned by women.

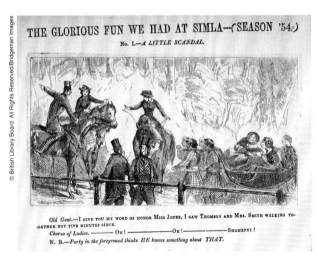

Of the many Himalayan hill stations created by the British, Simla was the most prominent. By the early nineteenth century, it had become the government's principal summer retreat. With its gymkhanas, amateur theatricals, 'fancy fairs' and, of course, flirtations and gossip, it was, wrote one observer, 'more English than anything I have seen in this country'.

The Uprisings of 1857, known to the British as The Mutiny, are now widely thought of as India's First War of Independence. Fighting first broke out at Meerut, the headquarters of the Bengal Artillery, on an otherwise sleepy Sunday afternoon, 10 May 1857. Despite the atrocities committed on that day, many servants and some Indian sepoys went out of their way to protect British families from the mob.

The shattered Residency at Lucknow after the siege. Lucknow, the capital city of the recently annexed Kingdom of Oudh (Awadh), was considered the 'jewel in the crown' of British India, which in 1857 was still controlled by the East India Company. The siege of the British Residency, which lasted from May to October, left many hundreds of women and children dead, not only from shell shot, but also from cholera, dysentery, scurvy and malnutrition.

*In Memoriam*, by Sir Joseph Noel Paton, caused a sensation when it was first exhibited at the Royal Academy in 1858. The massacres at Cawnpore (Kanpur), particularly that of the 73 women and 124 children held captive in a house known as the Bibighar, had become a collective trauma for the British in the wake of the Uprisings. Their reprisals against Indians – whether or not they were guilty of collaborating with the 'Mutineers' – were every bit as brutal.

After the debacle of the Uprisings, in 1858 the East India Company was stripped of its powers and disbanded. Control of its Empire – from now on known as the Raj – was transferred to the British Crown, represented by the newly created positions of Viceroy and Vicereine. The Imperial Assemblage of 1877, just outside Delhi, at which Queen Victoria was formally declared Empress of India, was attended by a hundred thousand guests.

Despite the deep scars left by the Uprisings, for most memsahibs life went on much as before. Women and children, sometimes very young ones, were regularly entrusted into the sole care of servants or bearers, often travelling hundreds of miles 'up country', with no more than their names and address on a piece of paper (and in at least one case, not even that).

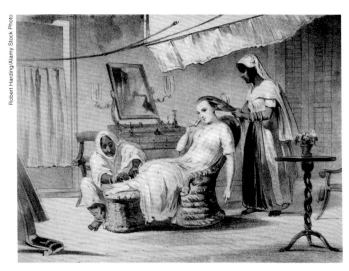

A young woman at her toilette, being 'shampooed' (massaged) by her Indian ayahs. In all eras, India offered women endless opportunities for re-invention. Those of modest, and even working-class, backgrounds often found themselves with fine houses, carriages and dizzying numbers of servants at their command. Sometimes their newly elevated social status went to their heads.

temperament, and as someone 'who always looks on the bright side and raises everyone's spirits': a valuable friend in those dark times.

For Kate Bartrum, the lowly wife of a surgeon, siege life was proving very different. In the tiny, stifling room all her time was spent in 'nursing, washing clothes, cups and saucers, fanning away flies, which have become a fearful nuisance, and cleaning the rooms, for most seem too ill mentally and bodily to care whether things are clean or dirty'. She did not mind that others laughed at her for being a maid of all work, 'for never was an independent and energetic spirit needed more than now'. Not for her were the moments of reprieve such as the ones Julia Inglis had time to take, walking on the rooftops of the Residency to enjoy the cooler air and beautiful views, when 'everything looked so calm and peaceful, it was difficult to think it could ever be a scene of war'.[7]

Only too soon it was exactly that. By the end of June, the enemy were only eight miles away, near the town of Chinhut (Chinhat). On 30 June a force of British and Indian troops led by Sir Henry Lawrence was soundly routed. First, the native cavalry had deserted their officers, quickly followed by the native artillery. It was a devastating setback. Rousing herself from her sickbed (she was recovering from smallpox) to watch from the Residency windows, Julia Inglis witnessed 'the greatest excitement and consternation' as the wounded soldiers returned. They came straggling back in twos and threes, 'some riding, some on guns, some supported by their comrades'. The enemy were now close enough for her to make out large groups of them on the banks of the river opposite and see the sinister flash of their muskets. 'A few minutes afterwards John came in, he was crying; and, after kissing me, turned to Mrs Case, and said, "Poor Case!" Never shall I forget the shock his words gave me, or the cry of agony from the poor widow.'

There was little time to mourn. The British losses were catastrophic: 365 men were reported either killed, wounded or missing. With the rebels at the door, the defence of the Residency now began in earnest. The compound, always dangerously overcrowded, was by now full almost to bursting point. Altogether three thousand people are estimated to have taken refuge there at the beginning of the siege, including 1280 women, children and their servants. On that first day, 30 June, Julia Inglis described how shot flew so thickly outside the walls that it was impossible even to think of venturing outside for air or exercise. Gone were the pleasant evenings of reprieve, taking the air on the rooftops. Before long she realised that it was too dangerous even to remain in their relatively comfortable quarters in the upper storey of the house (it was later completely demolished by a shell), and she and her family took refuge instead in one of the small underground rooms, where they remained all day, listening to the musketry fire outside.

The following day, 1 July, the fighting was heavier still. Early that morning 'John came in and told us we should soon hear heavy firing,' Julia Inglis wrote in her diary; 'his words were verified, and in a few minutes the cannonading and musketry firing were most terrific.' A Miss Palmer had one of her legs blown off by a roundshot. It took her two days to die. On 2 July there was consternation when Sir Henry Lawrence was fatally wounded by a shell from the howitzer they had lost at Chinhut. His thigh bone and pelvis were shattered beyond hope of recovery, and he died some days later, 'after suffering fearful pain, which he bore nobly', still wearing the miniature of his wife Honoria around his neck.*

At the height of the bombardment, although they were hardly able to breathe from fear, Julia Inglis and her friend Mrs Case read prayers to one another, trying not to imagine the terrible death that would befall them if the enemy managed to breach the walls. They later discovered that they had only been saved on that particular night because of the wholesale looting of the city of Lucknow that took place that evening. 'We heard the dreadful shouting and screaming in the city,'

---

*One of the survivors of the later Cawnpore massacres, Amy Horne, or Haines, who was taken into captivity by an Indian *sowar*, recounted what she overheard her captors saying about the British. 'The only man for whom they had any respect was Sir Henry Lawrence,' she wrote; 'they would have spared his life when they took the Residency. And that while he lived they were afraid to build their hopes too high!' See the *Narrative of Amy Horne*.

Julia Inglis wrote. 'Afterwards we learned they had been plundering and committing the most dreadful atrocities.'

The day after Sir Henry's death came a different kind of noise altogether: the jubilant celebrations as the twelve-year-old Birjis Qadr was crowned King of Oudh.

From now on, the women who had taken shelter within the Residency walls found themselves under constant fire, both day and night. Casualties were frequent, even within the relative safety of the compound. 'Mrs Dorin killed today at the Gubbins's house; she was helping to carry some things upstairs, when a very small bullet struck her in the forehead and went through her head, causing instantaneous death.' Julia Inglis herself narrowly missed being killed by a fragment of one of their own shells, which had recoiled and fallen inside the entrenchments. 'This evening I was standing outside the door with baby in my arms, talking to the ayah, when I felt something whiz past my ears,' she wrote on 23 July. 'I rushed inside, and when my alarm had subsided, ventured out again to discover what it was. I found a large piece of shell embedded about ten inches deep in the earth. It had fallen on the exact spot where I had been standing.' The soldiers were now sleeping with their arms next to them, so that their throats were not cut in the night.

Even under this most desperate of situations, some aspects of life went on with surreal normality. Unlike the overworked Kate Bartrum, many women still had numerous servants with them,* who would stay loyal to them throughout. Julia Inglis and her husband were able to breakfast and dine together every day. This was despite the fact that their rations were now down to a pound of meat and a pound of flour per man, and three quarters per woman. Very little else was procurable, 'no bread, butter, milk, eggs, wine, beer or tobacco'. Vegetables were a distant memory for everyone, no matter what their rank.

The Inglis family had access to an outhouse, considered a great luxury, but even then it was only with the greatest difficulty that they

---

*It was considered an extraordinary fact that 'several ladies have had to tend their children, and even wash their own clothes, as well as to cook their scanty meals entirely unaided'. See N. A. Chick, *Annals of the Indian Mutiny*.

were able to keep themselves clean. The flies continued to be a terrible torment to everyone. 'They covered our tables, filled our dishes and cups, and prevented the children getting rest during the day. Every kind of insect, fleas etc, abounded, and rats and mice ran about the room in broad daylight, the former of an immense size.'

Perhaps worst of all, however, was the appalling stench from the dead bodies that had not been properly buried, and also from the carcasses of animals. As the siege progressed and their supplies of food began to run out, scurvy or 'garrison disease' also took hold, causing loose teeth, swollen heads and painful eruptions under the skin.

There were daily fatalities. Even in rooms where it was thought it would be impossible for a bullet to penetrate, women and children were regularly shot dead. At one point, a large section of the Residency simply collapsed in on itself. With the increasingly cramped living conditions, sickness and disease became killers too, with deadly outbreaks of cholera, smallpox and dysentery. Almost everyone suffered from excruciating boils.

As ever, children were especially vulnerable. On 14 August Julia Inglis wrote: 'A poor woman, Mrs Beale by name, whose husband, an overseer of roads, had been killed during the siege, came today to ask me to give her a little milk for her only child, who was dying for the want of proper nourishment. It went to my heart to refuse her; but at that time I had only enough for my own children, and baby could not have lived without it. I think she understood that I would have given her some if I could.'

In Kate Bartrum's tiny room, people began to die. The first to go from their 'little band' was Mrs Hale, who died of cholera, leaving a little daughter, Katie, behind. The second, just two weeks later, was Mrs Thomas, who was taken by smallpox. She too left a little girl who looked 'as if she would not long outlive her'. On 20 July Mrs Clark gave birth to a baby girl. The labour was mercifully short, but the mother was so weak she was unable to nurse the newborn. The only thing Kate Bartrum had to give either was a little arrowroot mixed with water. By now all their children were ailing in some way. 'This was a time of distress which it is impossible to describe.'

Two days later it became clear that Mrs Clark was sinking fast. Not only was she physically weak, but her mind had also begun to wander. 'She tells me to come and sit beside her for she has much to tell me,' wrote Kate Bartrum in her diary. 'She fancies her husband is dead, that she shall soon see him ... I have been listening to her for most of night – and she frequently exclaims: "Lighten my darkness, I beseech thee, Oh Lord!" This is dreadful and I can do nothing for her. She takes no notice of little Teddie or Baby; both these little ones are suffering for want of proper food ... the baby *cannot* live.'

A week later Mr Harris, the chaplain, was sent for, who said prayers and baptised the baby. On 30 July Mrs Clark died, followed two days later by the infant. Teddie died in his sleep soon after.

Kate Bartrum had no time to mourn her friend and her two dead children. Bobbie now contracted cholera and she was told that he could not live. Although he was barely conscious, she nursed him feverishly, giving him brandy and opium at ten-minute intervals. Bobbie gradually recovered, but at this point his mother was taken ill too. 'Oh! the intense misery of that time,' she wrote. 'No husband near, my child so ill, and no-one to nurse him, and I almost too weak to do anything.' But 'God took pity on me and spared me for Baby's sake'.

By 8 August, when she was next able to write in her journal, Kate Bartrum recorded that there were only three of them left in the once overcrowded room. They looked at one another 'as if to say, "who will be the next to go"'.[8]

One day, one of the other women, Mrs Martin, asked Julia Inglis the question which was now on everyone's minds: whether, in the event of the enemy getting in, 'self-destruction' would be justifiable. She answered that she thought that should that ever happen, God 'would put it into our hearts how to act'. Nonetheless, several of the ladies were known to keep a supply of poison at hand.* There were

*In Delhi, Harriet Tytler, too, kept a bottle of laudanum close by her at all times, if the worst should happen: 'I quite made up my mind to give each of my children a good dose and drain the bottle myself, telling my husband to avenge our deaths until he dropped himself.'

several suicides, including that of Captain Graham, who shot himself in the head, leaving his young widow behind to fend for herself.

By the middle of August their situation was truly desperate. John, now Brigadier Inglis, and chief commander at Lucknow, showed his wife their method of getting messages over enemy lines: a very small paper rolled up into a quill, less than an inch across and sealed at both ends. The letter inside was written in Greek, so that if it fell into enemy hands they could not read it.

On 15 August, one such message reached them. The long-awaited relieving force was now at Mungulwar, and was expected to be with them in four days. Since their numbers were very few, the instructions now came that the Brigadier was to cut his way out of the Residency to join them. It was an impossible request. Not only was his weak and shattered force in no condition to leave their defences, but he was also further hampered with 'upwards of 120 sick and wounded, and at least 220 women and about 250 children, and no carriage of any description'. Their provisions could only last another month at best.

On 28 August, after two more weeks of waiting, news came that relief would not now come for another twenty-five days. 'My first thoughts were, "All is over with us; we can't hold out till then,"' Julia Inglis wrote.

Somehow, they staggered on. On 23 September, 'the sound of distant guns struck my ear', Julia Inglis recorded, 'and I shall never forget the thrilling sensation of hope and joy that filled my heart. Each boom seemed to say, "We are coming to save you."'

24th September: Distant guns were heard during the day ... I could not sleep from excitement and anxiety.

Friday 25th September: A day never to be forgotten. Heavy firing all round, and towards the middle of the day our relieving force could be descried. It was evident they were having a hard struggle, though the enemy could also be seen leaving the city in large numbers, swimming the river and crossing bridges ... John had ordered us to remain in the room at the end of the court, and not to let the children out. It was almost impossible to remain quiet ...

At 3pm John told us that hard fighting was going on near the bandstand, not far from our houses. At 6pm tremendous cheering was heard, and it was known our relief had reached us.[9]

Soon after, 'a short, quiet-looking, grey-haired man, who I knew at once was General Havelock' came in, accompanied by her husband. 'He shook hands with me, and said he feared we had suffered a great deal. I could hardly answer him,' Julia Inglis wrote. 'I longed to be with John alone, and he shared my feelings, for erelong he returned to me, and never shall I forget his heartfelt kiss as he said, "Thank God for this!" Yes, we were safe, and my darling husband spared me.'

Kate Bartrum, too, was about to be reunited with her husband. She also had heard the 'almost overwhelming' noise, confusion and cheering that greeted Havelock's troops. Taking Bobbie in her arms, she rushed to the Baillie Guard Gate, 'watching the face of everyone that came in'. She was told that her husband was indeed with the incoming troops, but the heavy artillery that he accompanied would not be there till the next morning. 'I could not sleep that night for joy at the thought of seeing him so soon.'

The next morning she was up at daybreak. Like many other women, she had kept one clean dress ready for the occasion, both for herself, and for her child. It was good news. 'I ... met Mr Freeling who told me that dear Robert was just coming in, that they had been sharing the same tent on the march, and that he was in high spirits at the thought of meeting his wife and child again,' Mrs Bartrum wrote. 'I waited, expecting to see him, but he did not come, so I gave baby his breakfast and sat at the door to watch for him again full of happiness. I felt he was so near me that at any moment we might be together again.'

She watched for him all day. In the evening, she went up to the top of the Residency, from where she could get a good view of the road, 'but I could not see him coming and returned back to my room disappointed'.

The following day, 27 September, she watched again, this time with a heart 'growing very sick with anxiety'. That afternoon Dr Derby came in to visit her. 'He looked so kindly and sadly into my face, and I said to him, "How strange it is that my husband has not come in!" "Yes," he said, "it *is* strange!" and turned and went out of the room. Then the thought struck me: Something has happened which they do not like to tell me! But this was agony too great almost to endure, to hear that he had been struck down at our very gates. Of this first hour of bitter woe I cannot speak ... My poor little fatherless boy! Who is to care for us now, baby?'

Robert Bartrum had been just stepping into the courtyard at the entrance of the Baillie Guard Gate when he was struck in the temple by a stray bullet. Falling across the body of his companion, he died instantly. His body was never recovered.

The hysteria and jubilation at their relief was short-lived. Havelock's forces were not sufficient to enable the women and children to be escorted out of the ruins of Lucknow safely, and they would be trapped inside for at least another month. With the relief forces came other, even less welcome news. Among the many atrocities that had been taking place around them, none were so terrible as the accounts that now reached them of what had happened at Cawnpore. As one witness wrote at the time: 'Nothing has ever happened in the world like this.'[10]

# CHAPTER 21

Cawnpore (Kanpur), on the banks of the River Ganges, lies just forty-five miles from Lucknow. At the time of the Uprisings it was one of the largest British stations in India. It was also one with the smallest ratio of British to Indian troops (outnumbering them by seventeen to one). Living here, and a friend to many Britons in Cawnpore, was Nana Govind Dhondu Pant, known familiarly as the Nana Sahib, the adopted son of Baji Rao II, the last Peshwa of the Maratha Confederacy. Like the adopted son of the King of Oudh, the Nana Sahib too had been deprived of his inheritance under Dalhousie's Doctrine of Lapse.

At the beginning of June, at the outbreak of hostilities in Cawnpore, the commanding officer, Major-General Sir Hugh Wheeler, had ordered all women and children to seek refuge in two large barracks in an open space at the centre of the cantonment. The barracks were surrounded by a hastily thrown-up three-foot-high mud wall, known as Wheeler's entrenchment. It was pitifully exposed, scarcely bullet-proof, and was never meant to withstand any kind of siege. But this is what the nine hundred people who now took refuge in this tiny space were about to endure.

On 6 June, the Nana Sahib sent General Wheeler a polite letter, informing him that the attack on the entrenchment would commence at ten o'clock that morning. Amy Horne, the eighteen-year-old step-daughter of an agent with the North-Western Dak (Mail) Company, who was living in Cawnpore with her mother and numerous young siblings, later wrote this rare first-hand account of the bombardment:

> The site of our entrenchment was surrounded by large and substantial buildings from three to eight hundred yards distant, occupied by the rebels, and from roof and window, all day, a shower of bullets poured down upon us in our exposed position. Shell likewise kept falling all over the entrenchment, and every shot that struck the barracks was followed by the heart-rending shrieks of the women and children, who were either killed outright by the projectiles, or crushed to death by the falling beams, masonry, and splinters. One shell killed seven women as it fell hissing into the trenches and burst. Windows and doors were soon shot off their sockets, and the shot and shell began to play freely through the denuded buildings.[1]

Over the three weeks that followed, their situation became increasingly desperate. At its greatest intensity, the shots were fired approximately every eight seconds. 'The agonies we endured during the siege are indescribable,' Amy Horne would remember. It was not only the fire from the heavy guns now fixed on the entrenchment, but the blistering June heat that made conditions unbearable (the highest temperature during that time was said to be 138°F, or 59°C).

The lack of food and water also caused them unbelievable distress. The only supply of water was from a single well, 'which soon became the target of rebel artillery, and it was only at risk of life that water could be drawn'. Despite the danger, men would still make dashes to it, 'rather than see us perish from thirst'. So great did their thirst become that on one occasion they gladly drank water that had been contaminated with human blood. It had seeped into their vessel 'from the wounds of a native nurse ... who, while standing near by, had both her legs carried away by the bursting of a shell'.

Soon, it was clear that they were running out of food, too. 'Our last meal was a horse, which was lying wounded. His flesh was converted into soup, and many cheerfully partook of it.' Others, including Amelia Horne's little siblings, 'poor wee things', were by this time close to starving, and would by this stage have eaten even 'the most loathsome thing' if it had been served up as food. Mrs White, the wife of a private and the mother of baby twins, had both elbows shattered by the same shot that killed her husband, who had been standing next to her. Unable to hold her babies, she was reduced to lying on the filthy floor, a child at each breast, in a desperate attempt to suckle them. Both mother and babies died soon after.

Sickening spectacles such as this could now be witnessed on an almost daily basis. General Wheeler's injured son, also a soldier, had his head blown off by a roundshot. Two little girls, aged eight and nine, had been left by their parents in the safety (or so they thought) of an inner room, when a shell came through the roof and exploded. The parents' agony, when they came back to find that all that was left of their children was 'bones, brains and flesh' which were strewn all over the floor, 'and not a step could you take without treading on some portion of their remains', is hard to imagine.

The same went for Lydia Hillersdon, the pregnant wife of the Collector, a 'sweet, calm, gentle woman' who was much loved for her many attempts to soothe and help those around her. Days from giving birth, she witnessed her husband's death by a roundshot which hit him full in the stomach, splattering her from head to foot with his bloody entrails. She too lost her life only days later when a cannon ball hit the inner veranda where she was lying, and buried her in rubble (one account claims she was in labour at the time). They managed to haul her out, but her skull had been crushed, and both she and her half-born child died within hours.

By this time, so many horrors had been witnessed that they became to some degree inured to them. Decorum and etiquette, once so highly prized, were things of the past. Most of the women were now dressed in little more than rags, their dresses having been torn up to make bandages. Amy Horne often woke up to find an exhausted soldier sleeping next to her on her *charpoy*.

And so the horrors went on. On 12 June, the thatched roof of one of the barracks which was being used as a makeshift hospital caught fire, causing pandemonium among the two hundred women, children and injured who were sheltering there. Both Amy Horne and her mother were hit on the head by falling debris; her little five-year-old sister had her leg fractured, and their ayah had 'half of one foot torn off'. In the same fire their entire stock of medicine was destroyed.

As at Delhi and Lucknow, the stench from dead bodies and the accompanying plague of flies were unbearable. According to Amy Horne's account many of their number had by now 'lost their reason', her own seven-month-pregnant mother among them. 'I used to sit and listen to her ravings, muttered in broken sentences. Her one theme was her mother whom she wanted to see. At one moment she would be calling for a conveyance to take her to her mother, and the next her mind would wander away to something else. Her dreadful affliction rendered me heartbroken, and her cries haunt me still. There was a clergyman among us who died raving mad through the combined effects of heat, exposure, and fear, and used to walk around stark naked. His condition was pitiful to see.'[2]

Others, knowing that the odds against them were hopeless, wrote their last letters home. One of the few to have survived the siege was written by Emma Larkins, the wife of an artillery major, who wrote to her sister, the aptly named Henrietta Coffin:

Wheelers Entrenchment, Cawnpore, 9th June.

I write this, dearest Henrietta, in the belief that our time of departure is come – the whole of the troops rose here and we took refuge in a barrack. We are so hemmed in by overpowering numbers that there seems no hope of escape, only about forty European soldiers are left out of one hundred and twenty men, a sad, sad number to hold out against such an awful enemy ... They have six guns against us, the walls are going, this is an awful hour my darling Henrietta. Jessie, Emily and Georgie [her children] cling to us ... Give my love to my sweet girls [her daughters back *in England]* ... Connie darling, your Mama has longed to see and know you ... Alice, my sweet child, remember your Creator in the days of your youth ... Ellen, my little lamb, I must not see you again in the flesh but remember I will look for you where sorrow and disappointment can never enter. Henry, dear boy, my heart grieves over you, oh dear boy if you saw the position your little brother and sisters are in at this moment ...

Dearest Henrietta, we leave them all in the hands of God, and your tender watching – my dying love to all my dear friends.[3]

Inscribed on the back of the envelope, which is preserved in the archives of the British Library, is the following note, written in a different hand: 'Given to her faithful ayah, who escaped through the Sepoy Troops. After many vicissitudes this letter reached England a year and nine months after the massacre. On reaching Calcutta, Col. William Larkins [a relative of her husband's], sitting on a court martial, refused to see her, giving no credence to her tale. Bursting into tears she called on Heaven to witness her Faithfulness, gave the packet to a servant and weeping turned away never to be heard of again.'[4]

Just when they thought their last days had come, a reprieve came from an unexpected quarter. On 25 June a short message was brought to the entrenchment from the Nana Sahib. It was addressed, with the same curious formality as before, to 'The Subjects of Her Most Gracious Majesty Queen Victoria', and stated: 'All those who are in no way connected with the acts of Lord Dalhousie, and are willing to lay down their arms, shall receive a safe passage to Allahabad.' Given their situation – only three days' rations left, no medicine, and the two barracks so charred and peppered with shot that they were on the point of collapse – they had little choice but to accept.

The truce was greeted with euphoria by the emaciated, stinking, tattered survivors, although the eerie silence, after so many weeks of bombardment, was thought by some to be almost painful. 'Only the occasional hushed note of warning was struck: "Will they really let us go down to Allahabad in safety?"'[5]

The Nana was as good as his word. The following day at dawn he sent a consignment of elephants, palanquins and bullock carts to convey them all to the Satichaura *ghat* (steps leading down to a river). The survivors emerged from the entrenchment like so many ghosts. 'Many a woman and child whom I had seen enter with beautiful and smiling countenances now looked old, haggard, desperate and imbecile. There they stood, shoeless and stockingless, and destitute of all the finery so dear to the heart of a woman – objects fit to make the angels weep!'[6]

But what did they care? They had survived. They were going home.

When the bedraggled group finally arrived at the *ghat*, they found a number of boats made ready to take them upriver to Allahabad. Amy Horne described what happened next: 'After all had embarked – which took about two hours to accomplish – the word was given to proceed. Instead of the crew obeying these orders, a signal was given from the shore and they all leaped into the water and waded to the bank, after having first secreted burning charcoal in the thatch of most of the boats. Immediately a volley of bullets assailed us, followed by a hail of shot and grape which struck the boats . . .'[7] It was an awful realisation. They were not going home after all. It was a trap.

Within a few minutes 'pandemonium reigned'. Several of the boats were soon a roaring mass of flames in which the sick and wounded were quickly burned to death. Those who tried to escape by jumping overboard were picked off by musket fire from the sepoys standing on the bank. Others were simply drowned in the mad scramble to escape. Those who tried to swim for the opposite bank soon found that the shore was 'alive with rebels' also armed with guns. The few who succeeded in pushing their boats to the other side of the river were mercilessly slaughtered.

Those who remained on boats now had to contend with the cavalry, who waded into the water with their swords drawn, slashing wildly at those who were still alive. 'The air resounded with the shrieks of the women and children and agonised prayers to God for mercy. The water was red with blood and the smoke from the heavy firing of the cannon and muskets and the fire from the burning boats lay like dense clouds over and around us. Several men were mutilated in the presence of their wives, while babies and children were torn from their mother's arms and hacked to pieces, the mothers being compelled to look on the carnage! Many children were deliberately set fire to and burned, while the sepoys laughed and cheered, inciting each other to greater acts of brutality!'[8]

Amy Horne's family – her mother, step-father and five brothers and sisters, all of whom had survived the siege – were the next in line. In the scramble to board the boats, Mrs Horne had become separated from the others, and they could soon see that her boat was one of the ones on fire. There was clearly no chance of survival. 'I cowered on the deck overwhelmed with grief,' Amy wrote, 'not knowing what horrible fate the next moment had in store for me.'

One of her little sisters, the same child whose leg had been fractured during the fire, was sitting next to her 'moaning piteously' and crying out, 'Oh, Amy, don't leave me!' But then a sepoy climbed on board their boat, and seizing Amy by the waist, tossed her overboard. 'The cries of my poor little sister, imploring me wildly not to leave her, still ring in my ears; and her last look of anguish ... has haunted me ever since.' Amy Horne would never see her sister, or any of her family, again.

It seems amazing that there could possibly have been any survivors after the massacre at Satichaura Ghat, but there were. Those who had not perished in the river were rounded up and taken back to Cawnpore. The men and older boys were immediately shot. In a state of complete shock, the remaining captives, all of them women and small children, were led away. This time they were not taken to the shattered entrenchment, but to a little bungalow known as the Bibighar, close to where the Nana Sahib, who was proclaimed the new Peshwa on 1 July, now had his headquarters.

As its name suggests, the Bibighar ('the *bibi*'s house') had originally been built for the long-forgotten mistress of a British officer. Here, in a series of small rooms, nearly two hundred women and children were now incarcerated.

They nearly survived. After two weeks, and twenty-five more deaths from cholera and dysentery, news came that General Havelock and his relieving forces were only a few marches away. The prospect of deliverance for the captives in the Bibighar would now prove their undoing: from being valuable hostages, they became instead potential witnesses to the atrocities that had taken place in Cawnpore.

On 15 July, orders came from the Nana Sahib that they were all to be shot. Although some sources would later attest to his reluctance on the matter, the order went out nonetheless that they should all be executed.

The squad of sepoys who were first called upon to undertake this task were forced to line up outside the building, but when ordered to fire on the Bibighar, they refused.* No amount of threats, including being blown from guns if they did not obey their orders, had any effect. In their place, an execution squad of five civilians was eventually found to finish the job: three Hindus in the Nana's employ, including one of his bodyguards, and two Muslim butchers from the town. All were carrying *tulwars*, curved swords, in their hands.

One of the only witnesses to what happened next was a Eurasian named John Fitchett, a drummer who was held captive in a nearby shed. Fitchett described how the five executioners entered the Bibighar with their weapons drawn. After that he could not see what happened, only hear the 'fearful shrieks' coming from inside the bungalow.

What was happening was butchery on a scarcely comprehensible scale. At one point the bodyguard's sword broke, and he had to replace it with a fresh one from the Nana's headquarters. This, too, soon broke, so he replaced it with a third. After half an hour their work was done and they left the building, locking the doors behind them.

Not all their victims – 73 women and 124 children – were dead. John Fitchett would later testify that, from his shed just fifteen yards from the main bungalow, he heard groans coming from the Bibighar all night.

The following day four sweepers arrived, together with a huge crowd from the city who had gathered to watch the proceedings. The

---

*According to one witness, one volley was initially fired, but it was aimed at the ceiling.

sweepers had been given orders to dispose of the bodies by throwing them down a dry well near the house. This they proceeded to do, dragging the women and children there, one at a time, stripping them of their clothes and then tipping them down the well.

Six people were found to be still alive: three women, and three little boys between the ages of five and seven, who ran hysterically round and round the well trying to escape. When they were finally caught they were simply tossed into the well with all the rest. 'No one said a word or tried to save them,' Fitchett would recall in his deposition. 'They simply stared as the six were buried alive in the mountain of naked corpses.'[9]

The next morning, on 17 July, Havelock's relieving forces arrived in Cawnpore. It is hard to imagine their feelings when they came across the gruesome remains in what would become known as the Slaughter House. 'I felt as if my heart was stone and my brain fire, and that the spot was enough to drive one mad,'[10] wrote Second Lieutenant Arthur Lang in his journal. Major Bingham of the 64th, one of the first officers to arrive on the scene, wrote this entry in his diary: 'The place was literally running ankle deep in blood, ladies' hair torn from their heads was lying about the floor, in scores, torn from them in their exertions to save their lives no doubt; poor little children's shoes lying here and there, gowns and frocks and bonnets belonging to these *poor, poor* creatures scattered everywhere.'[11] '[I found] quantities of dresses, clogged thickly with blood,' wrote another witness, 'children's frocks, frills and ladies underclothing of all kinds, also boys' trousers, leaves of Bibles, and of one book in particular, which seems to be strewed over the whole place, called *Preparation for Death*, also broken daguerreotype cases, and hair, some nearly a yard long, bonnets all bloody, and one or two shoes. I picked up a bit of paper with on it, "Ned's hair, with love," and opened it and found a little bit tied up with ribband.'[12]

Even more terrible than these pathetic remnants was the track down which the bodies of the dead women and children had been dragged from the Bibighar to the well. Thorny bushes were found to have 'entangled in them scraps of clothing and long hairs. One of the large trees ... had evidently had childrens' brains dashed out against its trunk ... and an eye glazed and withered could plainly be made out.'

Perhaps the most poignant item of all, discovered in the Bibighar among the torn hair and children's shoes, was a list written by Caroline Lindsay on a tiny scrap of paper:

Mamma died, July 12th
Alice died, July 9th
George died, June 27th
Entered the barracks, May 21st
Cavalry left, June 5th
First shot fired, June 6th
Uncle Willy died, June 18th
Aunt Lily died, June 17th
Left barracks, June 27th[13]

Caroline Lindsay was killed, together with her sister Frances, at the Bibighar on 15 July.

Even for these hardened soldiers, well used to the sickening brutalities of war, it was a sight they could scarcely believe. 'I have looked upon death in every form, but I could not look down that well again,' one of them later wrote.[14]

Augusta Becher, Harriet Tytler, Julia Inglis, Kate Bartrum and Amelia Horne all survived the Uprisings of 1857, although none of them was ever quite the same again.

Augusta Becher and her children managed to reach Bombay, from where they took a ship back to England. Although she was spared the worst atrocities of the Uprisings, her hair had overnight turned completely grey on that first dash from Simla, and it was a long time before she lost her 'scared expression'. Years later, when contemplating those times, she came to believe that those who had not themselves witnessed those terrible events of '57 at first hand would suffer from the effects of 'long suspense and fearful anxiety' far more than those who had, who seemed 'to have cast it by as an evil dream'.

Julia Inglis and Kate Bartrum, survivors of the siege of Lucknow, would not have agreed. After the arrival of Havelock's forces they endured nearly a month of further waiting within the Residency compound, and it was not until 18 November, with the arrival of more troops under the command of Sir Colin Campbell, that it was possible for them to be safely evacuated.

Julia Inglis had strangely mixed feelings when the moment came. 'We were indeed thunderstruck, and truly grieved, to think of abandoning the place we had held so long with a small force, now that it seemed to us we could have driven the enemy completely out of Lucknow, re-established our supremacy and marched out triumphantly.'

Just days before the retreat, one of the ayahs had been shot in the eye, and in order to extract the bullet it was necessary to remove her whole eyeball. Her employer, Mrs Bruere, 'actually held her while it was being performed', Julia Inglis recorded, adding: 'It was astonishing how accustomed, I will not say hardened, one had become to sights which once even to talk of would have sickened one. We were, alas! too familiar with the sight of blood to turn away from it.'[15]

The Lucknow women were affected by their release in different ways. The ecstatic welcome they received on first arriving at the British station at Allahabad was overpowering for many; and simply being in a proper house again, 'with all the appurtenances of civilization' around them, a strangely unsettling experience.

Julia Inglis was bewildered to find five months of correspondence from home waiting for her, including letters from her mother in which it was clear that she did not expect them ever to reach her. Mrs Case, Julia's great friend whose husband had been killed at Chinhut (Chinhat) early on in the siege, and who had borne her loss so bravely, now suffered a complete collapse. 'It was as if the blow had just struck her; she became thoroughly prostrate, and had no energy or wish to move.'

On Christmas Day, Julia Inglis gave a dinner for the remaining women and children of her husband's regiment, the 32nd. 'It was anything but a festive sight to me,' she wrote. 'There were now only 17 women, and nearly all were widows, and every child present had lost one or both parents.' The children, in particular, now 'ran wild', traumatised by the appalling events they had witnessed.

Despite having survived the siege together, Kate Bartrum and Julia Inglis met only once, on the boat that took them from Allahabad to Calcutta, from where they would both make the journey back to England. It was on this journey that Mrs Inglis came to hear the sad story of how Robert Bartrum had been shot through the head just outside the Residency, his wife waiting for him in vain at the Baillie Guard Gate. 'She had one little child with her,' Julia Inglis would remember, 'dreadfully weak and thin, but she hoped it would live to get home, as it was her only comfort'. But Bobbie did not survive. She later learned that the little boy had succumbed to illness,* and had died just the day before their ship sailed for England, leaving an utterly bereft Kate Bartrum to make the journey home alone.

Harriet Tytler survived with all her children, her baby, Stanley, in particular becoming something of a celebrity, with people making the pilgrimage for years after to see the spot where he had been born.† Mrs Leeson, on the other hand, while reunited with her husband, would later search in vain for the bones of her murdered children.

The siege of Delhi came to an end on 14 September. Harriet Tytler never forgot the death-like silence that greeted them when they finally entered the city again. 'The first thing which struck me so forcibly on entering . . . Delhi, only a few months before so crowded, was that it was now a city of the dead . . . All you could see was empty houses where the household hearths had ceased to burn, and not a living creature, except now and then a starved-looking cat, would show

---

*No reason is given for his death, either by Julia Inglis or by Kate Bartrum herself. It was later believed that the deaths of many children were caused by starvation, as was quite likely the case with Bobbie.

†It was not until their return to Delhi that Stanley could be baptised. There was some debate about his name: the soldiers wanted him to be called Battlefield Tytler. In the end a compromise was reached and he was instead saddled with the name Stanley 'Delhi Force'.

itself, and empty cages were to be seen here and there with their once-beloved occupants laid dead below.'

As Julia Inglis's had been, Harriet Tytler's emotional response was an unexpected one. Despite the gruesome sight of dead bodies, picked over by vultures and feasted on by gorged flies, the 'utter stillness' of the place, after the incessant booming of the guns and the constant rain of shot and shell during those four months of siege, struck her as 'indescribably sad'. It seemed to her 'as if something had gone out of our lives. Truly, living in the midst of incessant firing, it had become music to one's ears. Even my baby on a bed of straw slept through it as soundly as the most luxurious baby could have done in a feather bed in a palace, proving how we can become accustomed to anything.'[16]

Perhaps the strangest tale of all, however, belongs to Amy Horne, her family's only survivor from the first Cawnpore massacre at the Satichaura Ghat. After she was thrown into the river, the anguished cries of her little sister growing fainter and fainter in the distance, she had somehow swum to the opposite side of the river, where she was dragged on to the bank by a passing *sowar*. She was later able to identify this man as Mahommed Ismail Khan, from the 3rd Native Cavalry. 'His face was badly pitted with pock, and was adorned with a black beard divided in the centre. His eyes were the most striking feature in his face, being black and piercing, and capable of driving fear into one.'[17] Her description of him is of a stock, almost panto-mime villain, but here the comparison ends. The *sowar* gave her a set of Indian clothes to wear, and she was eventually taken before two *maulvis*,* Muslim holy men, and made to undergo a forced conversion. Men stood by with drawn swords, she would recall, 'to sever the heads of any who refused'.

For ten months Amy Horne was made to accompany her captor. At one point she ended up in Lucknow, where she was concealed in a

---

*One of these, Liaqat Ali, had been one of the chief instigators of the Uprising at Allahabad. Fourteen years later, when he was eventually brought to trial, he would use this episode, which he claimed had saved Amy Horne's life (this was certainly true), as a mitigating factor in his defence. It worked. Instead of the death penalty he was given a life sentence and sent to the penal colony at Port Blair, in the Andaman Islands.

hut within sight of the Residency. Little suspecting what was happening behind those beleaguered walls, she wrote, 'had I been mistress of worlds I would have given them to be in that Garrison'. But perhaps even that would have been better than her trials at the *sowar*'s hands.

While there is no suggestion in her narrative of her having been used as his sex slave – Victorian proprieties would almost certainly have prevented her from alluding to it – there seems no other convincing reason why he should have taken such risks to keep her with him, since it was death to harbour an English woman in what was regarded by her captor (and many others) as a jihad, a holy war, against the British. 'No person who has not actually heard them, will ever credit the low opinion of the talents of our officials,' Amy Horne wrote; 'no-one can ever describe the contempt in which they held our Government, our rulers, and even our Sovereign.'

Whatever the real reasons for Amy Horne's survival, in April 1858 she eventually ended up in her captor's village, Goothnee (Gothni), not far from Allahabad. Even there, the horror did not end. 'Mutilating was common among them,' she recalled, and she was told 'to feel grateful to them for having spared not only my hands, but nose and ears; and that I had been more fortunate than our poor old General Sir Hugh Wheeler, whose hands were cut off as soon as he was brought from the boat.'

With the Uprisings now nearly at an end, she persuaded him to release her, and somehow made her way into the nearby city, where some relatives, the Flouests, a family of indigo-planters, were still living. Her unexpected appearance was as if a ghost had appeared from the past. 'Ten long months of suffering, together with my native costume, had so altered my appearance that even when I gave my name they could scarce believe that one they had numbered with the dead stood before them.'[18]

# PART FIVE

Peter Newark Military Pictures/
Bridgeman Images

# IN THE AFTERMATH OF THE
# UPRISINGS: KAISAR-I-HIND

*In which the East India Company is disbanded – the British government takes over direct rule of its Indian territories – and Queen Victoria is declared Kaisar-i-Hind, Empress of India.*

# CHAPTER 22

In September 1857 Delhi was indeed a city of the dead.

The ancient city became the locus of some of the most terrible acts of revenge perpetrated against the Indians by the British. Retribution was swift, merciless, and every bit as savage as the actions of the rebels. Despite various attempts to rein in the worst of the reprisals – most notably by the Governor-General of the time, George Canning, who earned himself the unflattering sobriquet 'Clemency Canning' – the majority of the British public, both in India and at home, howled for blood.

Within days of Delhi Force troops entering the metropolis there was not a house that had not been systematically ransacked and looted.* Of the few remaining, half-starved inhabitants, those who were suspected of collaborating – including many innocent people who had not – were bayoneted, shot or hanged. Gallows were erected throughout the city, and soon there was hardly a neighbourhood that did not boast its own gruesome spectacle. Jeering crowds of soldiers gathered to watch the hangings, or went to gawp at the last of the Mughal emperors, the elderly and increasingly frail Bahadur Shah Zafar, now imprisoned in a tiny, dirty room in a bazaar backstreet.

*For the unfortunate citizens of Delhi, this was the second time that this had happened: the first ransacking was carried out by the rebel sepoys from Meerut who had arrived in Delhi just four months previously.

While having been the figurehead around whom the original mutineers from Meerut had first rallied in May, Zafar's agency in the Uprisings seems always to have been an ambivalent one. He was eventually sent into exile in Rangoon. Other members of the nobility, including Zafar's three sons who had commanded the Mughal forces fighting against the British, were not so fortunate. Mirza Mughal, Mirza Khizr Sultan and Mirza Abu Bakr were stripped naked and shot at point-blank range.

Many others were tortured before they were executed, often by deliberately making them break their caste. Some were force-fed with pork; others were made to get down on their hands and knees and lick the blood of their victims off the floor with their tongues. The sheer vindictiveness of the vengeance meted out by the British was deeply shocking to many.

From Calcutta, Lord Canning wrote to Queen Victoria raising his concerns about the 'violent rancour of a very large population of the English Community against every native Indian of every class. There is a rabid and indiscriminate vindictiveness abroad, even amongst many who ought to set a better example, which is impossible to contemplate without something like a feeling of shame for one's fellow countrymen. Not one man in ten seems to think that the hanging and shooting of 40 or 50,000 Mutineers beside other rebels, can be otherwise than predictable or right.'[1]

British women, even the mildest-mannered, most sympathetic ones such as Harriet Tytler, agreed with them. War had brutalised and hardened them all.

Indian women were mainly spared the fate of their men, but many were forced from their homes. For those who witnessed it, this was a strange and striking sight. 'What an experience it was to behold the myriads of women and children coming out of the Kashmir and Mori Gates,' wrote Harriet Tytler, 'women who had never seen the outside of their *zenana* walls or walked but a few steps across their tiny courtyards, surrounded only by their own family or their slaves, now to have to face the gaze of European soldiers as well as their own, all but strangers ... I was sorry for the poor things, more specially for the poor high-casted Hindu women to whom it was agonising pain to be jostled along with sweeperesses and other women of low birth and caste.' Some of these were driven so mad with grief and shame that, in an eerie echo of the fate of the British women at Cawnpore, they drowned themselves and their children in their own wells.

Even Zafar's wives, those 'unfortunate ladies, to whom no guilt could be attached, were exposed to the gaze of officers and soldiers who could go into the room where they were at their pleasure', wrote one observer. Mrs Coopland, who took her turn at going to stare at the prisoners, noted that the women all turned their faces to the wall whenever a man came into the room. 'It seemed absurd to humour thus their silly prejudices,' she wrote spitefully, 'when they had spared no European in their power any indignity or insult.'[2]

The once beautiful city, full of palaces, mosques and secret, fountain-filled gardens scented with jasmine and tuberose, had become a stinking charnel house, choked with dead bodies and the rotting carcasses of animals. Fearful of yet more outbreaks of disease, the British turned large numbers of the remaining civilian population out into the countryside, to scavenge as they could, or die.

At times it seemed as though even the city itself was to be punished. Calls for Delhi to be completely obliterated from the map, its ancient buildings razed to the ground regardless of beauty or antiquity, were only narrowly resisted.* Even then, large swathes of the city, especially around the Red Fort, were demolished anyway.

In one respect at least, the rebels did get what they wanted. The East India Company, with its once 'quiet trade' as advocated by Thomas Roe in the early seventeenth century, could not survive the debacle of the Uprisings. Under the provisions of the Government of India Act of 1858, the huge paramilitary corporation was nationalised, and effectively disbanded. Its possessions, administrative powers and machinery, even its armed forces, were taken from it. From now on

---

*Canning had initially agreed to the plan, but was persuaded against it by John Lawrence, Henry Lawrence's brother and Honoria Lawrence's brother-in-law. See Dalrymple, *The Last Mughal*.

the government in London would rule India directly. The role of Governor-General was replaced by that of the Viceroy,* the Queen's direct representative, who was sworn into office sitting on a throne made from the state howdah that had once belonged to Tipu Sultan.

Far from being ousted by the Uprisings, the British had only tightened their grip on their conquered dominions.

Only twenty years after the siege, Harriet Tytler would have been able to look down from the exact spot where her bullock cart had once stood and seen a sight every bit as incredible as the burning cantonments and shell-shattered bastions of Delhi during the Uprisings. For it was here on the outskirts of the city, not so long ago the principal theatre of war, that Queen Victoria was declared Kaisar-i-Hind, Empress of India.†

To mark the occasion, on New Year's Day 1877, an estimated hundred thousand people gathered together in an extraordinary durbar to mark the occasion. It became known as the Imperial Assemblage. Not since the height of the Mughal Empire had such an immense assemblage been gathered together on Indian soil. A city of tents, specially set up for the occasion, stretched over four miles. Chief among the guests were the sixty-three rulers of the Native States and their retinues. Each prince had pitched his own individual camp within the tented metropolis, each one sumptuously bedecked with cloth of blue, scarlet and gold.

During the day the streets of this tented city hummed and thronged with hundreds of horses, elephants, camels, and the myriad servants who attended the princely retinues.‡ At night thousands of lamps flickered between parterres of artificial flowers.

In addition to the sixty-three rulers were eight hundred titular princes and nobles; the Khan of Khelat and his Sirdars; the Prince of Arcot; the

---

*The last Governor-General, Lord Canning, was also the first Viceroy.
†This was a deliberate echo of Kaisar-i-Run, the Indian name for the Roman emperors.
‡In an attempt to keep numbers from becoming too surreal, each chief had been limited to bringing five hundred personal attendants. This did not include ordinary servants.

Princess of Tanjore; and the Imam of Muscat. Ambassadors came from Burma, Siam and Nepal; deputations from Yarkand (Yarkant), Chitral, Yasin and Kashgar. The Governors-General of Goa and Pondicherry were present, as were all the foreign consuls and senior British officials, fifteen thousand British troops, and the correspondents of no fewer than fourteen European newspapers and twenty-four Indian publications, as well as artists from the *Graphic* and the *Illustrated London News*.

Although their numbers were few, these last were of particular importance. The Imperial Assemblage was a deeply political piece of performance art. Its chief orchestrator, the Viceroy Lord Lytton,* was absolutely clear about its purpose, which was to secure the Indian aristocracy, and rally them round the British crown as its feudal head.† It was for this reason that he had taken the special precaution of inviting the editors of all the 'respectable' newspapers, both British and Indian, together with their wives and daughters. As he would later write in his despatch to the Queen, it had 'the happiest effect upon the tone of the whole press'.

On 23 December, a week before the proclamation was to take place, the Viceroy and the Vicereine and their entourage arrived in Delhi. Edith Lytton kept a detailed account of their extraordinary proceedings, vividly describing the crowds who gathered to watch as they processed on elephants through the streets of Delhi: a press of onlookers so vast that it took two and a half hours under the burning midday sun for them to reach the encampment.

The Lyttons, and their two daughters, Connie and Betty, were preceded by four aides-de-camp, three detachments of cavalry and

---

*Robert Lytton, son of the novelist Bulwer Lytton, had been a strange choice for Viceroy, and quite unlike his predecessors. A friend described him as 'a born Parisian with a pleasant touch of Bohemian added'. He was also a published poet.

†'They are a powerful aristocracy,' Lytton wrote in a letter to Lord Salisbury on 11 May 1877. 'To secure completely, and efficiently utilize, the Indian aristocracy is, I am convinced, the most important problem now before us. I admit that it is not easy of immediate solution, we require their cordial and willing allegiance, which is dependent on their sympathies and interests being in some way associated with the interests of British Power, on the other hand we certainly cannot afford to give them any increased political power independent of our own. Fortunately,' he added, patronisingly, 'they are easily affected by sentiment, and susceptible to the influence of symbols to which facts very inadequately correspond.'

twelve trumpeters. Behind them marched the retinues of the Indian rulers and princes, which among the myriad animals and weaponry they brought with them included the Gaekwad of Baroda's solid gold and silver cannons, each one resting on a carriage with golden wheels, drawn by bullocks with golden-tipped horns.

'Nothing I ever saw or have dreamed of could equal the rush of native chiefs' elephants that closed the procession ...' wrote one observer, who watched the entire procession from one of the specially constructed stands at the steps of the Jama Masjid, the city's principal mosque. 'Their courtiers and retinues ... jostled and pushed together in a most glorious confusion of dress, drapery and umbrella ... A double line of elephants lined the way, swaying backwards and forwards ... On their backs magnificent *howdahs*, and in the *howdahs* a motley crew – men in armour, men with shields and large swords, men with trumpets eight feet long, all sorts of wild men, shouting and scuffling; and behind all the golden sunset.'[3]

The following week was given over to greeting and entertaining the dignitaries. At the heart of the tented city was the great Durbar Tent, in which Lord Lytton received each and every one of the ruling chiefs, accompanied by their retinues, for three days solidly, from ten o'clock in the morning until seven o'clock at night. He also made return visits of protocol to those princes who were entitled by their rank to a visit by the Viceroy. A considerable amount of this time was taken up by the gun salutes with which each visit was marked. To honour the occasion, seven of the Indian rulers had their salutes raised to twenty-one guns, which delighted them greatly, as this would have put them on an equal footing with the Viceroy himself – until they discovered that Lytton had raised his own salute to thirty-one guns. (The Queen Empress, as Victoria was about to become, received a 101-gun salute.) The noise and clouds of gunpowder that ensued were as great as that on any battlefield.

Edith Lytton's duties were almost as punishing as those of her husband. She received the European ladies attending the ceremony between three and five o'clock each afternoon. The lone Indian woman among them was the Begum of Bhopal, the only female ruler of state: a 'scruffy little woman', Edith wrote, who wore 'little shoes like galoshes'. Each night there was a State Banquet at which Lady Lytton presided, and in the days in between a succession of other ceremonials. These included yet more visits, receptions, a march-past of troops both Indian and British (which took a punishing five hours) and the distribution of the medals specially cast for the occasion.

On the day itself, the family travelled by carriage from the Durbar Tent to a specially constructed Place of Assemblage: an enormous wrought-iron dais, painted red, gold, white and blue, beneath which Lord Lytton, as the Queen's representative, would be enthroned. Facing it was a two-hundred-foot semi-circular covered stand for the princes and other dignitaries.

The Lyttons dressed carefully for the part. As the Queen's (soon to be Queen Empress's) representative, the Viceroy wore the flowing robes of the Grand Master of the Star of India, 'a beautiful blue velvet embroidered with gold flowers and an ermine cape' (so heavy that it would take two sturdy pages to hold it up), on the front of which was pinned the insignia of the Star of India. Edith Lytton herself did not wear imperial ermine, but her dress was equally regal: 'a lovely gown of purple blue silk and velvet stamped with blue velvet brocade' designed especially for her in Paris by Worth.* Around her neck she wore a pearl and diamond choker, and her bonnet was stitched over with feathers and pearls.

To the strains of the march from *Tannhäuser*, the Viceroy made his way slowly to the dais, to the throne that had been placed there for the occasion. 'I walked after him,' Edith Lytton recorded, 'with a little girl on each side [her daughters] and the staff, a very brilliant one, fell in after us and so we all walked solemnly up to the dais. Having never walked except in a funeral procession and being rather shy I am afraid I felt very serious but the whole thing was most properly solemn.

*To have a gown designed by the Parisian couturier Charles Worth was a famously expensive affair. A simple day dress cost 1600 francs (£3000) while the evening gowns in which he specialised could cost as much as 2500 francs (£5000).

R's [Robert's] chair was, of course, put rather forward and mine at his right and the children at his left just behind. The Chiefs were in front in a semi-circular covered stand, and their new banners, gold umbrellas, and dress made it a splendid sight, but the British uniforms pervaded very much amongst these. Our Governors, Lieutenant-Governors and Members of Council were all facing the throne also.[4]

The Chief Herald, Major Barnes, 'an enormous man of, I am sure, seven feet', climbed the steps and then, facing the spectators, read out the Queen's Proclamation. A second aide followed, and read the same in Urdu. After this came the thundering sound of the Queen's 101-gun salute, which lasted a full twenty minutes. Lord Lytton then rose to make his speech, which ended with the words 'God save Victoria, Queen of the United Kingdom and Empress of India'.

It was, as Edith Lytton would record with both complacency and complete historical amnesia, 'the greatest day of our lives'.

In addition to the feasting and jubilation in Delhi itself, all over India gold and silver commemorative medals were distributed, honorary titles and certificates of honour conferred, salaries increased, and food and clothing distributed to the poor, but despite this careful exercise in diplomacy not everyone was happy.

The scars caused by the Uprisings of 1857 were deep and long-lasting. For all the apparent jubilation, a strong undercurrent of hatred and resentment towards the British, fuelled by bitter memories of their reprisals, would soon give rise to a growing political restlessness among the Indian professional classes, and sow the first seeds of Indian Nationalism – but all this was in the future. At the time of the Imperial Assemblage it seemed an impossibility that British rule would ever now come to an end.

In Edith Lytton's day, the imperial high noon of the British Raj, there was little to ruffle the calm waters of the average memsahib's life. External tensions, such as the growing threat from Russia along India's north-west frontier, and internal ones, such as the famine which raged throughout parts of India in the same year as the Assemblage, were not of nearly such pressing concern to many of them as the changes that they would now be required to make to their evening dress.

An order had gone out from the Lord Chamberlain's office in London which decreed that all ladies attending viceregal evening parties were to wear court trains – an announcement immediately denounced in the Calcutta *Statesman* for the unnecessary extravagance and expense it would create, adding a thousand rupees to the sartorial costs of the average family* (the order was subsequently modified, making it optional to wear one).

By the time the Marchioness of Dufferin and Ava took up her position as Vicereine, less than a decade later, Government House had all the trappings and ceremonies of monarchy. Lady Dufferin held regular Drawing Rooms, modelled along the same lines as Queen Victoria's at Buckingham Palace. Ladies wore their court trains, 'to say nothing of lappets and feathers', and queued to be formally presented to her. 'I got rather hot with the exercise of making so many curtseys,' she wrote.†[5] The transformation from a few fly-blown factories to an imperial court, with a king and queen (or, in the Lyttons' case, a complete royal family) at its head, was complete.

Much of the criticism that has been levelled at memsahibs stems from this period, and it is easy to see why. Before the Uprisings, most British women had regarded Indians from a hazy, uncomprehending distance; now there was an element of mistrust, even fear, in their dealings with them, which translated only too readily into hardened racism. The scars caused by the Uprisings were deep on both sides. Never before had British women and their children been casualties of war in such numbers, and the memory of it would last for generations.

At the same time, both physically and psychologically, India had never been nearer. The telegraph had been introduced to the public in India in 1854. Steam ships, first introduced in the 1830s, had already cut many

---

*The estimate was made for one wife and two daughters.
†At least the sight of so many heads bobbing up and down did not make her seasick, as it did Queen Victoria.

months off the length of the voyage, which after the opening of the Suez Canal in 1869 was four and a half thousand miles shorter than it had previously been. The tiny trickle of women, first started in 1617 by that pioneering trio Mrs Hudson, Mrs Towerson and Mrs Steele, had become a tidal flood, ebbing and flowing with the many steamers that made their way across the oceans.

A new form of literature now sprang up, almost literally, in the new-comers' wake. Unlike the Cherry sisters who in 1821 had had nothing but their father's anxious letter to advise them during the long voyage, a flurry of handbooks now came into existence to advise prospective memsahibs on their new lives.

One of the earliest of these was a little volume entitled *The Englishwoman in India*, put together anonymously by 'A Lady Resident' in 1864 (just three years after Mrs Beeton's ground-breaking *Book of Household Management* first appeared, which had done much the same thing for their stay-at-home sisters). 'How much I should have saved myself and my friends, had there been a little book of useful practical advice on the wants of an Indian lady then available,' wrote the author in her preface. This Victorian equivalent of a Lonely Planet guide for women contained:

Information for the Use of Ladies Proceeding to, or Residing in
The East Indies, On the Subjects of Their
Outfit, Furniture, Housekeeping,
The Rearing of Children,
Duties and Wages of Servants, Management of the Stables,
And
Arrangements for Travelling
To which are added
Receipts for Indian Cooking

Even a cursory glance at these handbooks makes it clear that Victorian memsahibs did not travel light. The extensive wardrobe and equipment now deemed necessary seems to have been in exactly inverse proportion to the length of the voyage. Although the average journey to India now took between three and four months, the underclothing considered absolutely necessary for a lady traveller would, on its own, have taken up several trunks. The Lady Resident's list includes 'four dozen day chemises, four dozen night chemises, three dozen gauze flannel or thick merino vests (if worn), and four dozen pairs of drawers'. This adds up to a total of 180 separate garments, all of which should be made 'of the best fine longcloth, not linen'.

*The Complete Indian Housekeeper and Cook*, published in 1888, included an even more substantial dress list. This one was deemed suitable for a woman travelling to north-west Punjab:

6 warm nightgowns (silk or wool)

6 nightgowns (silk or thin wool) for hot weather

6 calico combinations

6 silk or wool combinations

6 calico or clackingette slip bodices

6 trimmed muslin bodices

12 prs tan stockings

12 prs Lisle thread stockings

6 strong white petticoats

6 trimmed petticoats

2 warm petticoats

4 flannel petticoats

36 pocket handkerchiefs

4 pairs stays

4 fine calico-trimmed combinations for evening

2 winter morning dresses

2 winter afternoon dresses

2 tennis dresses

evening dresses [number not specified]

6 summer tea gowns

4 summer tennis gowns

2 summer afternoon gowns

1 riding habit, with lighter jacket

1 Ulster [a kind of coat]

1 Handsome wrap

1 umbrella

2 sunshades

1 evening wrap

1 Mackintosh

2 pairs walking shoes

2 pairs tennis shoes

evening shoes

4 pairs house shoes

2 pairs strong house shoes

In the past, passengers had always been responsible for fitting out their own cabins, but the modern steam ships now came fully equipped with all the necessary furniture, including sleeping berths, mattresses and pillows, washstands, lamps, blankets and linen. This did not prevent handbooks from suggesting alarming quantities of extra items to make the voyage comfortable. 'Take one or two folding chairs, cane ones, and an air cushion,' suggested the Lady Resident; 'also some swing trays, which could easily be made up by a carpenter ... A bag of hooks and brass-headed nails of all sizes is quite indispensable, together with a hammer and chisel; also a chintz curtain with rings and a cord to run through them, for in the tropics this will avoid the necessity of shutting the cabin door at night.'

Whether cabin furniture was provided or not, 'a really well-made set of marching drawers should be taken', she advised, 'as they are invaluable in India. They should divide into two parts, and be brass-bound."* In addition, a large foot-tub and a small bath were 'highly necessary', the latter preferably with its own can, as it would not do to depend upon the ship's buckets for fetching water.

Women travelling with young children were urged to provide themselves with 'a small tin kitchen' to take with them on board. This comprised 'a lamp, kettle, and saucepan, and wicks and oil, or spirit, to burn in it'. Also, 'some arrow root, patent barley, biscuit powder etc' and a canister or two of good white sugar, 'as that given out for children is often inferior and sometimes positively unwholesome'. For the adults she suggests 'a few bottles of the very best wine that can be procured', and a supply of champagne, which 'has been known to allay sickness when all else failed'. By this she means her previous suggestion of chloroform taken with a little water.

Good 'port wine' was known to alleviate the weakness and depression following seasickness: it was generally impossible to procure it on board, 'so a few bottles would be worth any money'. Somewhat

---

*When I first married, I was given one of these by my mother-in-law. I wondered at it for years: a strange sawn-off thing with no legs, which I later realised was the top half of one such travelling chest of drawers.

less cheering is her suggestion of a couple of jars of chloride of lime and several packets of Allnutt's fumigating powder, which together with camphor and camphorated spirits of wine were sure to see off the worst of the vermin and insect life on board. The failsafe remedy of corrosive sublimate dissolved in turpentine was not recommended, being both poisonous and inflammable, and, not surprisingly, 'in every way unsafe'.[6]

Were Victorian memsahibs any different from their Jacobean, Caroline and Georgian predecessors? The tone taken by Major S. Leigh Hunt (Madras Army) in his handbook for women in the tropics, *Tropical Trials*, first published in 1883, certainly implies as much. 'Many and varied are the difficulties which beset a woman when she first exchanges her European home and its surroundings for the vicissitudes of life in the tropics,' he begins portentously. 'Few can realise the sacrifices they will be called upon to make in taking such a decided step ... The sudden and complete upset of old-world life, and the disturbance of long existing associations, produces, in many women, a state of mental chaos, that utterly incapacitates them from making due and proper preparations for the contemplated journey.'[7]

In addition to being completely feeble-minded herself, the future memsahib's friends were likely, in the Major's view, to be just as bad. He warns his readers darkly against 'the dear, kind, sympathising female friend [who] sees her opportunity and eagerly proffers advice, which, though doubtless prompted by the best of intentions, from its utter impracticability, only serves further to complicate the situation.'

Clearly the Major had never come across Flora Annie Steel. It was Mrs Steel who was the co-author, together with her friend Grace Gardiner, of *The Complete Indian Housekeeper and Cook*, a best-seller in its day, and certainly one of the most famous publications of its kind. It came with a fulsome dedication: 'To the English girls to whom fate may assign the task of being house-mother in Our Eastern Empire this little volume is dedicated'.[8] The acerbically practical advice and the vast range of subject matter that make *The Complete Indian Housekeeper and Cook* such a joy to read today suggest a very different kind of memsahib from the feather-brained, hysterical dim-wit imagined by the Major, unable even to board her ship without 'a cool-headed male relation or friend' by her side to prevent her from swooning away.

The kind of woman that Mrs Steel and her friend Mrs Gardiner were writing for was made of very different stuff. Not only would the Steel-Gardiner memsahib happily cast off her stays in the hot season if it were practical to do so, but she would think nothing of setting off to the hills with her three children and all her possessions loaded on to a camel caravan (a long list, of both possessions and camels, helpfully provided). Had the Steel-Gardiner memsahib ever come across the Major's memsahib, she would have had a cure for hysteria immediately at her fingertips ('whisky and water with a little chlorodyne' – a popular medicine of the day which had a soothing, mildly narcotic effect – 'and a little wholesome neglect'). She would have been scathing in the extreme of any woman who professed never to go into her own kitchen 'for fear that her appetite might be marred by seeing a servant using his toes as an efficient toast rack . . . or the soup strained through a greasy turban'.

While the Major's memsahib was fussing about with her lifetime supply of tulle, net, lace, ruffles, frillings, white and coloured collars and cuffs, artificial flowers and ribbons (as suggested in *Tropical Trials*), the Steel-Gardiner memsahib would have been efficiently rustling up home remedies for 'bumble-foot' in chickens and sore udders in cows, and dosing her recalcitrant servants with castor oil – on the (dubious) grounds that there must be some physical cause for their complete inability to remember instructions.

The range and depth of the Steel-Gardiner memsahib's knowledge was magisterial. There was almost nothing she did not know, from where to procure the best water filter (the Berkefeld Patent Traveller's and Army Pump Filter) or the best baby's bottle (Paget's Germ-Free Feeding Bottle) to how to prevent leather chairs from cracking in the heat (rub them with egg white beaten thin with water), and even what to do in case of snake bite ('if the snake is known to be deadly, amputate the finger or toe at the next joint').

The Steel-Gardiner memsahib was particularly good at looking after the sick, both children and adults, and had every type of home remedy at her fingertips. She could have passed on hopeful recipes for champagne jelly and chicken soup for convalescents, antidotes perhaps to an alarming-sounding concoction called 'Cannibal broth' (made from minced beef and hydrochloric acid – God alone knows what effect that had).

She could even be quite brutal when the situation required. If the tooth of a teething child were visible through the gums, she could with perfect sang-froid have followed the advice to 'take the child's head between your knees, its body being held firmly by another person, and with a small, sharp, lancet or penknife and a steady hand, cut the gum through to the tooth. This affords great relief . . .'

If some of her recipes seem to be rather desperate gropings in the dark (for the relief of cholera she recommends a mixture of sulphuric and nitric acid mixed in with a tablespoon of vinegar and a teaspoon of Worcester sauce), for the most part her suggestions are practical, sensible and brisk. For example, she would have agreed with Mrs Steel that breakfast should be a family meal, and that it was not necessary 'to have a tribe of servants dancing around the table ready to snatch away your plate at the least pause'. The *khitmatgar* (butler), in particular, 'should be generally discouraged from making [the butter] a medium for a display of his powers in the plastic art; it is doubtless gratifying to observe such yearning after beauty, even in butter, but it is suggestive of too much handling to be pleasant'.

The stereotype of the British memsahib, apathetic, indolent and pleasure-seeking, simply collapses under this onslaught of advice and endeavour. In its place an image comes to mind of an eager young housewife armed with hammers, tacks, brass nails, a goodly supply of Bon Accord enamel, Japanese black, varnish, beeswax, Putz Pommade and, above all, a formidable amount of energy: a woman, in fact, not unlike Flora Annie Steel herself.

# CHAPTER 23

Except that no one was quite like Flora Annie Steel.

A photograph of her in old age shows a small, eager-looking woman in dusty widow's weeds sitting in a chair. Her hair is snow white beneath a black cap, and the expression on her face suggests she is about to burst out laughing. One of her arms is raised, her forefinger half pointing at something just out of our view. An imperfectly blacked pair of boots? A scrap of cobweb, invisible to anyone but her, still hanging from the rafters? Or the unfinished manuscript of one of the many novels that she went on to write, at top speed, sometimes churning out more than one a year, after her return from India?

While the *Complete Indian Housekeeper and Cook* is by far her most famous work, running into many editions in her own lifetime, Mrs Steel was also well known for those novels, almost forgotten now (if the ones I read during my research are anything to go by, with good reason). The subjects she tackled were mostly about the British experience in India: the Uprisings (*Bread Upon the Waters*), missionary work (*The Hosts of the Lord*), the effects of a cholera epidemic (*Voices in the Night*), and many others besides. What makes her novels unusual is her willingness to depict a wide range of Indian characters as well as English ones: prostitutes from the bazaar, *nautch* girls, young begums cloistered in their *zenanas*, journalists, traders, holy men, nobles down on their luck. She was particularly good at showing the cultural ambiguities faced by ambitious and newly educated (in the English way) young Indian men, some of whom even marry English women (with disastrous consequences).

For all of this she drew upon her own experiences of twenty-two years living and working in India, wonderfully chronicled in her autobiography *The Garden of Fidelity*. The tone leaves us in no doubt that this is the same author who co-wrote the *Complete Indian Housekeeper*.

She wrote, I suspect, almost exactly as she would have spoken – not always a comfortable experience.* 'Of course I was born,' she snaps at us on the first page, 'everyone is.'[1] And indeed she was: in Harrow, on the outskirts of north London, in 1847. Her parents, the Websters, were Scots and literary (they were friends of the novelist Thackeray), her large tribe of siblings 'all healthy strong Scottish children'. Her mother had been a considerable heiress, but somehow the family money was lost, and the young Flora Annie was brought up frugally.

Flora Annie Steel had great admiration for her mother – 'a real charmer, who kept the whole family going' – whose ideas about childrearing seem to have been of the 'wholesome neglect' variety. Wishing to encourage her children's imagination, Mrs Webster disapproved of all bought toys, and her children were obliged to invent them for themselves. One of her daughter's earliest memories was of burning, hanging and torturing an effigy of the Nana Sahib that she had made herself (a popular pastime, apparently, in English nurseries all over the country at that time). Her mother wrote plays for them to act in, their servants providing the audience. Her other entertainments included making peepshows (charging a halfpenny a peep) and being taken out shooting with her brothers, dressed in boy's clothing.

There was a healthy streak of eccentricity in the Webster household. Instead of having set birthdays, each sibling was encouraged to choose their own day of celebration, one or other of them simply announcing at the breakfast table 'tomorrow is my birthday', whereupon everyone

---

*She reminds me of one of my great-aunts, a contemporary of Phyllis's but as unalike her as possible: a formidable woman who annoyed many of her peers with her superior competence at just about everything, but who was adored by us children. We were oblivious to her rudeness, and thrilled by her anarchic ways.

in the family would write them an ode. Later, when there was no more money to pay for a governess, Flora Annie was left to educate herself, which she did by reading books in the attic: 'it was', she wrote, 'an excellent education'.

Even as a young child the future Mrs Steel always did what she set out to do 'with quite appalling energy', and the same was true of her in later life. At fifteen, when her mother fell ill, she took on singlehandedly the running of the family household, and at eighty-two, the year she wrote her memoir, was still making all her own clothes.

Her marriage to Henry William Steel, a member of the Indian Civil Service, was something of a mystery, even to her. They met when she was twenty. 'Why I married I cannot say: I never have been able to say,' she wrote. 'I do not think either of us was in love. I know I was not; I never have been. That is a sad fact, but it has to be faced.'

Another mystery for a twenty-year-old, even a fiercely competent one, was how to prepare for the voyage to India. Like the Lady Resident before her, she too must have longed for a little book of friendly practical advice to see her on her way. Having (mortifyingly) somehow lost most of her luggage en route, the newly-wed Mrs Steel arrived in Calcutta with only a small cabin trunk and a lot of cold-weather clothes, and was obliged to buy a complete new trousseau from the European shops.* The heat was tremendous, and she was instantly bitten all over so badly by mosquitoes that she was soon covered with blisters.

Although still not much more than a child – 'round-faced, high-coloured, with my hair still in curls though tied up at the back with a bit of ribbon' – she was entranced by what she found. Stopping off in Madras en route, she found even the surf an exciting adventure. 'It was exhilarating,' she wrote of the experience. 'Something quite new; something that held all possibilities. A boat that had not a nail in it; dark-skinned boatmen with no clothes on, who did not look naked, a surf such as I had never seen before, thundering on yellow sands.'

---

*She claims to have done so from one of the Whiteaway-Laidlaw department stores, but the first of these was not founded until 1877, ten years after her arrival.

From Calcutta came a journey up the Grand Trunk Road: 'inconceivably straight, broad, and white, inconceivably monotonous, inconceivably dusty. Then every ten miles the huge, square caravanserais built in the time of the Mughal Emperor, set back from the road, so that just one long wall was visible in the moonlight, pierced by one tall shadow of a wide arch. Dusky forms, queer-shaped camels, all jumbled together ... Was it any wonder that ... I was watching, watching, watching, listening, listening, listening ...'

The Steels' first Indian home was in Ludhiana, in the Punjab, two hundred miles north of Delhi. Their house – 'very sparsely furnished, as all up-country houses were in those days – matting, a table or two, a few chairs ... a Stuttgart piano' – was shared with a Scots doctor, who became a close friend. There were no other European women and very few amenities, although ice was delivered to them daily, by special post from Lahore.

Eventually their lost luggage turned up. Mrs Steel waited for it eagerly, 'agog with the unexpected delight of seeing our wedding presents once more', but when she opened the boxes it was to find yet another mystery: despite the weight of their trunks, most of the contents had simply vanished.

'Well! There were five ivory-handled dinner knives, and a sufficiency of small stones to make up the weight on the first tray. Below, more and larger stones, and the three stoppered bottles of the cruet stand; the fourth had gone, doubtless because being the pepper castor, it had a silver tip.

'What do I see next? Two people laughing like children, and being joined by a burly Scotsman, who positively threw himself into our only rocking chair and kicked his heels up in the air, as was the dear man's wont at any screaming jests.'

For all this merriment, adjusting to life in India was not easy. It was, she wrote, 'a hard country for Westerners to grip', but she threw herself wholeheartedly into trying to understand it, well aware that some of her endeavours, such as when she insisted on sitting down to talk to some holy men, made the local people think she was quite mad; 'but that is always a passport in India' was her only observation.

The loneliness and boredom that Flora Annie Steel experienced were common to many women living in India, particularly in its wilder outposts. Under these circumstances, to have married the wrong man was a personal catastrophe. Some of the accounts in which this is implied are quite heartbreaking. 'Except for the buzzing of mosquitoes, the sound of native tom-toms in an adjoining village, or my husband's voice, talking in Hindustani, the silence, as I retraced my steps to the hot veranda, was like that which a prisoner must feel immured in solitary confinement,'[2] wrote one nineteen-year-old bride bleakly of her experience living on a remote tea plantation in Assam.

Marriages in India were made with notorious rapidity, sometimes within only weeks of a couple having met. Young women, with little or no real understanding either of the men they had married or of the demands of married life, were especially vulnerable to this custom. Flora Annie Steel wrote about the difficulties with admirable candour. She had, she wrote, 'an inborn dislike to the sensual side of things'. Like almost all young women of her day, she had married 'knowing nothing: absolutely nothing' save what she had learned from books. On being introduced to the intimacies of marriage on their honeymoon, 'I simply stared,' she remembered. 'I accepted everything as part of the Great Mystery of humanity and the world.'

Not everyone could be so sanguine. The same nineteen-year-old tea-planter's wife was so traumatised by her husband's sexual demands ('It is for *this* that girls are given wedding presents and congratulations, actually congratulations!' she exclaimed with horror) that the marriage stood precious little chance of success. Some simply gave up and went home. Most had little choice but to soldier on.

Although her marriage to Henry was to prove a happy and enduring one, even Mrs Steel found her first few years in India hard, especially after her first child, a daughter, was stillborn. Of their posting in Kasur, in the Punjab, she wrote: 'I found myself absolutely alone, save for a busy husband. I should never have frittered away my time ... But there was literally no one but the natives. There was nothing but the garden to care for. Therefore I had no choice. I had to observe – or die, since that, without some work, I should die was a foregone conclusion.'

The fact that there were no other British women there to keep her company proved an unexpected blessing. She learned languages, several of them, and was, she claimed, one of the only European women in the Punjab, apart from the missionary ladies, to be able to converse in the vernacular. One of her many gifts seems to have been her willingness not only to talk to people, both men and women of every creed and caste, but to listen to them too. One of the happy results of all this was her first book, *Wide Awake Tales*, a collection of folk stories gathered during her many wanderings through India.

Her eccentric childhood, during which she had been thrown entirely upon her own resources for entertainment, stood her in good stead. Like many people in the Indian Civil Service, Henry was relocated frequently. In their first three years in India, the Steels moved house nine times.

In Kashmir, they lived for a while in a hill station so tiny that many of the country people had never seen a white woman before. Mrs Steel had no hesitation in befriending the wives of their fellow officials, who were all 'country bred' (in other words women of mixed race): 'such dear, good, more-British-than-the-British women'. Only one of them had ever been to England, so she had endless topics of conversation readily to hand.

Before long she was organising reading parties, in which she read aloud Thackeray, Dickens, Scott and George Sand novels, translating the latter as she went along. 'It improved my French, which I had almost forgotten.' She also had numerous pets, including two squirrels called Tweedledum and Tweedledee, 'handsome souls no bigger than small rats'. They hated it when she sat at her desk to write, and would try to grab the pen from her, and even to lick the ink from the page as she wrote.

But reading parties and pet squirrels were never going to be enough to satisfy Mrs Steel's super-abundant energies. It was in teaching that she really found her vocation.

# CHAPTER 24

Teaching, particularly the teaching of Indian women and girls, was an area in which British women already regarded themselves as uniquely well qualified. In the eighteenth century, a period not usually known for British philanthropic endeavours, a number of schools and orphanages for girls had been founded, but it was not until the beginning of the nineteenth that their efforts really got going.

With the renewal of the East India Company's charter in 1813, the way was opened for the first time to missionaries, who frequently doubled as teachers; and when the Company charter was renewed again in 1833, the gates were opened still further, this time to anyone regardless of their background, which soon included 'secular' teachers, governesses and, occasionally, female companions for the daughters of the elite.

Those who were most dogged with respect to education were the missionaries who came flooding to India almost as soon as the ink on the 1813 charter was dry.* Although there were converts to Christianity, there are many stories, at once heroic and tragicomic, of missionaries living forlornly for years in India without achieving a

---

*Within a very few years of that 1813 charter, five intrepid souls – Mrs Mead and Mrs Mault of the London Missionary Society, and Mrs Norton, Mrs Baker and Mrs Bailey of the Church Missionary Society – had set up schools in Travancore in south India. A free girls' school was established by the bleakly named Sarah Loveless in Madras in 1816, and many others quickly followed in other parts of India throughout the 1820s and 1830s.

single convert. Proselytising alone was likely to be a dispiriting experience. Education, they quickly realised, was the key.*

While their desire to convert the 'heathens' of India is distasteful to our modern sensibilities, missionary-teachers were important in that they were among the first to realise that the seclusion of Indian women belied their immense influence and power. 'The importance of educating the native girls is very considerable . . .' wrote the wife of a Wesleyan Methodist clergyman, in 1816. '*The heathen females are the main support of paganism.*'[1] While never fully comprehending what they considered to be a degraded way of life, they were quick to appreciate that Indian women were the key to their success, and made concerted efforts to reach them behind their purdah screens.

Feminist historians have been critical of these endeavours, believing that these teachers, missionaries and the philanthropic wives of British administrators stereotyped Indian women as 'voiceless, helpless, and ignorant, and as invariably trapped in a "pitiable" state, requiring the benevolent gestures of their Western sisters'[2] to break out from behind their pagan bars. But this was not invariably the case, and there were many who used this opportunity to make profound connections with the women they reached.

Flora Annie Steel started out, as so many women did, by teaching in her own home. Later she went on to found several small schools. With this experience under her belt, and with her gift for languages, she was invited by the government a few years later to become an Inspectress of Schools in the Punjab. The area of her remit was a vast one: 141,000 square miles, stretching from Peshawar to Delhi. By the time went home to England in 1889, she estimated that twenty thousand girls had passed through her hands.

Her methods were often controversial. When she declared that she would refuse a grant to any school (mostly these were the ones

---

*The very first attempt to found European-style schools, for both boys and girls, was at a Danish mission in Tranquebar (Tharangambadi) in the early eighteenth century. An Englishman, the Rev. C. S. John, made similar attempts in Madras in the 1770s. For a more detailed account of missionary activity in India see Rosemary Raza's excellent *In Their Own Words: British Women Writers and India*.

founded by missionaries) that paid its pupils to attend, there was an outcry. Mrs Steel was unwavering, but even she admitted to having occasional doubts. 'The spectacle of a pretty young girl of sixteen nursing her own baby and puzzling her brains out over fractions in the upper class gave me qualms, especially when I found out she was married to an absolutely ignorant man.' Not even she could deny that the six rupees a month the young mother was paid for her scholarship 'was an efficient aid to the family finances'. But she stayed true to her principles, noting only 'we got a much better class of girl'.

The custom of 'prizes for all' at the end of the school year was another issue with which she disagreed: 'a sort of reward for coming to the school at all, which did not suit my ideas about the dignity and honour of education'. When she tried to abolish it there was another outcry. 'No mother would consent to send her daughter to a school where she did not get a prize.' So after trying to reason with them, with no success, she decided on another method:

> A big meeting of mothers was convened in the largest courtyard where I announced, in order to meet their wishes, I had hit on a plan. The first prize would be given to the best scholar, the second to the worst, and so on. It did not take long for my audience to perceive the drift of this; smiles grew, until there was a burst of laughter, and amid much good-natured chaff as to whose daughter would get second prize, the meeting dispersed, satisfied that whatever was ordered would be just. Of course it goes without saying that at the first prize-giving there were an enormous number of consolations and not a few gifts!

Mrs Steel's strong views, and her 'autocratic ways', while enjoyed by many, did not endear her to everyone. 'I was a distinctly independent critic,' she explained; 'my tongue has always run faster than it should for what is called charity, and, despite my appointment as Inspectress, I was not a *persona grata* with the innermost circle.'

'Why don't you keep your wife in order?' wrote a despairing official once to Henry Steel. 'Take her for a month and try!' he wrote back. On one occasion, Mrs Steel discovered a cabal working against her, trying to implicate her on corruption charges.* Although she would later have to give evidence in front of a commission, and was proved innocent, she never discovered the source of the cabal.

Her greatest supporters throughout this difficulty turned out to be the women themselves, and on one occasion even her pupils, girls ranging in age between four and fourteen. While not knowing the particulars of the case, they had come to have an inkling that she was in some kind of trouble.

I was solemnly informed that they wished to set a watch for me. I inquired what that was, and was told I should see in good time. All I had to do was to come down to the big school at daybreak – not a minute later. There I should find the door barred and a noise as of singing birds within. So I was to chant, 'Little birds, little birds, why do you sing all the night long?' And the answer would come back as a chorus, 'We sing for freedom, for freedom. Let us go! Let us go!' Then I had to unbar the door with the words, 'Fly away, little birds,' and the rest would follow. It did follow with a vengeance. Such a squeal of four hundred children never was. Helter-skelter, shrieking, laughing, chattering, and as they passed me they flung at me the spools of cotton which the elder ones had spun during the long night during which *every one of them*, babies and all, had sat up, hungry, thirsty, singing hymns. I was literally snowed under. Afterwards they gathered the spools up, they wove them, they dyed the cloth, they embroidered it, and oh! the delight when I actually came down to school in a dress made by them. I have it still, and I shall wear it when my time comes to pass on and find out what life has really meant.[3]

---

*The University of the Punjab was found to have been selling its diplomas. She had been offered a bribe of a sapphire ring – presumably to turn a blind eye to this – but had refused.

However much she might have fought against government policy, Mrs Steel was nonetheless working from within an already existing system. She also had many years' experience of living in India behind her, and spoke several languages. Another woman who made the education of girls in India her vocation, Florence Wyld, had no such advantages.

In 1909, Florence Wyld was appointed principal of the first ever school for girls in Hyderabad. Unlike Flora Annie Steel, whose pupils were mainly from the lower castes, Miss Wyld would be teaching families of the elite, who observed strict purdah.

Her first experiences were disastrous. She arrived to find that the English friend on whose recommendation she had taken the job was nowhere to be found. It soon became clear not only that there was no school to speak of for girls in Hyderabad, 'but that there had been no school for some considerable time'; in fact, 'no school had ever really existed'.

To add to her difficulties, it soon dawned on her that even if she were to create a school, there would be no demand for its services. The only real enthusiasm for the project had come from two or three families who had recently moved to Hyderabad from Bombay (and were often more liberal in their views). Among the city dwellers of Hyderabad not only was there no desire to have their girls educated, but the likelihood was that they would actually oppose such a thing. 'Education for girls was not only entirely unnecessary in their sight, but might also prove to be dangerous.' Since in those days all high-caste women were brought up in seclusion, the possibility now arose 'that in the course of time it could even lead to a condition in which the strictures of *purdah* might be loosened', Florence Wyld would later recall. 'A desire for freedom might arise, and this possibility must be prevented.'[4]

Despite the fact that the building she was eventually allocated was of the most rudimentary kind (there were no lavatories, for example) and the number of her pupils totalled only four, Miss Wyld did succeed in opening a school of sorts, thanks in large part to the help of

Khujista Begum, a member of the royal family who championed her 'with wonderful foresight, vision and ambition for Indian girls.'*

Over time, many more pupils were persuaded to come, and conditions in the school slowly improved, but all her pupils remained in the strictest purdah throughout, a situation that for a western woman such as Florence Wyld, who had never travelled east and was completely unfamiliar with its customs, made for some surreal moments. She was amazed by the screens that were hastily erected to form a pop-up corridor each time a pupil arrived at the school, stretching all the way from their carriage doors to the entrance to the girls' compound.

One day an enormous cavalcade suddenly appeared at the entrance: 'a very large carriage was preceded by two outriders in special livery, two more outriders bringing up the rear', from which emerged 'three beautifully dressed girls ... decked in precious jewellery'. They turned out to be the daughters of the city's principal nobility, and added great prestige to the school.

For all these advances, there were setbacks too. Miss Wyld soon caught on to the fact that 'scarcely anyone living in a *purdah* household had any idea of time', and the idea that school had a fixed timetable would be all but impossible to impress on anyone. Pupils came if they felt like it, or not at all, as they wished. It took rather longer to get used to the idea that ayahs expected to sit on the floor next to their charges (who knows, maybe they learned something too), and that any girl who wished to sit a piano exam (the idea of learning a musical instrument at all being in itself the most revolutionary idea) had to do so wearing full-length gloves.

Most disconcerting of all was the difficulty of teaching young pupils who had no knowledge of the world outside their own homes. 'Most of the conditions and things which are familiar to us from earliest childhood, and which we take for granted as part of our natural existence were unknown to these children, or their mothers,' Florence Wyld wrote.

*The role played by Khujista Begum, and many other pioneering Indian women like her, is unfortunately beyond the scope of this book.

As Mrs Meer Hassan Ali had discovered in the 1820s, nature, and animal life, proved particularly difficult to explain. How was Miss Wyld to teach geography, including such concepts as trade winds and geographical strata, when none of them had ever seen any life beyond their home compound? While she was able to make good use of pictures to help her explain some ideas, 'a moment's thought is enough to make one realise that pictures alone, if one has never seen or known the original, are flat and lifeless', she wrote.

> A painting of a meadow with cows grazing and a stream running through, or another of a landscape showing hills and valley, what would that mean if we had never seen a meadow or a cow, a stream or a hill? A tree in a picture is tall and still. The real beauty of a tree standing forty to sixty foot high, with its great branches waving in the wind, the sun shining on rounded trunk and colourful leaves, of this a picture alone can tell nothing. But of all the beauties of nature that I found most impossible to describe was that of running water ... The swift current of a river, the light and shade on the surface, the water running over rocks, the glint of the sun on the ripples flowing over the pebbles, the fascination of watching this is beyond possibility of description.

Other subjects, such as history, were difficult to teach for quite different reasons. 'Miss Ma', as the girls called her, wanted her pupils to learn Indian history, but could find no English textbooks on the subject, while British history, hardly surprisingly, 'took a lot of explaining'. Back in England, she had taught history without a qualm, and not until now 'had I so strongly wanted to leave out so much!'

Her reminiscences about her own life were equally mixed. Her one English friend in Hyderabad, whom she refers to only as Mrs X, the same woman who had recommended her for the job, dropped her as soon as she arrived. As a result Florence Wyld's first few months in the city were extremely unhappy ones: unhappy, and uncomprehending. The practical problems of getting herself settled might have been

easily solved if she had had someone to advise her, but this kind of
help was not forthcoming. At first she could not understand why Mrs
X not only failed to call on her, but left her, with 'utter callousness', to
shift for herself. During those first few months in Hyderabad she felt
'completely isolated, lost and helpless'.

She had been given rooms, but they had no furniture. Worse, she
had no means of transport, and as a complete *griffin* in India had not
anticipated that it would be far too hot to walk anywhere. (At this
point, Mrs Steel's handbook might have come in useful, but even
her massive compendium did not include any hints for how to set up
a purdah school.) Even the food was mystifying. There was no beef
or pork to be had, only *muttony-beef-fish-steak*, all referred to in one
word. The actual result of this verbal effort, she would later record,
would usually turn out to be goat, 'an impossibly tough proposition'.
Later, when she contracted typhoid, she dosed herself with too much
quinine, which turned her temporarily stone deaf. In those days there
was still no idea that typhoid was infectious. 'One just lived or died,'
she wrote stoically. 'I lived.'

Most dispiriting of all, however, was the gradual realisation that as
a single woman, and a teacher, she had somehow lost caste among her
fellow Britons. Back in England, she had mixed socially with Mrs X,
as they were both from similar backgrounds – 'people of the ordinary
type of gentlefolk' – and they naturally met on these terms. In addition to being a gentlewoman, Miss Wyld was both highly intelligent
and extremely well-educated, having been one of the first women to
read for a degree at Oxford (perhaps this was part of the problem, as
'bluestockings' were still considered a curious and not especially lady-
like breed). She was also a tennis blue. Despite these credentials, it was
soon clear that in India, Mrs X and her friends were treating her as a
social inferior: a prejudice, Miss Wyld observed, that would take years
to overcome.

Perhaps it was as well that she did not understand her new position
all at once. Instead it was a gradual, and cruel, let-down. Florence
Wyld had three other young Englishwomen helping her at the school,

and she felt responsible for helping them to adjust to their new surroundings; but however hard she tried, it seemed impossible to get to know other English people. 'Nearly all the English community lived six to twelve miles away, and these were long distances, when one's only means of getting about was by buggy or Victoria.'

Eventually, the dreadful 'Mrs X', after a good deal of prodding, produced a Garrison Directory, in which she had reluctantly marked six names in pencil, and suggested that Miss Wyld should call on them. 'Call on them? What did that mean?' It later transpired that the correct etiquette would have been to put her card in the person's letterbox, and then wait for them to return her visit. 'These things would have been quite simple if I had known about them ... but as a stranger in the land I found it very confusing.'

Equally confusing were her enquiries about the Club.* When she asked about joining it, her friend became conveniently vague. 'The Club? There is not the least need for you to bother about the Club. It's too far for you, it would not interest you at all,' she told her, and promptly changed the subject.

The fact that Miss Wyld was a single woman was another mark against her, it being 'an accepted fact that all women would have a man attached'. On one of the few occasions when she was invited to a tennis party, and several other single women turned up, she tentatively suggested that they should make up a women's four: 'they just laughed'.

In the earlier part of the nineteenth century, Julia Maitland had written about the rivalry between the British who belonged to the covenanted Civil Service (the so-called 'heaven blessed') and those who belonged to the military. By the second half of the nineteenth century both were happily united in their invincible snobbery towards everyone else: missionaries, teachers, medics, and even the traders, planters and merchants, whose forebears had once formed the backbone of the East India Company (and without whom, had they but known it, none of them would have been there in the first place).

*The Secunderabad Club in Hyderabad, then known as the Garrison Club, was founded in 1878, and is one of the five oldest of its kind in India.

In this many women were eagerly complicit, closing ranks if necessary to keep 'outsiders' in their place.

Before the events of 1857, the civil and military hierarchies imposed by the East India Company had naturally extended to include wives, who on marriage came to assume their husbands' ranks. In the second half of the nineteenth century, with a Viceroy and Vicereine presiding at Government House, society in India had become ever more alert to these divisions. Many women described 'the everlasting jealousy of precedence' that governed social life in India: 'enough to try the patience of any chamberlain who had to regulate the etiquette of a German Court for twenty years'.[5]

Another guidebook of sorts to come into existence in this period was the Warrant of Precedence, which set out the exact ranking of everyone within the administration, right down to the lowliest post-office official. Except for the very wealthy or aristocratic, those who were outside the system found themselves in a social no-man's land.

Florence Wyld was quite astute enough to appreciate the subtleties of the situation. 'As time went by I came to realise that quite a number of wives had not before marriage had very much social standing, and now, finding themselves in a land where they had servants at their constant beck and call, they thought themselves rather more important than they really were,' she observed. Despite this, she claimed, the majority of the English women in Hyderabad were 'exceedingly nice'.

Whether or not this was true – and by her own admission it would take many years to overcome their prejudice – in the meantime she took refuge in her work. After its painful beginnings, the purdah school that she founded, the Mahbubia School,* was not only a success but would become famous for its groundbreaking work. In this 'Miss Ma' was helped by the ambitions of her pupils themselves. Eventually she was able to prepare several of the older ones to sit for the Senior Cambridge Exams. When the results came through, she went to tell them the news immediately.

*Named after the old Nizam of Hyderabad. It exists today, and even has its own Facebook page.

I did not let them wonder for one moment. 'You have passed! You have all passed!' It would spoil things if I attempted to tell of the happy exuberance that followed. They had won. They had always meant to win from the start. It was I, knowing more of the pitfalls, who had been fearsome. This was no result of an ordinary prosaic Examination. It celebrated, for the first time over the passage of years, a worthwhile victory won by a group of girls living under the condition of *purdah*, through their own sustained and determined effort.

Medicine was another area in which British women were able to make a significant contribution. The first is thought to have been a Miss Chaffinch, a Baptist nurse, who was working in India as early as 1812, although no details are known about her. In the 1880s the Vicereine, Lady Dufferin, launched the Countess of Dufferin's Fund for Supplying Female Medical Aid to the Women of India, which aimed to found purdah hospitals for women all over India. Not everyone approved. Flora Annie Steel (of course) pronounced that she thought the nurses and 'lady doctors' that were being brought in were a mistake. 'They perpetuated a vicious circle by bolstering up the *purdah*,' was her forthright opinion. 'But for the fact that Mahomet, as it were, went to the mountain, the mountain would indubitably have come to Mahomet.'[6]

But the fact remained: female British doctors and nurses had never been in such demand. One of these, Hester May Dowson, travelled to India to work as a nurse in Bombay during the plague of 1897–8. Unlike both Miss Wyld and Mrs Steel, who spent many years of their lives in India, Hester Dowson was brought in as part of an emergency government scheme to provide medical relief during the epidemic, an experience that she recorded in letters to her family that were later printed for private circulation.

Her voyage to India did not augur well. While the male doctors were given first-class accommodation on board the ship, the nurses were put, three to a cabin, in the smallest, hottest third-class cabins, located at the very bottom of the ship. The air was so stifling, temperatures in Hester's cabin reaching over 90°F, that eventually it made her ill. Taking pity on her, two officers chivalrously gave up their cabin to her until she recovered. Even before she had boarded the ship, on the train between Calais and Paris, she had made friends with one of the other nurses, Harriet McDougall, who as luck would have it had been appointed to the same hospital in Bombay. It was a friendship that would see them through many of the difficulties ahead.

The Arthur Road Hospital in Bombay had been commandeered as part of the government scheme to treat victims of the plague, although when the two young women finally arrived, the 'hospital' proved to be not much more than a row of low-roofed sheds. The conditions inside were not much better. The beds consisted of Indian *charpoys*, 'short four-legged bedsteads made of cane, like a cane bottomed chair, about a foot from the ground. Over the cane is laid a cotton blanket, then the patient, and over him a cotton blanket (white) and a dark, warmer rug which he pulls over him when cold. There is no mattress or bedding.'

In one of her first letters home, dated 19 December 1897, Hester Dowson described her daily routine. 'Well! We have been on duty two days now,' she wrote. 'Get up at 6am and after a light breakfast, drive to the hospital, a mile and a half. There work hard till 12, when we have lunch with tea in a tent which is like an oven, as the sun pours on it all day. Then, one day we go back to the ward until 4, and off the rest of the day, and the alternate day we go back to quarters after tiffin lunch, rest till 3.30, then back on duty till 8pm, and back to dinner at 8.30.'[7]

It was a punishing schedule. There were many new cases of plague every day and deaths were frequent. Most of the actual nursing was done by Indian orderlies, the 'ward boys' as she refers to them, 'as we only have time to take Drs orders, give medicines (which are all 2 hourly and some every half an hour), take temperatures; give feeds; and see that the boys do their work'.

One of the difficulties the two women were completely unprepared for was dealing with the different castes and religions among their patients. 'Some of them don't like us to touch them, and most refuse to take food from our hands. We have to try to get hold of the ward boy of the same caste before they will take it – unless they are delirious.' Few, if any, of the doctors were so respectful of these feelings. Hester Dowson hated to see how 'the little "caste" and religious prejudices of the people are despised and trodden on, especially by these young men fresh from England, who know nothing of the language of the natives. The people who have been out longer are more tolerant,' she observed, 'but the superior way these young Doctors have, when talking of the natives, is abominable.'

Christmas and New Year came and went, but the two women were working so hard they barely noticed. On a personal level, the situation improved when they were moved together into a four-roomed bungalow, a little way from the main hospital. It was sparsely furnished – a table, washstand, beds and a cupboard – and had no windows, so the only light came in through the door. In the early mornings it was so dark they could barely see to eat their breakfast, but gradually they made it into a home.

Soon they had their own servant, a Goan boy called Peter, who did housework, cooked them breakfast, and brought them tea in the morning. Best of all he drew baths for them, sometimes two a day – a wonderful luxury, especially when the weather grew cold. Later they were also able to employ a cook, who proved to be extraordinarily resourceful. From 'an old hovel of a hut', the first meal he provided for them was 'a most excellent clear soup; beef olives, with a thick gravy; potatoes and kidney beans; an entrée made of eggs; stewed apricots, custard and coffee'. To their delight, this feast arrived 'all beautifully hot and punctual to the minute'.

Although the twenty-seven-year-old Harriet McDougall was by far the more experienced – she had been a Gold Medallist at St Bart's Hospital in London – the friendship between the two young women continued to grow. They looked after one another when they were ill, and arranged things so that they would always be on duty together. If Hester ever felt homesick, Harriet would read to her from her favourite authors: George Eliot, George Meredith, and the poems of Robert Browning.

'Work here much harder than I expected,' Hester Dowson wrote home. 'Miss McDougall, straight from a smart hospital like "Barts", where everything is just tip top, finds it most terribly harassing to be obliged, for the want of necessary materials, to allow things to slide, and perhaps only do for the patients a little better than would be done in their own home.'

As the weeks went on, and there was no sign of the epidemic abating, Hester Dowson's views on the way the government was handling the situation grew increasingly critical. She had come to have a real admiration for her patients and their families – 'a most affectionate people' – many of whom were poor migrant workers from the countryside, living in overcrowded, slum-like quarters where all diseases, not only the plague, could quickly spread. In an effort to quarantine them, most had been taken to the hospital against their will, and were frightened by a medical system that they did not understand. Hester Dowson was deeply sympathetic to their plight:

I feel dreadfully for the poor patients here, taken by force, by an alien race, out of their homes and obliged to enter our Hospitals and be treated and drugged by any young English doctor who may have only lately come out, and who can try pretty nearly any treatment he chooses. Then, though a certain number of families are always allowed to visit them, many dare not come into a hospital put apart for the plague, though they would be willing, no doubt, to sit by their own relations at home. The poor things are forced, every two hours, to take nauseous medicines, which many of them genuinely believe to be poison, to drink milk whether they like it or not, and generally made miserable for the little time the majority of them have left in this life.

Most of all she regretted her inability to speak to them. 'Of course, we sisters do not understand them when they speak to us, and consequently they are practically dependent on the rough ward boys, who having become familiar with death and disease, have grown sometimes callous to suffering, and who are often, I am afraid, far from kind to the poor suffering creatures. It is ... terrible work.'

The epidemic continued to grow, and was proving to be 'of a very fatal kind'. On a single night twenty-four patients died, and nine more the following day. On another occasion, six of her patients died within half an hour of each other.* All were delirious, and had to be tied down to their beds to stop them escaping. The two women were desperate not to be able to do more for them. Basic supplies, such as sheets and blankets, were in short supply, and those that they had were frequently stolen by the dhobi-wallah. Two of their fellow nurses were taken ill themselves, which greatly increased their workload, not helped by the less than efficient contributions of the 'ward boys'.

'Good nursing is out of the question as, in the men's wards, it has to be done by the native ward boys, who are very rough material and who seem to have ingrained in them the importance of doing nothing they can avoid doing,' Hester Dowson wrote. 'You have to tell them each separate thing you want doing, every time, and how to do it. They are always disappearing, and you find them asleep or smoking round the corner, and they either don't, or pretend they don't, understand what you mean, and then take three times as long to do it as you would yourself.'

It was exhausting work. The night shifts made her ill. Fortunately, since she had Harriet, who looked after her 'ever so well', she always recovered.

Despite death and suffering all around, there were occasional moments of reprieve. She came to relish her surroundings. In the early mornings, faint blue mist hung between the trees; while 'in the evenings, in the starlight, it is like a fairy scene here, with our hanging

---

*In one week in March 1898 alone, the government recorded 2184 deaths, representing 136.4 per thousand of the population.

trees and the wild shrubberies and the palms scattered about'. Bombay itself she thought 'a beautiful town, full of fine buildings'. The station and the General Post Office, in particular, were 'as good as anything in London', the latter 'very well kept with beautiful palms and grass plots in front'.

Thanks to Harriet McDougall, who had introduced her to a young Englishman whom she refers to as Mr P—, Hester was occasionally able to venture into the bazaars to go shopping. Not only could Mr P— speak the language, he was also intending to learn Sanskrit to enable him to study Indian religions. 'In a land where most English men and women "run down" the natives, and seem to have boundless contempt for them', he was to prove the perfect chaperone.

Hester Dowson certainly thought so. 'It is a treat to come across one like him, who really seems to know them and yet to like and admire them; he is very anxious we should not despise them,' she wrote. 'He seems quite at home with them, and is very good at managing them and bargaining, but yet so gentle and manly, and not in the least rough spoken to them, though it is a wonder he is not, for a mob of at least ten men follow him about the market from stall to stall, pestering him to carry parcels etc, and hoping for *bakhsheesh*. It needs someone pretty calm and collected not to lose one's temper, and yet get away without being fleeced.'

Mr P— and his friend Lieutenant S— were, she wrote approvingly, 'two very good specimens of the British officer'.

The same could not be said of the English doctors at the Arthur Road Hospital, whose high-handed behaviour and 'insolence and ignorance' towards their patients made her blood boil; but as nurses, there was nothing either of them could do about it. They had now been working almost without a break for several months. Even the super-efficient Harriet McDougall was beginning to feel the strain.

Outside the hospital compound there was an ugly atmosphere. Many people had already fled the city; those who were left were becoming increasingly hostile towards the methods the British were using to contain the epidemic. The forced removal of women was particularly controversial with the Muslim population, as was the inspection of corpses, and the delays to the performance of funeral rites. Again, Hester Dowson was full of sympathy for them. 'I think it is awfully hard on them,' she wrote, 'all these regulations being enforced, simply because we have the power. I am sure that most of them do not understand or believe that it is done from a disinterested motive, or for their good.'

Troops were now stationed in the city 'as they are afraid of rioting, owing to the very strict house to house visitation that is now going forward, in the fruitless hope of stopping the ravages of the plague'.* One day one of the nurses from the Arthur Road Hospital had stones thrown at her when she walked down the street. 'I'm afraid a good many of the natives hate us,' Hester Dowson wrote; 'it's all connected to this plague business'.

Despite poor pay and rudimentary accommodation, their situation was better than that of many of the nurses who were shipped out from England in 1897. One 'poor nurse' was sent to Surat, where there were hardly any other Europeans. 'She writes me to say her quarters and everything are appalling, and she would give all she possesses to get away, and yet she has knocked about the world a good deal, in Egypt and elsewhere.'

The news from Peshawar, close to the Afghan border, was even worse. The nurses there reported that the only way to keep safe was to lock themselves into the hospital every night. 'No Europeans are allowed to walk about after dark as the Afridis [a Pashtun tribe] used to come right up to the town and shoot the men lying down, or in camp, whenever they could.'

Closer to home, disaster struck in a different form. In her next letter she wrote with the news that 'Miss McDougall has a poisoned eye and

---

*She was subsequently proved right. On 11 March, Reuters reported that fifteen thousand dockers, labourers and cartmen employed at railway goods stations had gone on strike. On the same day the Governor of Bombay sent a telegram which read: 'Plague disturbances began with attempted removal of Mahommedan female plague patients to hospital. Mob collected and became dangerous that police had to fire on them. Firing dispersed mob in that locality, but were smaller disturbances in other places.' Many people were killed.

is off duty ... But no reason to be alarmed.' In fact, there was every reason to be alarmed. A patient she had been attending, delirious and in the last stages of pneumonia, had coughed in her face. Some of the sputum had entered one of her eyes, and it was this that had caused the infection. The doctor had been to see her, and told her not to go back to work. 'He had found a gland [in her neck], and was anxious but said nothing to her.

'We went to bed as usual, but at 5am she called me, and I found that she had been up all night, walking about, and her temperature was 102, but her eye feeling better. She would not wake me in the night, she was always so unselfish. She had made up her mind that it was the plague, and by 12 o'clock her temperature was 104.'

The following day her temperature had reached 106.2°F. It was very unlikely that she would now survive. 'We still hoped her good constitution would pull her through, but Dr Dimmock, who was most kind, walked up the road with me a little way and said it was just a fight for life, and I must let her friends in India know.'

At this point, possibly from the distress her friend's illness had caused her, Hester Dowson also began to feel unwell. She reported a fit of shivering, aching in her bones, and could take no food. Fortunately, a huge dose of quinine seemed to set her right; but while she began to recover, it became clear that there was nothing more that could be done for her friend. 'Everything possible was tried for Miss McDougall, but she became very delirious and was difficult to feed, though she still seemed to know me and drank when I told her to.'

That night she could not sleep from wanting to be with her friend. At nine in the morning the nurse who had been put in charge of Miss McDougall came to say that there had been a change. 'I ran in and found her un-conscious, unable to swallow, and only breathing now and then. She did not know me, and all that day I sat by her, hardly moving from her bedside, hoping for a gleam of consciousness, that she might see and know me ... I kept moistening her lips, but she couldn't swallow, and gradually she got worse in pulse and breathing. I was all alone with her at 4pm, when the nurse went to tea, when suddenly she struggled for breath and died.'

Hester Dowson was devastated. 'I was only so thankful that I was the one there to stroke her face, and gently straighten the poor limbs for the last time. The Doctor was there the whole time, but no one else, and he was kindness itself.' What was particularly hard for her was that she had not been able to speak to Harriet towards the end. 'I wish she had been more conscious,' she wrote forlornly. 'One longs to have said a few of the things one had to say, the last opportunity of expressing all the love one feels ... But everything seemed so strange and rapid. She was so strong, tall and pretty, with lovely hair, and so full of character and determination.'

In recognition of her outstanding nursing work, Harriet McDougall was given a first-class naval funeral. On the day, a white hearse appeared at the door of their little bungalow drawn by milk-white horses. Her coffin was carried out by a naval brigade, also wearing white. Although many people were in attendance, Hester Dowson was not present.

Instead, she went back to her room to be alone, and to think it all over. 'I wandered around the grounds till I saw Dr Dimmock's carriage coming back,' she recalled. 'He made me get in there and then, and said he would take me for a drive, which I felt was just what I should like. We drove on and on and it seemed to me, into the dusk of evening, and at last I found we had got to his bungalow on Malabar Hill, and his sweet pretty young wife came and kissed and "mothered" me. They would not let me go back but telephoned I was sleeping there ... And I slept for the first time since she was taken ill.'

In a letter to her family a few days later, Hester Dowson wondered how it might have been if it had been her, and not her friend, who had died that day. 'It seems so strange that all I have been living through this last week was unknown to you ...' she wrote on 28 February, 'and that I might be dead and buried from plague, almost before you could know that I was ill. Miss McDougall's death has made me feel more than ever how near death may be to any of us; and how terrible to feel that if one got the plague, all the longing in the world would not make it possible to communicate with any of you again.'

# CONCLUSION

I had not thought to find a connection between the first women adventurers and the last in this book, but perhaps one is contained in Hester Dowson's lament.

When she wrote about the last days of her friend Harriet McDougall, dying so far away from home, we can imagine that the situation would have been not so very different from that of any of the women who travelled to India in the seventeenth century. A twelve-year-old child, plucked from Christ's Hospital and sent to Bombay in the 1680s, her life expectancy no more than 'two mussouns', might have experienced something very similar when her end came. In fact, Hester Dowson's description – 'the little sweltering hot bungalow, the tiny little room, the foreign ayah (though no one could have more faithfully watched and fanned the flies off than she did)'[1] – might have described the dying moments of any number of British women, tormented by 'the impossible longing' to bid farewell to friends and family back home.

While it is true that many of the women I write about here – Augusta Becher, Fanny Parkes and Flora Annie Steel, to name but a few – would end their lives peacefully back home, for countless others this was not an option. For them, India *was* home. From the colonisation of Bombay in the 1660s, whole generations of Britons had been born and brought up there. Eliza Draper, for example, born in Bombay in 1744, was the third generation of an Anglo-Indian family that could trace their antecedents back to the beginning of the eighteenth century. Yet even Eliza Draper, and others like her, remained in some sense 'aliens under one sky'.

We are used to thinking of memsahibs as being part of a colonising race, but in the early centuries their experience was much closer to that of immigrants than that of colonisers. Indians themselves not only did not welcome them, but often despised them for their strange, improper ways. And like outsiders everywhere, they clung together. Some of the more outrageous-sounding pieces of British flummery – the Vicereine's Drawing Rooms in the late nineteenth century for example – start to make a little more sense when you consider what they had grown out of: a tradition of hospitality, going back centuries, which all Britons could rely on, even in the remotest trading outposts.

Even the oh-so-British hill stations, with their fancy fairs, their amateur dramatic societies and their houses with suburban names, begin to seem a little less ludicrous when we remember what the alternatives were. Who can forget the lone woman in a society consisting only of men, half crazed with loneliness and boredom, whom Emily Eden encountered on her way to Simla?

But power corrupts. Little by little, as the influence and reach of the East India Company grew, so too did the arrogance and racism of the British. It is inevitable that the personal histories of the women I have written about rub up, often unhappily, against some of the most shameful episodes in our colonial past. This is particularly true of the period after the Uprisings of 1857. For example, at the same time that Edith Lytton stood in her diamonds and pearls with all the pomp and circumstance of the Imperial Assemblage around her, many millions of Indians were starving to death in the famine that raged throughout south India. Her husband's role in the matter was much criticised, not least because of the vast amount of money that had been spent on a durbar that, in the opinion of many, would have been far better used to bring relief to the victims of that famine.

But these stories provide us with other more positive ways of looking at our shared history. Generalisations about a group tend to unravel when individual lives are scrutinised. As individuals, British women struggled to make sense of a world that was not only indescribably alien, but also frequently hostile to them. They died in shipwrecks and storms, and of frightening illnesses they did not understand. They lost their children to war and disease, or, what is perhaps worse, had the loving bonds between them severed by too-long separations. Even the simplest female avocations – keeping house, buying food, dealing with servants – were beset with difficulties of which their friends and relations back in England could have had only the vaguest possible notion . . . but criticised them for it nonetheless.

In much the same way as when I was concluding *Daughters of Britannia* and *Courtesans*, I am left wondering about the myriad women whose stories it has not been possible to tell. Those who left some record of their lives, even if it was only a shopping list, were mostly middle-class and educated – even if this turned out to be a nimble feat of self-promotion on the voyage out. There were many more, from humbler backgrounds, whose stories are lost to us forever: the soldiers' wives, the lady's maids, the shopkeepers. I long to know how Poll Puff and her exquisite apple pies came to be in Calcutta at all; to hear the full story of Eliza Draper's grandmother, captured by pirates; and to unearth more details about the gentlewomen among whom the 'itch of gaming' had spread in the 1720s, to the ire of the EIC. I wonder, too, about the nameless women in the family photograph albums I studied all those years ago, whose stories I will never know.

A great deal depended, as it always does, on the energies of the individual. The best of them connected to India in ways that were both true and profound. 'Oh, the pleasure of vagabondizing through India,' you will recall Fanny Parkes writing. 'With the Neapolitan saying "Vedi Napoli, e poi mori", I beg leave to differ entirely, and would rather offer *this* advice – "See the Taj Mahal, and then – see the Ruins of Delhi." How much there is to delight the eye in this bright and beautiful world! Roaming about with a good tent and a good Arab, one might be happy for ever in India.'

Whatever their fate might have been, none of the women who went to India could fail to be changed by it. They saw death and suffering, but they saw marvels, too. If many of their stories are about the ordinary warp and weft of life, then so much the better. There is a truthfulness about them that still speaks to us today, and that illuminates our long history which is forever entwined.

# ACKNOWLEDGEMENTS

I would like to thank my agent, Caroline Michel, and everyone at Peters, Fraser & Dunlop Literary Agency. At Virago, my warmest appreciation goes to Nithya Rae, Linda Silverman, Daniel Balado and – of course – my wonderful editor, Lennie Goodings.

# BIBLIOGRAPHY

## Manuscript and Unpublished Sources

Katherine Bartrum, *Manuscript Copy of a diary kept between 7th June 1857 and 12th February 1858, by Mrs Katherine Bartram, wife of surgeon Robert Henry Bartram (1831–1857)*. British Library Mss Eur A69.

Hester Mary Dowson, *Bombay During the Plague: nurse at the Arthur Road Hospital, Bombay, describing her voyage to India, her experiences during the plague of 1897–1898, and the death from plague of her friend Harriet McDougall*. (Printed for private circulation only.)

Margaret Fowke's Papers. British Library Mss Eur D 546/xi.
Joseph Fowke's Papers. British Library Mss Eur D 546/xii.
Sophia Plowden Papers. British Library Eur Mss B 187.
Emily Royal and George Dawson. British Library Photo Eur 262.
Lady Florentia Sale. British Library Mss Eur 186.

## Newspapers and Periodicals

*Hickey's Bengal Gazette*

## Published Sources

Ali, Mrs Meer Hassan, *Observations on the Mussulmans of India: Descriptive of their Manners, Customs, Habits and Religious Opinions. Made During a Twelve Years' Residence in Their Immediate Society*. (2 vols, London, 1832).
Allen, Charles, *Plain Tales from the Raj*. (London, 1975).
Allen, Charles (ed), *A Glimpse of the Burning Plain: Leaves from the Indian Journals of Charlotte Canning*. (London, 1986).
Balfour, Lady Betty, *The History of Lord Lytton's Indian Administration 1876–1880*. (London, 1899).

Barr, Pat, *Memsahibs: The Women of Victorian England.* (London, 1976).

Barr, Pat, *Dust in the Balance: British Women in India 1905–1945.* (London, 1989).

Becher, Augusta, *Personal Reminiscences of Augusta Becher.* (London, 1930).

Blum, Dilys, *Englishwomen's Dress in Eighteenth-Century India: The Margaret Fowke Correspondence, 1776–1786.* (London, 1983).

Brendon, Vyvyen, *Children of the Raj.* (London, 2005).

Burney, Fanny, *A Busy Day.* (London, 1795).

Calendar of State Papers (W. Noel Sainsbury ed) *Colonial Series, East India, China and Japan, 1617–1621, preserved in Her Majesty's Public Record Office and elsewhere.* (London, 1870).

Calendar of State Papers (W. Noel Sainsbury ed) *Colonial Series, East Indies China and Japan, 1622–1624, preserved in Her Majesty's Public Record Office and elsewhere.* (London, 1878).

Calendar of State Papers (W. Noel Sainsbury ed) *Colonial Series, East Indies, China and Persia, 1625–1629, preserved in Her Majesty's Public Record Office and elsewhere.* (London, 1884).

Calendar of State Papers (W. Noel Sainsbury ed) *Colonial Series, East India and Persia, 1630–1634, preserved in the Public Record Office and the India Office.* (London, 1892).

Chick, N.A., *Annals of the Indian Rebellion 1857–8, Containing narratives of the outbreaks and eventful occurrences and stories of personal adventures.* (Calcutta, 1859).

Clemons, Eliza, *The Manners and Customs of Society in India; Including Scenes in the Mofussil Stations; Interspersed with Characteristic Tales and Anecdotes; and Reminiscences of the late Burmese War. To which are added Instructions for the Guidance of Cadets, and other Young Gentlemen, During their First Year's Residence in India.* (London, 1841).

Clive, Henrietta, *see* Shields, Nancy

Colley, Linda, *The Ordeal of Elizabeth Marsh: A Woman in World History.* (London, 2007).

Dalrymple, William, *White Mughals: Love and Betrayal in Eighteenth-Century India.* (London, 2002).

Dalrymple, William, *The Last Mughal: The Fall of a Dynasty, Delhi 1857.* (London, 2006).

Dalrymple, William, *Return of a King: The Battle for Afghanistan* (London, 2013).

de Courcy, Ann, *The Fishing Fleet: Husband Hunting in the Raj.* (London, 2012).

Diver, Maud, *The Englishwoman in India.* (London, 1909).

Dodwell, Henry, *The Nabobs of Madras.* (London, 1926).

Draper, Eliza, *see* Wright, Arnold and Sclater, William Lutley

Dufferin, Countess of, *Our Viceregal Life in India: Selections from my Journals 1884–1888.* (2 vols, London, 1889).

Dunbar, Janet (ed), *Tigers, Durbars and Kings: Fanny Eden's Indian Journals 1837–1838.* (London, 1988).

East India Company (Danvers, F.C. and Foster, William eds), *Letters Received by the East India Company from Its Servants in the East: Transcribed from the Original Correspondence series of the East India Company Records.* (6 vols, London, 1896–1902).

Eden, Emily, *Up the Country: Letters written to her sister from the Upper Provinces of India.* (London, 1866).

Eden, Fanny, *see* Dunbar

Edwardes, Michael, *The Nabobs at Home.* (London, 1991).

Fay, Eliza, *Original Letters From India, 1779–1815, with introductory and terminal notes by E. M. Forster.* (London, 1925).

Ferguson, Niall, *Empire: How Britain Made the Modern World.* (London, 2003).

Foote, Samuel, *The Nabob: A Comedy in Three Acts.* (London, 1773).

Foster, William (ed), *The English Factories in India 1618–1669: A Calendar of Documents in the India Office, British Museum, and Public Record Office.* (13 vols, London, 1906–27).

Fraser, Antonia, *The Weaker Vessel: A Woman's Lot in Seventeenth-Century England.* (London, 1984).

Gascoigne, Bamber, *A Brief History of the Great Moghuls, India's Most Flamboyant Rulers.* (London, 1971).

Gaughan, Joan Mickleson, *The 'Incumberances': British Women in India 1615–1856.* (Delhi, 2013).

Gilmour, David, *The Ruling Caste: Imperial Lives in the Victorian Raj.* (London, 2005).

Graham, Maria, *Journal of a Residence in India.* (Edinburgh, 1813).

Hickey, William, (Alfred Spencer ed), *Memoirs of William Hickey.* (4 vols, London, 1923).

Inglis, Julia, *The Siege of Lucknow: A Diary.* (London, 1892).

Jasanoff, Maya, *Liberty's Exiles: The Loss of America and the Remaking of the British Empire.* (London, 2011).

Kaye, M. M., *The Golden Calm: An English Lady's Life in Moghul Delhi. Reminiscences by Emily, Lady Clive Bayley, and her father Thomas Metcalfe.* (Exeter, 1980).

Keay, John, *The Honourable Company: A History of the East India Company.* (London, 1991).

Kincaid, Dennis, *British Social Life in India 1608–1937.* (London, 1938).

Kindersley, Jemima, *Letters from the Island of Teneriffe, Brazil, the Cape of Good Hope and the East Indies.* (London, 1777).

A Lady Resident, *The English Woman In India.* (London, 1864).

Lawrence, Honoria, (Lawrence, John and Woodiwiss, Audrey eds), *The Journals of Honoria Lawrence: India Observed 1837–1854.* (London, 1980).

Leigh Hunt, Major S., *Tropical Trials: A Handbook for Women in the Tropics.* (London, 1883).

Login, Lena, *Lady Login's Recollections of Court and Camp Life: 1820–1904.* (London, 1916).

Losti, J.P. and Roy, Mahini, *Mughal India: Art, Culture and Empire.* (London, 2012).

Lutyens, Mary, *The Lyttons in India: An Account of Lord Lytton's Viceroyalty 1876–1880.* (London, 1979).

Lytton, Robert, (Lady Betty Balfour ed), *Personal and Literary Letters of Robert, First Earl of Lytton.* (London, 1906).

Macfarlane, Iris, *Daughter of Empire: A Memoir of Life and Times in the British Raj.* (London, 2012).

Macmillan, Margaret, *Women of the Raj.* (London, 1988).

Maitland, Julia, *Letters from Madras During the Years 1836–1839.* (London, 1843).

Markham, Clements R. (ed), *The Hawkins' Voyages During the Reign of Henry VIII, Queen Elizabeth I, and James I.* (London, 1878).

Marsh, Elizabeth (Khalid Bekkaoui ed) *The Female Captive: A Narrative of Facts which Happened in Barbary in the Year 1756, Written by Herself.* (Casablanca, 2003).

Marshall, P.J., 'The Private Fortune of Marian Hastings', *Bulletin of the Institute of Historical Research*, Vol 37, November 1964.

Micklethwait, John and Wooldridge, Adrian, *The Company: A Short History of a Revolutionary Idea.* (London, 2003).

Milton, Giles, *Nathaniel's Nutmeg: How One Man's Courage Changed the Course of History.* (London, 1999).

Nussbaum, Felicity (ed), *The Global Eighteenth Century.* (Baltimore, 2003).

Nugent, Maria, *A Journal from the Year 1811 til the Year 1815, Including a Voyage to and Residence in India, with a Tour to the North-Western parts of the British Possessions in that Country, under the Bengal Government.* (2 vols, London, 1839).

Parkes, Fanny, (William Dalrymple ed), *Begums, Thugs and White Mughals: The Journals of Fanny Parkes.* (London, 2002).

Parkes, Fanny, *Wanderings of a Pilgrim in Search of the Picturesque, During Four-and-Twenty Years in the East; with Revelations of Life in the Zenana.* (2 vols, London, 1850).

Postans, Marianne, *Western India in 1838.* (2 vols, London, 1839).

Raza, Rosemary, *In Their Own Words: British Women Writers and India, 1740–1857.* (New Delhi, 2006).

Robinson, Jane, *Angels of Albion: Women of the Indian Mutiny.* (London, 1996).

Sattin, Anthony (ed), *An Englishwoman in India: The Memoirs of Harriet Tytler, 1828–1858.* (Oxford, 1986).

Shields, Nancy (ed), *Birds of Passage: Henrietta Clive's Travels in South India 1798–1801.* (London, 2009).

Smart, Jane, *Letter from a Lady at Madrass to her friends in London: Giving an*

*Account of a Visit, made by the Governor of That Place, With his Lady and Others, to the Nobob (Prime Minister to the Great Moghul) and his Lady, etc, in which their Persons and Amazing Richness of Dress, are particularly described. With some Account of the Manners and Customs of the Moors in general.* (London, 1743).

Smith, Hilda (ed) *Women Writers and the Early Modern British Political System.* (Cambridge, 1998).

Stanford, J.K., *Ladies in the Sun: The Memsahibs' India 1790–1860.* (London, 1962).

Steel, Flora Annie, and Gardiner, Grace, *The Complete Indian Housekeeper and Cook.* (London, 1888).

Steel, Flora Annie, *The Garden of Fidelity: Being the Autobiography of Flora Annie Steel 1847–1929.* (London, 1929).

Trollope, Joanna, *Britannia's Daughters: Women of the British Empire.* (London, 1983).

Tytler, Harriet, *see* Sattin, Anthony

Venning, Annabel, *Following the Drum: The Lives of Army Wives and Daughters, Past and Present.* (London, 2005).

Wright, Arnold and Sclater, William Lutley, *Sterne's Eliza: Some Account of her Life in India: with her Letters Written Between 1757 and 1774.* (London, 1922).

Wright, Jonathan, *The Ambassadors: From Ancient Greece to the Nation State.* (London, 2006).

# NOTES

**Introduction**

1  Shashi Tharoor, *Inglorious Empire: What the British Did to India*. (London, 2017).

2  Henry Dodwell, *The Nabobs of Madras*. (London, 1926).

3  Antonia Fraser, *The Weaker Vessel: A Woman's Lot in Seventeenth-Century England*. (London, 1984).

4  Susan Stave, 'Investments, Votes and Bribes: Women as Shareholders in the Chartered National Companies'. In Hilda Smith (ed), *Women Writers and the Early Modern British Political Tradition*. (Cambridge, 1998).

5  William Hickey (ed Alfred Spencer) *Memoirs of William Hickey*. (4 vols, London, 1923) Vol 3.

6  Maud Diver, *The Englishwoman in India*. (Edinburgh and London, 1909).

**Chapter 1**

1  East India Company (Danvers and Foster eds), *Letters Received from its Servants in the East*. (6 vols, 1896–1902) Vol. VI, 9 July 1617.

2  John Keay, *The Honourable Company: A History of the East India Company*. (London, 1991).

3  Henrietta Clive to George Herbert, 2nd Earl of Powis, 23 July 1799, quoted in Nancy K. Shields (ed), *Birds of Passage: Henrietta Clive's Travels in South India 1798–1801* (London, 2009).

4  Quoted in Keay, op. cit.

5  East India Company, *Letters Received*. Vol VI, 28 December 1617.

6  Letters Received, Vol II, 19 June 1615.

7  Letters Received, Vol VI, 3 November 1617.

8  Ibid., 8 November 1617.

9  Ibid., 6 December 1617.

10  Ibid.

11  East India Company, (W. Foster ed), *The English Factories in India 1618–1621*. (13 vols, London, 1906–27) Letter from Matthew Duke, in Pring's fleet at sea, to the Company, 16 March 1618.

12  Clements Markham (ed), *The Hawkins' Voyages During the Reign of Henry VIII, Queen Elizabeth I, and James I*. (London, 1878).

13  Ibid.

14  Ibid.

15  Calendar of State Papers, 17 February 1614.

16  Letters Received, op. cit. Vol VI, 28 December 1617.

17  Ibid., 18 December 1617.

18  *The English Factories in India*, 1618–1621.

19  East India Company (N. Sainsbury ed), *Original Correspondence of and Minutes of Court of Committees*. (London, 1862–92), 17 September 1619.

20  J. Talboys Wheeler (ed), *Early Travels in India: Being Reprints of Rare and Curious Narratives of Old Travellers in India in the Sixteenth and Seventeenth Centuries*. (Calcutta, 1864).

**Chapter 2**

1  Calendar of State Papers, Vol. V, 1630–1632.

2  Quoted in Keay, *The Honourable Company*.

3  Ibid.

4  Ibid.

5   East India Company (N. Sainsbury ed),
    *Original Correspondence of and Minutes
    of Court of Committees, 1668–1670*, 30
    December 1668.
6   Court Minutes, 1674–1676, 10 February
    1675.
7   Ibid., 8 December 1675.
8   Ibid., 18 February 1676.
9   Quoted in Keay, op. cit.

**Chapter 3**

1   Hickey, *Memoirs*. Vol 3 (1782–1790).
2   Ibid.
3   Ibid.
4   Ibid.
5   Quoted in Keay, *The Honourable
    Company*.
6   Eliza Fay, *Original Letters from India,
    1799–1815*. (London, 1925).

**Chapter 4**

1   Emma Roberts, quoted in Rosemary
    Raza, *In Their Own Words: British Women
    Writers and India 1740–1857*. (New Delhi,
    2006).
2   Fanny Parkes, *Wanderings of a Pilgrim
    in Search of the Picturesque, During
    Four-and-Twenty Years in the East; with
    Revelations of Life in the Zenana*. (London,
    1850).
3   Emily Eden, *Up the Country: Letters
    Written to her Sister from the Upper
    Provinces of India*. (London, 1866).
4   Augusta Becher, *Personal Reminiscences
    of Augusta Becher, 1830–1888*. Ed H. G.
    Rawlinson (London, 1930).
5   Fay, op. cit.
6   Henrietta Clive, (ed Nancy K. Shields),
    *Birds of Passage*.
7   Arnold Wright and William Lutley
    Sclater (eds), *Sterne's Eliza: Some Account
    of her Life in India with her Letters
    written between 1757 and 1774*. (London,
    1922).
8   Jemima Kindersley, *Letters from the Island
    of Teneriffe, Brazil, the Cape of Good Hope
    and the East Indies*. (London, 1777).
9   Quoted in Linda Colley, *The Ordeal of
    Elizabeth Marsh: A Woman in World
    History*. (London, 2007).
10  Fay, *Original Letters from India,
    1779–1815*.
11  Kindersley, op. cit.
12  Fay, op. cit.

13  Jane Smart, *Letter from a Lady at Madras
    to her friends in London*. (London, 1743).
14  Ibid.
15  Quoted in Colley, op. cit.
16  Kindersley, op. cit.

**Chapter 5**

1   Wright and Sclater, *Sterne's Eliza*.
2   Hickey, *Memoirs*.
3   *Bengal Gazette*, 28 April 1781.
4   Quoted in Raza, *British Women Writers
    and India*.
5   Hickey, *Memoirs*. Vol. 2 (1775–1782).
6   Katie Hickman, *Courtesans*. (London,
    2003).
7   Keay, *The Honourable Company*.
8   E. M. Forster's introduction to Fay,
    *Original Letters from India, 1779–1815*.
9   Cited in John Keay, *India Discovered*.
    (London, 1981).
10  Hickey, *Memoirs*. Vol. 3.

**Chapter 6**

1   Fay, *Original Letters from India,
    1779–1815*.
2   Mr Hickey's *Bengal Gazette*, 18 November
    1780.
3   Quoted in Dilys Blum, *Englishwomen's
    Dress in Eighteenth-Century India:
    The Margaret Fowke Correspondence
    1776–1786*. (London, 1983).
4   Margaret Fowke to Mrs Weelock, 27
    December 1781 (British Library, Eur F.2,
    106).
5   Fay, op. cit., Letter XIV, 13 April 1780.
6   Quoted in Blum, op. cit.
7   Mr Hickey's *Bengal Gazette*, February
    1780.
8   Fay, op. cit.
9   Ibid., Letter XV, 29 May.
10  Felicity A. Nussbaum (ed), *The Global
    Eighteenth Century*. (Baltimore, 2003).
11  P. J. Marshall, 'The Private Fortune of
    Marian Hastings', in the *Bulletin of the
    Institute of Historical Research*, Vol 37,
    November 1964.
12  Mr Hickey's *Bengal Gazette*, 25
    November 1780.
13  Fay, op. cit., Letter XVI, 29 August.
14  Beth Fowkes Tobin, 'The English
    Garden Conversation Piece in India', in
    Nussbaum (ed), op. cit.
15  Hickey, *Memoirs*.
16  Fanny Burney, *A Busy Day*. (London, 1795).

## Chapter 7

1 The Fowke Correspondence (British Library, Eur Mss D 546/XI).
2 Ibid.
3 Ibid., Eur Mss D.546/XII, Joseph Fowke to Mr Henchman, Calcutta, 12 January 1781.
4 Keay, *The Honourable Company*.
5 Ibid.
6 This, and all the following quotations, are from Eliza Fay, *Original Letters from India*.

## Chapter 8

1 Kindersley, *Letters*.
2 Anthony Sattin (ed), *An Englishwoman in India: The Memoirs of Harriet Tytler 1828–1858*. (Oxford, 1986).
3 Hickey, *Memoirs*, Vol 3.
4 Ibid.
5 Ibid.
6 Letter from Mrs Sophia Plowden giving news of her life in Calcutta, 1783. (British Library Mss Eur B.187).
7 Hickey, *Memoirs*, Vol 3.
8 Fay, *Original Letters from India, 1779–1815*.
9 Ibid., Part Second, Letter III, 19 February 1815.
10 Calendar of State Papers, Colonial Series, 18 February 1614.
11 East India Company, Court Minutes, 4 December 1668.
12 Quoted in Dodwell, *The Nabobs of Madras*.
13 This, and all the following quotations in Eliza Draper's story, are from Wright and Sclater, *Sterne's Eliza*.
14 Abraham Parsons, *Travels in Asia and Africa*. (London, 1808).

## Chapter 9

1 Elizabeth Marsh's Indian Journal is quoted extensively in Colley, *The Ordeal of Elizabeth Marsh*.
2 Cited in William Dalrymple, *White Mughals*. (London, 2002).
3 Ibid.
4 Ibid. Dalrymple is quoting from Anna A. Suvorova, *Masnavi: A Study of Urdu Romance*. (Karachi, 2000).
5 See Raza, *In Their Own Words*. She is quoting from *The Journal of the Families in British India Society*, Number 10, Autumn 2003.

6 See Dalrymple, op. cit.
7 Parkes, *Wandering of a Pilgrim in Search of the Picturesque*.
8 Ibid.
9 Shields (ed), *Birds of Passage*, Henrietta Clive to Lady Douglas, 31 August 1800.
10 Ibid, Henrietta Clive to Lord Clive, 16 March 1800.
11 Maria Graham, *Journal of a Residence in India*. (Edinburgh, 1813).
12 Mrs Meer Hassan Ali, *Observations on the Mussulmans of India, Descriptive of their Manners, Customs, Habits and Religious Opinions*. (London, 1832).
13 Parkes, op. cit.
14 Mrs Meer Hassan Ali, op. cit.
15 Ibid.
16 E. Dalhousie Login (ed), *Lady Login's Recollections: Court Life and Camp Life: 1820–1904*. (London, 1916).
17 Ibid.
18 This quotation, and all the above, are taken from Login (ed), *Lady Login's Recollections*.
19 Parkes, *Wandering of a Pilgrim in Search of the Picturesque*.

## Chapter 10

1 Emily Royal (British Library, Mss Eur 262).
2 Shields (ed), *Birds of Passage*.
3 *The Cherry Papers*. This, and all following quotations, are reproduced in J. K. Stanford, *Ladies in the Sun: The Memsahibs' India 1790–1860*. (London, 1962).
4 Ibid.
5 *The Baker Papers*, quoted in Stanford, op. cit.
6 Raza, *In Their Own Words*.
7 Charles Grant, 'Observations on the State of Society among the Asiatic Subjects of Great Britain', quoted in Niall Ferguson, *Empire: How Britain Made the Modern World*. (London, 2003).
8 Maria Graham, *Journal of a Residence in India*.
9 Parkes, *Wanderings of a Pilgrim*.
10 David Gilmour, *The Ruling Caste: Imperial Lives in the Victorian Raj*. (London, 2005).

### Chapter 11

1   Shields (ed), *Birds of Passage*.
2   Ibid.
3   Parkes, *Wanderings of a Pilgrim*.
4   Julia Maitland, *Letters from Madras During the Years 1836–1839*. (London, 1843).
5   Shields, op. cit.
6   Maitland, op. cit.
7   Ibid.
8   Honoria Lawrence (John Lawrence and Audrey Woodiwiss eds), *The Journals of Honoria Lawrence: India Observed 1837–1854*. (London, 1980).
9   Ashley L. Cohen (ed), *Lady Nugent's East India Journal*. (Oxford, 2014).
10  Shields, op. cit., Henrietta Clive to Lady Douglas, 24 August 1798.
11  Ibid.
12  Anne Barnard, *The Letters of Lady Anne Barnard to Henry Dundas from the Cape and Elsewhere 1793–1803*. (Rotterdam, 1973).

### Chapter 12

1   Shields (ed), *Birds of Passage*, Henrietta Clive to Lady Douglas, 20 December 1797.
2   Ibid.
3   Ibid., Henrietta Clive to Lady Clive, 22 January 1800.
4   Ibid., Henrietta Clive to Lord Clive, 15 March 1800.
5   Ibid., Henrietta Clive to Lord Clive, 2 August 1800.
6   Ibid., 13 June 1800.
7   Ibid., 4 May 1800.
8   Ibid., 2 October 1800.
9   Ibid., 26 April 1800.
10  Ibid., 23 September 1800.
11  Ibid., Henrietta Clive to Lady Douglas, 31 August 1800.
12  Ibid., Henrietta Clive to George Herbert, undated.
13  Henrietta Clive's Journal, 12 August 1800.
14  Ibid., Henrietta Clive to Lady Douglas, 31 August 1800.

### Chapter 13

1   Colley, *The Ordeal of Elizabeth Marsh*.
2   Elizabeth Marsh (Khalid Bekkaoui ed), *The Female Captive: A Narrative of Facts which Happened in Barbary in the Year 1756, Written by Herself*. (Casablanca, 2003).

3   Ibid.
4   Elizabeth Marsh's Indian Journal, quoted in Colley.
5   Ibid.
6   Ibid.

### Chapter 14

1   Maitland, *Letters from Madras*.
2   Ibid.
3   Ibid.
4   Janet Dunbar (ed), *Tigers, Durbars and Kings: Fanny Eden's Indian Journals 1837–1838*. (London, 1988).
5   Emily Eden, *Up the Country*.
6   Maitland, *Letters from Madras*.
7   Eliza Clemons, *The Manners and Customs of Society in India*. (London, 1841).
8   Fanny Parkes, *Wanderings of a Pilgrim in Search of the Picturesque*.
9   Ibid.
10  Ibid.
11  Emily Eden, *Up the Country*.
12  Fanny Eden, Dunbar (ed).

### Chapter 15

1   Fanny Parkes, *Wanderings of a Pilgrim in Search of the Picturesque*.
2   Honoria Lawrence (John Lawrence and Audrey Woodiwiss eds), *The Journals of Honoria Lawrence*.
3   Harriet Tytler, Sattin (ed.)
4   Dunbar (ed), *Tigers, Durbars and Kings*.
5   Maria Nugent (Ashley L. Cohen ed), *East Indian Journal*.
6   Cited in Dalrymple, *White Mughals*. Dalrymple is quoting from Amin Jaffer's *Furniture from British India and Ceylon*. (London, 2001).
7   Augusta Becher, *Personal Reminiscences*.
8   Raza, *In Their Own Words*.
9   Parkes, *Wandering of a Pilgrim in Search of the Picturesque*.
10  Quoted in Margaret Macmillan, *Women of the Raj*. (London, 1988).
11  Honoria Lawrence, op. cit.
12  Wright and Sclater, *Sterne's Eliza*.
13  Macmillan, op. cit.
14  Dunbar (ed), op. cit.
15  Maria Nugent, op. cit., Letter to Lord Temple, March 1812.
16  Honoria Lawrence, op. cit.
17  Fanny Parkes, op. cit.

## Chapter 16

1  This quotation, and those that follow, are from Dunbar (ed), *Tigers, Durbars and Kings: Fanny Eden's Indian Journals 1837–1838.*
2  Emily Eden, *Up the Country.*
3  Dunbar (ed), op. cit.
4  Ibid.
5  Emily Eden, op. cit.
6  Dunbar (ed), op. cit.
7  Emily Eden, op. cit.
8  Dunbar (ed), op. cit.
9  Isabella Fane, *Miss Fane in India*, ed. John Premble (Gloucester, 1985).
10 Dunbar (ed), op. cit.
11 Emily Eden, op. cit.
12 Ibid.
13 Dunbar (ed), op. cit.
14 Emily Eden, op. cit.
15 Ibid.
16 Dunbar (ed), op. cit.

## Chapter 17

1  See Raza, *In their Own Words.*
2  Maria Nugent (Ashley L. Cohen ed), *East Indian Journal.*
3  Ibid.
4  Ibid.
5  A Lady Resident, *The Englishwoman in India.* (London, 1864).
6  Letter from Sophia Plowden giving news of her life in Calcutta, 1783. (British Library Mss Eur B.187).
7  Emily Eden, *Up the Country.*
8  Sattin (ed), *An Englishwoman in India.*
9  Quoted in Colley, *The Ordeal of Elizabeth Marsh.*
10 Letters from Emily Royal and George Dawson. (British Library Photo Eur 262).
11 Quoted in Wright and Sclater, *Sterne's Eliza.*
12 Emily Eden, op. cit.
13 Augusta Becher, *Personal Reminiscences of Augusta Becher.*
14 This and all the quotations below from Sattin (ed), *An Englishwoman in India.*
15 Honoria Lawrence (John Lawrence and Audrey Woodiwiss eds), *The Journals of Honoria Lawrence.*

## Chapter 18

1  Login (ed), *Lady Login's Recollections.*
2  Quoted in Lawrence, *The Journals of Honoria Lawrence.*

3  Ibid.
4  Ibid.
5  Becher, *Personal Reminiscences.*
6  Sattin (ed), *An Englishwoman in India.*
7  Lawrence, op. cit.
8  Sattin (ed), op. cit.
9  Ibid.
10 Ibid.
11 Saul David, *The Indian Mutiny.* (London, 2002).
12 Lieutenant Alfred Mackenzie, quoted in ibid.
13 Ibid.
14 Emily Eden, *Up the Country.*

## Chapter 19

1  Mrs Muter, *My Recollections of the Sepoy Revolt.* (London, 1911).
2  Ibid.
3  Quoted in David, *The Indian Mutiny.*
4  Quoted in Jane Robinson, *Angels of Albion: Women of the Indian Mutiny.* (London, 1996).
5  David, op. cit.
6  This and all the following quotations are from Harriet Tytler's memoirs, Sattin (ed).

## Chapter 20

1  William Howard Russell, *My Diary in India*, Vol 1. (London, 1957).
2  David, *The Indian Mutiny.*
3  Julia Inglis, *The Siege of Lucknow: A Diary.* (London, 1892).
4  Jane Robinson, *Angels of Albion: Women of the Indian Mutiny.* (London, 1996).
5  Martin Gubbins, *An Account of the Mutinies in Oude.* (London, 1858).
6  Kate Bartrum, Manuscript copy of a diary kept between 7 June 1857 and 12 February 1858. (British Library, Eur Mss A 69).
7  Julia Inglis, op. cit.
8  Bartrum, op. cit.
9  Inglis, op. cit.
10 Robinson, op. cit. She is quoting from Fred Roberts, *Letters Written during the Indian Mutiny.* (London, 1924).

## Chapter 21

1  Manuscript copy of the narrative of Amy Haines or Horne. (British Library, Add Mss 41488.f.64). She is referred to here as Amy Haines, but in other versions of her narrative she goes by the name of Horne.

2    Ibid.
3    Emma Larkins to Mrs Henrietta Coffin, 9 June 1857. (British Library, Eur Mss photo 233).
4    Ibid.
5    Horne narrative, op. cit.
6    Ibid.
7    Ibid.
8    Ibid.
9    David, op. cit.
10   Ibid.
11   Ibid.
12   Quoted in Robinson, *Angels of Albion*.
13   Captain Mowbray Thomson, *The Story of Cawnpore*. (London, 1859).
14   Robinson, op. cit.
15   Inglis, op. cit.
16   Sattin (ed), *An Englishwoman in India*.
17   Horne narrative, op. cit.
18   Ibid.

## Chapter 22

1    Quoted in Dalrymple, *The Last Mughal*.
2    Ibid.
3    From Edith Lytton's unpublished diaries; quoted in Mary Lutyens, *The Lyttons in India: An Account of Lord Lytton's Viceroyalty 1876–1880*. (London, 1979).
4    Ibid.
5    Lady Dufferin, *Our Viceregal Life in India: Selections from my Journal, 1884–1888*, Vol 1. (London, 1889).
6    A Lady Resident, *The Englishwoman in India*. (London, 1864).

7    Major Leigh Hunt, *Tropical Trials: A Handbook for Women in the Tropics*. (London, 1883).
8    Flora Annie Steel and Grace Gardiner, *The Complete Indian Housekeeper and Cook*. (London, 1888).

## Chapter 23

1    This and all the following quotes are taken from Flora Annie Steel, *The Garden of Fidelity: Being the Autobiography of Flora Annie Steel 1847–1929* (London, 1929).
2    Margaret Smith, *A Different Drummer*. (London, 1931).

## Chapter 24

1    Quoted in Raza, *In Their Own Words*.
2    Shampa Roy, *Feminist Review*, No. 94, 2010.
3    Flora Annie Steel, *The Garden of Fidelity, Being the Autobiography of Flora Annie Steel, 1847–1929*. (London, 1929).
4    Miss F. M. Wyld, *Memoirs*. (British Library, Mss Eur B 320).
5    Elizabeth Elton Smith, *The East Indian Sketchbook*. (London, 1833).
6    Steel, op. cit.
7    *Bombay During the Plague – Privately printed extracts from the letters of Hester May Dowson*. (BL Mss Eur B 385).

## Conclusion

1    Hester Dowson, *Bombay During the Plague*.

# INDEX

*A Busy Day* (Fanny Burney) 90–1
Abu Bakr 320
actresses 122
Afghanistan 237
Agra 22fn, 24, 27, 35, 36, 225
Ahmedabad 22
Akbar Shah 210
alcohol consumption 83fn, 114
Allahabad 165, 224, 261, 307, 313
Ambala 275, 285
Amboyna Massacre 34fn
Amritsar 237–8
Andhra Pradesh 193
Anglo-Indians
   children 207, 219, 220–2
   Indian-born British 66, 124
   marriages 221–2, 223
   mixed descent 124fn, 207
   prejudice against 220–1, 222
Angrey, Khanhoji (Angria) 94–5,
   124
Anjediva 40
Anjengo 93, 94
Annandale 269, 270
Anson, General Sir George 271,
   275
Arcot 181
armies (EIC) 93, 159, 266, 268

Bengal Army 280, 291
   fighting strength 268
   Indian soldiers, British treatment
      of 209
Arracan 267
Asaf ud-Daula, Nawab of Lucknow
   62
Assam 267
attar of roses 236
Auckland, Lord 211, 228, 229, 230,
   231, 232, 234–5, 270
Augusta, Princess 139, 140
Aurangzeb, Emperor 71
ayahs 7, 165, 222, 244, 276, 307,
   313, 345, 359
Ayres, Captain 103

Baghput 284
Baker, Caroline 156–9
balls 117, 118, 172–3, 178, 210–11,
   222, 240
bandits 232
Bangalore 181–2, 184, 198–200
Barahmahal 186
Barbary corsairs 191
Barnard, General 286
Barry, Charlotte 2–3, 5–6
   see also Hickey, Charlotte

Bartrum, Kate 294, 295, 297, 298,
    299, 301–2, 312–13, 314
Bartrum, Robert 294, 314
Baxter, Sarah 122
Becher, Augusta 216, 249, 250, 253,
    268, 269, 271
    and the Indian Uprisings 271,
        275–7, 312
    travels through India 263, 264, 266
Becher, Septimus 275, 276, 277
Benares 229, 234
Bengal 72, 73, 93
Bengal Army 280, 291
*Bengal Gazette* 77, 79, 80, 86–7
Bentinck, Lord William 237
Betaizor 224
betel nut 61–2, 119
*bibis* (Indian mistresses) 136–7, 138,
    217, 218
Biddulph, William 22
Bihar 72
Bingham, Major 311
Bird, William Hamilton 120
Birjus Qadr 297
bluestockings 347
Bombay 10, 39–43, 57, 65
    Arthur Road Hospital 351–4, 355
    Byculla School 222
    first EIC sovereign settlement
        39–40
    plague 350, 351–4, 355–6
    population growth 43, 127
    social life and entertainment
        65–6, 127
    women traders 123
Britain
    Anglo-Maratha Wars 197
    Anglo-Mysore Wars 140, 141, 179,
        186–7, 197, 267
    Carnatic Wars 71–2

English Civil War 39
India Act, 1784 160, 267
Regulating Act, 1773 73
Seven Years War 72, 190–1
see also East India Company
Broach 22fn
Brodnax, John 123
Buckingham, Lady 243
budgerows 76
Burhanpur 22fn
Burney, Fanny 90, 201

Calcutta 5, 10, 11–12, 57, 65, 72, 73,
    76–7
    'Black Hole' of Calcutta 77
    church services 174
    daily life in 77
    garden houses 76, 77, 118
    Government House 117, 220
    growth of 212
    Harmonicon 76, 84
    Kidderpore Orphanage 221, 222
    Presidency 76
    St John's Church 55fn
    social life and entertainment
        83–4, 117–18, 172–3
    women traders 123
Calicut 102–11
Campbell, Sir Colin 313
Canning, George 319, 320, 321fn,
    322fn
card games 83, 101
    gambling 120–2
careers and business ventures,
    women and 11–12, 122–3
    see also medical profession;
    schools
Carnatic Wars 71–2
Case, Mrs (Lucknow resident)
    294–5, 296, 313

cashmere shawls 215
caste system 164, 171, 209
Catherine of Braganza 39
Cawnpore (Kanpur) 210, 254, 293
　Bibigarh 309–11
　Indian Uprising 303–12
　massacres 308–12
　siege of 303–7
Chaffinch, Miss (Baptist nurse) 350
Chambers, Charlotte 279
Chambers, Sir Robert 84, 246
Charles II 39, 40
Charlotte, Queen 172fn
Charnock, Job 76, 160
Cherry, Georgiana 150fn, 156
Cherry, Peter 150, 151, 152–6, 159
Chevillard De Montesson, Monsieur
　52–3
childbirth 253, 286
children
　Anglo-Indian 207, 219, 220–2
　child mortality 242
　during the Indian Uprisings
　　282–3, 285–6, 287–9, 294,
　　298, 299, 305, 309, 311, 313
　education see schools
　hardships experienced by 246–7,
　　250–2, 282–3, 285–6, 287–9,
　　294, 298, 299, 305, 309, 311,
　　313
　health risks 244, 253
　'Indianisation' 244
　natural 136
　newborns 253–4, 296
　orphanages 221–2, 223
　separation from 7, 242–8, 250–2,
　　262
　travels around India,
　　unaccompanied 249
Chinhut (Chinhat) 295

chlorodyne 332
chloroform 330
cholera 113, 114, 298, 299, 310, 333
Christmas celebrations 117–18
Christ's Hospital, London 42
church services 174
Clapham Sect 161
Clemons, Eliza 209
Clerke, Sir John 130, 194
Clive, Charlotte 151, 152, 176, 180,
　182
Clive, Lord Edward 175–6, 182
Clive, Lady Henrietta 9, 20, 151,
　174–6, 177–9, 180, 242
　early life 175
　on her fellow countrywomen
　　177–8
　intellectual pursuits 178, 183–6
　mineral collection 178, 185fn
　plant collecting 183–4, 185
　travels around India 140–1, 179,
　　180–8, 198
　visits zenanas 140–1, 187–8
Clive, Henrietta (Harry) 151, 176,
　180, 182
Clive, Robert 72, 73, 92, 124, 181
cloth trade 24fn
Codrington, Captain 231, 233
Coimbatore 185
Colaba 94
companions, female 123
The Complete Indian Housekeeper
　and Cook (Flora Annie Steel)
　329, 331–3, 334
conjurors 205
Cornwallis, Lord 187, 207fn
Coromandel Coast 58, 71, 194
corruption 74–5, 160
Cossimbazar (Kasimbazar) 75
Crisp, James 191, 192, 193

Cromwell, Oliver 39
Cross, Mary 123
cultural adjustment 56–7, 58–9
cultural gulf 8, 204–6, 209–11
Cuttack 196

Dacca (Dhaka) 88, 114, 193, 194, 195
*dak* bungalows 265
Dalhousie, Lord 267
Dalrymple, William 137, 206,
     207fn, 217fn, 321fn
dancing
   balls 117, 118, 172–3, 178, 210–11,
      221, 222, 240
   Indian view of 210–11
   nautch women 62, 119–20, 210,
      215
*dandee* (hammock) 264
Danish traders 71
Dasgaon 127
Dawson, George 247–8
Day, Francis 57
Delhi 197, 218, 229
   Flagstaff Tower 282, 283–4
   Imperial Assemblage 322–6, 360
   Indian Uprisings 271, 281–8, 314,
      319–21
   massacres 271, 283, 284, 285–6,
      288–9
   Red Fort 285, 321
Delhi Force 288fn, 319
demi-monde 54–5, 68, 73–4
*dhoolie* (covered litter) 264
dinner parties 200–1
disease and sickness
   children 244, 253
   cholera 113, 114, 298, 299, 310, 333
   dysentery 21, 253, 286, 298, 310
   malaria 113
   scurvy 298

   on ships 20–1
   smallpox 298
   typhoid 113, 347
Diver, Maud 13
divorce 85
*diwani* (revenue-raising powers)
   72–3
Doctrine of Lapse 267, 290, 303
Dowson, Hester May 350–8, 359
Drake, Francis 26
Draper, Daniel 124, 125, 128, 130,
   135
Draper, Eliza 124–31, 135–6,
   359–60
   elopement 130–1, 135
   friendship with Laurence Sterne
      126
Drawing Rooms, Vicereine's 360
duels 53fn, 122
Dufferin, Lady 12, 230fn, 327, 350
Duke, Matthew 25
Dundas, Robert 161fn
Dutch East India Company 34fn
Dutch traders 10, 70–1
dysentery 21, 253, 286, 298, 310

East India Company
   administrative structure 73
   annexation of territory under the
      Doctrine of Lapse 267–8,
      290–1
   armies 93, 159, 266, 268
   cessation of commercial
      transactions 267
   Civil Service 203
   civilian–military relations 204,
      348
   corruption 74–5, 160
   Court of Directors 118
   in crisis 38–9, 91–3

disbanded 321–2
*diwani* 72–3
early days of 10, 18, 21–33
factories in the 17th century (map) 16
female shareholders 11
female traders 11, 24, 36, 123
ferman 70, 72, 93
first sovereign Indian possession 39–40
Governor-General role 73, 322
growing power, Parliamentary checks on 160
industrial enterprise 38
lucrative emoluments 74–5, 160
male environment 21–4
permanent charter 39
policies on religion 160–1
policies on women 21–5, 41–4, 54, 150
Presidencies 57
racist edicts 207
rivals 70–1
Supreme Council 73
Supreme Court of Judicature 73
territorial expansion 9, 71, 186, 197, 267–8
territories 1765 (map) 46
territories 1805 (map) 134
territories 1857 (map) 274
verge of bankruptcy 39, 93
Eden, Emily and Fanny 207–8, 210–11, 215, 220, 221, 269–70, 360
travels around India 228–41, 248–9
Egypt 95–8
encampments 31, 229–30, 322–6
English Civil War 39
*The Englishwoman in India* (anon) 244, 328–9

entertainment *see* social life and entertainment
entomology 186, 201
etiquette 151
see also handbooks and instruction manuals; social precedence
eunuchs 143, 146
Evangelical movement 161, 206–7

famines 195, 234, 326, 360
Fane, Isabella 236
fashion 78–80, 86, 158, 239
court dress 325, 327
gala events 117
Indian attire 37, 61, 214–15, 216–17, 235
Fatehgunj 238
Fay, Anthony 104, 106, 108, 109, 110, 111
Fay, Eliza 80–6, 87, 95–111, 112, 117, 122, 123, 157, 167, 246
accomplishments 80–1
captivity in Calicut 102–11
on the demi-monde 55
on fashion 79
on Marian Hastings 84–6
travels to India 20, 95–102
Fenwick, Edward 118
*ferman* (royal decree) 70, 72, 93, 120
Ferozepur 261–2
*fête champêtre* 118
Finch, William 26
First Afghan War 12, 261
First Sikh War 262
'fishing fleets' 8, 124
Fitchett, John 310, 311
floods 38
flywhisks 88, 235fn

food and drink 82–3
  alcohol consumption 83fn, 114
  dak bungalow food 265
  English foodstuffs, availability of
    212–13
  Indian 209–10, 213–14
  onboard ships 102, 154, 157–8
  rules/taboos 209–10
Foote, Samuel 89
Forster, E. M. 55fn, 73, 81, 84fn
Fowke, Joseph 93
Fowke, Margaret 13, 78–80, 92–3
France
  Carnatic Wars 71–2
  Seven Years War 72, 190–1

Galle 57
gambling 120–2
Ganjam 194
garden conversation piece (art) 88
garden houses 76, 77, 118, 176, 182
garden parties 118
Garden Reach 77, 118
Gardiner, Grace 331–3
Gardner, Colonel William Linnaeus
    217, 218–19, 223, 225
Gardner, James 219, 226fn
George III 117
Germon, Maria 292
Ghaziuddin Haider 138
gift exchanges 27–8, 37, 62, 202,
    235
Gonda 294
Goothnee 316
Gorakhpur 259, 260, 261
Goulding, Mr (preacher) 25, 35
governesses 123
Graham, Maria 141, 162
Grand Trunk Road 265, 337
Grant, Charles 161

Graves, Brigadier 283fn, 284
Greathead, Eliza 277, 279
Greville, Lord 203
*griffinage* 168, 208, 347
Gubbins, Mr (financial
    commissioner) 292, 293
Gujarat 38
Gyfford, William 94

Hapsburgs 71
handbooks and instruction manuals
    150–1, 152–6, 209, 328–33
Hare, John 101–2
Hastings, Marian 81, 82, 84–6, 88,
    95
Hastings, Warren 73, 81, 86, 88
  impeachment 86, 160
Havelock, General 301, 310, 311
Hawkins, William 25–34, 70
  death of 34
  marriage to Maryam 33–4
  visit to Mughal court 27–33
Hayes, Mrs (London madam) 68–9
heat, tolerance of 56, 113
Hickey, Charlotte 167
  death of 115–17
  former courtesan 2–3, 67–8
  introduction into Calcutta society
    67–8
  prisoner of the French 52–4
  travels to India 1–3, 47–51, 114
Hickey, William
  on British status in India 92
  on corruption 75
  and death of his wife 115–17
  friendship with Robert Pott 70,
    73, 74
  gambling losses 121–2
  Indian mistress 138fn
  observations of women 12, 68, 69

prisoner of the French 53, 54
    return to England 89
    on the Setting Up Ceremony 66
    travels to India 1–3, 5, 47–51
Hill, Diana 122
hill stations 56, 198–200, 207, 249,
    268, 339, 360
    see also Simla
Hillersdon, Lydia 305
'Hindustani Airs' 120
homosexuality 136
hookahs 214
Hopkins, Captain 246
Horne, Amy 296fn, 303–5, 306,
    308–9, 315–16
horseracing 83
horses and stables 170
Hudson, Mrs (trader) 11, 17, 18–19,
    21, 24, 35, 36
hunting 128
hurricanes 47–51, 167, 247–8
husbands, search for 8, 123–4, 175
    Anglo-Indians 221–2
Hyat-ool-Nissa Begum 226
Hyder Ali 102, 103, 107, 128, 140,
    184, 187, 197
Hyderabad 197, 218, 344, 346–7
    Mahbubia School 349
    Secunderabad Club 348fn

Ichapur 194
Imhoff, Baron Carl von 85
Imperial Assemblage 31fn, 322–6,
    360
India Act 1784 160, 267
Indian Uprisings (1857) 148, 255,
    268–9, 270–1, 275–316
    aftermath 319–21, 327
    attack on Delhi 280–4
    British retribution 319–21

causes of 280
    Cawnpore massacres 308–12, 315
    Delhi massacre 271, 283, 284,
        285–6, 288–9
    Enfield rifles controversy 268–9,
        280
    Meerut Uprising 271, 277
    outbreak of 271
    siege of Cawnpore 303–7
    siege of Delhi 286–9, 314–15
    siege of Lucknow 290–302
Indian women
    adornment 60–1, 143
    clothing 37, 61, 214–15, 216–17, 235
    encounters with 36–7, 59–64,
        120, 139, 142, 145–6, 149,
        187–8, 226–7, 235–6
    high-ranking women 36–7, 60–3,
        139, 143, 144, 145–6, 235–6
    medical treatment 146–7
    mistresses of British men 136–7,
        138, 217, 218
    nautch women 119–20, 149
    perspective on European women
        63–4, 142
    purdah schools 344–7, 349–50
    seclusion of 59–61, 63, 137–47,
        148–9
    social and political influence 144
    zenanas 59–61, 137–47, 187, 209,
        225, 226, 235–6
'Indianised' children 244
'Indianised' Englishmen 137, 217–
    18, 219
indigo trade 11, 24, 308
Inglis, Julia 292, 293, 294, 295,
    296–8, 300–1
    and the Indian Uprisings 312–14
Inglis, Lieutenant-Colonel John
    292, 295, 296, 300–1

interracial liaisons 94, 137, 138–40, 206
  children of 221–2
  fake marriage certificates 220
  marriages 218–20, 223
  mistresses 136–7, 138, 218
Isaacs, Martha 122
isolated postings 238–40

Jahangir, Emperor 19fn, 22, 27–33, 144
James I 27
Jasanoff, Maya 172fn
Jesuits 28, 32
jewellery, Indian 30, 61
Jhansi 267
John, Revd C.S. 341fn
'John Company' see East India Company
Johnson, Kitty 167
Jourdain, John 20–1
Jutog 275

Karwar 93
Kashmir 262, 339
Kasur 338
Keay, John 18
Keeling, Thomas 23
Kerridge, Thomas 22, 23, 24, 25
Khair un-Nissa 137
Khan, Mahommed Ismail 315–16
Khan-i-Khana 63
Khanum Jan 120
Khasganj 217, 225
Khizr Sultan 320
Khujista Begum 345
Kindersley, Jemima 59, 113, 114, 176, 177, 189
Kipling, Rudyard 251
Kirkpatrick, James Achilles 137, 218

Kumbakonam 183

Lang, Second Lieutenant Arthur 311
Larkins, Emma 306–7
Larkins, Colonel William 307
Lawrence, Sir Henry 253, 254, 255, 256–7, 261, 291, 295, 296
Lawrence, Lady Honoria 253–4, 255–66, 290
  death of 291
  early life 256–8
  travels around India 259–63, 264, 265, 266
  travels to India 257–8
Lawrence, John 321fn
Leeson, Mrs (teacher) 288–9, 314
Leigh Hunt, Major S. 331
Liaqat Ali 315fn
Lindsay, Caroline 312
Lindsay, Frances 312
Linnaeus, Carl 217
Login, Lady Lena 144–8, 255
loneliness and boredom 8, 226, 338, 360
love poetry 137
Lucknow 145, 148, 210, 262
  Indian Uprisings 290–302, 312–13
  Residency 291–302, 312–13
  siege of 290–302
Ludhiana 337
luxury goods 86–8, 212
  European commodities 212
  see also fashion; jewellery
Lytton, Bulwer 323fn
Lytton, Lady 13, 323, 324–5, 360
Lytton, Lord 323–4, 325–6, 360

McDougall, Harriet 351, 352–3, 355, 356–7, 359

Madras 10, 43, 57–8, 74, 176–7, 200, 336
  architecture 176
  'crossing the bar' 58, 156
  French attacks on 71
  numbers of Englishwomen in 65, 175
  social life and entertainment 178–9
  women traders 123
Mahé 110fn
maidservants 123, 124, 171
Maitland, Julia 198–206, 208, 242
Malabar 186
malaria 113
Malika Gaytee 145–6, 147
Malle, Captain 52
Maratha Wars 197
Marathas 93, 94, 195, 196, 197, 267
Marsh, Elizabeth 13, 88, 135–6, 167, 246
  early life 190
  in North Africa 191–3
  travels around India 189–90, 193–6, 215
Mason, Betty 167
masquerades 118–19
Masulipatam (Machilipatnam) 135, 194
medical profession 350–8
medical supplies 330, 332, 333
Meerut 268–9, 271, 277, 284, 286
memsahibs 6–10
  handbooks and instruction manuals 328–33
  snobbery and racial prejudice 8, 207, 308–9, 327
  stereotypes 8, 333
Methodism 162
mineral collecting 178, 185fn

Minto, Lord 172, 173
Mirzas Mughal 320
missionary activity 161–2, 204, 223–4
  education 340–1
mistresses, Indian *see bibis*
*mofussil see* rural provinces, life in the
monarch's birthday celebrations 117, 172, 178
money-lending 123
Monox, Edward 21, 22, 35
Moore, Kate 277
morality, new 159, 174, 175, 223
Morgan, Mary 62
Mughal court 19fn, 22, 24, 26, 27–33
  decadence 31–2
  disintegration of 71
  encampments 31
  wealth and luxury 29–31
Mulka Begum 210, 216, 217, 219
Mundy, Peter 38
Mungulwar 300
Munro, Thomas 161fn
Murshidabad 74–5
*mussoola* boats 58
Mussoorie 249
Muter, Mrs Dunbar Douglas 277–8
Myers (travelling salesman) 213
Mysore 188, 197
Mysore Wars 140, 141, 179, 186–7, 197, 267

*The Nabob* (Samuel Foote) 89–90
Nabobs 70, 162, 172
  satirising of 89–90
Nagapatam 57
Nagpur 267–8
Nana Sahib (Nana Govind Dhondu Pant) 303, 307, 308, 310, 335

*Nathalia* (ship) 55, 100–4
nationalism, Indian 326
*nautch* women 62, 119–20, 210, 215
Nepal 262
*New Year's Gift* (ship) 17–18, 19–20, 25
Nugent, Sir George 169, 171–2, 173,
    203, 222, 243
Nugent, Lady Maria 169–74, 175,
    208, 213, 214, 220, 222, 244
  depression 172, 243
  early life 171–2
  on religious observances 173–4
  separation from her children 172,
    242–3
  on servants 169–71
Nur Jahan 144
nurses 350–8

Oakley, Lady 187
Ochterlony, Sir David 218
O'Hara (school-fellow of William
    Hickey) 74
opium 161fn, 164, 225
oral tradition 143
Orissa 72, 195–6
orphanages 221–2, 223
Osborne, William 229, 232, 270
Oudh 138, 139, 145, 290–1

palanquins 88, 264
Parkes, Fanny 9, 210, 213, 219, 361
  encounters with Indian women
    142, 149, 216–17, 226–7
  on missionary activity 223–4
  travels around India 142, 224–7,
    228, 231–2, 240–1
patronage 203
Pegu 267
*Personal Reminiscences* (Augusta
    Becher) 263

Peshawar 264, 356
pets 151, 178, 233–4, 339
Phyllis (author's relation) 6–7
plague 350, 351–4, 355–6
plant collecting 183–4, 185
Plassey, Battle of 72, 92
Pley, Constance 11
Plowden, Elizabeth 62
Plowden, Sophia 119–20, 244–5
Poll Puff 11–12
Pondicherry 71
Popham, Joseph 191
portrait painters, female 122, 178fn
portrait painting 88
Portuguese traders 10, 26–7, 32, 70
Pott, Emily 68–70, 153
Pott, Robert 68, 69–70, 73, 74–5,
    116, 160
Pott's Folly 70
Powell, Lady 19fn
Powell, Sir Thomas 19fn
profligacy 73–4, 162
prostitution, London 68–9
Punjab 267, 339, 341
Purchas, Samuel 36
purdah hospitals 350
purdah schools 344–7, 349–50
Puri 195

quadrille (card game) 101
quadrille (dance) 211fn, 225, 240

racism 8, 57, 63, 141, 206, 207, 360
railways 229
Raj
  detrimental effects of 9
  imperial arrogance 206, 327,
    360
  Raj nostalgia 9
Rajahmundry 200, 201–3

Rajasthan 262
Ramsay, Allan 190
Rangherry 181
Ranjit Singh 237
Rawalpindi 230fn
*Raynha de Portugal* (ship) 1, 2, 3, 6,
    47–51, 52, 114
Read, Catherine 122
Regulating Act, 1773 73
religion 160–1, 173–4, 175, 204
    see also missionary activity
Resident, post of 74–5, 267
returning to England 88–9
    children 7, 242–8, 250–2, 262
Reynolds, Sir Joshua 69, 176
Ripley, Colonel 284
Roe, Sir Thomas 22, 23–4, 25,
    28fn, 35, 70, 71, 144
Ross, Johanna 123
Royal, Emily 247, 248
Rumbold, Lady 121
Rumbold, Sir Thomas 121
rural provinces, life in the 198, 200,
    213, 238–40, 337–9
    see also hill stations; travels
        around India
Russian interests in Asia 237, 326

Salé 191
Sale, Lady 12
sale of possessions 263
Salem 186
Salmon, Nathaniel 17, 18
Sambhalpur 267
San Thomé 57, 71
Satara 267
schools 122, 248–9, 340–1
    in England 250–1
    for girls 122, 340–8
    missionary teachers 340–1

native pupils 341–7, 349–50
    purdah schools 344–7, 349–50
Sclater, James 127, 129
scurvy 298
Seringapatam 112, 179, 186–7, 197
servants 7, 82, 163–71, 173, 180, 201
    deference 163, 208
    dilatoriness 168
    English 123
    female 123, 124, 171
    incivility to 208
    livery 169, 170
    multitude of 163, 164–6, 169–70,
        333
    salaries 165–6
    see also slaves
Setting Up Ceremony 66–7, 175, 200
Seven Years' War 72, 190–1
Shah Alam II 120
Shah Jehan 34
ships
    cabin furniture and fittings 151,
        330
    child passengers 150–6, 246–8
    food 102, 154, 157–8
    life on board 20, 100–2, 152–8,
        194, 350–1
    livestock 152
    medical supplies 330
Shirley, Sir Robert 19fn
shopkeepers, female 122
shopping 213
Short, Mary (Sultan Mariam
        Begum Sahiba) 138
Sidi Muhammad 191, 192
siestas 83
Sikh Kingdom 236, 237–8, 262,
    267
Simla 207, 221, 228, 236, 240, 268,
    269–71, 275–6

Sind 267
Siraj-ud-Daulah, Nawab of Bengal 72
sitar 225
slaves 143, 166, 167, 191
smallpox 298
Smart, Jane 59–62, 63, 140
Smith, George 189, 193, 195, 196
Smythe, Sir Thomas 28fn
snobbery 8, 207, 348–9
    see also social precedence
social life and entertainment
    balls 117, 118, 172–3, 178, 210–11, 222, 240
    card games 83, 101
    Christmas 117–18
    dinner parties 200–1
    gambling 120–2
    garden parties 118
    horseracing 83
    hunting 128
    masquerades 118–19
    monarch's birthday celebrations 117, 172, 178
    nautches 119–20
    Setting Up Ceremony 66–7, 175, 200
    social calls 65–7, 83–4, 348
    theatrical productions 122, 178–9
social mobility 54–5, 84
social precedence 65, 129, 231, 347, 348–9
    see also caste system
spa town 127
spice trade 34fn, 38
Srikakulam 195
Starke, Mariana 67
stays 215, 216
steam ships 327, 330
Steel, Flora Annie 331–9, 341–4, 350

autobiography 335
    *The Complete Indian Housekeeper and Cook* 329, 331–3, 334
    eccentric childhood 335–6, 339
    educational activities 341–4
    folk story collection 339
    novels 334
    travels to India 336
Steel, Henry William 336, 338, 343
Steele, Frances (née Webb) 18–19, 21, 23–4, 34, 35fn
    encounters with Indian women 36–7, 62–3
    travels to India 17–18, 21
Steele, Richard 17–18, 22, 24, 34, 36
Sterne, Laurence 125–6, 127
storytelling 143
Suder Khan 103, 105, 107, 109, 111
Suez Canal 328
sunstroke 56, 283fn
Surat 10, 11, 19, 21–2, 26, 38–9, 129, 356
*Sutlej* (ship) 247–8
Swedish traders 71

Taj Mahal 225, 229
Tamil Nadu 193
Tanjore (Thanjavur) 183
tataravan 98
tax collecting 72–3
Taylor, Mr (merchant) 99, 101
technological advances 327–8
telegraphy 327
Tellicherry 93–4, 127–8
Tenasserim 267
Tharoor, Shashi 9
theatrical productions 89–91, 122, 158, 178–9

Timms, Biddy (Mrs Meer Hassan Ali) 139–40, 141–2, 143–4
Tipu Sultan 140, 141, 179, 186, 187, 197, 322
Tiretta, Mr (architect) 70fn
Tonelli, Anna 178, 182
Towerson, Gabriel 24, 34, 35
Towerson, Maryam 17, 18–19, 21, 24, 25–6, 33–4, 35
traders, female 11–12, 123
Tranquebar 341fn
travel to India
  journey time 19, 150
  overland route 95
  perils 19, 47–51, 96–7, 150, 152, 248
  see also ships
travels around India
  army wives 253–4, 259–62, 263–6
  Augusta Becher 263, 264, 266
  children 249
  discomforts 263, 264, 266
  Elizabeth Marsh 189–90, 193–6, 215
  Emma and Fanny Eden 228–41, 248–9
  entourages 180, 229, 261
  Fanny Parkes 142, 224–7, 228, 231–2, 240–1
  Harriet Tytler 265–6
  Henrietta Clive 140–1, 179, 180–8, 198
  Honoria Lawrence 259–63, 264, 265, 266
  Jemima Kindersley 189
  luggage and supplies 264–5, 328–30
  modes of transport 180, 229, 260, 264

  perils 232, 261
  rest stations 265
  road conditions 233, 263
  safety 266
  tent-palaces 229–30
Trincomalee 51
Tropical Trials (Major Leigh Hunt) 331, 332
Tulloh, Mr (Calcutta auctioneer) 55fn
Tulloh, Mrs 55, 100, 107, 108, 112
turbans 215, 239
typhoid 113, 347
Tytler, Harriet 155fn, 249–2, 263, 266, 275fn
  and the Indian Uprisings 279fn, 280–8, 289, 299fn, 314–15, 320–1
  travels through India 265–6
Tytler, Captain Robert 280–1, 282, 284, 285, 287

uncovenanted clerks 220–1
Untouchables 171
Up the Country (Emily Eden) 228

Vellore 181, 187
Viceroy, role of 322
Victoria, Queen 146fn, 199fn, 320, 327fn
  Empress of India 13, 322, 324, 326

waltz 211
War of the Austrian Succession 71
Warrant of Precedence 65, 349
Warren, Emily see Pott, Emily
water gardens 29–30
Webb, Frances 17, 18
  see also Steele, Frances

weddings, Indian 219
Wellesley, Colonel 187
wet nurses 164
Wheeler, Major-General Sir Hugh 303, 316
White Mughals 160, 218, 219, 227
Whitehall, John 135, 136, 221
Wilberforce, William 161
Willcock, Captain Frank 288
Worth, Charles 325fn

Wortley-Montagu, Lady Mary 59fn
writers (EIC employees) 88, 238–9
Wuzeeroolniza Begum 148
Wyld, Florence 344–8, 349–50

Zafar Bahadur Shah 280, 319–20, 321
*zenanas* 59–61, 137–47, 187, 209, 225, 226, 235–6
Zoffany, Johann 55fn, 88